Extending Microsoft Dynamics NAV 2016 Cookbook

Make the most of your NAV deployment by extending and customizing it with a variety of expert tools

Alexander Drogin

Packt>

BIRMINGHAM - MUMBAI

Extending Microsoft Dynamics NAV 2016 Cookbook

First published: January 2017

Production reference: 1130117

Published by Packt Publishing Ltd.
Livery Place
35 Livery Street
Birmingham
B3 2PB, UK.
ISBN 978-1-78646-060-8

www.packtpub.com

Credits

Author

Alexander Drogin

Reviewer

Oleg Romashkov

Commissioning Editor

Aaron Lazar

Acquisition Editor

Sonali Vernekar

Content Development Editor

Siddhi Chavan

Technical Editors

Dhiraj Chandanshive

Bhavin Savalia

Copy Editor

Safis Editing

Project Coordinator

Vaidehi Sawant

Proofreader

Safis Editing

Indexer

Mariammal Chettiyar

Production Coordinator

Arvindkumar Gupta

About the Author

Alexander Drogin started working with Navision Attain version 3.01 in 2002 as a software developer at a consulting company. After 7 years of development, he shifted his focus to end-user support. In 2012, he joined the Microsoft Russia development team as a software engineer in testing, and worked on NAV test automation. Currently, he leads the sustained engineering team in the Supply Chain Management area at Microsoft.

I would like to thank my colleagues who helped me in my work on this book--Oleg Romashkov, for reviewing the book and testing the code samples, whose valuable feedback on the content helped improve the quality of the book; and Sergey Iazovskiy, who helped me in designing numerous .NET examples and solving issues with .NET Interoperability.

About the Reviewer

Oleg Romashkov has been a NAV developer since 2001. He worked for eight years with Microsoft by developing new features and country localizations for NAV 4.00 – NAV 2015. Also he spent 7 years working for a few MS partners where he implemented NAV for more than 20 customer projects.

www.PacktPub.com

For support files and downloads related to your book, please visit www.PacktPub.com.

Did you know that Packt offers eBook versions of every book published, with PDF and ePub files available? You can upgrade to the eBook version at www.PacktPub.com and as a print book customer, you are entitled to a discount on the eBook copy. Get in touch with us at service@packtpub.com for more details.

At www.PacktPub.com, you can also read a collection of free technical articles, sign up for a range of free newsletters and receive exclusive discounts and offers on Packt books and eBooks.

Mapt

https://www.packtpub.com/mapt

Get the most in-demand software skills with Mapt. Mapt gives you full access to all Packt books and video courses, as well as industry-leading tools to help you plan your personal development and advance your career.

Why subscribe?

- Fully searchable across every book published by Packt
- Copy and paste, print, and bookmark content
- On demand and accessible via a web browser

Customer Feedback

Thank you for purchasing this Packt book. We take our commitment to improving our content and products to meet your needs seriously—that's why your feedback is so valuable. Whatever your feelings about your purchase, please consider leaving a review on this book's Amazon page. Not only will this help us, more importantly it will also help others in the community to make an informed decision about the resources that they invest in to learn.

You can also review for us on a regular basis by joining our reviewers' club. **If you're interested in joining, or would like to learn more about the benefits we offer, please contact us**: customerreviews@packtpub.com.

Table of Contents

Preface

Microsoft Dynamics NAV 2016 is a modern enterprise resource planning application that covers a wide range of user demands. The NAV technical platform gives end-users and applications developers access to cutting-edge technologies, while the front-end business application meets most of the daily needs of small and medium-sized companies. Still every business is individual and must face unique challenges, and it is impossible to foresee all demands from business users to the ERP software.

To satisfy the requirements of each unique company, NAV offers a wide variety of tools to extend standard functionality. This toolset includes the internal development environment that enables developers to tailor the business application to individual needs. Besides, in this book you will find multiple recipes guiding you through the integration of external libraries developed in .NET languages, into NAV applications.

With the recipes in this book, you will customize NAV applications, develop business logic, extend user interfaces, and organize solutions with custom role centers arranged specifically for each functional role in the organization.

The book then proceeds to reporting tools, which are the essential part of any enterprise software. You will build informative and interactive reports with built-in NAV tools, and use Visual Studio reporting tools and SQL Server Reporting Services to design and publish reports. Readers not so skillful in application development, but proficient in Excel or Power BI, will learn how to load data from NAV into their favorite reporting system and model comprehensive reports.

System administrators will find useful recipes on different aspects of NAV server configuration and security features.

What this book covers

Chapter 1, *Writing Basic C/AL Code*, describes NAV 2016 server and client installation and configuration and introduces the NAV 2016 development environment along with the basics of the NAV application language, C/AL.

Chapter 2, *Advanced C/AL Development*, delves deeper into C/AL development and NAV application objects. You will learn how to store your data in tables, present the data in UI with pages, export, import, and structure the data in XMLPorts and queries, and write efficient and reusable code.

Chapter 3, *Reporting and Data Analysis*, introduces the reader to NAV reporting capabilities. The chapter begins with an in-depth description of C/SIDE Report objects, shifting to integration with external tools in the second part. You will learn how to present NAV data in different reporting systems, including Power BI, SQL Server Reporting Services, and MS Excel.

Chapter 4, *.NET Interoperability in C/AL*, covers the integration of .NET assemblies into the NAV client application language. Recipes in this chapter give an overview of the DotNet data type in NAV, various extensions of C/AL aimed at supporting the .NET interoperability and development of custom .Net assemblies and their integration into NAV.

Chapter 5, *Extending C/AL with COM Components*, walks the reader through developing COM components and the integration of COM into the NAV application.

Chapter 6, *SharePoint Integration*, provides an overview of corporate web portals on the SharePoint platform and various ways to integrate NAV elements into the corporate sites.

Chapter 7, *Control Add-ins*, covers extending the NAV user interface with custom controls written in .NET languages, such as C#, or in JavaScript.

Chapter 8, *Web Services*, covers publishing SOAP and OData web services from NAV to expose data and functionality through standard communication interfaces over the Web. You will learn how to publish and consume NAV web services and protect web service endpoints from unauthorized access.

Chapter 9, *Events and Extension Packages*, covers the events which have been introduced in NAV 2016 to allow application developers to extend NAV functionality without modification to the base application code. We will go through subscribing to different types of events to receive notifications of changes in database, user actions, and events in the app business logic. The chapter then covers developing extension packages that utilize the idea of events to bind third party extensions to NAV application code.

Chapter 10, *PowerShell*, gives an overview of the reach set of PowerShell cmdlets available in NAV shell.

What you need for this book

Microsoft Dynamics NAV 2016

Microsoft SQL Server 2012 Service Pack 2 Express, Standard, or Enterprise

Microsoft Visual Studio 2012 Professional, Premium or Ultimate edition

Instead of Visual Studio 2012, you can use its free version, Visual Studio Code, to develop .NET code in C#

To design report layouts, Visual Studio is also required. VS report designer can be replaced with the free Microsoft SQL Server 2012 Report Builder

Microsoft Office 2016. The book covers different aspects of integration between NAV and Office applications.

Power BI is required for data analysis in Chapter 3, *Reporting and Data Analysis*.

The R language environment. Two recipes in Chapter 3, *Reporting and Data Analysis,* use R scripts for statistical analysis of NAV data. These will require R.

SharePoint Server 2016 or SharePoint Online subscription

Java SE Development Kit 8 and an IDE for Java development, for example, Eclipse.

Windows Management Framework 3.0 must be installed to use features of PowerShell 3.0. Installation is required on Windows 7 or Windows Server 2008. In Windows 8, Windows Server 2012 and higher versions, PowerShell 3.0 is integrated into the operating system.

Who this book is for

This book is intended for NAV developers, administrators, and advanced users who want to take the most from NAV implementation. The reader is expected to be familiar with basic programming and have a good knowledge of NAV business application. Understanding of object-oriented principles, as well as some experience of programming in C# and/or Java would be helpful.

Sections

In this book, you will find several headings that appear frequently (Getting ready, How to do it, How it works, There's more, and See also).

To give clear instructions on how to complete a recipe, we use these sections as follows:

Getting ready

This section tells you what to expect in the recipe, and describes how to set up any software or any preliminary settings required for the recipe.

How to do it...

This section contains the steps required to follow the recipe.

How it works...

This section usually consists of a detailed explanation of what happened in the previous section.

There's more...

This section consists of additional information about the recipe in order to make the reader more knowledgeable about the recipe.

See also

This section provides helpful links to other useful information for the recipe.

Conventions

In this book, you will find a number of text styles that distinguish between different kinds of information. Here are some examples of these styles and an explanation of their meaning.

Code words in text, database table names, folder names, filenames, file extensions, pathnames, dummy URLs, user input, and Twitter handles are shown as follows: "Open the `ClientUserSettings.config` file located in the `AppData` directory."

A block of code is set as follows:

```
SalesLine.SETFILTER(
  "Document Type",'%1|%2',
  SalesLine."Document Type"::Order,
  SalesLine."Document Type"::Invoice);
```

Any command-line input or output is written as follows:

```
Install-NAVApp -ServerInstance DynamicsNAV90 `
  -Name "ILE Posting DateTime"
```

New terms and **important words** are shown in bold. Words that you see on the screen, for example, in menus or dialog boxes, appear in the text like this: "Click **Next**, then select the option **Do not export the private key**."

> Warnings or important notes appear in a box like this.

> Tips and tricks appear like this.

Reader feedback

Feedback from our readers is always welcome. Let us know what you think about this book-what you liked or disliked. Reader feedback is important for us as it helps us develop titles that you will really get the most out of.

To send us general feedback, simply e-mail `feedback@packtpub.com`, and mention the book's title in the subject of your message.

If there is a topic that you have expertise in and you are interested in either writing or contributing to a book, see our author guide at `www.packtpub.com/authors`.

Customer support

Now that you are the proud owner of a Packt book, we have a number of things to help you to get the most from your purchase.

Downloading the example code

You can download the example code files for this book from your account at `http://www.packtpub.com`. If you purchased this book elsewhere, you can visit `http://www.packtpub.com/support` and register to have the files e-mailed directly to you.

You can download the code files by following these steps:

1. Log in or register to our website using your e-mail address and password.
2. Hover the mouse pointer on the **SUPPORT** tab at the top.
3. Click on **Code Downloads & Errata**.
4. Enter the name of the book in the **Search** box.
5. Select the book for which you're looking to download the code files.
6. Choose from the drop-down menu where you purchased this book from.
7. Click on **Code Download**.

You can also download the code files by clicking on the **Code Files** button on the book's webpage at the Packt Publishing website. This page can be accessed by entering the book's name in the **Search** box. Please note that you need to be logged in to your Packt account.

Once the file is downloaded, please make sure that you unzip or extract the folder using the latest version of:

- WinRAR / 7-Zip for Windows
- Zipeg / iZip / UnRarX for Mac
- 7-Zip / PeaZip for Linux

The code bundle for the book is also hosted on GitHub at `https://github.com/PacktPublishing/Extending-Microsoft-Dynamics-NAV-2016-Cookbook`. We also have other code bundles from our rich catalog of books and videos available at `https://github.com/PacktPublishing/`. Check them out!

Errata

Although we have taken every care to ensure the accuracy of our content, mistakes do happen. If you find a mistake in one of our books-maybe a mistake in the text or the code-we would be grateful if you could report this to us. By doing so, you can save other readers from frustration and help us improve subsequent versions of this book. If you find any errata, please report them by visiting http://www.packtpub.com/submit-errata, selecting your book, clicking on the **Errata Submission Form** link, and entering the details of your errata. Once your errata are verified, your submission will be accepted and the errata will be uploaded to our website or added to any list of existing errata under the Errata section of that title.

To view the previously submitted errata, go to https://www.packtpub.com/books/content/support and enter the name of the book in the search field. The required information will appear under the **Errata** section.

Piracy

Piracy of copyrighted material on the Internet is an ongoing problem across all media. At Packt, we take the protection of our copyright and licenses very seriously. If you come across any illegal copies of our works in any form on the Internet, please provide us with the location address or website name immediately so that we can pursue a remedy.

Please contact us at copyright@packtpub.com with a link to the suspected pirated material.

We appreciate your help in protecting our authors and our ability to bring you valuable content.

Questions

If you have a problem with any aspect of this book, you can contact us at questions@packtpub.com, and we will do our best to address the problem.

1
Writing Basic C/AL Code

In this chapter we will cover the following recipes:

- Installing NAV Development Environment
- Application object triggers
- NAV Development environment – C/SIDE
- Compiling objects and error handling
- Importing and exporting application objects
- Basic C/AL programming
- Accessing the database
- Configuring NAV Server
- Configuring Web Server

Introduction

Microsoft Dynamics NAV 2016 has a rich toolset for extending functionality. Additionally, a wide number of external tools can be connected to the NAV database to enrich data processing and analysis experience. But C/AL, the internal NAV application language, is still the primary means of enhancing user experience when it comes to developing new functionality.

This chapter will introduce you to the basics of NAV Client Application Language development, from installing the development environment and configuring the server to the fundamentals of data manipulation with C/AL.

C/AL Development is framed around objects representing different kinds of functionality and designers associated with each object type. While the details of design for each type of objects will be covered in the next chapter, this chapter will introduce readers to the concept of objects and triggers and present the integrated development environment.

In the last recipe we will concentrate on secure access to the NAV server from the web and mobile client.

Installing NAV Development Environment

This introductory recipe describes the basic steps of installing the C/SIDE – NAV development environment. This is the initial requirement for all recipes involving the development of NAV objects.

Getting ready

Microsoft Dynamics NAV 2016 server and development environment can be installed on a computer running Windows 7 Home edition or higher versions. But the recommended minimum requirement is Windows 7 Service Pack 1 Professional edition. Some of the features described in this book are supported only on Windows 7.1 Professional or higher versions.

If you need detailed instructions on system requirements, refer to the MSDN article *System Requirements for Microsoft Dynamics NAV 2016*. Further in this book, we will assume that the minimum requirements described in this article are satisfied.

How to do it...

1. Run `setup.exe` from the installation media.
2. After accepting the licensing terms, you will have two setup modes to choose from:

   1. **Install Demo**: This installs a preconfigured set of components for the demonstration environment without manual configuration.

   2. **Choose an installation option**: You can choose which components to install and manually configure setup options.

3. Click the **Choose an installation** option. **Install Demo mode** is convenient for a quick unattended setup, but it won't install all components required for the recipes in this book.

4. In the list of installation options, choose **Developer** and click **Customize**. Options that should be installed include:

- **Client**
- **Development Environment (C/SIDE)**
- **Microsoft Office Excel Add-in**
- **Administration Tool**
- **Server**
- **Microsoft Office Outlook Integration**
- **SQL Server Database Components**
- **Demo Database**
- **Microsoft Office Outlook Add-in**
- **Web Server Components**

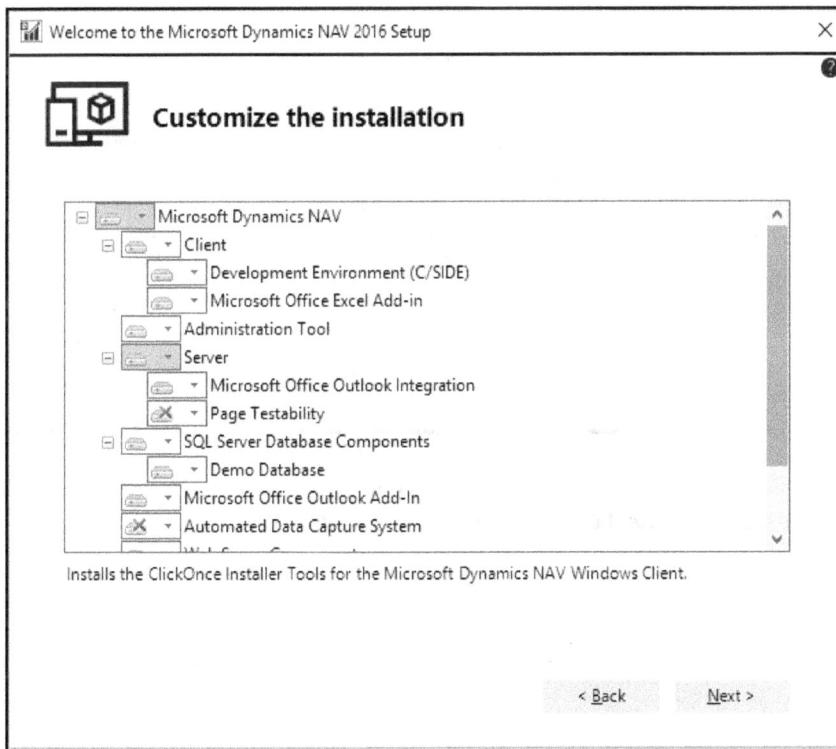

5. Click **Next** and review the installation parameters.

6. If you have the Microsoft SQL Server installed on your development computer, all parameters can be left with their default values. Otherwise specify the SQL Server name and SQL Server instance name.

7. Click **Apply** to run the installation.

8. After installation completes, run the Dynamics NAV 2016 Development Environment from the **Start** menu. C/SIDE client will connect to the SQL Server database created during the installation process.

9. The following is the **Object Designer** window that opens when you connect to the database in the NAV Development Environment:

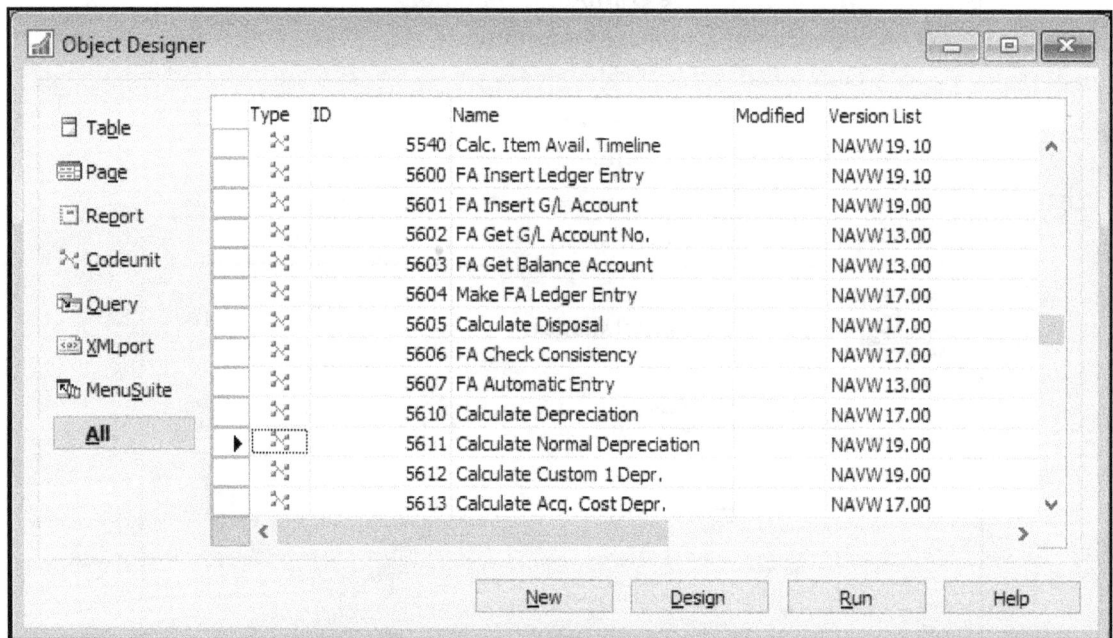

If you don't see this window after connecting to the database, click **Object Designer** in the **Tools** menu or press *Shift + F12*.

How it works...

We chose to install Dynamics NAV 2016 components required for the recipes in this book. Extended testability options, automated data capture system, and click **Once installation are not covered in the book and remain optional**.

The help server must be installed if you intend to use local help files. If you prefer looking for information on MSDN or online communities, it can be skipped. All reference documents installed along with the help server are available online.

Installation will create and start a service named `DynamicsNAV90`. You can find it in your computer's services list as **Microsoft Dynamics NAV Server [DynamicsNAV90]**.

To verify the service installation, run the Dynamics NAV 2016 Client from the **Start** menu, click **Select Server** in the application menu, and enter the server address:

```
localhost:7046/DynamicsNAV90
```

The web server components installation creates a web site called `DynamicsNAV90` in the Internet Information Services.

Dynamics NAV can now be accessed in a web browser on the following address:

```
http://localhost:8080/DynamicsNAV90
```

Application object triggers

Trigger is a piece of code that is executed in response to some external action. All objects in NAV, except Menu Suite, have a set of triggers that can be programmed to respond to certain user's or system actions. For example, when a page with data is displayed on the screen, a sequence of triggers are fired in the application.

- `OnInit`: Page object is initialized
- `OnOpenPage`: Page is displayed
- `OnAfterGetRecord`: Table record displayed on the page is read from the database
- `OnAfterGetCurrRecord`: Table record currently selected is read from the database

There are other triggers reacting to UI elements, data modifications or to external events from .NET components. We will delve deeper into different types of objects and corresponding triggers later in the book. Now let's create a code module (called a codeunit in NAV) with a single trigger that fires when the object is executed.

How to do it...

1. In the left column of the object designer, click on the codeunit object.
2. Click the **New** button in the bottom part of the **Object Designer** form. A new codeunit object is created.
3. Each object in NAV must have a unique name and number that are assigned to the object when it is saved in the database. Click **File** | **Save** and fill in the **ID** and **Name** fields in the **Save As** dialog. Leave the **Compiled** option checked:

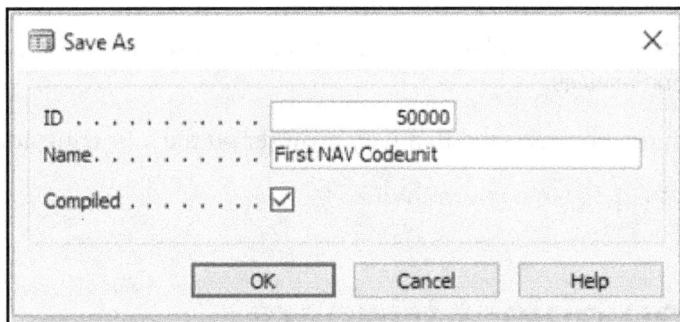

Save As	✕
ID	50000
Name.	First NAV Codeunit
Compiled	☑

OK   Cancel   Help

4. The new codeunit has two system-created triggers. Position the cursor in the empty line below Documentation and write a short description of your new codeunit. For example, This is my first NAV codeunit:

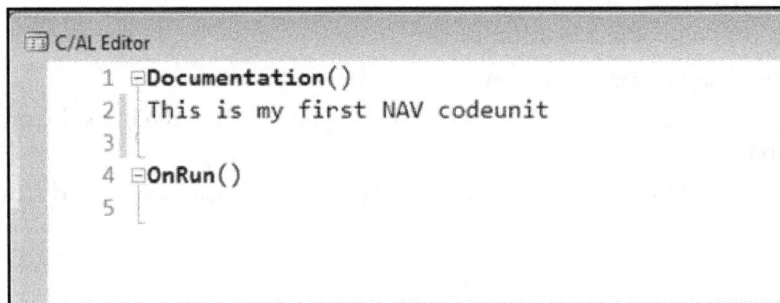

```
C/AL Editor
1  ⊟Documentation()
2  │ This is my first NAV codeunit
3  │
4  ⊟OnRun()
5  │
```

5. Move the cursor to the OnRun trigger and enter a line of code that will be executed when the trigger fires:

```
MESSAGE('Codeunit OnRun trigger');
```

6. Save the codeunit and close the editor window.

7. In the object designer, select the codeunit 50000 and click the **Run** button located under the list objects. This action will start the role-tailored client and execute the codeunit. Execution of the codeunit fires its OnRun trigger. When run, it will show a message box with the codeunit **OnRun** trigger in it.

8. In the **Object Designer** window, create another codeunit, save it with ID 50001 and name it NAV Codeunit Runner.

9. Write a line of code in the OnRun trigger that will invoke the first codeunit:

```
CODEUNIT.RUN(CODEUNIT::"First NAV Codeunit");
```

10. Close the code editor and run codeunit 50001 from the object designer. The same message box with the codeunit **OnRun** trigger will be shown.

How it works...

In most cases all triggers supported by an object are available in the C/AL code editor as soon as the new object is created. There are several exceptions when a trigger must be explicitly declared as a function having specific signature, but these triggers are outside the material covered in this chapter. All application triggers we are going to work with will be created by the C/SIDE without developer's intervention.

All NAV objects that can execute C/AL code (that is, all objects except Menu Suite), have the **Documentation** section. This object section is often referred to as a trigger, and looks like a function in the code editor, although it is never executed. Documentation is used to comment the object – usually comments applicable to the object in general are placed here.

Codeunit objects support only one trigger OnRun that is called when the object is executed. In Step 7 we run the codeunit manually from the object designer. In the steps, Step 8 to Step 10, the same trigger fires when execution of the codeunit is initiated from another codeunit's OnRun trigger. This way, triggers can be chained, when the execution of an object can cause another trigger to fire.

To run the codeunit we use the system function CODEUNIT.RUN which takes the codeunit ID as the parameter. It can simply be a number (50000). Or we can refer to the codeunit by its name, making the code more human-readable.

NAV Development Environment – C/SIDE

C/SIDE is the NAV integrated development environment where we create application objects, design the user interface, and write code. The next recipe gives an overview of the environment and presents some new features introduced to the IDE in NAV 2016.

How to do it...

1. Open **NAV Object Designer** and create a new codeunit.
2. In the **C/AL Code Editor** window, click **C/AL Globals** in the **View** menu to access the list of global variables, text constants, and functions.
3. Select the **Functions** tab in the **C/AL Globals** window and type the function name. Name the new function Multiply. By default, a new function is created with the Local attribute. Local functions are visible only inside the object where they are declared and cannot be called from other objects.
4. Close the declarations window. Now you can see the new function Multiply in the C/AL editor.
5. Position the cursor on an empty line inside the function and open the **C/AL Locals** window. Here you can declare local variables available inside the function, as well as the function's parameters and return type.
6. In the **Parameters** tab, enter the name and the type of a new function parameter you want to declare. Create a parameter X of type Integer. To do this, enter X in the **Name** field and choose Integer from the drop-down list in the **DataType** field.

7. Add one more integer variable, Y:

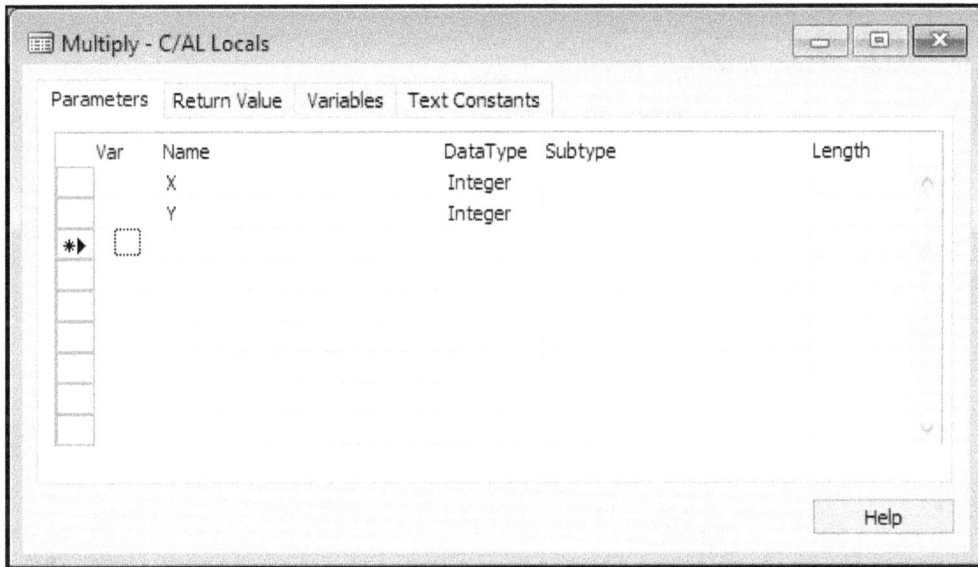

8. Switch to the **Return Value** tab and fill the **Return Type** field. Select **Integer** in the list of types. Close the window and review the changes to the function in the code editor. Now you have declared a function that takes two Integer parameters and returns an Integer result.

9. We want this function to return the result of the multiplication of two parameters X and Y. EXIT statement serves this purpose, so the function's code should consist of one line: EXIT(X * Y). Start typing the first statement EXIT. As you type, IntelliSense will suggest possible language structures:

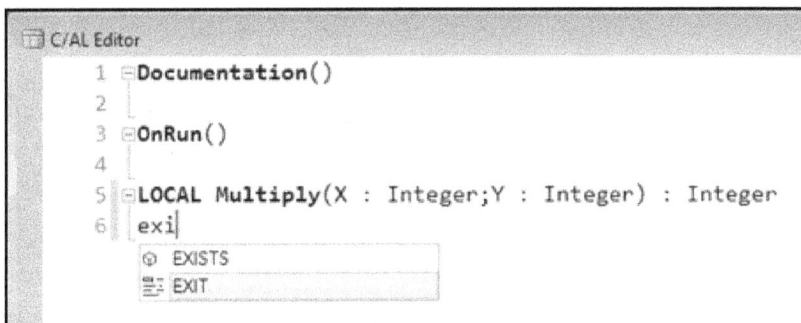

When you see the function **EXIT** in the suggested autocompletion list, select it by pressing the up and down keys on the keyboard and press *Enter* to confirm the selection.

10. Complete the function. Enter the line `EXIT(X * Y);`.

11. Move to the `OnRun` trigger, declare a local Integer variable `z` and start typing the invocation of the function `Multiply: Z := Multiply(5,8)`. As you type the first symbols of the function name, IntelliSense will show a list of suggestions. After you type the opening bracket before entering the function arguments, IntelliSense will show the parameter names and types along with the function return type:

```
C/AL Editor
  1  Documentation()
  2
  3  OnRun()
  4  Z := Multiply(|
  5              [ Integer := ] Multiply(X : Integer,Y : Integer)
  6  LOCAL Multiply(x : integer;y : integer) : integer
  7  EXIT(X * Y);
```

How it works...

Unlike many other programming languages, like C++, C# or Java, variables and functions declaration in C/SIDE are separated from the program text. All global and local declarations are accessed in the code editor via the main menu.

Variables and text constants declared in the C/AL Locals can be used only in the function where they are created. C/AL Globals declarations are accessible from any function in the same object.

Functions can only be created in the C/AL Globals and can be accessed from anywhere in the same object. Function do not have to return a value and can be declared without any return type. If you want the function to return a result, you must assign a return type to it and use the `EXIT` statement to return a value to the caller function.

In the steps from Step 7 to Step 11 we demonstrate how IntelliSence integrates with the NAV development environment. IntelliSense is a Microsoft code completion feature widely used in Visual Studio. It aides a developer in coding by suggesting possible variable and function names, function parameters, and many other things. Such code hints speed up coding and reduce the risk of typos, and many plain coding mistakes.

Compiling objects and error handling

The C/AL code in NAV objects is not executable itself. Before a C/AL object can be used in the application, it must be compiled into binary code that can be run.

The C/AL compiler is a part of the C/SIDE development environment, and can be run either from the object designer or in the code editor while writing the application code.

How to do it...

1. Open NAV object designer and create a new codeunit.
2. In the OnRun trigger, declare a local variable CurrDate of type Integer:

Name	DataType
CurrDate	Integer

3. Add two code lines in the OnRun trigger:

```
CurrDate := TODAY;
MESSAGE('Today is %1,CurrDate);
```

4. The preceding code contains two errors. Let's try to compile it. Press *F11* or click **Compile** in the **Tools** menu to compile the code. A message will inform you about an incorrect type conversion and position the cursor in the line containing the first error.
5. Click **Save** in the **File** menu, assign an ID and name to the new codeunit, uncheck the **Compiled** checkmark in the dialog box, and click **OK**:

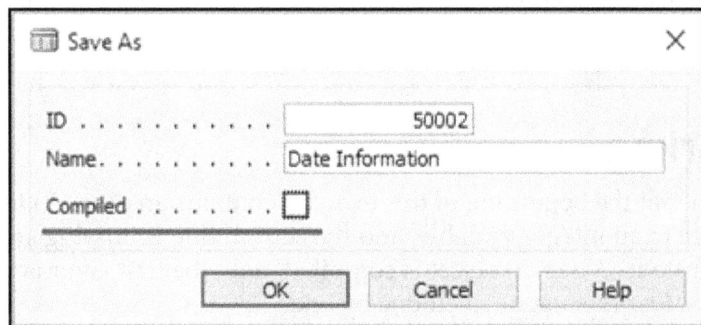

6. The object is saved without compiling. The **Compiled** column in object designer does not have a checkmark, which indicates that the object is uncompiled:

Type	ID	Name	Modified	Version List	Date	Time	Compiled
		9900 Data Upgrade Mgt.		NAVW19.00	15.09.15	12:00:00	✔
		9990 Code Coverage Mgt.		NAVW19.10	28.06.16	12:00:00	✔
		50002 Date Information	✔		25.07.16	22:55:25	
		130400 CAL Test Runner		NAVW19.10	28.06.16	12:00:00	✔
		130401 CAL Test Management		NAVW19.10	28.06.16	12:00:00	✔
		130402 CAL Command Line Test Runner		NAVW19.10	28.06.16	12:00:00	✔

Uncompiled objects cannot be executed.

7. Select the codeunit `50002` and click **Run** in the object designer. An error message will inform you that the object must be saved in the compiled form before it can be run.
8. Close the message dialog and click **Design**.
9. To fix the first error in the code, open C/AL Locals in the `OnRun` trigger and change the data type of the `CurrDate` variable. Replace **Integer** with **Date**.
10. After fixing the error, Click **Compile**. This time, compilation will stop on the second line informing you about a syntax error.
11. Insert the missing apostrophe to close the text constant and fix the erroneous line. The following is the correct function code:

```
CurrDate := TODAY;
MESSAGE('Today is %1',CurrDate);
```

12. Save the object, this time with the **Compiled** option, and run it from the object designer.

How it works...

Each of the two lines at the beginning of this exercise contains an error. In the first line we are assigning a date to an integer variable, and the second line is missing an apostrophe closing the text constant. When an object is compiled, only the first error is shown if the compilation breaks. Errors must be fixed one by one.

In Step 5 we are saving the object without compiling. This option is often used in the middle of the development process, when the object is incomplete and not syntactically correct yet.

It is not necessary to open objects in the code editor to compile them one at a time. It is possible to compile multiple objects in one batch. Select all objects you want to compile in the object designer and press *F11* – it will run compilation for all selected objects. If several objects are selected and there are compilation errors in any of them, the list of errors will be displayed in a summary table.

Importing and exporting application objects

Dynamics NAV application objects can be exported in plain text format and edited with external tools. Although editing code outside C/SIDE is not as convenient as doing it in the C/SIDE code editor, this may be useful when, for example, you need to compare different versions of the same object with a file comparison program or export the source file into a code repository.

Objects can also be exported and imported in binary format as `.fob` files. Binary files cannot be edited directly, so the format is convenient when you do not want to disclose the internal application code. Besides, `.fob` files do not require a developer's license to be imported, and therefore are used to deploy objects on the customer's site.

How to do it...

First let us export an object into a text file and edit it outside C/SIDE editor.

1. Open NAV object designer and create a new codeunit.
2. In the `OnRun` trigger, add a single line of code:

```
MESSAGE('Hello World');
```

3. Click **Save**, fill in the **ID** and **Name** fields: **50003 HelloWorld**, close the code editor.
4. Select the codeunit `50003` in the object designer and click **Export** in the **File** menu.
5. Choose the folder where you want to export the codeunit to and name the file `COD50003.txt`.
6. Select **Text Format** (`*.txt`) in the **File Type** drop-down list and click **Save**.

7. In a file manager, locate the file `COD50003.txt` and open it in a text editor. This is how the exported object looks in a text editor:

```
OBJECT Codeunit 50003 Hello World
{
  OBJECT-PROPERTIES
  {
    Date=22.07.16;
    Time=23:44:09;
    Modified=Yes;
    Version List=;
  }
  PROPERTIES
  {
    OnRun=BEGIN
    MESSAGE('Hello World');
    END;

  }
  CODE
  {

    BEGIN
    END.
  }
}
```

8. In the object text locate the line `MESSAGE('Hello World');` and replace the message text, `MESSAGE('Exported NAV object');`.

9. Save the object and close the editor.

10. Return to NAV object designer, click **Import** from the **File** menu, select **Text Files** in the file type filter, and choose the file `COD50003.txt`.

11. Click **Design** in the object editor window and review the object code. It contains code modified outside of the C/AL editor.

If the object you are importing already exists in the application, it will be replaced with the new version without warning. Any changes made to the object will be lost.

12. In the object designer, select the codeunit `50003` we created in the previous step and click **Export** in the **File** menu.

13. Select **Dynamics NAV Object Format (*.fob)** in the **File Type** drop-down list.

14. Choose the folder where you want to export the codeunit to and name the file `COD50003`. It will be automatically assigned an extension `.fob`. Save the file.

15. Back in the object designer click **Design** to edit the codeunit and replace the message text with the empty string: `MESSAGE('')`. Then save the codeunit and close the code editor.

16. In the object designer, click **Import** from the **File** menu. In the **Import Objects** dialog, select **Dynamics NAV Object Files** in the file type filter, locate the file `COD50003.fob`, and click **Open**.

17. C/SIDE will warn you that there is an object with conflicting versions in the database. Click **OK** to switch to **Import Worksheet**:

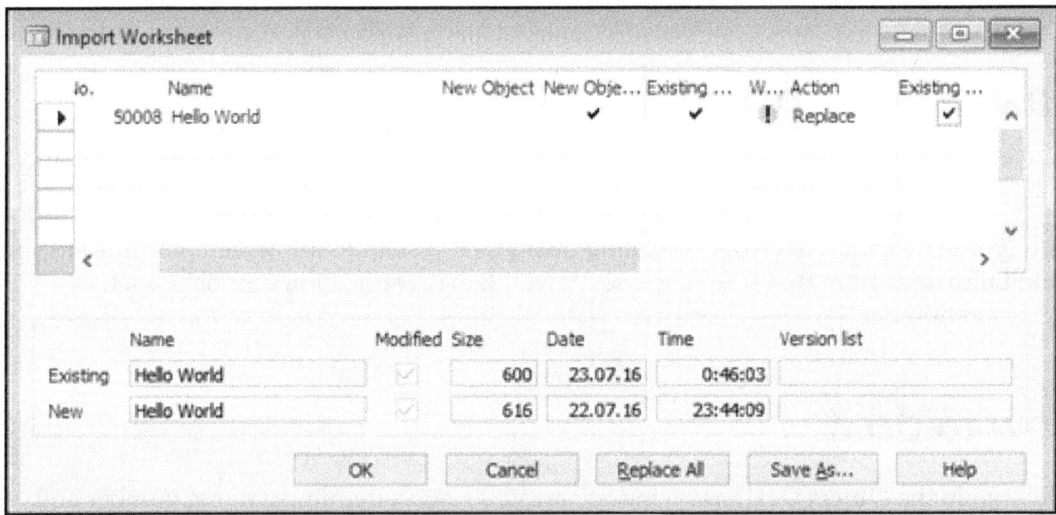

18. Click **OK** to import the object replacing the codeunit existing in the database.

How it works...

When importing application objects in plain text format, C/SIDE does not check objects for possible conflicts. Merging code must be done manually by the developer.

Binary files are automatically checked for conflicts during the import if there are objects with the same ID in the database and in the file being imported. If both files have the **Modified** flag checked, this is considered as a conflict that must be resolved in the **Import Worksheet** dialog. In the **Action** field, you can choose how to handle conflicting objects. Possible options are:

- **Replace** to replace the object in the database with the new one.
- **Skip** to leave the existing object unchanged and ignore the new object.
- **Merge** to automatically merge changes from both objects (only applicable for tables)

Basic C/AL programming

As an example, let's create a simple function that receives a checksum as a parameter and verifies if a check sum satisfies given criteria.

It is a typical task for a developer working on an ERP system to implement verification such as the **Luhn algorithm** that is widely used to validate identification numbers, such as a credit card number.

How to do it...

1. In the **Object Designer** window, create a new codeunit. Assign a number and name (for example, `50000`, `Luhn Verification`).
2. Click **View**, then **C/AL Globals**; in the **Globals** window open the **Functions** tab.
3. In the first line of the table enter the function name, `SplitNumber`.

   The verification function receives a BigInteger number as an input parameter, but the algorithm works with separate digits. Therefore, before starting the validation we need to convert the number into an array of digits.

4. Position into the `Split` function, the number you just declared, and click **View**, then **C/AL Locals**. First tab in the **Locals** window is **Parameters**. Enter the first parameter of the function:
   - `Name`: Digits
   - `DataType`: Byte
   - `Var`: Set the checkmark in this field

5. Still in the **C/AL Locals** window, click **View, Properties** to open the variable properties and set **Dimensions** = 11.

6. Close the variable properties window and add the second function parameter **AccountNumber** with type **BigInteger.**

   The **Parameters** window with the list of properties for the variable Digits is shown in the following screenshot:

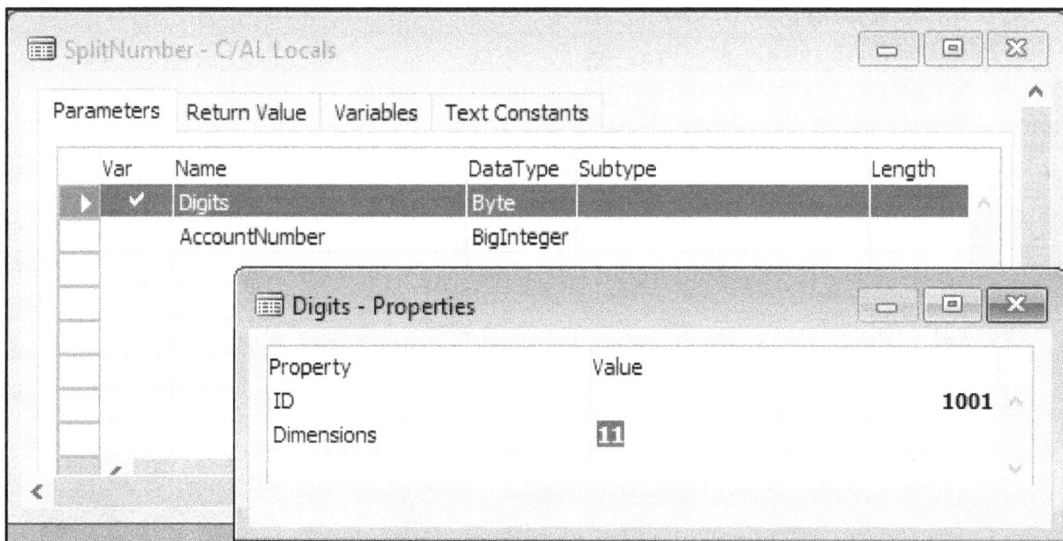

7. Next, navigate to the **Variables** tab. Insert a variable **i** of **Integer** type.

8. Close the local declarations window to return to the code editor and type the function code:

```
FOR i := 11 DOWNTO 1 DO BEGIN
   Digits[i] := AccountNumber MOD 10;
   ccountNumber := AccountNumber DIV 10;
END;
```

9. Open the **C/AL Globals** window again and insert the second function `VerifyCheckSum`. This is the main function that implements the verification algorithm.

10. In the **C/AL Locals** window, insert a single parameter of this function `AccountNumber` of type `BigInteger`.

11. Navigate to the **Return Value** tab and fill in the **Return Type** field. In this case, the type should be **Boolean**.

12. In the **C/AL Locals** window, declare three local variables as follows:

Name	Data Type
Digits	Byte
CheckSum	Integer
i	Integer

13. Select the **Digits** variable, open its properties, and set **Dimensions** to 11.

14. Type the following function code:

```
SplitNumber(Digits,AccountNumber);
FOR i := 1 TO 10 DO BEGIN
   IF i MOD 2 = 1 THEN
      CheckSum += (Digits[i] * 2) DIV 10 +
         (Digits[i] * 2) MOD 10;
END;
CheckSum := 10 - (CheckSum * 9) MOD 10;
EXIT(CheckSum = Digits[11]);
```

15. In the OnRun trigger, place the code that will call the verification function:

```
IF VerifyCheckSum(79927398712) THEN
   MESSAGE(CorrectCheckSumMsg)
ELSE
   MESSAGE(WrongCheckSumMsg);
```

16. To present the execution result to the user, OnRun uses two text constants that we have not declared yet. To do it, open the **C/AL Globals** window in the **View** menu. In the **Text Constants** tab, enter the values as in the following table:

Name	Value
CorrectCheckSumMsg	Account number has correct checksum
WrongCheckSumMsg	Account number has wrong checksum

How it works...

The SplitNumber function, described in Step 1 through Step 8, uses a FOR...DOWNTO loop with a loop control variable to iterate on all digits in the BigInteger number, starting from the last digit. In each step the number is divided by 10 using the integer division function DIV. The modulus division function MOD returns the remainder of this division that is placed in the corresponding element of an array.

The Dimensions property of the parameter Digits tells that this variable is an array consisting of 11 elements (value of Dimensions is the number of elements. A variable with undefined dimensions is a scalar).

When a function is called, it can receive arguments either by value or by reference. Var checkmark in the parameter declaration means that the argument will be passed to the function by reference, and all changes made to the Digits array in the function SplitNumber will be reflected in the function VerifyCheckSum that calls SplitNumber. Arrays cannot be function return values in C/AL, so passing an array variable by reference is the only way to send arrays between functions.

The VerifyCheckSum function defined in Step 9 to Step 13 calls the helper function SplitNumber and then uses the same loop type, but iterates from the first digit to the last (FOR 1 TO 10). This loop computes the checksum, which is compared to the last digit of the account number. If the two values match, the checksum is correct. Finally, the function returns the Boolean value conveying the verification result, TRUE or FALSE.

Based on this result, the `OnRun` function in the codeunit will display one of the two text constants in a message. In the given example, the checksum is incorrect, so the message will look like this:

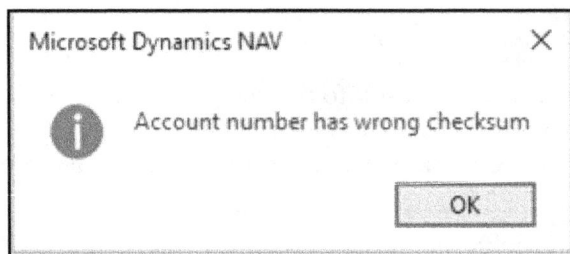

To see the message for the correct result, replace the last digit in the account number with 3. The correct number is **79927398713**.

Messages shown in the dialog box are declared as text constants in Step 16. The same text can be written within C/AL code without declaring constants, but in general, it is recommended to use named constants, because they allow to store text values in different languages and easily switch to any available language layer. Hardcoded text values in the C/AL code cannot provide such flexibility.

Accessing the database in C/AL

Microsoft Dynamics NAV is an information system, and its primary purpose is to collect, store, organize, and present data. Therefore C/AL has a rich set of functions for data access and manipulation.

The next example will present a set of basic functions to read data from the NAV database, filter and search records in a table, and calculate aggregated values based on database records.

In this example, suppose we want to calculate the total amount in all open sales orders and invoices for a certain customer in a specified period.

How to do it...

1. In the NAV Object Designer, create a new codeunit object.
2. Open the codeunit you just created in code designer, position it in the OnRun trigger, and open the local declarations window (**C/AL Locals**). Declare the following local variables:

Name	DataType	Subtype
SalesLine	Record	Sales Line
StartingDate	Date	
EndingDate	Date	

3. Close the local variables window and declare a global text constant in the **C/AL Globals** window:

Name	ConstValue
SalesAmountMsg	Total amount in sales documents: %1

4. Return to the code editor and type the function code:

```
StartingDate := CALCDATE('<-1M>',WORKDATE);
EndingDate := WORKDATE;

SalesLine.SETRANGE("Sell-to Customer No.",'10000');
SalesLine.SETFILTER(
  "Document Type",'%1|%2',
  SalesLine."Document Type"::Order,
  SalesLine."Document Type"::Invoice);
SalesLine.SETRANGE(
  "Posting Date",StartingDate,EndingDate);
SalesLine.CALCSUMS("Line Amount");
MESSAGE(SalesAmountMsg,SalesLine."Line Amount");
```

5. Save the changes, then close the code editor and run the codeunit.

How it works…

A record is a complex data type. Variable declared as record refers to a table in the database. A variable contains a single table record and can move forward and backward through the recordset. A C/AL record resembles an object in object-oriented languages, although they are not exactly the same. You can call record methods and read fields using dot notation.

For example below are valid statements with the `Customer` record variable:

```
Customer.Name := 'New Customer';
IF Customer.Balance <= 0 THEN
   MESSAGE
```

The variable we just declared refers to the table `Sales Line`, which stores all open sales documents lines.

Since we want to calculate the sales amount in a certain period, first of all we need to define the date range for the calculation.

The first line in the code example finds the starting date of the period. In this calculation we refer to the system-defined global variable `WORKDATE`. If you are an experienced NAV user, you know what a workdate is; this is the default date for all documents created in the system. It does not always match the calendar date, so in the application code we use `WORKDATE` as the pivot date. Another system variable `TODAY` stores the actual calendar date, but it is used much less frequently than workdate.

Workdate is the last date of the period we want to analyze. To find the first date, use the `CALCDATE` function. It calculates a date based on the formula and the reference date. `CALCDATE('<-1M>',WORKDATE)` means that the resulting date will be one month earlier than the workdate. In the NAV 9.0 demo database workdate is 25.01.2017, so the result of this `CALCDATE` will be 25.12.2016.

The next line sets a filter on the `SalesLine` table. Filtering is used in C/AL to search for records corresponding to given criteria. There are two functions to apply filters to a table: `SETFILTER` and `SETRANGE`. Both take the field name to which the filter is applied, as the first parameter.

`SETRANGE` can filter all values within a given range or a single value. In the code example we use it to filter sales lines where the customer code is '10000'. Then we apply one more filter on the **Posting Date** field to filter out all dates less than **StartingDate** and greater than **EndingDate**.

Another filter is applied on the **Document Type** field:

```
SalesLine.SETFILTER(
  "Document Type",'%1|%2',
  SalesLine."Document Type"::Order,
  SalesLine."Document Type"::Invoice);
```

We want to see only invoices and orders in the final result, and we can combine these two values in a filter with the SETFILTER function. '%1|%2' is a combination of two placeholders that will be replaced with actual filter values in the runtime.

The last database statement in this example is the CALCSUMS function. SETRANGE itself does not change the state of the record variable – it only prepares filters for the following records search or calculation. Now CALCSUMS will calculate the result based on the record filters. It will find the sum of the **Line Amount** field in all records within the filtered range.

Only sales lines in which all filtering conditions are satisfied will be taken into account:

- Customer No is '10000'
- Document Type is Order or Invoice
- Posting Date is between 25.12.2016 and 25.01.2017

Finally, we will show the result as a message with the MESSAGE function. Placeholders "%1" in the message text will be replaced with the second parameter of the function (SalesLine."Line Amount"):

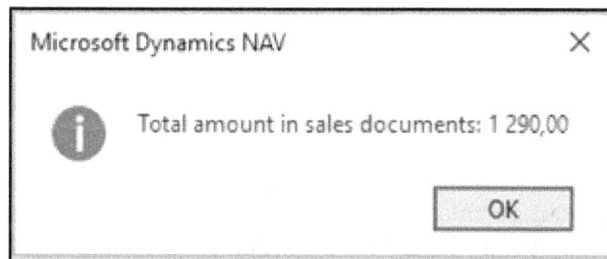

Configuring NAV Server

After installing the demonstration or development configuration, you can access the NAV database without any additional setup – just run the Role-Tailored Client. Now let's see how to change default settings and connect to NAV Server with NAV user credentials instead of Windows domain authentication.

Getting ready

The NAV User Password authentication method requires an SSL certificate that must be installed on both server and client computers. For testing purposes, you can generate a self-signed certificate with the **New-SelfSignedCertificateEx** PowerShell cmdlet that can be downloaded from Microsoft TechNet.

How to do it...

1. Run **Role-Tailored Client** and connect to your NAV Server instance.
2. In the main application menu, navigate to **Administration | IT Administration | General | Users** to open the list of user accounts and click **New**.
3. Fill in the user card. The first field to enter is **User Name**. Enter here the login name the user will enter when connecting to the server.
4. Leave **Windows User Name** blank and move to the **Microsoft Dynamics NAV Password Authentication** tab, click on the **assist edit** button in the **Password** field, and enter a new user password.
5. Move to **User Permission Sets** tab and assign one or more permission sets to the user account.

> Users without permission sets won't be able to login to the server. At least one user account must have the **SUPER** permission set assigned to it.

6. From the **Start** menu, run the Windows PowerShell console with administrator credentials. To do this, open the start menu, type `PowerShell`, right-click on the application name, and choose the command **Run as administrator**.

7. Change the current directory to the folder where you saved the `New-SelfSignedCertificateEx.ps1` cmdlet.

8. Load the contents of the `New-SelfSignedCertificateEx.ps1` file into the shell:

```
. .\New-SelfSignedCertificateEx.ps1
```

9. Run the function `New-SelfSignedCertificateEx` with the following parameters, replacing "`<Server Name>`" with the name of your computer hosting the web server:

```
New-SelfSignedCertificateEx -Subject "CN=<Server Name>"
  -IsCA $true -Exportable -StoreLocation LocalMachine
```

The following screenshot shows the output generated:

```
PS C:\> cd c:\Dynamics NAV
PS C:\Dynamics NAV> . .\New-SelfSignedCertificateEx.ps1
PS C:\Dynamics NAV> New-SelfSignedCertificateEx -Subject "CN=localhost" -IsCA $true -Exportable -StoreLocation LocalMach
ine

Thumbprint                                Subject
----------                                -------
1551A2CF7C766AFEF8EC5C4476BAF04269C2380C  CN=localhost


PS C:\Dynamics NAV> _
```

10. Run **Microsoft Management Console**: open the **Application** menu and type mmc.

11. Click **Add/Remove Snap-in** in the **File** menu.

12. Select **Certificates** in the list of available snap-ins, click **Add**, then choose **Computer Account**, and then **Local Computer.**

13. Unfold the **Personal | Certificates** folder under the **Console Root** and locate the certificate you just created. You can easily identify it by the **Issued To** and **Issued By** fields. They both will have the name of your computer.

14. Right-click on the certificate, select **All Tasks | Manage Private Keys**. Add **Read** permission for **NETWORK SERVICE** account.

15. Copy the certificate from **Personal | Certificates to Trusted Root Certification Authorities | Certificates**.

16. Double-click on the certificate name or choose **Open** from the drop-down menu. Open the **Details** tab and scroll to the **Thumbprint** field:

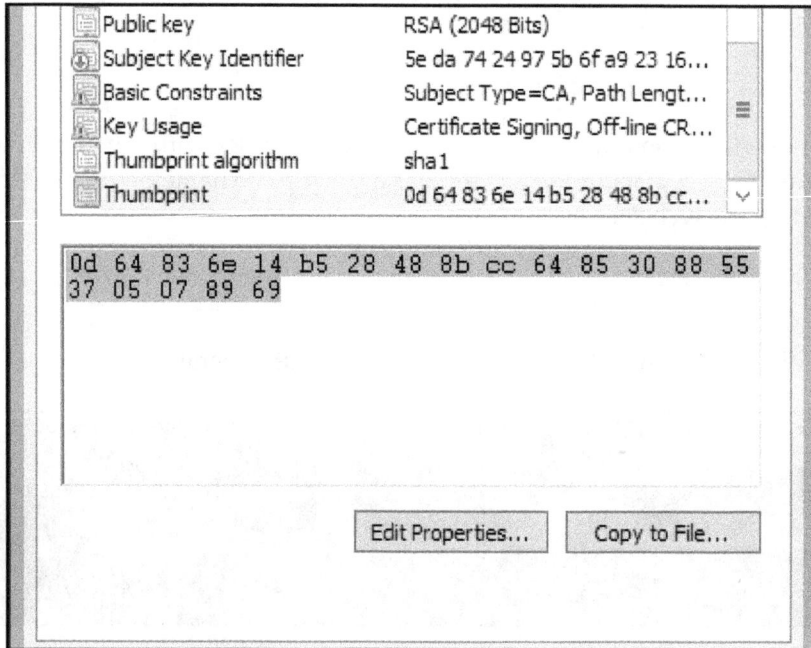

17. Copy it to a text editor and remove all white spaces from it. The correct certificate thumbprint must be a 40-digit hexadecimal number. For example, `0d64836e14b528488bcc64853088553705078969`.

> This number is only an example. Your certificate will have a different thumbprint.

18. Keep the value, it will be required in the next step.
19. From the **Start** menu, run **Dynamics NAV 2016 Administration**.
20. Unfold the **Microsoft Dynamics NAV (local)** snap-in under the console root and choose your server instance name. If you accepted the default name when installing the server, it should be **DynamicsNAV90**.
21. Click **Edit** in the configuration pane. Change the value of the **Credential Type** field from **Windows** to **NAVUserPassword**.

22. Fill the **Certificate Thumbprint** field. Copy the value you received from the self-signed certificate. Make sure you delete all spaces between digit groups. The certificate thumbprint must be exactly 40 characters long.

23. Click **Save** – you will be warned that the service must restart before the new settings will be activated.

24. To restart the service, click on the snap-in name (**Microsoft Dynamics NAV**), then choose the service instance in the middle pane of the management console. After that, the **Restart** button will be available in the **Actions** pane on the right. Click **Restart** and wait for the action to complete:

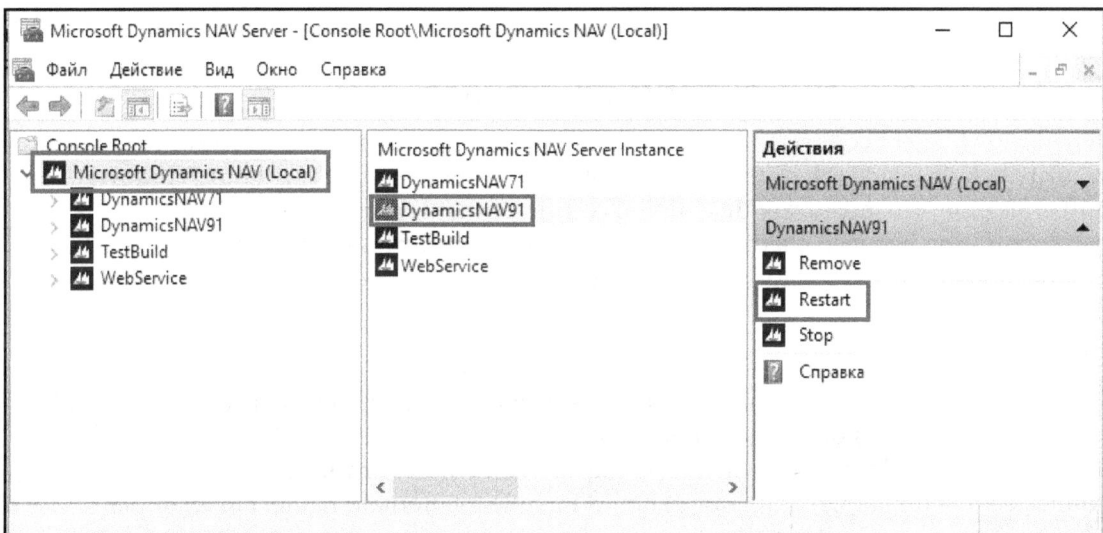

25. Open the `ClientUserSettings.config` file located in the `AppData` directory. Its default location is `C:\Users\<UserName>\AppData\Roaming\Microsoft\Microsoft Dynamics NAV\90\ClientUserSettings.config`.

26. Change the value of the `ClientServicesCredentialType` key from `Windows` to `NavUserPassword`:

```
<add key="ClientServicesCredentialType"
  value="NavUserPassword" />
```

27. Run the Role Tailored Client. You will be requested to enter a user name and password. Enter a user name and password of the user you created earlier. You will be connected to NAV with the NAV user credentials instead of your domain account.

How it works...

Changing the authentication method requires a number of changes in configuration on both the server and client side.

Creating a NAV user account

Since we want to change the server authentication type, first of all we need to create a user account that will be able to connect to the server after the new configuration takes effect. Step 1 to Step 5 create a new user that will connect with new credentials.

Generating a self-signed certificate

When a NAV client connects to a server with Windows authentication, Windows hides all security details inside the Kerberos protocol. If we want to connect without Windows authentication, we must provide a digital certificate that will ensure security of communication between client and server. Real-life certificates are issued by a trusted certification authority, but for development and testing purposes you can create your own certificate.

Step 6 and Step 7 will create such a self-signed certificate. When generating a certificate, make sure that the server name passed to the cmdlet exactly matches the computer's full name, as shown in its properties. If you don't know the server's full name, open the Windows File Explorer, right-click on **Computer**, and select **Properties**. If your computer is connected to a domain, its full name should include the domain name. For example: `mycomputer.domain.com`.

Obtaining the certificate thumbprint

After running the `New-SelfSignedCertificateEx` cmdlet, your new certificate is created in the **LocalMachine** certificate store. Each SSL certificate has a so-called thumbprint, a hexadecimal number generated by a hash algorithm from the certificate content. This number must be provided to both the NAV server and client to establish a secure connection.

Changing the server configuration

Step 15 to Step 20 modify the server instance configuration. We simply change two keys in the server setup, but this would not work without long preparation work made in previous steps.

A final modification in the client configuration file is required to ensure that client and server will use the same authentication protocol.

Configuring web server

Web server configuration requires proper attention, because the setup must ensure security of the data sent over the Internet. This recipe will explain how to access your NAV Server from a web browser using a secure connection with the HTTPS protocol. In conclusion, we will see how to connect to NAV from a mobile device will simple additional steps.

Getting ready

Several prerequisites must be met before you can connect to your NAV server over the Web.

- Microsoft Dynamics NAV Web Server must be installed and connected to the NAV Server instance which you want to be accessible from the phone client. Web server and NAV Server can be running on separate computers, but the web server must have access to the NAV instance.
- To generate a self-signed security certificate you will need the `New-SelfSignedCertificateEx` PowerShell cmdlet that can be downloaded from Microsoft TechNet.
- To connect to the NAV server from a mobile device, as per the *There's more* section, NAV Phone Client must be installed on your device. The installation path depends on the OS version of your mobile device. For example, on an Android device, tap the **Google Play** icon and type Dynamics NAV in the **Search** window. Then choose the Dynamics NAV application from the search result and follow the on-screen installation instructions.

How to do it...

1. From the Start menu, run the Dynamics NAV Administration Shell or Windows Powershell and change the active directory to the folder where you saved the `New-SelfSignedCertificateEx.ps1` cmdlet.

2. Run the cmdlet with the following parameters, replacing `"<Server Name>"` with the name of your computer hosting the web server:

   ```
   .\New-SelfSignedCertificateEx.ps1 -Subject "CN=<Server Name>"
   -IsCA $true -Exportable -StoreLocation LocalMachine -StoreName My
   ```

3. Run Microsoft Management Console. Open the **Application** menu and type `mmc`.

4. Click **Add/Remove Snap-in** in the **File** menu.

5. Select **Certificates** in the list of available snap-ins, click **Add**, then choose **Computer Account**, and then **Local Computer**.

6. Unfold the `Personal / Certificates` folder under the Console Root and locate the certificate you just created. You can easily identify it by the **Issued To** and **Issued By** fields. They both will have the name of your computer.

7. Right-click on the certificate, select **All Tasks | Manage Private Keys**. Add **Read** permission for **NETWORK SERVICE** account.

8. Copy the certificate from **Personal | Certificates** to **Trusted Root Certification Authorities | Certificates**.

9. Double-click on the certificate name or choose **Open** from the drop-down menu. Open the **Details** tab and scroll to the **Thumbprint** field.

10. Copy it to a text editor and remove all white spaces from it. The correct certificate thumbprint must be a 40-digit hexadecimal number. For example: `0d64836e14b528488bcc64853088553705078969`.

11. Right-click on the certificate name and choose **All Tasks | Export**. Accept the default values for all options in the certificate export master: do not export the private key, choose the **X.509 in DER encoding** as the certificate format. Specify the file's location and name; this is the file you will need to copy to the client connecting to NAV.

12. In the Microsoft Management Console, click **Add/Remove Snap-ins,** choose **Microsoft Dynamics NAV** in the snap-ins list, and add it to the console root.

13. Right-click on the **Microsoft Dynamics NAV** snap-in and choose **Add Instance**.

14. In the **Server Instance** window, specify the new instance name and services ports. For this demo, we will name the instance `WebLogin`. When setting ports for services, make sure they are not used by other NAV instances.

15. Select **Network Service** as the service account:

16. Click **OK** to accept the settings and create the service instance. Still in the management console, click the **Edit** button in the right pane to change the configuration setting of the new service:

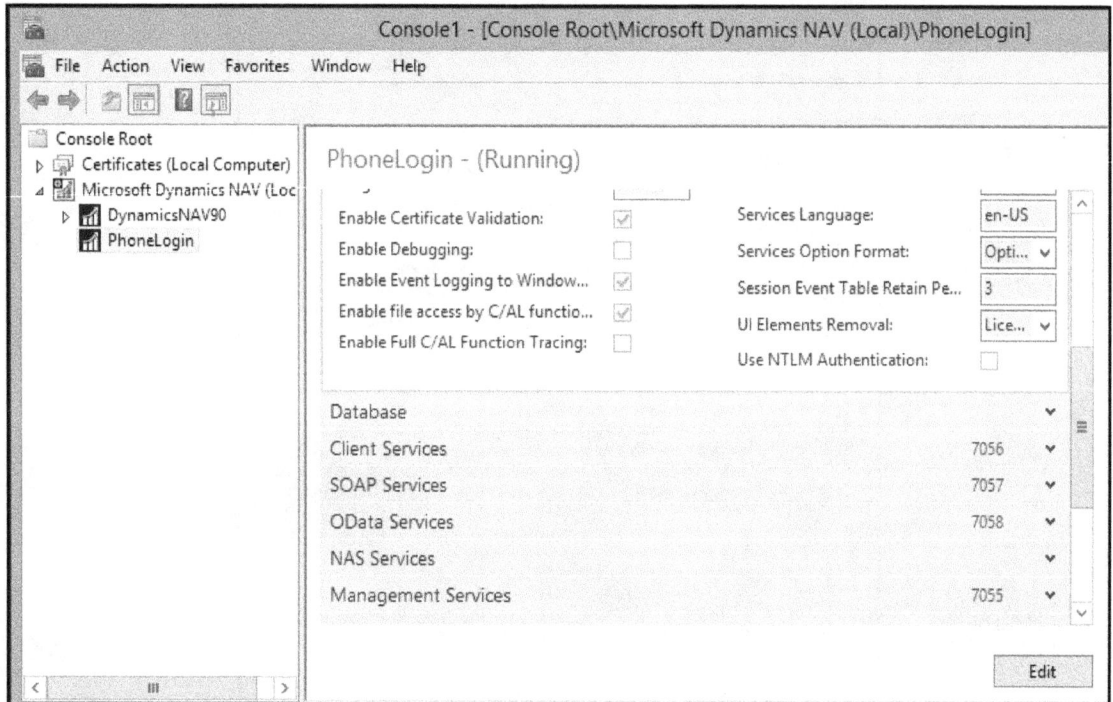

17. The first parameter that should be changed is **Credential Type**. The default value is **Windows**; select **NavUserPassword** in the dropdown list.

18. You also need to provide the certificate thumbprint in the **Certificate Thumbprint** field. To obtain the thumbprint value, return to your certificate created in the first step and double-click on the certificate name or choose **Open** from the drop-down menu. Open the **Details** tab and scroll to the **Thumbprint** field.

19. Copy the thumbprint to the NAV service setup. Don't forget to remove all white spaces from it, or the value will not be accepted.

20. Add the **Internet Information Services** snap-in to the Microsoft Management Console. Click **Add/Remove Snap-in** and select **Internet Information Services**.

21. In the `Sites` folder locate `Microsoft Dynamics NAV 2016 Web Client`. Select the site root and click on **Bindings** in the **Actions** pane.

22. Add site binding for HTTPS protocol: choose **https** for **Type** and leave the default port as `443` for HTTPS connections. In the **SSL certificate** option choose the certificate you created in the first step, from the drop-down list.

23. In the IIS management console, select the `DynamicsNAV` folder under the `Microsoft Dynamics NAV 2016 Web Client` site and then click on **Explore** action in the **Actions** pane. This action will open the folder in which web site files are located. Alternatively, you can open this folder in a file manager. The default files location is `C:\inetpub\wwwroot\DynamicsNAV90`.

24. Open the `web.config` file in a text editor, change the following three configuration keys, and save the file:
    - `ServerInstance.` `New value:` WebLogin
    - `ClientServicesCredentialType.` `New value:` NavUserPassword
    - `ClientServicesPort.` `New value:` 7056

25. Connect to the NAV server with the role-tailored client and open users setup: `Administration | IT Administration | General | Users`.

26. Create a new user. Enter a user name and set the password in the **Microsoft Dynamics NAV Password Authentication** tab. Leave the **Windows User Name** field blank.

27. Assign permission sets of your choice to the user. At least one user in the database must have the **SUPER** permission set.

28. Install the certificate on the client computer.

29. Run the web browser and open the page by typing this URL, `https://localhost:8080/DynamicsNAV90/`.

You will required to enter the user name and password:

Microsoft Dynamics NAV

User name

PHONELOGIN

Password

$\rightarrow$

30. After successful authentication, you will be redirected to the default role center:

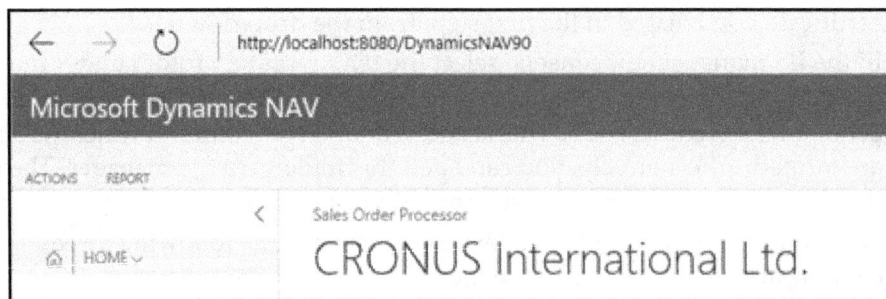

How it works...

In Step 1 through Step 8 we generate a self-signed SSL certificate the same way we did in the previous recipe of this chapter, *Configuring NAV Server*. The certificate is required whenever we need to establish a secure connection with authentication type other than Windows.

After running the `New-SelfSignedCertificateEx` cmdlet, your new certificate is created in the **LocalMachine** certificate store. A client computer connecting to the server must hold a copy of this certificate. To copy it to the client PC or mobile device, you need to export the certificate file. Step 9 exports the security certificate into a file that will be installed on client. A new NAV Server instance is created and configured in Step 10 to Step 17. We need two service instances here to redirect web requests to a separate service and leave Windows users unaffected. The user login type in NAV is defined by the server-side setup, and once a service is configured for `NAVUserPassword` credential type, it cannot authenticate users with the Windows credential type; they will receive a "`Protocol mismatch`" error. Since web users are outside of the corporate domain and cannot access the server with Windows credentials, we must change the authentication type they use. But we still want domain users to be able to login with their Windows domain account. And this is why we need the second service instance. Users within domain will be connecting to the service `DynamicsNAV90`, nothing will change for them. On the other hand, web requests will be redirected to the `WebLogin` service. Since both services point to the same database, all users will work with the same data and application.

Our front-end is the web server published by the **Internet Information Services** (**IIS**), and the IIS service must forward all incoming requests to the correct back-end service. Now let us configure the web service.

The final setup on the web server side is to configure authorization requests from IIS to the NAV instance that will serve them.

There's more...

With the web server configuration complete, you can connect to the same service from a mobile device running NAV Tablet Client or Phone Client.

Your mobile device must have the SSL certificate registered, same as the Windows Role-Tailored Client. To install the certificate on the mobile device:

- Copy the exported certificate file to the mobile device, locate it, and click on the file.
- Give a name to the certificate when asked. This name is independent of the server or client name and can be any text as shown in the following screenshot:

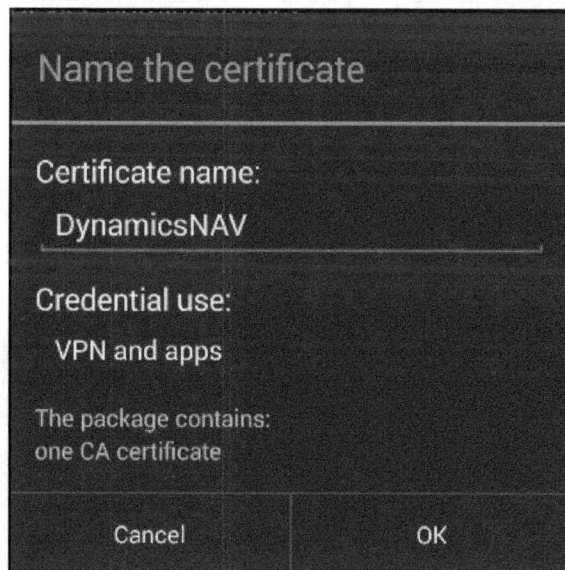

Name the certificate

Certificate name:

DynamicsNAV

Credential use:

VPN and apps

The package contains:
one CA certificate

Cancel   OK

After the certificate is successfully installed, you will see a confirmation. Then locate the Dynamics NAV phone client shortcut in your applications and click it. You will be prompted to enter the service name:

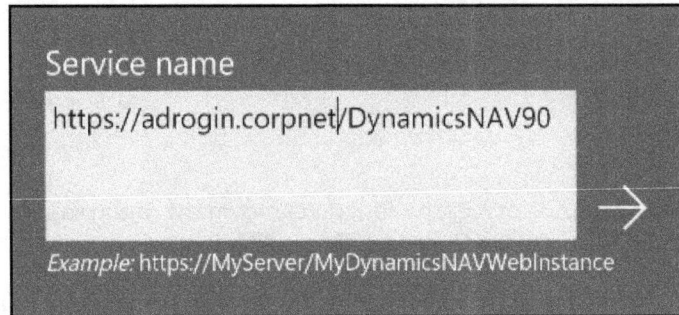

Service name

https://adrogin.corpnet/DynamicsNAV90

Example: https://MyServer/MyDynamicsNAVWebInstance

Enter the server name and the web instance name and connect to the server. You will be asked to enter a user name and password. These are the name and the password of the user created in the previous step.

Now you are connected to the NAV server:

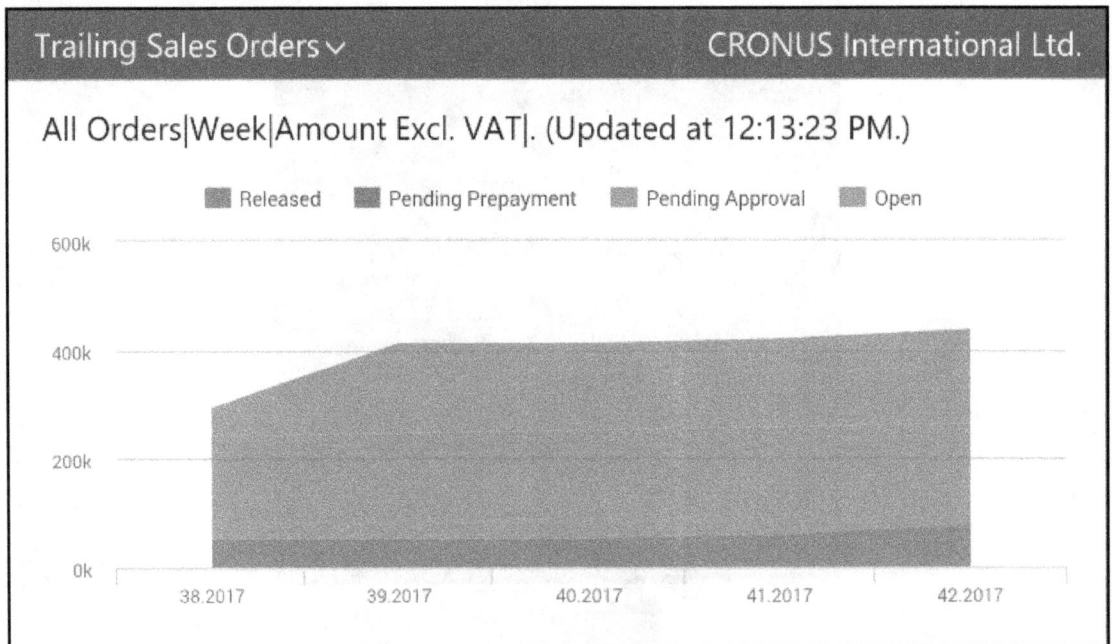

Trailing Sales Orders ⌄   CRONUS International Ltd.

All Orders|Week|Amount Excl. VAT|. (Updated at 12:13:23 PM.)

▨ Released   ▨ Pending Prepayment   ▨ Pending Approval   ▨ Open

600k				
400k				
200k				
0k				
38.2017	39.2017	40.2017	41.2017	42.2017

If you are configuring a web server inside your corporate network, it is possible that you won't be able to perform this step and connect to the server from a mobile phone. Corporate security policies often block connections to internal resources from outside. In this case, discuss possible solutions with your company's system administrators.

See also

- The *Configuring NAV Server* recipe

Advanced C/AL Development

2

In this chapter we will cover the following recipes:

- Creating custom tables
- Understanding database triggers
- Implementing a user interface with pages
- Linking datasources in subpages
- Working with page triggers
- Presenting related data in FactBoxes
- Designing reusable code
- Accessing temporary tables
- Role-Tailored client and role centers
- Assigning role centers to user profiles
- Simplifying data access with queries
- Improving performance with table indexes
- Linking datasources with advanced queries
- Exchanging data with XMLPort objects
- Designing user menu
- Referencing records and fields via RecordRef and FieldRef
- Working with single instance codeunits
- Running tasks in background sessions

Introduction

Each object type in Dynamics NAV has a designer associated with it. So far, we dealt with only one type – codeunit designer where you could write C/AL code. But different tasks, such as describing a table structure or designing a user interface in pages, require different tools. In this chapter we will have a closer look at all types of object designers presented in NAV development environment.

To make all the examples consistent, recipes in this chapter are presented in a form of a small add-on, each recipe expanding its functionality. We will see how to create a data model, present data in pages, move common code into codeunits, and create custom menus and a role center for the add-on.

Examples will be centered around a fictitious company selling goods that require a quality certificate to be sold. We will create a solution to store certificates, keep track of their validity, and block sales documents posting for items with an expired or invalid certificate.

Creating custom tables

Data is the core of any business application. We will start developing our solution from designing the data model. The first recipe will show how to create custom tables, set up field references and configure FlowFields that are calculated by the NAV platform based on table data.

How to do it...

In this recipe, we design the data model for the solution.

1. Open Object Designer and select **Table** in the list of object types. Click **New**. Table designer will open.
2. Each table field must have a number, a name, and a data type. Number 1 is already assign automatically. In the **Field Name** field enter No. and choose **Code** as **Data Type**. Finally, enter 20 in **Length**. This will create a **Code[20]** field.
3. Move to the next empty line. **Field No.** will automatically increment. Enter CA Code in **Field Name**, **Code** in **Data Type**, and 20 in **Length**.

4. Create other fields as given in the following table:

Field No.	Field Name	Data Type	Length
1	No.	Code	20
2	CA Code	Code	20
3	Item No.	Code	20
4	Issued Date	Date	
5	Last Prolonged Date	Date	

5. Click **File | Save** to save the table. You will be prompted to enter table ID and name. These fields are common for all objects, as well as the next field compiled. We have already seen the same fields when saving new codeunits. Save the object as table `50010Item Certificate`.

6. The last field in the **Save As** dialog box, **Synchronize Schema**, is unique for tables, it is not applicable for other objects. This value indicates the method of metadata synchronization between NAV and SQL Server. Select the default value **Now – with validation**:

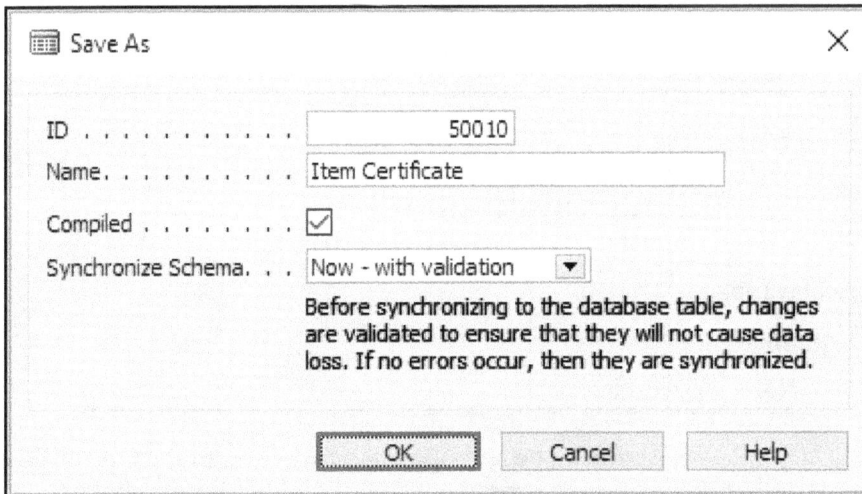

7. Select field number 3 **Item No.** and open **Properties** from the **View** menu or press *Shift + F4*.

8. Find the property `TableRelation` and click on the **assist** button in the column **Value**. In the **Table** column, enter the table name as `Item`, then field name `No.` in the **Field** column.

9. Click the **assist** button in the **Table Filter** field to open the filter setup window. Set values as follows:

Field	Type	Value
Type	CONST	Inventory

10. Click **OK** after configuring the relation filter. In the **Table Relation** setup window click **OK** again. When table relation setup is complete, the **TableRelation** field in the table designer should have the value:

```
Item.No. WHERE (Type=CONST(Inventory))
```

11. Create a **50011 Certification Authority** table. Add fields as in the table:

Field No.	Field Name	Data Type	Length
1	Code	Code	20
2	Name	Text	50

12. Create table **50012 Item Certificate Action**. Create fields as in the table:

Field No.	Field Name	Data Type	Length
1	Certificate No.	Code	20
2	Action Date	Date	
3	Action Type	Option	
4	Expiration Date	Date	
5	Item No.	Code	20

13. Select the field 3 **Action Type** and open its properties. In the **OptionString** property set value: **,Issued,Prolonged,Revoked** (the first symbol before the comma is a space, it is important for the field to be presented correctly in pages).

14. When all tables are created, we can set up key references between them. Open table **50010 Item Certificate** in table designer and open properties for field **No. 2 CA Code**. This is the reference to the authority issuing the certificate (table Certification Authority). Locate the property **TableRelation** and enter `"Certification Authority"` (with quotation marks).

15. Open properties for the field 4 **Issued Date**. Set **Editable = No, FieldClass = FlowField**. In the **CalcFormula** property, click the **assist** button to open the **Calculation Formula** setup. Fill the values as follows:

- **Method: Lookup**
- **Table: 50012**
- **Field: Action Date**

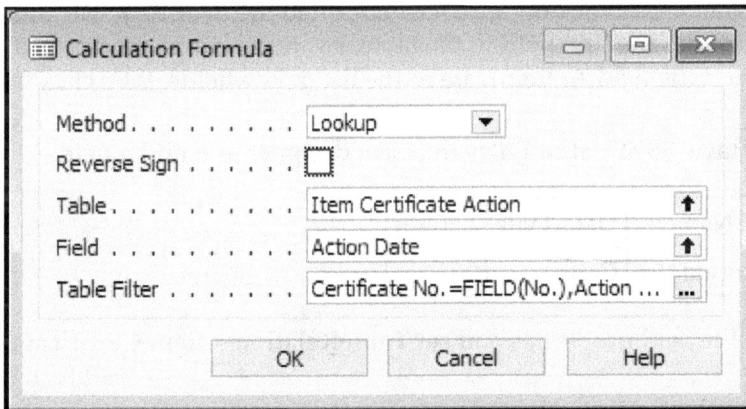

16. In the **Table Filter** field, click the assist button and fill the filtering parameters:

Field	Type	Value
Certificate No.	FIELD	No.
Action Type	CONST	Issued

17. Click **OK** in the filtering parameters, then in the calculation formula setup. **CalcFormula** should be evaluated to the code:

```
Lookup("Item Certificate Action"."Action Date" WHERE
    (Certificate No.=FIELD(No.),Action Type=CONST(Issued)))
```

[51]

18. Setup the field 5 **Last Prolonged Date** the same way: set **Editable** to **No**, **FieldClass** property to **FlowField**, and **CalcFormula** to:

```
Max("Item Certificate Action"."Action Date" WHERE
    (Certificate No.=FIELD(No.),Action Type=CONST(Prolonged)))
```

You can set up the formula step-by-step or simply copy the preceding line into the property value. After configuring **Last Prolonged Date**, save the table and close the designer.

19. Setup field properties in the table 50012 **Item Certificate Action**. Open the table in table designer and open properties for the field 1 **Certificate No**. Set **Editable = No** and **TableReference = 50010**.

20. Change the primary key for the table **Item Certificate Action**. Click **Keys** in the **View** menu and click on the **assist** button in the field **Key**. The default primary key includes the first field in the table. For our example, we need a compound key. Add the field **Action Date** to the list of key fields, then click **OK** and save the table.

21. Open table 5802 **Value Entry** in object designer and add a field:

Field No.	Field Name	Data Type	Length
50000	Certificate No.	Code	20

22. Open the field properties and set **TableRelation = Item Certificate**.

How it works...

In this recipe we are creating tables for our small add-on. To see the whole picture, let's look at the ER diagram of the data model as follows:

Item Certificate

PK	No.
	CA Code
	Item No.

Certification Authority

PK	Code
	Name

Value Entry

PK	Entry No.
	Item No.
	Certificate No.

Item Certificate Action

PK	Certificate No.
PK	Action Date
	Action Type
	Expiration Date
	Item No.

Item

PK	No.
	Description

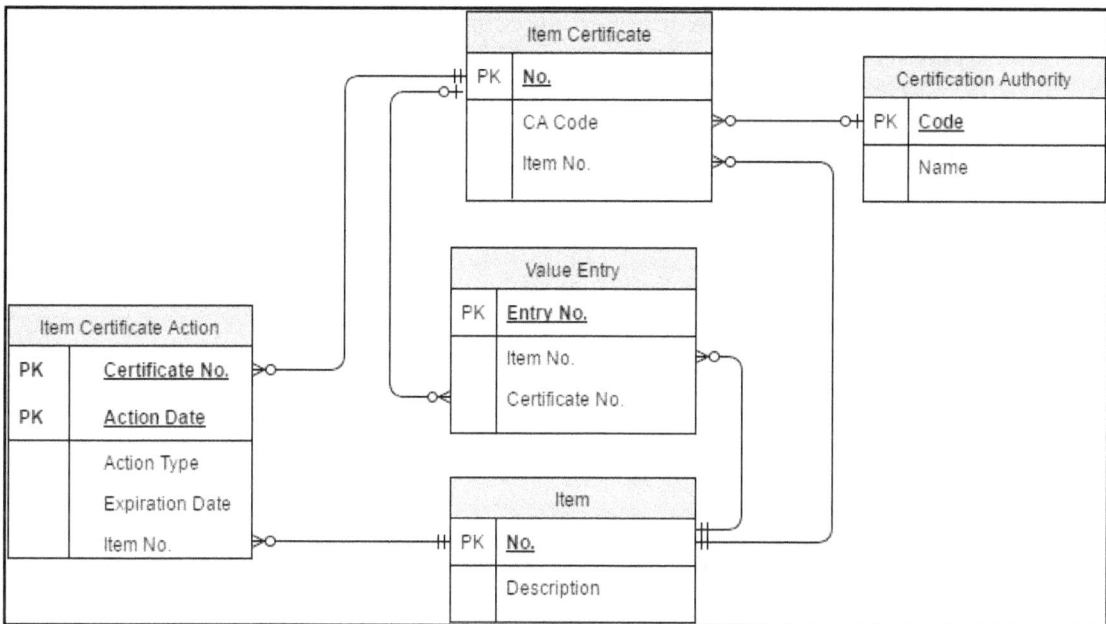

Each NAV Table object is mapped to an actual table in SQL Server database, and most of the fields have their representation as fields in database tables. But, as you can see, some of the fields declared above are missing in the diagram. Skipped are fields that have **FieldClass** property equal to **FlowField**. Actually, only fields with **FieldClass = Normal** are stored in the database.

The **FlowField** field is a special type of field that is not saved in the database, but is calculated "on-the-fly" according to the formula described in the **CalcFormula** property. For example, formula we configured in the **Issued Date** field of the table **Item Certificate** uses method **Lookup** on the **Item Certificate Action** table to retrieve the field value. **Lookup** means that whenever the field's value is calculated, NAV will find the first record in the **Item Certificate Action** table that corresponds to the set of filters and return the value of the field **Action Date**.

To get the value of a **FlowField** field in the application code, we use the function CALCFIELDS. For example, to calculate the field for a certificate number 12345:

```
ItemCertificate.GET('12345');
ItemCertificate.CALCFIELDS("Issued Date");
```

When table objects are saved in the designer, a specific option in the **Save** dialog appears that requests the schema synchronization option. This option is here, because table is the only C/SIDE object mapped to SQL Server metadata. While pages, reports and other objects are internal C/AL entities, tables must maintain schema mapping. Every time a table is compiled, the corresponding SQL table must be updated accordingly:

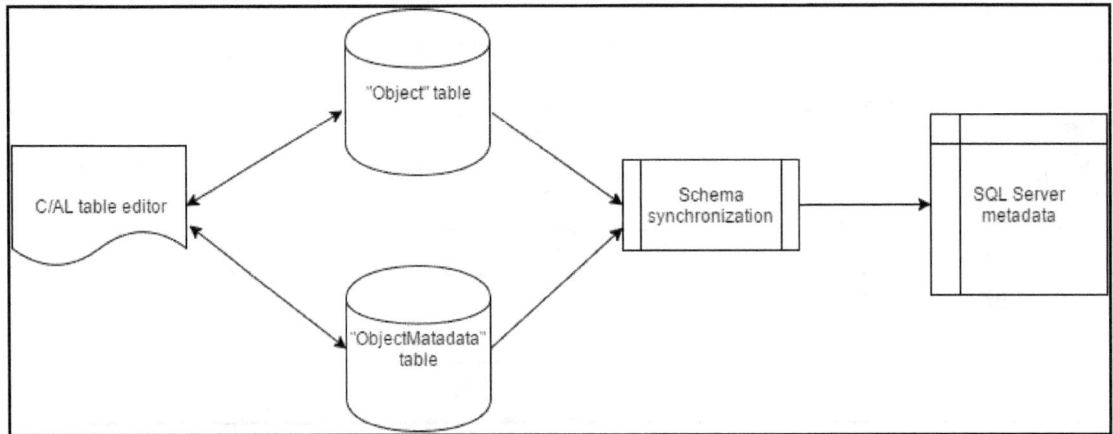

The synchronization procedure issues a SQL DDL statements to update affected database tables. But before applying modifications, Dynamics NAV Server will verify that the modification will not cause data corruption.

If potentially destructive factors are detected during verification, it will attempt to run all upgrade triggers defined for the table to safely update data. If no upgrade trigger exists, synchronization will fail and changes will not be propagated to the SQL server.

Changes that are considered destructive are:

- Table deleted
- Table field deleted
- Length of a text field reduced
- Data type of a field changed, and implicit conversion is impossible (for example, data type changed from Text to Integer or vice versa)
- Field is removed from a compound primary key

Available options for schema synchronization are as follows:

- **Now – with validation**: Table synchronization will be executed immediately. Cannot be done if the Dynamics NAV Server service is unavailable.
- **Later**: Table modifications will be saved in the **Object** and **ObjectMetadata** tables, but will not be synchronized with the SQL Server metadata. Changes must be synchronized later.
- **Force**: With this option, modifications will not be validated, no upgrade triggers are executed. Any data affected by the modification will be deleted.

> The **Force** option is for development and testing environment. Do not use it on production server, since it may result in data loss.

Only when all tables are saved, we can set up table relations. This is done in Step 14 and Step 19. Besides, it means that the reference will be automatically checked for consistency every time a new value is assigned to the field **Item** in the **Item Certificate** table. The verification procedure performed by NAV platform will ensure that the item no. is a valid item code existing in the **Item** table.

The C/AL code can override this verification. Assignment statements such as `ItemCertificate."Item No."` `:=` `'NewItem'` will set the new value even if it is inconsistent (item with code `'NewItem'` does not exist in the **Item** table). To ensure verification is executed, assign new values through the `VALIDATE` function: `ItemCertificate.VALIDATE("Item No.", 'NewItem')`. In case of inconsistent assignment the `VALIDATE` function will fail with error.

Step 20 creates a compound key for the **Item Certificate Action** table. When a new table is created, it always receives the primary key — NAV tables cannot be created as a heap, without the clustered index. First key in the list of table keys is always the primary key, all other are table indexes. Any key can be made compound:

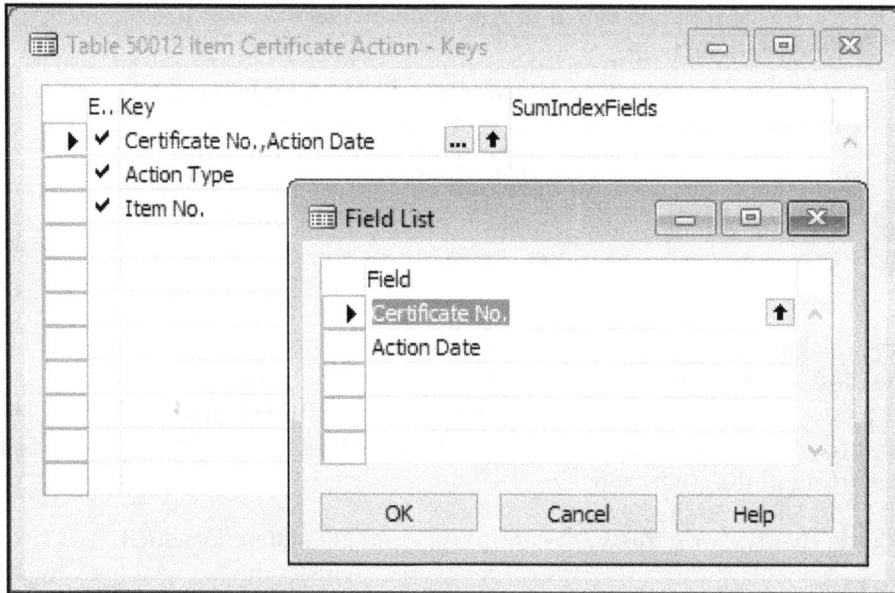

Step 21 and Step 22 add a reference to the item certificate from the **Value Entry** table. Later in this chapter we will add code to fill this field while posting sales documents, and use the updated value to calculate sales amounts related to particular certificate.

Understanding database triggers

Data in the database is constantly changed – records are inserted, updated, deleted. Almost any user action results in data modification, and all modifications of data run application triggers.

How to do it...

In this recipe we will learn how to use some of the most important and frequently used table triggers to control data flow.

1. Open table 50010 **Item Certificate** in object designer. Click **C/AL Code** in the **View** menu or press *F9* to open table code. Open **C/AL Globals** and create two functions, DeleteCertificateActions and UpdateItemOnActions.

2. Position cursor in the DeleteCertificateActions variable and declare a local record variable ItemCertificateAction:

Name	DataType	Subtype
ItemCertificateAction	Record	Item Certificate Action

3. This is a simple function with lines of code in it:

    ```
    ItemCertificateAction.SETRANGE("Certificate No.","No.");
    ItemCertificateAction.DELETEALL;
    ```

4. Move to the function UpdateItemOnActions. Declare a local record variable ItemCertificateAction. It has the same type and subtype as the previous variable. You can copy it from the function DeleteCertificateActions.

5. Place the function code under the function name:

    ```
    ItemCertificateAction.SETRANGE("Certificate No.","No.");
    ItemCertificateAction.MODIFYALL("Item No.","Item No.");
    ```

6. Locate the table trigger OnModify and place the following code in it:

    ```
    IF "Item No." <> xRec."Item No." THEN
      UpdateItemOnActions;
    ```

7. Under the OnDelete trigger place one line:

    ```
    DeleteCertificateActions;
    ```

8. Open table 50012 **Item Certificate Action** in the object designer. This table has a bit more code in triggers than other tables in this example. I won't write it all here – you can always download code files from the web site. Let's look at one important trigger we did not employ before.

Select the field **Expiration Date** and press *F9*. In the empty line in the `OnValidate` trigger insert code:

```
IF "Action Type" = "Action Type"::Revoked THEN
  TESTFIELD("Expiration Date",0D)
ELSE IF "Expiration Date" < "Action Date" THEN
  FIELDERROR("Expiration Date",
    ' cannot be earlier than ' + FIELDNAME(
    "Action Date"));
```

9. Open table 27 **Item** in the object designer, switch to table **C/AL Code**, and create a function `DeleteItemCertificates`.

10. Declare a local variable in the new function:

Name	DataType	Subtype
`ItemCertificateAction`	Record	Item Certificate Action

11. Insert function code as follows:

```
ItemCertificate.SETRANGE("Item No.","No.");
ItemCertificate.DELETEALL(TRUE);
```

12. Locate the local function `DeleteRelatedData` in the **Item** table and call your new function `DeleteItemCertificates` from it. Insert the last line, after all existing code in `DeleteRelatedData` as follows:

```
DeleteItemCertificates;
```

How it works...

We start by accessing trigger code in a table. In the first recipe of this chapter we dealt with table designer only to create new table fields and configure calculation formulas for **FlowFields**. But behind the scenes, tables have associated code that can be allocated in triggers or user-defined functions. Triggers execute normal C/AL code, but they cannot be called explicitly — triggers are invoked by the platform in response to associated events.

Applies a filter as follows

When a new table is created, it has all supported triggers in place. Any code written in the triggers will be executed when the corresponding database event occurs:

- OnInsert: A new record is inserted in the table
- OnModify: A record is modified
- OnDelete: A record is deleted from the database
- OnRename: One of the primary key fields of the record is modified

The first database event we want to handle is data modification in the table 50010 **Item Certificate**. If the **Item No.** field in the certificate is changed, modification must be propagated to all linked certificate actions to maintain data consistency.

The OnModify trigger is called when any of the table fields are changed, so first we make sure that the field that caused this trigger to fire is indeed **Item No**.

We do it by comparing the value of two global variables Rec and xRec. These are system variables maintained by the NAV platform, they can be accessed in any C/AL function in a table.

The Rec variable always refers to the current value of the record.

In the OnModify trigger variable xRec will contain the value of the record before the modification. If, for example, value of **Item No.** is changed from *1110* to *1120*, the OnModify trigger is called with Rec."Item No," = 1120, and xRec."Item No." = 1110.

```
IF "Item No." <> xRec."Item No." THEN
```

This verification before modifying data is not required. If we update item code that has not been changed, we will just change a field value with exactly the same value. But this is a good style to skip unnecessary data modifications to reduce database server workload when possible. One comparison operation can save us a database query that is much more expensive in terms of computational resources.

When we are sure that the value is in fact changed, and related records must also be updated, we filter the **Item Certificate Action** table by the value of the **Certificate No.** field and modify all records.

```
ItemCertificateAction.SETRANGE("Certificate No.","No.");
```

Applies a filter as follows:

```
ItemCertificateAction.MODIFYALL("Item No.","Item No.");
```

The `MODIFYALL` function will update all records in the table **Item Certificate Action** which fall under the filtering criteria.

In the previous recipe I already mentioned the `VALIDATE` function. It should be used when assigning values to record fields to perform data validations. Besides running platform verification for referential integrity, it will also execute the `OnValidate` trigger for the field.

The `DeleteItemCertificates` function in Step 9 to Step 11 deletes all certificates assigned to an item when the item is deleted. Here, function `DELETEALL` is called with a `boolean` parameter `TRUE`. This parameter indicates that the `OnDelete` trigger in the table **Item Certificate** will be called. If the parameter value is `FALSE` or it is omitted, trigger will not be executed. The `DELETEALL(FALSE)` trigger is faster that `DELETEALL(TRUE)` trigger, because it will issue only one SQL query, while the latter will delete each record separately.

Implementing a user interface with pages

The foundation of the user interface in Dynamics NAV, is the `Page` object. Pages can be used to represent table data, receive user input, and exhibit actions buttons.

C/AL code can be executed in pages to format data and process data received from the input.

How to do it...

In this recipe, we will implement the user interface based on pages, and write C/AL code formatting data in the page.

1. In the object designer, select **Page** in the object types list and Click on **New** — this action button will open the page designer.
2. In the **Table** field of the page wizard, select table 50010 **Item Certificate** as the source table for the page, or just enter its name or ID manually.

3. Chose **Create a page using wizard** option and select **Card** in the list of page types. Click **OK**:

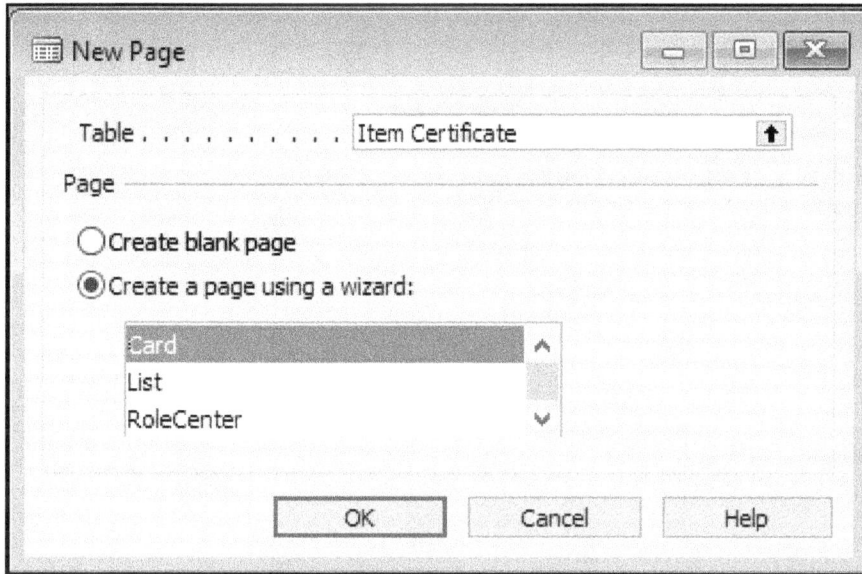

4. Next step in the wizard will suggest you to create FastTabs on the page. Leave one tab named **General**, as per the default setup, then click **Next**.
5. In the next step, we select table fields that will be presented on the page. Move all fields from the **Available Fields** pane to the **Field Order** pane.
6. Next step is **FactBox** setup. The **Item Certificate** card does not have any fact boxes, so click **Finish** here to complete the wizard.

7. Click **Preview** to make sure:

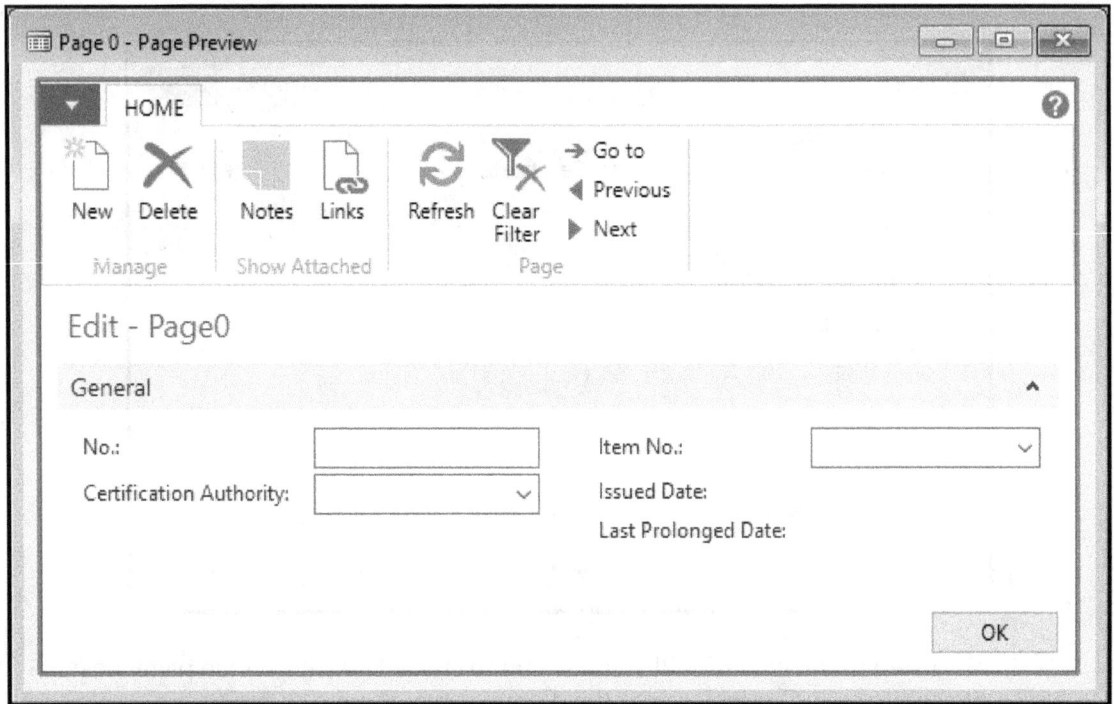

Page 0 - Page Preview

| | HOME | | | | | | |

New Delete Notes Links Refresh Clear Filter Go to Previous Next

Manage Show Attached Page

Edit - Page0

General

No.:

Certification Authority:

Item No.:

Issued Date:

Last Prolonged Date:

OK

8. Close the preview and save the page 50010 **Item Certificate Card**. Close the page designer.

9. Back in the object designer, create another page. Enter the same table 50010 as the page source, choose **Create a page using a wizard**. But instead of **Card**, select the **List** page type. Other steps of the wizard are identical to the **Card** wizard, except the **FastTtabs** definition. **FastTabs** cannot be created in a list page, so this step will be skipped:

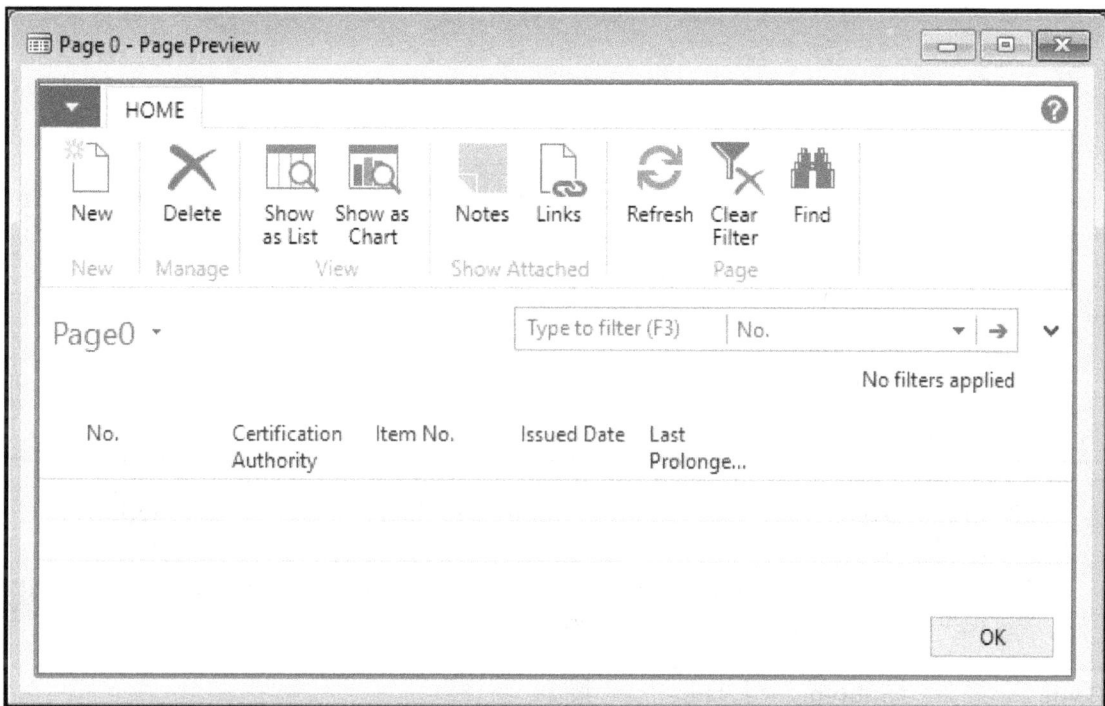

10. Save the new page with ID 50013 and name Item Certificate List.

11. Step in the empty line below all fields in the designer and open **Page-Properties**. In the **Editable** property select **No** from the drop-down list as shown here:

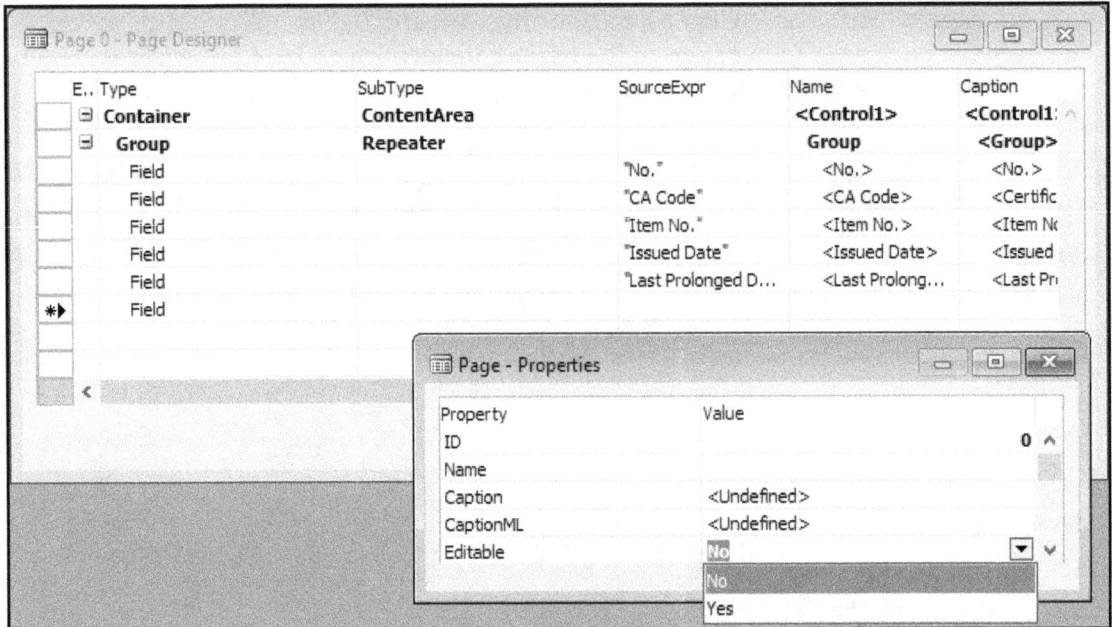

E.. Type	SubType	SourceExpr	Name	Caption
⊟ Container	ContentArea		<Control1>	<Control1:
⊟ Group	Repeater		Group	<Group>
Field		"No."	<No.>	<No.>
Field		"CA Code"	<CA Code>	<Certific
Field		"Item No."	<Item No.>	<Item No
Field		"Issued Date"	<Issued Date>	<Issued
Field		"Last Prolonged D...	<Last Prolong...	<Last Pr
Field				

Page - Properties

Property	Value
ID	0
Name	
Caption	<Undefined>
CaptionML	<Undefined>
Editable	No
	No
	Yes

12. In the next step, we will add action buttons to the page. **Select Page Actions** in the **View** menu or press *Ctrl + Alt + F4* to open the page **Action Designer**.

13. Before creating action buttons, you need **ActionContainer** where the actions will reside. In the action designer, insert the container line:

Type	Subtype	Name
ActionContainer	ActionItems	Certification

14. Add action items below the container and ensure actions are indented under the **ActionContainer** type as shown here:

E..	Type	SubType	Name	Caption
⊟	**ActionContainer**	**ActionItems**	**Certification**	**<Certification>**
	Action		IssueCertificate	Issue Certificate
	Action		ProlongCertificate	Prolong Certificate
▶	Action		RevokeCertificate	Revoke Certificate

15. Select the first action **IssueCertificate** and open **C/AL Code**. You will see the function called `IssueCertificate - OnAction`. This is the C/AL trigger that is executed when the user clicks the action button. Place one line of code in this trigger:

    ```
    IssueCertificate;
    ```

16. Create a local function `InsertCertificateAction`. This is a low-level function that fills the `Item Certificate Action` table:

    ```
    WITH ItemCertificateAction DO BEGIN
      VALIDATE("Certificate No.","No.");
      VALIDATE("Action Date",WORKDATE);
      VALIDATE("Action Type",ActionType);
      IF ActionType <> "Action Type"::Revoked THEN
        VALIDATE("Expiration Date",CALCDATE('<1Y>',WORKDATE));
      VALIDATE("Item No.","Item No.");
      INSERT(TRUE);
    END;
    ```

17. The function `InsertCertificateAction` accepts one parameter and uses a local variable.

    Declare the parameter `ActionType` of type `Option`. Do not add any option values.

Open the list of local function variables and add a variable:

Name	DataType	Subtype
ItemCertificateAction	Record	Item Certificate Action

18. Now let's create the function that is called from the action trigger. Declare the function `IssueCertificate`; it should be local as follows:

```
IF NOT IsCertificateIssued THEN
    InsertCertificateAction(
        ItemCertificateAction."."Action Type"::Issued);
```

19. Declare one local variable in the function:

Name	DataType	Subtype
ItemCertificateAction	Record	Item Certificate Action

20. The `IsCertificateIssued` function called here is declared in the table 50010 **Item Certificate** that is the data source for the page 50013 **Certificate List**. Open the table 50010 in table designer and declare the function `IsCertificateIssued`. Change its return type to `Boolean`, then add a local variable `ItemCertificateAction` referencing the record `Item Certificate Action` (see Step 19).

21. The function itself contains only one line calling another method, `CertificateActionExists`:

```
EXIT(CertificateActionExists(
    ItemCertificateAction."Action Type"::Issued));
```

22. The `CertificateActionExists` function should be declared in the same table 50010. Its return type should be `Boolean`, and the function takes one parameter `ActionType` of type `Option`.

23. Declare a local variable `ItemCertificateAction` in the function `CertificateActionExists`. This is a record type variable with subtype `Item Certificate Action`.

24. The function itself returns the Boolean value indicating if there are any actions of the given type in the table:

```
WITH ItemCertificateAction DO BEGIN
   SETRANGE("Certificate No.","No.");
   SETRANGE("Action Type",ActionType);

   EXIT(NOT ISEMPTY);
END;
```

25. Close the code editor and return to the action designer. Open properties for the IssueCertificate action and click on the **lookup** button in the **Image** property.

26. Select the image **ReleaseDoc** from the list of image resources. Click **OK**, then close the action properties.

27. Below the new action, add another action container, select **RelatedInformation** in the **SubType** field. Insert another action item under the new container, name it Item. This action button will open a card for the item linked to the certificate:

E.. Type	SubType	Name	Caption
⊟ **ActionContainer**	**ActionItems**	**Certification**	**<Certification>**
▶ ☐ Action		IssueCertificate	Issue Certificate
Action		ProlongCertificate	Prolong Certificate
Action		RevokeCertificate	Revoke Certificate
⊟ **ActionContainer**	**RelatedInformation**	**Related**	**<Related>**
Action		Item	Item
Action		ViewActive	View Active

28. Open properties of the **Item** action. Click on the **lookup** button in front of the **RunObject** property and select **Page 30 Item Card** in the list of objects.

29. Select the property **RunPageLink**. Click on the assist button in the **Value** field and set up the link for item that will be shown when the action is activated:

Field	Type	Value
No.	FIELD	Item No.

After the link is configured, the value of the **RunPageLink** property will be No.=FIELD(Item No.).

How it works...

Most NAV pages are linked to certain database tables and present data stored in the database.

How the fields are arranged in the page is defined by the **PageType** property. When a new page is created using a wizard, page type is set by the wizard. If a page is created without any wizard, default value **Card** is selected, then it can be changed manually. In Step 3 and Step 9 we create different types of pages by selecting the type in the page wizard.

In Step 4 FastTabs are added to the **Card** page. Each **Card** page must have at least one FastTab. The **Page** fields can be grouped in several tabs for logical presentation of data on large forms having many fields. We are now developing a small page, whose fields can be presented in a single tab.

Usually, tables contain a lot of data irrelevant for user, some fields used by the system internally that should not clutter the user interface. In Step 4, fields that will be shown on the page, are selected from the list of source table fields. You can rearrange the fields in the designer manually, but the final position of each field on the canvas will be defined automatically by the system depending on the page layout.

The **Card** page will display one table record at a time, while in the list page records are presented in a tabular form — one table line per record. List pages are convenient for searching data and quick overview, and cards come in handy when you need to scrutinize or edit a single record. In NAV, most of master tables containing entities such as **Customer**, **Vendor**, **Item**, or **Bank Account**, have at least two associated pages – a card and a list.

List pages are mostly made non-editable, assuming that records must be modified in the corresponding card page. This is what we do in Step 10 – the **Editable** property in the page specifies if records can be altered. When its value is FALSE, no modifications are allowed in the page. If the page is editable, the **Editable** property can be set for individual fields, enabling or disabling modifications for fields.

When you open properties, while a blank line is selected in the designer (like in the picture in Step 10), properties of the page object will open. Accessing **Properties** with the selection on a field or container will open properties of the selected item.

In the last part of this recipe we are enriching the page with actions. Actions buttons are created in a dedicated **Action Designer**. Simple actions that only run another object, such as page or report, do not require any coding. Object execution can be configured in action properties, including some simple logic – linked object can be filtered or positioned on a particular record.

If possibilities provided by object links is insufficient for your task, action logic must be programmed in the OnAction trigger.

Actions can be grouped in ActionContainers. Each container is presented as a tab in the page's action pane:

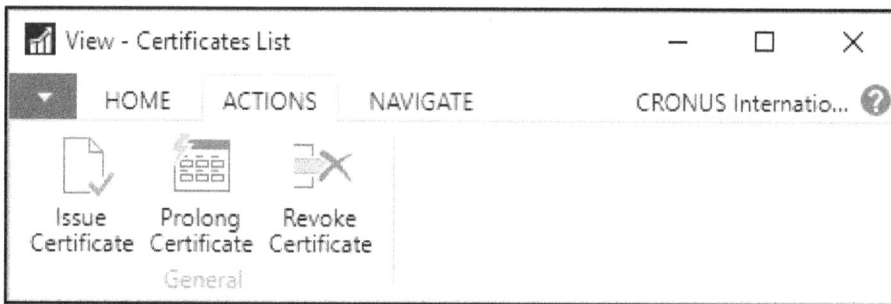

To be shown in the page, action must be included in an action container.

> Actions with the **RunObject** property undefined and no code in the OnAction trigger will not appear in the **Actions** pane on the page.

Linking datasources in subpages

Subpages are used to present related information linked to the master record shown in the page. A document header displayed in the main page with linked lines in a subpage is a typical example.

Subpage always has a rule linking it to its master page, and it is always updated in response to any action in the master page. In NAV 2016 it is possible to update the master page after modifying data in a subpage.

How to do it...

In current recipe, we will create a subpage presenting the list of actions performed on a certificate.

1. Create a new page in object designer.
2. Set table 50012 **Item Certificate Action** as a source table for the new page.
3. Choose the **Create a page using a wizard** option and select the **ListPart** page type.
4. Select the following fields to be presented in the page:
   - **Action Date**
   - **Action Type**
   - **Expiration Date**
5. Finish and save as page 50012 **Item Certificate Subform**.
6. Design the page 50010 **Item Certificate Card** and add a line below the last field:
   - **Type = Part**
   - **SubType = Page**
   - **Name = CertificateActions**
7. Make sure the new subpage part is indented on one level with the **Group** part. Use arrow buttons in the page designer to align the subpage position:

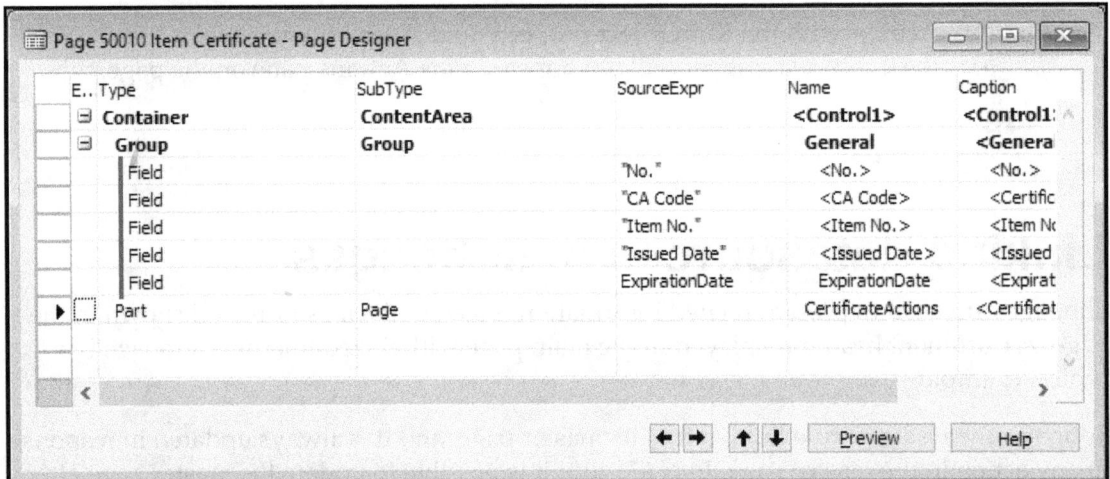

E..	Type	SubType	SourceExpr	Name	Caption
	Container	ContentArea		<Control1>	<Control1:
	Group	Group		General	<Genera
	Field		"No."	<No.>	<No.>
	Field		"CA Code"	<CA Code>	<Certific
	Field		"Item No."	<Item No.>	<Item Nc
	Field		"Issued Date"	<Issued Date>	<Issued
	Field		ExpirationDate	ExpirationDate	<Expirat
	Part	Page		CertificateActions	<Certificat

Page 50010 Item Certificate - Page Designer

← → ↑ ↓ | Preview | Help

8. Open the properties of the page part and set the value of the property `PagePartID` to `Item Certificate Subform`.

9. Select the page part and open its properties. Click the assist button in the **SubPageLink** property and set up a subpage filter as shown in the table:

Field	Type	Value
Certificate No.	FIELD	No.

After you have finished configuring the link and closed the filter setup form, the **SubpageLink** property should have its value as `Certificate No.=FIELD(No.)`.

Alternatively, you can enter this filter manually without the table filter setup form.

10. Set the value of the **UpdatePropagation** property to **Both** and save the changes.

How it works...

The subpage in this example will show all actions performed on a certificate. A list page is coupled with the certificate card created in previous walk-through. The page is created using the usual C/SIDE page wizard with **ListPart** for the type.

There are two page types intended for subpage controls:

- CardPart
- ListPart

These correspond to **Card** and **List** pages respectively, but their layout is optimized for embedding these pages into a parent control.

Step 6 inserts the subpage into the **Certificate** card page, which will be its host. Property **PagePartID** is the ID number of the subpage. Synchronization of data between two pages is controlled by the **SubPageLink** property:

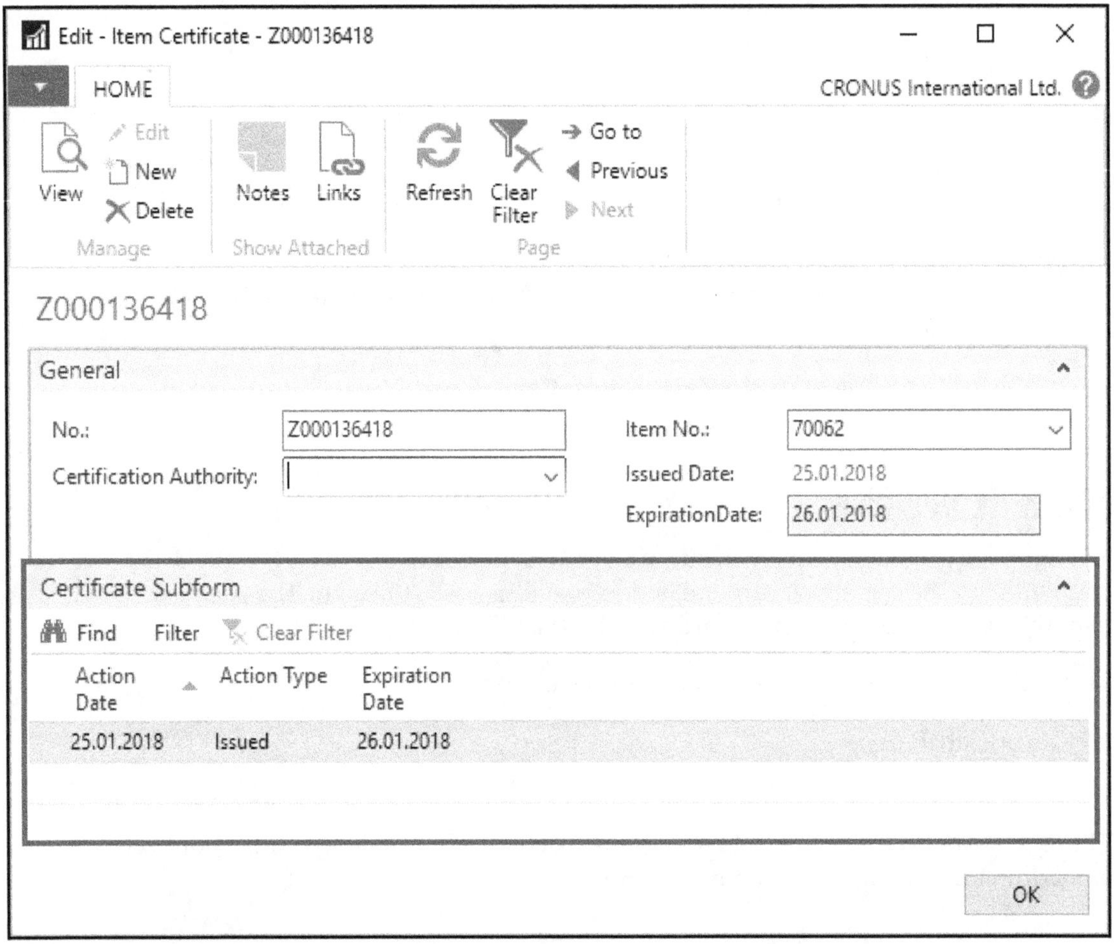

The parent page **Item Certificate Card** has the **Issued Date** and **Expiration Date** fields which are **FlowFields** calculated from related actions. This implies that these fields must recalculated when data in the subpage is modified. For example, if the user enters a new expiration date in the action line, we expect it to be updated in the certificate header as well.

Such updates in the parent page initiated from the child control must be enabled explicitly. We do it in Step 10 by modifying the property **UpdatePropagation**. The default value of this property is **SubPart**, which means that updates of the child page won't be forwarded to the parent. **UpdatePropagation = Both** enables forwarding of updates from the subpage to its parent page. The property does not update the page itself. To force the update propagation, you must call the function UPDATE on the subpage's data modification trigger. This is illustrated in the next recipe, *Working with page triggers*.

Working with page triggers

Page triggers are used to change the way page data is presented to the user. In this recipe, we will use triggers to calculate a value that will be displayed in the page "on-the-fly", when a record in retrieved from the database. Besides, trigger code will update the style of text boxes depending on the data displayed in them.

How to do it...

To illustrate the data presentation in a page, we write page trigger code highlighting expired certificates to draw user's attention to entries demanding immediate action.

1. Open the page 50010 **Item Certificate Card** in page designer. Declare a global variable ExpirationDate of the **Date** type.
2. Insert a new field in the General group, just below the field **Issued Date**. Set **SourceExpr = ExpirationDate** to make the ExpirationDate variable as the data source for the new field.
3. Open the **C/AL Code** page. Declare a function GetCertificateExpirationDate.
4. Open function parameters and add one parameter:

Name	DataType	Length
CertificateNo	Code	20

5. In the **Return Value** tab, select **Date** as the function return type.

6. Switch to the function's local variables and declare a variable:

Name	DataType	Subtype
ItemCertificateAction	Record	Item Certificate Action

7. The following is the function code that will find the expiration date for a given certificate:

```
WITH ItemCertificateAction DO BEGIN
  SETRANGE("Certificate No.",CertificateNo);
  SETRANGE("Action Type","Action Type"::Revoked);
  IF FINDLAST THEN
    EXIT("Action Date");

  SETRANGE(
    "Action Type",
    "Action Type"::Issued,"Action Type"::Prolonged);
  IF FINDLAST THEN
    EXIT("Expiration Date");
END;
```

8. Declare a global Boolean variable, IsCertificateOverdue.

9. Access the properties of the page field ExpirationDate, select property **Style** and choose **Attention** in its value. Property **StyleExpr** is located just below **Style**. Enter IsCertificateOverdue in the **StyleExpr** value.

10. In the OnAfterGetRecord trigger, insert this code:

```
ExpirationDate := GetCertificateExpirationDate("No.");
IsCertificateOverdue := ExpirationDate < WORKDATE;
```

11. Open the page 50012 **Certificate Subform** in page designer and switch to the **C/AL Code** page.

12. In the OnNewRecord trigger, declare a local variable as shown in the table:

Name	DataType	Subtype
ItemCertificate	Record	Item Certificate

13. Then add the following code to the trigger `OnNewRecord`:

```
ItemCertificate.GET("Certificate No.");
VALIDATE("Item No.",ItemCertificate."Item No.");
```

14. Enter this code in the `OnInsert`, `OnModify`, and `OnDelete` triggers as follows:

```
CurrPage.UPDATE(FALSE);
This step is required to force the modification propagation to
the parent page. Without UPDATE on the subpage, fields
displaying aggregated values will not be updated.
```

15. Create a function `CanEditExpirationDate` that returns a `Boolean` value:

```
EXIT("Action Type" <> "Action Type"::Revoked);
```

16. Declare a global `Boolean` variable `IsExpirationDateEditable` and write the code that will set the variable's value, in the `OnAfterGetCurrRecord` trigger:

```
IsExpirationDateEditable := CanEditExpirationDate;
```

17. Code the **ActionType** and **OnValidate** fields as in `OnAfterGetRecord`:

```
IsExpirationDateEditable := CanEditExpirationDate;
```

How it works...

First two steps in the recipe create a page field that uses a variable as a data source instead of a record field. When displaying a table field, we only need to link the table data with a page control, no other actions are required. Actual data binding is performed by the NAV platform. When displaying a variable, the task of updating its value on page updates, lies on the developer.

Therefore, in Step 3 through Step 7 we create a function that will find the value to be displayed.

Another important function of page triggers is controlling the appearance of UI elements. In Step 8, the style of the text box showing the certificate's expiration date is changed to **Attention**. Fields with the **Attention** style are displayed in a red italic font instead of a regular straight black. But we don't need all certificates to be highlighted, only those expired on the work date. To change the style dynamically, we assign a `Boolean` variable `IsCertificateOverdue` to the **StyleExpr** property. As a result, the **Attention** style will be applied to the text box only when the variable `IsCertificateOverdue` is evaluated to `TRUE`. If the variable's value is `FALSE`, text will be displayed in the normal style:

General			^
No.:	IC9276561093	Item No.:	1928-S v
Certification Authority:	v	Issued Date:	25.01.2016
		ExpirationDate:	15.12.2017

The value of the control variable should be updated every time the page displays another record. Corresponding page trigger that is run on each update of the record view is called `OnAfterGetCurrRecord`. Unlike a very similar trigger `OnAfterGetRecord` that fires each time a record is retrieved from the database, the `OnAfterGetCurrRecord` trigger is executed only on the record currently selected by the user.

Presenting related data in FactBoxes

FactBoxes are subpages presenting information related to the main page, but considered less important than the main content. This is an auxiliary page that can be minimized or completely removed from the view when it is not needed.

How to do it...

This recipe creates a FactBox to present information about item certificates in sales orders.

1. Create a new page in page designer.
2. Select the table 50010 **Item Certificate** as a source for the page. Choose **Create a page using a wizard** option and select the page type **CardPart**.

3. Add fields to the page:
   - **No.**
   - **Certification Authority**
   - **Issued Date**

4. The **FactBox** page must display the certificate expiration date the same way as it is shown in the **Item Certificate Card** page. In the next recipe we will see how to reuse the function we already have in page 50010. For now, let's copy the function to the new page.

5. Declare two global variables: `ExpirationDate` of type `Date` and `IsCertificateOverdue` of type `Boolean`.

6. Close variable declarations. Back in the page designer, insert a new field in the `General` group, just below the `Issued Date` field. In the field's properties, set `SourceExpr = ExpirationDate` to assign the variable `ExpirationDate` to the field's data source.

7. Enter the `OnAfterGetRecord` trigger code (same as in the **Item Certificate Card** page):

```
ExpirationDate := GetCertificateExpirationDate("No.");
IsCertificateOverdue := ExpirationDate < WORKDATE;
```

8. Open properties for the **ExpirationDate** field and set:
   - **Style = Attention**
   - **StyleExpr = IsCertificateOverdue**

9. Save the page as page 50014 **Item Certificate Factbox**

10. Design page 42 **Sales Order**

> To open this page in the designer you will require a license with the Solution Developer module, while for most other recipes a less expensive Application Builder license is sufficient.

11. Add a line below all existing page parts and set up a new part as follows:

Type	Subtype	Name	Caption
Part	Page	ItemCertificateFactbox	Item Certificate Details

Indentation matters in page part configuration, so make sure that the new part is aligned with other parts in the **FactBoxArea** container.

12. In the subpage properties, set the property **ProviderID = 58**.

13. Open the page part properties and fill in the value of the property `PagePartID`. Set the value to `Item Certificate Factbox`.

14. Set up the property **SubPageLink**. Click the assist button in the **Value** field and set up a table filter:
    - **Field**: Item No.
    - **Type**: FIELD
    - **Value**: No.
    - **OnlyMaxLimit**: Set the checkmark in this field.

    Click OK to accept the subpage link setup. Now the property value should look like this: **Item No.=FIELD(UPPERLIMIT(No.))**

15. Save the **Factbox** page and close the page designer. To review the result, run the page 42 **Sales Order**. The new factbox is shown on the bottom of the factbox area on the right side of the page:

How it works...

Factbox is a special type of a page, so designing a factbox, in general, is the same as designing a page with several specific actions required to link it with its parent page and synchronize the view.

A Factbox page data can be based on a source table, just like for any other type of page. In current example, the factbox uses the page 50010 **Item Certificate** as a data source. First three steps create a page via the page creation wizard and display table fields on the page.

In the subsequent steps, from Step 4 to Step 7, we declare a variable that will serve as a data source for the fourth page field. The value of the expiration date is stored in another table and must be retrieved dynamically in the trigger `OnAfterGetRecord`.

To synchronize the content displayed in the parent page and the factbox, the property `SubPageLink` must be configured. This is done in Step 13 and Step 14.

First, the property `ProviderID` identifies the page part which the factbox must be synchronized with. If you leave the default value 0, the factbox will be in sync with the Sales Order page itself. We need to link it to the currently selected item which is shown in the subpage `SalesLines`. Therefore, `ProviderID` must have the value of the `SalesLines` page part. To find the page part ID, select it and open its properties. The first property in the list is ID, and this is the value that must be copied to the `ProviderID` of the factbox. The ID of the `SalesLines` part is 58.

The link is established between the field `Item No.` in the subpage and the field `No.` of the `Sales Order` page. Whenever the new record is retrieved in the page `Sales Order`, the linked factbox page is updated to show a record with the matching item no. The filtering parameter `OnlyMaxLimit` is added to find the last certificate from the list.

Designing reusable code

Code modules in NAV are called codeunits. A codeunit does not have any user interface; the only purpose of a codeunit object is to store application code that can be called from other objects.

How to do it...

Now we will create a codeunit that will store functions common for objects in the current chapter, and move duplicated code from different objects into the codeunit.

1. Create a new codeunit in object designer. Save it as codeunit 50010 **Item Certificate Mgt.**
2. Declare a global function `GetCertificateExpirationDate`.
3. Select the function in **C/AL Globals** list and open its properties. By default, property **Local** is set to **Yes**. Change it to **No** to make the function accessible from other objects.
4. Open function parameters in **C/AL Locals** and declare one parameter:

Name	Type	Length
CertificateNo	Code	20

5. Still in **C/AL Locals**, add a local variable to the function:

Name	DataType	Subtype
ItemCertificateAction	Record	Item Certificate Action

6. Change the function return type to `Date` and return to the code editor.
7. Enter the following function code:

```
WITH ItemCertificateAction DO BEGIN
  SETRANGE("Certificate No.",CertificateNo);
  SETRANGE("Action Type","Action Type"::Revoked);
  IF FINDLAST THEN
    EXIT("Action Date");

  SETRANGE(
    "Action Type",
    "Action Type"::Issued,"Action  Type"::Prolonged);
  IF FINDLAST THEN
    EXIT("Expiration Date");
END;
```

8. We will need two more global functions in this codeunit to include certificate data into the posted ledger entries.

   In the same codeunit 50010 declare a global function `FindActiveItemCertificate`, change its return type to **Code**, and Length to `20`.

9. Add two function parameters:

Name	DataType	Length
ItemNo	Code	20
CertificateDate	Date	

10. Declare a local variable in the function `FindActiveItemCertificate`:

Name	DataType	Subtype
ItemCertificateAction	Record	Item Certificate Action

11. The function code is as follows:

```
WITH ItemCertificateAction DO BEGIN
  SETRANGE("Item No.",ItemNo);
  SETFILTER("Expiration Date",'>=%1',CertificateDate);
  FINDLAST;

  EXIT("Certificate No.");
END;
```

12. The last function in the codeunit 50010 is `VerifyActiveItemCertificateExists`. It does not return any value, so leave the return type blank. Two parameters and a local variable used in the function are the same as in the previously declared `FindActiveItemCertificate`. Copy both parameters `ItemNo` and `CertificateDate`, as well as the local variable `ItemCertificateAction` into the new function.

13. Besides the local variable, we will need a text constant for a UI message. Open **C/AL Globals**, switch to the **Text Constants** tab and create a constant:

Name	ConstValue
NoValidCertificateErr	Item %1 does not have a valid certificate

14. Place the following code in the function:

```
WITH ItemCertificateAction DO BEGIN
  SETRANGE("Item No.",ItemNo);
  SETFILTER("Expiration Date",'>=%1',CertificateDate);
  IF ISEMPTY THEN
    ERROR(NoValidCertificateErr,ItemNo);
END;
```

15. Save and close the codeunit and open the page 50010 **Item Certificate Card** in designer. If you followed the previous recipes in this chapter, page 50010 now has a local function `GetCertificateExpirationDate`.

16. Move to the trigger `OnAfterGetRecord` and declare a local variable:

Name	DataType	Subtype
ItemCertificateMgt	Codeunit	Item Certificate Mgt.

17. Replace all code in the `OnAfterGetRecord` trigger with an invocation of the codeunit:

```
ExpirationDate :=
  ItemCertificateMgt.GetCertificateExpirationDate("No.");
  IsCertificateOverdue := ExpirationDate < WORKDATE;
```

18. Place the same code in the page **Item Certificate Factbox** – the `OnAfterGetRecord` trigger.

How it works...

We are moving all code dealing with item certificates into a dedicated codeunit that will contain functions specific to this task. Codeunit 50010 will serve as a code library for the set of tasks related to our sample add-on, presenting code in a logical group. Besides, we will remove duplicated functions from two tables and place the code into the same codeunit, where it can be reused by different objects.

New functions in all C/AL objects are created with LOCAL modifier. To make a function visible from other objects, you need to change the modifier in the function's properties. This is done in Step 3.

See also

The *Working with page triggers* recipe.

Accessing temporary tables

Temporary tables, created in server memory instead of the database, are widely used to store the interim results of complex calculations. Temp tables can be used as buffers for data presented to the user, when the dataset cannot be obtained directly from a table.

An example of such dataset can be a list of certificates issued or prolonged in the past year, that have not been revoked and not yet expired. While it is possible to construct a SQL query that will collect this data from a join of several tables, C/AL code for this task will be a little more intricate and requires a temporary storage for the records.

How to do it...

In this recipe, a temporary table is used to store a list of certificates collected in a C/AL function. The table will be used as a data source for a page to present the data to the user.

1. Edit the codeunit 50010 **Item Certificate Mgt.** and declare a global function `CollectProlongedNotRevokedCertificates`. To allow the function to be called from other objects, access its properties and set **Local = No**.
2. Declare a function's parameter `TempItemCertificate : Record "Item Certificate"`.
3. Set the checkmark in the **Var** field.
4. In the local declarations inside the function, create the following variables:

Name	DataType	Subtype
ItemCertificateAction	Record	Item Certificate Action
ItemCertificate	Record	Item Certificate

5. First of all, the function should make sure that there are no residual records left in the recordset:

```
TempItemCertificate.RESET;
TempItemCertificate.DELETEALL;
```

6. Then it starts collecting data for the new recordset:

```
WITH ItemCertificateAction DO BEGIN
  SETRANGE("Action Date",
    CALCDATE('<-1Y>',WORKDATE),WORKDATE);
  SETFILTER("Expiration Date",'>%1',WORKDATE);
  IF FINDSET THEN
    REPEAT
  IF NOT TempItemCertificate.GET(
    ItemCertificateAction."Certificate No.")
  THEN
    IF NOT ItemCertificate.IsCertificateRevoked(
      "Certificate No.")
  THEN BEGIN
    ItemCertificate.GET(
      ItemCertificateAction."Certificate No.");
    TempItemCertificate := ItemCertificate;
    TempItemCertificate.INSERT;
  END;
  UNTIL NEXT = 0;
END;
```

7. The `IsCertificateRevoked` function, called in the code, should be declared in the table 50010 `Item Certificate`. Create the function, change its return type to `Boolean`, and add a local variable:

Name	DataType	Subtype
ItemCertificateAction	Record	Item Certificate Action

8. `IsCertificateRevoked` calls the function `CertificateActionExists` to find out if there is a `Revoked` action registered for the certificate:

```
EXIT(CertificateActionExists(
  ItemCertificateAction."Action Type"::Revoked));
```

9. Open the page 50013 **Certificates List** in the page designer and click **Page Actions** in the **View** menu to access the list of page actions.

10. Insert an action item in the **RelatedInformation** action container. Name it `ViewActive`.

11. Access the action's C/AL code and write the following code in the `OnAction` trigger:

```
ItemCertificateMgt.CollectProlongedNotRevokedCertificates(
    TempItemCertificate);
PAGE.RUN(PAGE::"Certificates List",TempItemCertificate);
```

12. The `TempItemCertificate` variable should be declared in the list of local variables in the `OnAction` trigger:

Name	DataType	Subtype
TempItemCertificate	Record	Item Certificate

13. Open the properties of the variable `TempItemCertificate` and set **Temporary** to **Yes**.

> Declaring a record variable as temporary means that the table will be stored in memory, and all data access and data modification statements will be executed against the in-memory instance of the table instead of the database.

14. Save the page, close the page editor, and run the page from the object designer.
15. Run the page 50013 **Certificates List** and execute the action **View Active**.

How it works...

The `CollectProlongedNotRevokedCertificates` function declared in codeunit **Item Certificate Mgt.**, will analyze item certificates within the given period range and insert the resulting dataset into the record parameter `TempItemCertificate`.

The function's parameter is declared as a record variable, but the variable passed to it from the action trigger in Step 11 has the `TEMPORARY` attribute. This property does not change the way the table is accessed in the C/AL code, but data manipulation functions, such as `FINDSET`, `INSERT`, `MODIFY`, and so on, called on this variable won't issue SQL queries. Instead, records will be retrieved, inserted, and modified in a recordset stored in memory, as we will see in the code sample.

First thing the function does, is remove all filters from the parameter variable and delete all data it may contain. We simply call `DELETEALL` on the **Item Certificate** record, this statement won't affect records in the database.

Double-check that the variable has the TEMPORARY key switched on. Otherwise DELETEALL will delete all data from the real database table.

After clearing the temporary buffer, we begin collecting data into it. For the sake of simplicity of the example, date range is limited to the period from work date – 1 year to the work date:

```
SETRANGE("Action Date",CALCDATE('<-1Y>',WORKDATE),WORKDATE);
```

This will filter out all certificates with no actions in the past year.

Next, we leave only certificates with an expiration date later than the application work date:

```
SETFILTER("Expiration Date",'>%1',WORKDATE);
```

Code will run a loop on all certificates' actions and rule out revoked certificates, inserting all active ones into the buffer.

Finally, from Step 9 to Step 13 we create a page action that will execute the function. First line in the action trigger calls the function CollectProlongedNotRevokedCertificates passing a temporary variable into which the records will be inserted as shown:

```
ItemCertificateMgt.CollectProlongedNotRevokedCertificates(
    TempItemCertificate);
```

In the next line, PAGE.RUN will open the page **Certificates List** with the temporary buffer as a source. The page will take the data to display from the buffer instead of the database:

```
PAGE.RUN(PAGE::"Certificates List",TempItemCertificate);
```

See also

It is possible to build a page based on a temporary table. The **SourceTableTemporary** page property tells that the page won't select data from the database, but will read a buffer that must be filled on page initialization.

For details, see the *Simpifying data access with queries* recipe where we will fill the temporary page source using a query object.

Role-Tailored client and role centers

Role center is a special type of page created through the page designer. Usually role centers include a number of subpages.

Typical role center is not a single page, but a container with a number of subbpages presenting different dataset under various angles. Therefore, creating and configuring a role center may be a complicated task that requires creating many auxiliary tables and pages.

How to do it...

In this recipe, we will develop a role center for our custom solution to present the most important information in one screen.

1. Create a table with the following fields:

Field No.	Field Name	Data Type	Length	Field Class
1	Primary Key	Code	10	Normal
2	Certificates – Total	Integer		FlowField
3	Certificates – Issued	Integer		FlowField
4	Certificates – Revoked	Integer		FlowField
5	Date Filter	Date		FlowFilter
6	Future Period Filter	Date		FlowFilter

2. Select field 2 **Certificates – Total** and change its **CalcFormula** property to `Count("Item Certificate")`. You can set up the calculation formula in a dialog, or enter the formula directly in the property value field. If you choose to set up the formula, click the assist button in the **Value** field, select **Count** in the **Method** field and **Item Certificate** in the **Table** field.

3. Select field 3 **Certificates – Issued**. Set up **Method = Count, Table = ItemCertificate Action**. Open table filters and setup two filters:

Field	Type	Value
Action Type	CONST	Issued
Action Date	FIELD	Date Filter

Alternatively, enter the formula directly in the **CalcFormula** property:

```
Count("Item Certificate Action" WHERE (Action
    Type=CONST(Issued),Action Date=FIELD(Date Filter)))
```

4. Set up the calculation formula for field 4 **Certificates – Revoked**:

```
Method = Count, Table = Item Certificate Action
```

Table filters setup:

Field	Type	Value
Action Type	CONST	Revoked
Action Date	FIELD	Date Filter

Calculation formula for field 4 is this:

```
Count("Item Certificate Action" WHERE (Action
    Type=CONST(Revoked),Action Date=FIELD(Date Filter)))
```

5. Save it as table 50013 **Item Certification Cue**.
6. In the page designer, create a new page. Select table **Item Certification Cue** as the source table for this page. Choose **Create a page using a wizard** and select **CardPart** as the page type.
7. In the **Card Part Page Wizard**, select 3 fields to be presented on the page: **Certificates – Total, Certificates – Issued, Certificates – Revoked**. The primary key and both flowfilters are internal fields that should not be shown to the user.

8. Finish the wizard and preview the page. Now it looks like a plain card page without role center's brick interface:

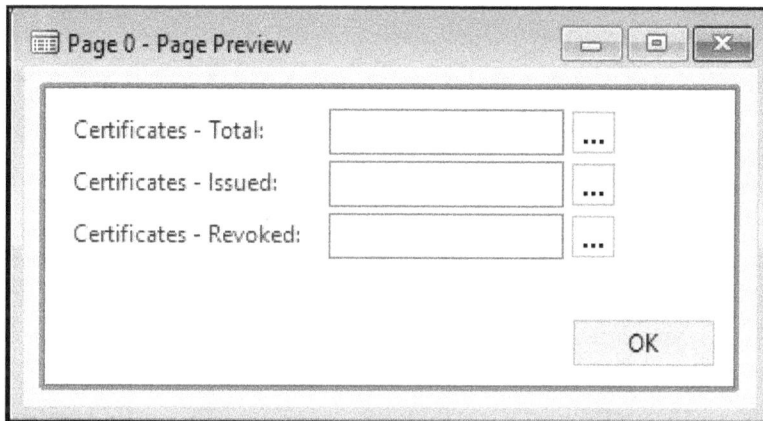

9. Save the new page with ID 50015 and name it `Item Cert. - Certificates`.
10. To change the fields' appearance, you need to include them in a **CueGroup** subtype:

   - In the page designer, insert a new line between **ContainerArea** and fields.
   - In the new line, select **Type = Group**, **SubType = CueGroup**
   - Select all fields and indent them one step to the right, so that the fields are aligned under the **CueGroup**:

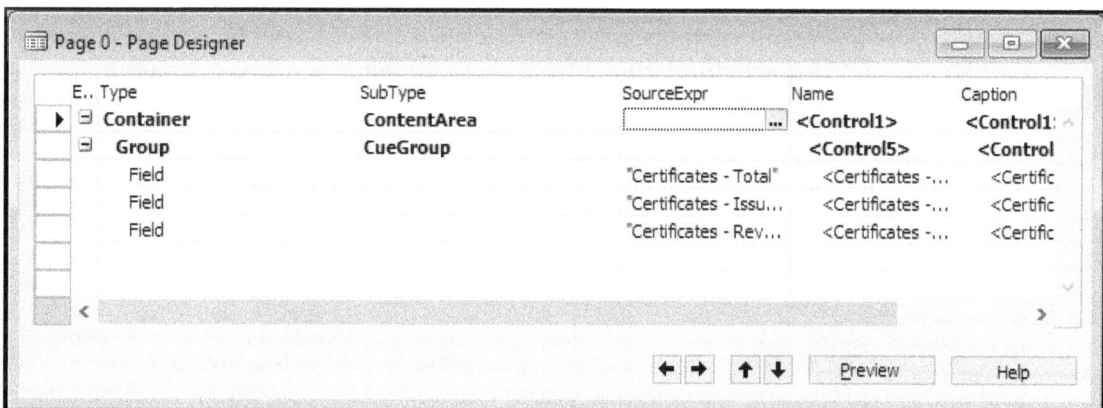

Preview the page. Now the fields will be presented as bricks instead of text fields:

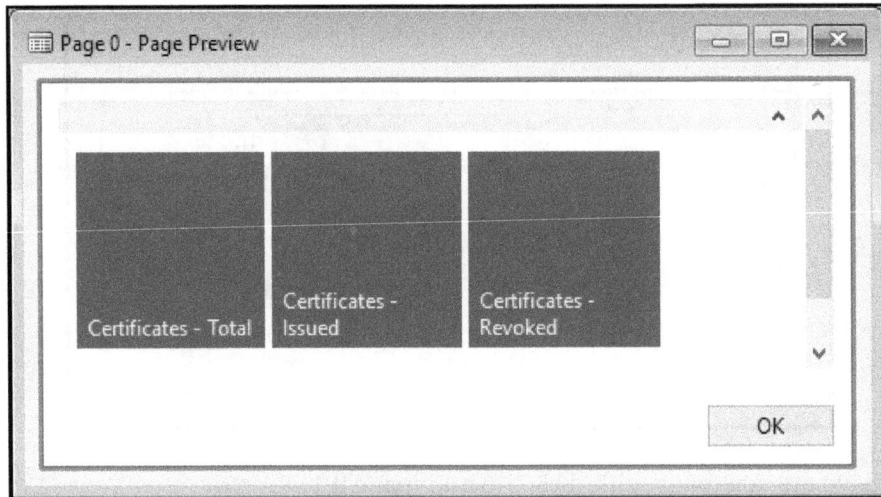

11. Still there is more data that can be presented in the role center's cue page. Create two global Integer variables in the page 50015:
    - ExpiredCertificates
    - CertificatesDueToExpire

12. Add another field in the page designer, under the field **Certificates – Revoked**. **Set Type = Field, SourceExpr = ExpiredCertificates**. And below this, another one: **Type = Field, SourceExpr = CertificatesDueToExpire**. The new field does not have a source in a table field, and the caption will not be inherited from the table. Fill the **Caption** field manually. Its value should be **Certificates – Due to expire**.

13. Open the C/AL code editor and enter code to initialize the cue table in the OnOpenPage trigger:

```
RESET;
  IF NOT GET THEN BEGIN
    INIT;
      INSERT;
  END;

  SETRANGE(
    "Date Filter",CALCDATE('<-1M>',WORKDATE),WORKDATE);
  SETRANGE(
    "Future Period Filter",
    CALCDATE('<1D>',WORKDATE),CALCDATE('<1M>',WORKDATE));
```

14. For now, only FlowFields will be calculated on page run – they have formulas evaluated automatically and don't require any further intervention. But there are two page fields whose values are presented in variables instead of tables fields, and these values have to be calculated by C/AL code. The code for counting certificates expired in the past month and certificates due to expire in the next month is very similar, so let's examine one of the two functions, the other is available for downloading from the site.

> In the page 50015, declare a local function `CountCertificatesDueToExpire`, set its return type to `Integer`.

15. Declare a local variable in the function:

Name	DataType	Subtype
ItemCertificateAction	Record	Item Certificate Action

16. Enter the function code that will count the number of records:

```
ItemCertificateAction.SETFILTER(
  "Expiration Date",GETFILTER("Future Period Filter"));
EXIT(ItemCertificateAction.COUNT);
```

17. In the `OnAfterGetRecord` trigger, enter the following code:

```
ExpiredCertificates := CountExpiredCertificates;
  CertificatesDueToExpire := CountCertificatesDueToExpire;
```

> The `CountExpiredCertificates` function won't be detailed here. It is very similar to `CountCertificatesDueToExpire` and is available in source files to this chapter.

18. Cue elements should also support drilldown to the underlying raw data. For the total count of certificates, drilldown is a simple property setup:

> Open properties for the page field **Certificates – Total** and set **DrillDownPageID = Certificates List**.

19. Other fields require special handling through C/AL code. Declare a local function in the page 50015 `FillTempCertificateBuffer`. This function has one parameter:

Name	DataType	Subtype
ItemCertificateAction	Record	Item Certificate Action

Parameter must by passed by reference, so set the checkmark in the **Var** field in the C/AL Locals.

20. Declare a local variable in the function:

Name	DataType	Subtype
`TempItemCertificate`	Record	Item Certificate

This is a temporary buffer for records to be shown in the drill down page. Open the variable's properties and set **Temporary = Yes**.

21. The function code is as follows:

```
IF ItemCertificateAction.FINDSET THEN
  REPEAT
    InsertCertificateBufferRecord(
      TempItemCertificate,
      ItemCertificateAction."Certificate No.");
  UNTIL ItemCertificateAction.NEXT = 0;

PAGE.RUN(PAGE::"Certificate List",TempItemCertificate);
```

22. Declare a function `InsertCertificateBufferRecord`. This is the function that will insert a record into the temporary record. The function takes two parameters:

Name	DataType	Subtype	Length
TempItemCertificate	Record	Item Certificate	
CertificateNo	Code		20

`TempItemCertificate` is passed by reference – set the checkmark in the **Var** field for this parameter.

[92]

23. The code for the `InsertCertificateBufferRecord` function is as follows:

```
TempItemCertificate."No." := CertificateNo;
    IF TempItemCertificate.INSERT THEN;
```

24. Create a function named `DrillDownDueToExpire`. It has one local variable:

Name	DataType	Subtype
ItemCertificateAction	Record	Item Certificate Action

And its code is as follows:

```
ItemCertificateAction.SETFILTER(
    "Expiration Date",GETFILTER("Future Period Filter"));
FillTempCertificateBuffer(ItemCertificateAction);
```

25. Select the field `CertificatesDueToExpire` and open its C/AL triggers. In the trigger `CertificatesDueToExpire - OnDrillDown` call the function declared in the previous step:

```
DrillDownDueToExpire;
```

Other brick elements must also have their `OnDrillDown` triggers handled. You can find the code of these triggers in source files.

26. Finally, the **Cue** page looks like it should, and with all the brick elements clickable:

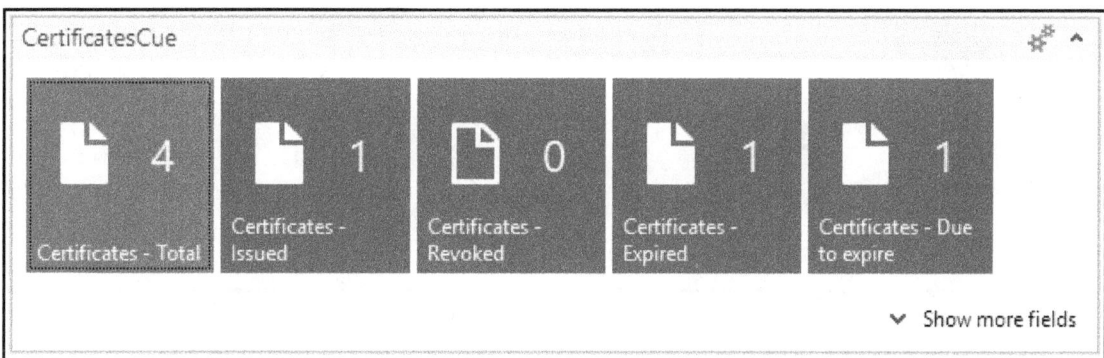

CertificatesCue

| 4 | 1 | 0 | 1 | 1 |
| Certificates - Total | Certificates - Issued | Certificates - Revoked | Certificates - Expired | Certificates - Due to expire |

Show more fields

27. Role center can contain other types of subpages besides cues. This can be any kind of information that has greater importance for the user and should always be at hand. List subpages are also often present in role centers. Let's enrich the role center with a list of certified items.

28. Create a new page in the page designer. Select the table **Item** for the page source, choose to create a page using a wizard, and pick **ListPart** for the page type.

29. In the list of table fields, pick **No**. and enter a description for the page, finish the wizard and save the new object as page 50016 **Item Cert. – Items**.

30. Declare the following global variables in the page:

Name	DataType	Subtype
ItemCertificateMgt	Codeunit	Item Certificate Mgt.
ExpirationDate	Date	
ItemCertificateOverdue	Boolean	

31. In the page designer, add a line to the fields list. Set **Type = Field, SourceExpr = ExpirationDate** and **Name = Expiration Date**:

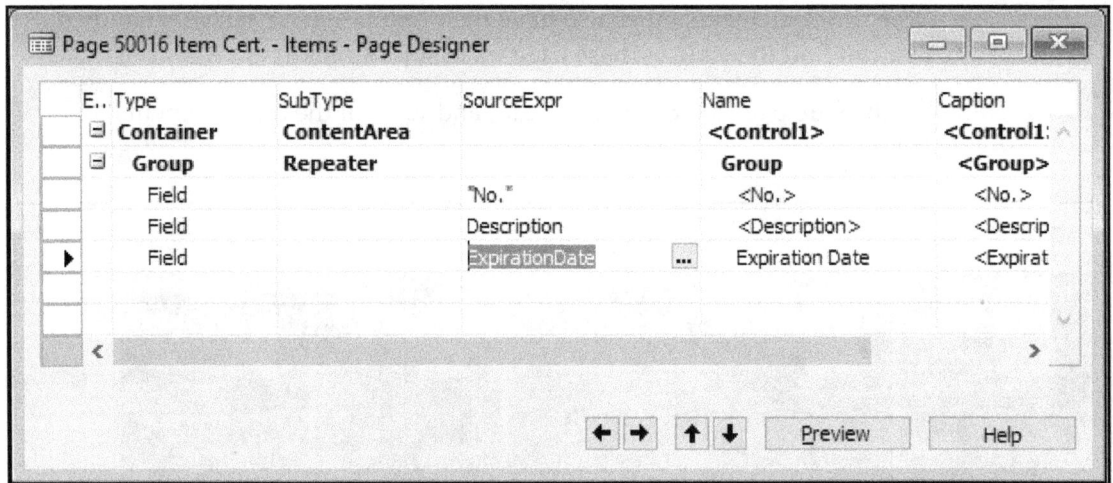

[94]

32. Select the field "**No.**" and open its properties. Set new values for the **Style** and **StyleExpr** properties to **Attention** and **ItemCertificateOverdue** respectively.

33. Close the field properties and set the same value for two remaining fields.

34. Open C/AL code for the page (click **C/AL Code** in the **View** menu or press *F9*) and add trigger code for the `OnAfterGetRecord` trigger:

```
ExpirationDate :=
   ItemCertificateMgt.GetItemCertExpirationDate("No.");
ItemCertificateOverdue := ExpirationDate < WORKDATE;
```

35. Save the page. Now all components are ready for the **Role Center** page itself.

36. Wrapping all subpage parts into a container is the simplest task in role center configuration. First you need to create the **Role Center** page.

37. Create a page in the page designer. Leave the **Table** field blank, but choose to use the wizard, and set **RoleCenter** for the page type.

38. Page designer will open. The new page has only one container control. Add a **Group** control under the **Container**, then two page parts in the group:

E.. Type	SubType
⊟ **Container**	**RoleCenterArea**
⊟ **Group**	**Group**
▸ ☐ Part	Page
Part	Page

39. Select the first page part and open its properties. Set **PagePartID = Item Cert. – Certificates**. This is the cue subpage created earlier.

40. Open the properties of the second page part and set its **PagePartID = Item Cert. – Items**.

41. Save the page with ID 50017 and name it `Item Certification Role Center`. Now the role center is ready. You can run it from the object designer to preview the result. In the next recipe we will assign this role center to a user profile to make it the application starting page:

How it works...

This recipe begins by creating a table that will serve as a data source for the **Cue** page. Cue is the central element in the role center that presents key indicators in a graphical form. These indicators are usually counters of some entities, most important for the user.

Cue table created in the first step does not actually store any data in the database. All its fields are either FlowFilters or FlowFields, which are calculated based on data from other tables. Cue table is just a convenient way to describe rules for the calculation of data presented in the role center, although its possibilities are limited to FlowField's **CalcFormula** property. More sophisticated computations require other means, such as C/AL functions executed on UI triggers.

The primary key is declared on this table simply because there is no way to create a NAV table without one. This is a dummy code that is always empty.

The integer fields from 2 through 4 are counters that will calculate different measures:

- **Certificates – Total**: Total number of item certificates in the database
- **Certificates – Issued**: Number of item certificates issued in the period defined by the field **Date Filter**
- **Certificates – Revoked**: Number of item certificates revoked in the period defined by the date filter **Future Period Filter**

The last two fields are date filters used as elements of calculation formulas in the FlowFields. These filters will be determined by the the C/AL code when the cue page is shown on the screen.

Step 2 through Step 6 will set up the calculation formulas for FlowFields, and in Step 7 the cue page that will display the graphics is created.

At first, the page doesn't look like a cue page – the fields are shown as simple text boxes. To turn them into graphic elements, you need to wrap the fields in a **CueGroup** element. And this is all you need to do to display cue controls based on table data.

Step 13 will initialize the cue table underlying the page. The OnOpenPage trigger is executed each time the page is displayed in the application. The purpose of the code in this trigger is to ensure that there is a record in the cue table, and to initialize the page filters.

Two date filters applied to **FlowFilter** fields in the OnOpenPage trigger, will limit the period for FlowFields with calculation formulas based on the date. Out of three FlowFields declared in the cue table, one (**Certificates – Total**) is independent of the date. Its **CalcFormula** property does not refer to dates, and the result will always be the total count of certificates.

Two other fields, **Certificates – Issued** and **Certificates – Revoked**, make use of the **Date Filter** field to limit the period. This period is defined by the following line:

```
SETRANGE("Date Filter",CALCDATE('<-1M>',WORKDATE),WORKDATE);
```

This means that the result produced by the **CalcFormula** property will include only certificates issued or revoked in the period from `WORKDATE - 1` month to `WORKDATE` inclusively. If you want to change the default period, this is the place to do it – just replace the date formula with your own.

Further on, in Step 11 to Step 16, we create two fields that will be updated by C/AL triggers. It is relatively simple to display data based on table fields, but the task becomes a bit more complicated when the capabilities of a FlowField formula are insufficient to calculate the field value, and we have to turn to C/AL. The idea is to simply use a global variable as a data source for a page field, and recalculate the variable value each time the page is updated.

The variables `ExpiredCertificates` and `CertificatesDueToExpire` declared in Step 11 will hold the values of the last two cue indicators we will calculate dynamically in C/AL. `ExpiredCertificates` will show the number of certificates expired in the past month, and `CertificatesDueToExpire` – number of certificates due to expire in the next month. Both periods will be limited by the table's FlowFilter values set in the `OnOpenPage` trigger. And here we will need the second filter field **Future Period Filter**, so far kept idle. One of the two functions performing this calculation is described in Step 14 to Step 16.

The function then must be called from the page trigger `OnAfterGetCurrRecord` to update the variable value each time the record is read from the database.

After this, all cue elements will be calculated and displayed in the page as graphic controls. Next thing, we are adding drill down functions to all of the controls to have the possibility to view data source for computed indicators. For the total count field this is a very simple trick – we only need to set the `DrillDownPageID` in the field. When the user clicks on the control, page identified by this property will open. If the field does not have a source in the table, drill down function must be programmed.

Step 19 to Step 26 describe the code changes that must be made to enable drill down in pure C/AL. In order to show the drill down page, we collect related records from the database into a temporary table and run a page with the temporary buffer as a substitute for the real table:

```
PAGE.RUN(PAGE::"Certificates List",TempItemCertificate);
```

This code will run page 50013 **Certificates List**, but instead of retrieving database records on opening, the page will take data from the buffer variable passed in the second parameter of `PAGE.RUN`.

Role centers are, by nature, aggregates of information, most important for the user in their job. A role center includes a number of subpages in one or several groups. Another example of a page part for the role center is a list of entities with which the user works. Step 28 to Step 35 create a list of items that presents information in a user-friendly manner, by highlighting items requiring immediate attention.

Finally, the last four steps assemble all parts into a practical role center page.

Assigning role centers to user profiles

The role center is the central access point to everyday tasks for the user. This is what he or she will see first when launching the application, and the role center page should be configured accordingly. Role centers are assigned to users in agreement with their roles in the organization.

Getting ready

In this recipe you will assign the role center created in the previous demo, to a user profile. In order to do it, you will need all object from the *Role-Tailored client and role centers* recipe imported and compiled.

How to do it...

Now we will assign the custom role center to a user account to make it the user's homepage:

1. In the application menu, open `/Departments/Administration/Application Setup/RoleTailored Client/Profiles`, or type `Profiles` in the **Search** field and select the **Profiles** page in the search results.
2. In the **Profiles** page, click **New** to create a new user profile.
3. Enter profile `ID`. `Name CERT MANAGER` and `Certification Manager` in the **Description**.

4. Click the lookup button in the field named **Role Center ID**. This button will open the list of all pages of type **RoleCenter**. Choose page 50017 **Item Certification Role Center**. You can also enter the page name or ID directly in the profile card, without lookup. Close the profiles page.

> Don't forget to setup the Role Center ID before assigning the new profile to a user account. Users with a missing role center ID in their profile won't be able to open the Role-Tailored client.

5. Open **Departments** | **Administration** | **Application Setup** | **RoleTailored Client** | **User Personalization**.
6. Create a new profile, select the ID of the user you want to assign the profile to in the **User ID** field. In the **Profile ID**, select the profile **CERT MANAGER**.
7. Setup **Language ID**, **Locale ID**, and **Time Zone** as per your preference:

8. Close the NAV client and login again under the user account you just configured. Now you will enter your workspace with your custom Role Center.

How it works...

Configuration of the role center begins from setting up of the appropriate user profile, because role centers are not assigned to user accounts directly, but through their profiles by navigating to **User Account** | **User Profile** | **Role Center**.

In the initial four steps we create and setup a user profile that will be associated with the role of a certification manager.

In the second part of the demo, in Step 5 to Step 7, a user account is associated with a profile that will run a custom role center on login. The same page will be shown when the user clicks the **Home** link in the menu.

Simplifying data access with queries

Structures of NAV client application language allow accessing only one table at a time, there is no C/AL structure that would enable a table join in one statement. This limitation often affects the performance of C/AL code, forcing the developer to use loops on table records where a single query would be sufficient. With a Query object, developers can overcome this limitation and create queries joining several tables.

How to do it...

In this recipe, we will create a query object calculating profit per item, and use the query as a data source for a page.

1. In the first step, we will add a field to the Item table that will specify if an item certificate is required to post an item entry. Open the table 27 Item in table designer and insert the field:

Field No.	Field Name	Data Type
50100	Certificate Required	Boolean

2. Save the modification in the table. Switch to the page designer and open the page 30 `Item Card`. Insert the field **Certificate Required** in the **Item** field group. Save the page.

3. Open the object designer, select object type **Query**, and create a new object.

4. Insert the first query data item – table **Item**. In the field **Type**, select **DataItem** and set **DataSource = Item**.

5. Select the data item line and open the properties. In the **DataItemTableFilter** property, click the **assist** button and setup the filter:

Field	Type	Value
Certificate Required	CONST	Yes

6. Close the formula editor. Now ensure that the value of **DataItemTableFilter** is **Certificate Required=CONST(Yes)**.

7. Close data item properties and insert two data item fields below the **Item** line:

Type	DataSource	MethodType
Column	No.	None
Column	Description	None

8. Under the **Item** table fields, add a linked data item **Value Entry**. Set **Type = DataItem** and **Data Source = Value Entry**.

9. Open properties for the **Value Entry** data item and configure the link to the **Item** table. Click the assist button in the **DataItemLink** field and setup the reference:

Field	Reference Data Item	Reference Field
Item No.	Item	No.

10. The **DataItemLink** property will receive the following value: **Item No.=Item."No."**.

11. Set **DataItemLinkType** to **Exclude Row If No Match**.

12. outIn the **DataItemTableFilter** property, open the filter editor and setup the filter as shown in the table:

Field	Type	Value
Item Ledger Entry Type	FILTER	Sale

13. Insert columns for the **Value Entry** table:

Type	Data Source	Name	Method Type	Method
Column	Invoiced Quantity	<Sum_Invoiced_Quantity>	Totals	Sum
Column	Cost Amount (Actual)	<Sum_Cost_Amount_Actual>	Totals	Sum
Column	Sales Amount (Actual)	<Sum_Sales_Amount_Actual>	Totals	Sum
Filter	Posting Date	<Posting_Date>		

Names for all data items and columns are assigned automatically by C/SIDE. You can change or accept the default values.

As soon as you select the `Totals` method in any of the columns all columns without totaling become grouping fields. The **Group By** property will be automatically checked for these fields.

14. Select the empty line under the last filter element and open the properties of the `Query` object. Setup the `OrderBy` property. Select **Sum_Sales_Amount_Actual** as the ordering field, and **Direction = Descending**:

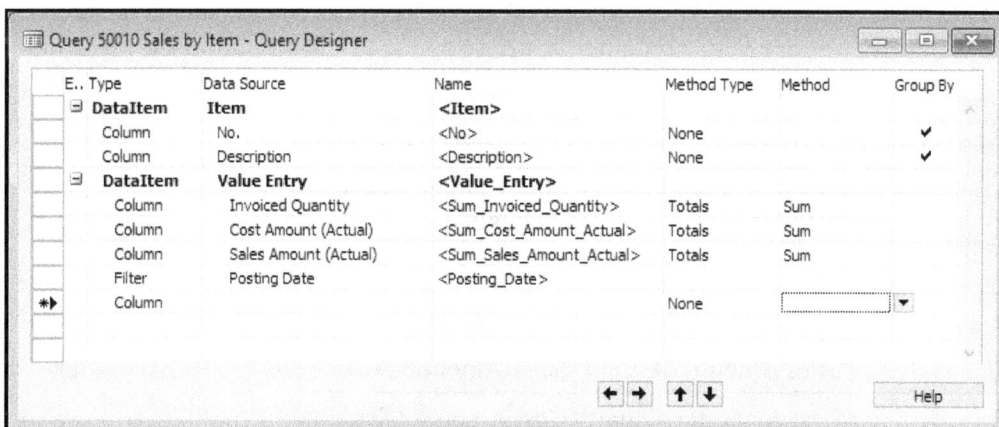

15. Save the Query with the ID 50010 and name it `Sales by Item`.

16. To verify the result, run the page 30 `Item Card` and set the checkmark `Certificate Required` for items **1928-S** and **1952-W**. Run the query and make sure that is returns sales and cost amounts for both items.

17. Create a page in the page designer. Select **Create a page using a wizard** and choose **Page type = Worksheet**. Select the table `Value Entry` as the page source.

18. Declare global variables:

Name	DataType
ProfitPct	Integer
FromDate	Date
ToDate	Date

19. Create a `ContentArea` container called **Item Profit**. Add a group named **DateFilters** in the container and insert two fields in the group. Link global variables `FromDate` and `ToDate` to source expressions of the fields:

Type	Subtype	SourceExpr	Name	Caption
Container	ContentArea		ItemProfit	Item Profit
Group	Group		DateFilters	Date Filters
Field		FromDate	FromDate	From Date
Field		ToDate	ToDate	To Date

20. In the `ContentArea` container insert a `Repeater` group and insert these fields:

Type	Subtype	SourceExpr	Name
Group	Repeater		Group
Field		Item No.	Item No.
Field		Description	Description
Field		Invoiced Quantity	Invoiced Quantity
Field		Sales Amount (Actual)	Sales Amount (Actual)
Field		Cost Amount (Actual)	Cost Amount (Actual)
Field		ProfitPct	ProfitPct

The final page layout will be as shown in the following screenshot:

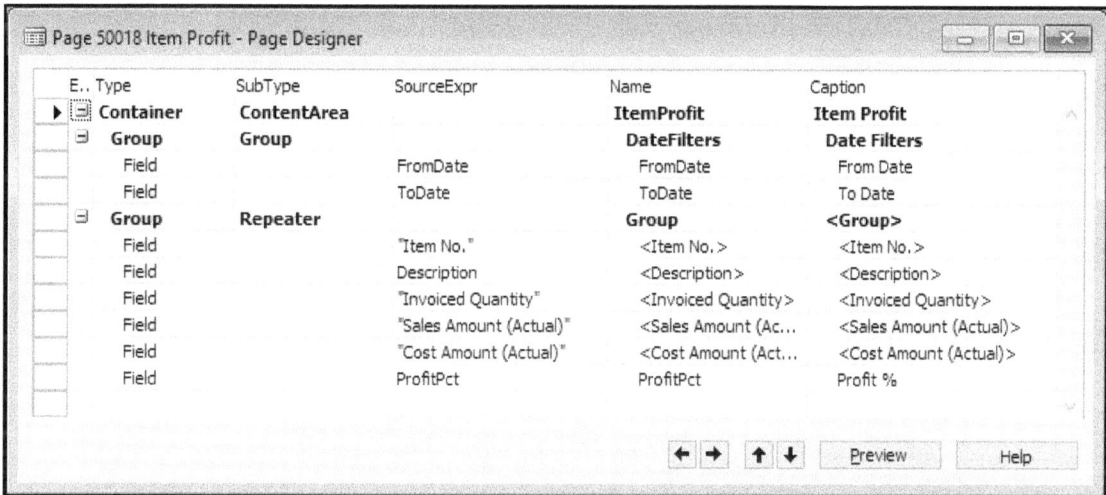

21. Access the page properties and set **SourceTableTemporary = Yes**, **ShowFilter = No**.

22. Select the repeater element and open its properties. Set **Editable = FALSE**.

23. Open page C/AL code in the code editor. In the `OnOpenPage` trigger call the function than will collect the list of items with related data:

    ```
    GetItems;
    ```

24. The `ProfitPct` variable should be updated in the `OnAfterGetRecord` trigger:

    ```
    IF "Cost Amount (Actual)" <> 0 THEN
      ProfitPct :=
        ROUND(("Sales Amount (Actual)" - "Cost Amount (Actual)") /
        "Cost Amount (Actual)" * 100,2);
    ```

25. Two filter fields should also update the page data. In triggers `FromDate - OnValidate` and `ToDate - OnValidate`, insert function call:

    ```
    GetItems;
    ```

26. The local variables are as follows:

Name	DataType	Subtype
SalesbyItem	Query	Sales by Item
EntryNo	Integer	

27. The code is as follows:

```
IF FromDate = 0D THEN
  FromDate := WORKDATE;
IF ToDate = 0D THEN
  ToDate := WORKDATE;

RESET;
DELETEALL;

EntryNo := 1;
SalesbyItem.SETRANGE(Posting_Date,FromDate,ToDate);
IF SalesbyItem.OPEN THEN
  WHILE SalesbyItem.READ DO BEGIN
    "Entry No." := EntryNo;
    "Item No." := SalesbyItem.No;
    Description := SalesbyItem.Description;
    "Invoiced Quantity" := -
        SalesbyItem.Sum_Invoiced_Quantity;
    "Sales Amount (Actual)" :=
        SalesbyItem.Sum_Sales_Amount_Actual;
    "Cost Amount (Actual)" := -
        SalesbyItem.Sum_Cost_Amount_Actual;
    INSERT;

    EntryNo += 1;
  END;
```

28. Save the page as 50018 **Item Profit**.

29. Run the page from the object designer. By default, the date filter is limited by the work date. Change the values of **From Date** and **To Date** and see how amounts are recalculated.

How it works...

On each page update, the query object is executed, and the resulting record set is copied into a temporary table.

The result described earlier could be achieved without a query object. The same amounts can be obtained by C/AL code. We only need to iterate on the list of items and calculate sums on each item in the loop:

```
IF Item.FINDSET THEN
  REPEAT
    ValueEntry.SETRANGE("Posting Date",FromDate,ToDate);
    ValueEntry.SETRANGE("Item No.",Item."No.");
    ValueEntry.CALCSUMS(
      "Invoiced Quantity","Sales Amount (Actual)",
      "Cost Amount (Actual)");
  UNTIL Item.NEXT = 0;
```

The main advantage of a query over this bit of C/AL code is performance. Query object requires only one server request. The function `Query.OPEN` will issue a singe SQL query, while C/AL loop above has to query the Item table to retrieve all records from it and then run a separate query for each item to calculate amounts.

Filters can be applied to a Query object before execution:

```
SalesbyItem.SETRANGE(Posting_Date,FromDate,ToDate);
```

The filtered field must be exposed in the query – it has to be in the returned result set, or declared as a **Filter** field.

Improving performance with indexes

Selecting data from a large table with millions of records can be a very slow process when records are scanned directly. A good index can drive search queries many times faster. We will see how to control table indexed from the NAV development environment.

How to do it...

This recipe shows how to create indexes in a table to improve the performance of queries from the previous recipe.

1. In the list of keys, move to the empty line below the primary key **No.** and click the **assist** button on the right.
2. Open table 50010 **Item Certificate** in object designer and click **View** I **Keys**.
3. In the **Fields List** window, add two fields to the index:
   - Item No.
   - CA Code
4. Click **OK**, then close key's list and save the table:

5. Open table 5802 **Value Entry** in table designer, go to key's definition.
6. Add a key containing two fields: **Item No.** and **Certificate No.**.

   Certificate No. is a custom field added in the recipe *Creating Custom Tables*.

7. Click the **assist** button in the **SumIndexFields** field and add two fields to the index: **Invoiced Quantity** and **Sales Amount (Actual)**.

How it works...

The **Keys** view shows all keys declared for a table. First key in the list is always the table's primary key. When a new table is created, the first field defined in it becomes its primary key and the clustered index. Clustered index can later be changed: it must be defined, but it can be any of the table keys.

The primary key can also be altered, but its position in the list cannot be changed – it is always the top one. All NAV table keys can have corresponding SQL indexes. Creating a table key in C/SIDE creates a SQL index with the same fields, unless you disable the SQL index manually by setting the property **MaintainSQLIndex** to **No**.

In Step 4 through Step 6 an index with **SumIndexFields** is created on a table 5802 **Value Entry**. Declaring **Invoiced Quantity** and **Sales Amount (Actual)** as **SumIndexFields** means that NAV will create an indexed view based on the contents on the **Value Entry** table.

If you open SQL Server Management Studio after saving the changes in table 5802 and connect to your NAV demo database, you can find in it an indexed view named **CRONUS International Ltd_$Value Entry$VSIFT$15** that contains the fields defined in the index.

Run the page 50018 from the previous recipe and compare the SQL queries that NAV issues to calculate the sums with and without the SIFT index.

If there is no SIFT index defined, this is a simple and straightforward SUM operation on **Value Entry** table:

```
SELECT SUM("Invoiced Quantity")
FROM "Demo Database NAV (9-0)".dbo."CRONUS International Ltd_$Value Entry"
WITH(READUNCOMMITTED)
WHERE ("Item No_"=@0 AND "Certificate No_"=@1)
OPTION(OPTIMIZE FOR UNKNOWN)
```

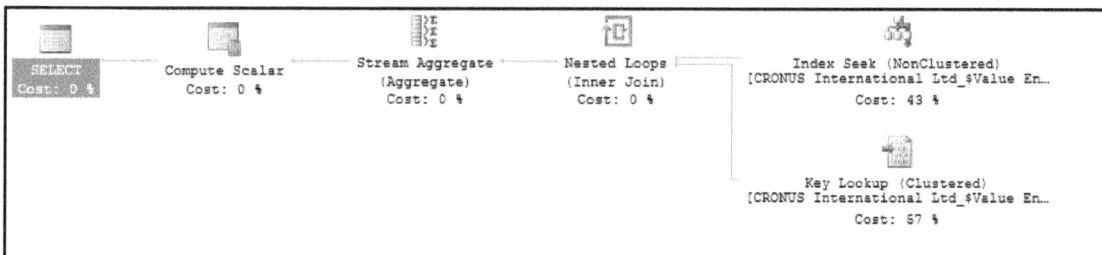

```
SELECT SUM("SUM$Invoiced Quantity")
FROM "Demo Database NAV (9-0)".dbo."CRONUS International Ltd_$Value
Entry$VSIFT$15"
  WITH(READUNCOMMITTED,NOEXPAND)
  WHERE ("Item No_"=@0 AND "Certificate No_"=@1)
  OPTION(OPTIMIZE FOR UNKNOWN)
```

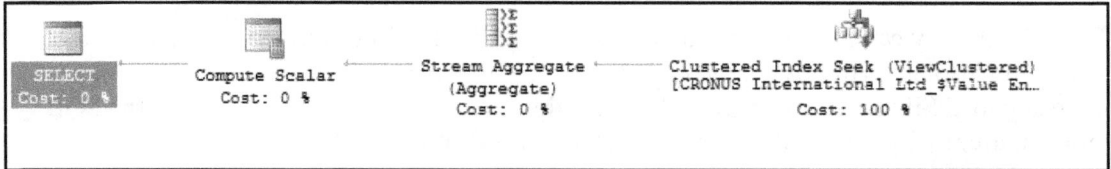

Linking datasources with advanced queries

The data item property **DataItemLinkType** specifies how the tables will be joined in the query. Besides two basic types, there is an option that allows the developer to enable advanced options and perform right outer joins, full outer joins, and cross joins.

How to do it...

In this recipe , we will build a Query object with full outer join between two tables to see detailed information on customer discount groups configuration:

1. Create a Query object in object designer.
2. Insert a data item with the **Customer** table as data source.
3. Include two columns from the **Customer** table: **No.** and **Name**.
4. Add another data item **Customer Discount Group**.

5. Include two fields from the **Discount** group: **Code** and **Description**:

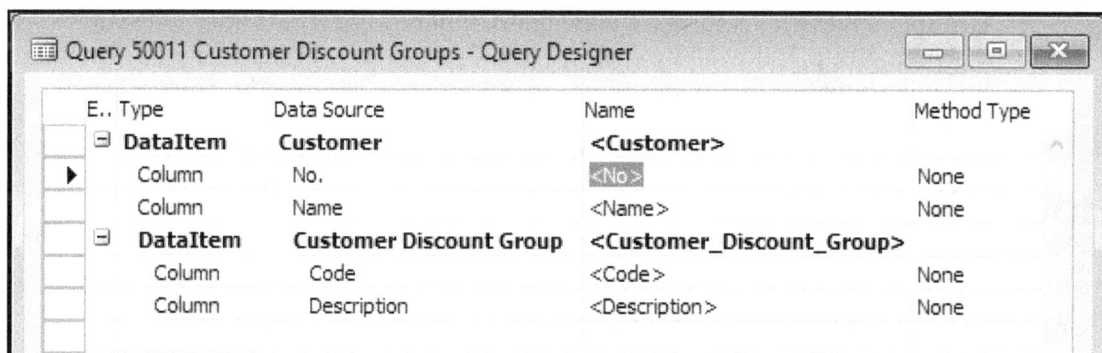

E..	Type	Data Source	Name	Method Type
⊟	**DataItem**	**Customer**	**<Customer>**	
▶	Column	No.	<No>	None
	Column	Name	<Name>	None
⊟	**DataItem**	**Customer Discount Group**	**<Customer_Discount_Group>**	
	Column	Code	<Code>	None
	Column	Description	<Description>	None

Query 50011 Customer Discount Groups - Query Designer

6. Open the properties for customer discount group data item and choose **SQL Advanced Options** in the **DataItemLinkType** property.
7. The new property, **SQLJoinType** will become available. Select **FullOuterJoin**.
8. Open link editor in the **DataItemLink** property and configure the link:

Field	Reference DataItem	Reference Field
Code	Customer	Customer Disc. Group

```
DataItemLink = Code=Customer."Customer Disc. Group"
```

9. Close the data item properties and open the Query object properties.
10. In the **OrderBy** field, click on the assist button and choose two fields for ordering:

Column	Direction
Code	Ascending
No	Ascending

11. Save the object as Query 50011 **Customer Discount Groups**. To test it, run the NAV client, navigate to /Departments/Sales & Marketing/Order Processing/Setup, open the **Customer Discount Groups** page and create a discount group, not assigned to any customer. Let it be named WHOLESALE.

12. Return to the object designer and run the query 50011 to preview the result. You will see the full outer join of two tables: **Customer** and **Customer Discount Group**. First entries returned by the query will represent customer without discount group, followed by customers with a discount group assigned. The final line will show the only discount group, WHOLESALE not used by any customer.

How it works...

Two basic join types available in a query configuration are:

- Use Default Values if No Match
- Exclude Row If No Match

They correspond to SQL right outer join and inner join, respectively. In the given example, tables will be joined using a full outer join statement to include data from both tables, even those records that don't have a matching pair on any side of the join statement.

The SQL query corresponding to the Query object is the following:

```
SELECT
    customer.No_, customer.Name,
    discount.Code, discount.[Description]
FROM
    dbo.[CRONUS International Ltd_$Customer] customer
FULL OUTER JOIN
    dbo.[CRONUS International Ltd_$Customer Discount Group] discount
    ON customer.[Customer Disc_ Group] = discount.Code
ORDER BY discount.Code, customer.No_
```

Exchanging data with XMLPort objects

XMLPort is a C/SIDE object used to exchange data with external applications in XML format or as plain text in CSV format. XMLPorts are easily configurable and allow us to execute more intricate logic in C/AL trigger. All these advantages make them a very handy tool when it comes to exporting reports in XML format or importing data from external sources.

How to do it...

Now we will create an XMLPort object to export a list of items with certificates in XML format.

1. In the C/SIDE object designer, select **XMLPort** in the object types and click **New**. This opens the XMLPort Designer.
2. Each line in the designer represents an XML node – either an element or an element's attribute.
3. Insert a line in the designer to create the root element ItemCertificates:

Node Name	Node Type	Source Type	Data Source
ItemCertificates	Element	Text	<ItemCertificates>

Text in angle brackets means default value assigned by the system. It can be left as-is, without changes.

The root XML element is a text constant that does not require any additional configuration.

4. Insert another line in the designer, following the root element:

Node Name	Node Type	Source Type	Data Source
Certificate	Element	Table	Item Certificate

This **XMLPort** element will export records from the data source table **Item Certificate**.

5. Under the **Certificate** element insert its child elements that will export certificate No., its issuing date, and expiration date:

Node Name	Node Type	Source Type
CertificateNo	Element	Field
IssuedDate	Element	Text
ExpirationDate	Element	Text

6. In the **Data Source** field of the **CertificateNo** element, click the lookup button and select the field **No**. The text fields should have default data sources.

7. Insert the **Item** element below the **ExpirationDate**. Its indentation level should be aligned with the **ExpirationData** element. This element is a child of the **Certificate** element:

Node Name	Node Type	Source Type	Data Source
Item	Element	Table	Item

8. Open the properties for the **Item** element and setup the data item link:
   - **LinkTable = Item Certificate**
   - **LinkFields = No.=FIELD(Item No.)**

   LinkFields property can be entered directly as text, or configured in a formula constructor.

   Still in the **Item** node properties, setup sorting for the data item: set property **SourceTableView = SORTING(No.)**

9. Insert the attributes of the **Item** element in the XMLPort designer:

Node Name	Node Type	Source Type	Data Source
ItemNo	Attribute	Field	Item::No.
ItemDescription	Attribute	Field	Item::Description

With all set up completed, the object structure looks as shown in the following screenshot:

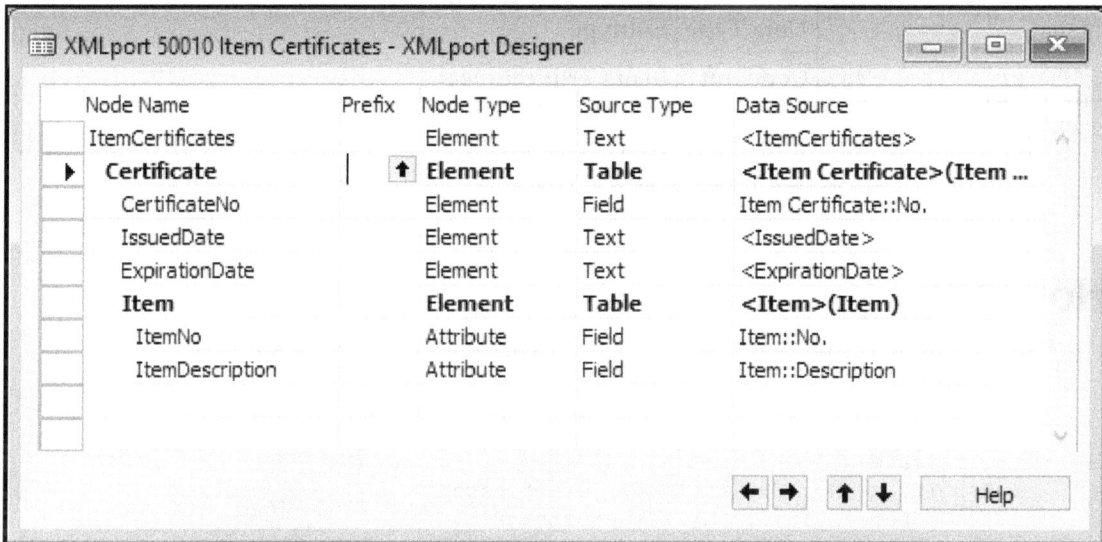

Node Name	Prefix	Node Type	Source Type	Data Source
ItemCertificates		Element	Text	<ItemCertificates>
Certificate		⬆ **Element**	**Table**	**<Item Certificate>(Item ...**
CertificateNo		Element	Field	Item Certificate::No.
IssuedDate		Element	Text	<IssuedDate>
ExpirationDate		Element	Text	<ExpirationDate>
Item		**Element**	**Table**	**<Item>(Item)**
ItemNo		Attribute	Field	Item::No.
ItemDescription		Attribute	Field	Item::Description

XMLport 50010 Item Certificates - XMLport Designer

10. This configuration is sufficient to export data taken directly from the source tables' fields. But there are two fields in our configuration that are not mapped to table fields and must be calculated. These are two date elements: `IssuedDate` and `ExpirationDate`. To assign values to a variable that must be exported in the XMLPort, open C/AL code and locate the trigger `Item Certificate - Export::OnAfterGetRecord`. Insert this code in the trigger:

```
"Item Certificate".CALCFIELDS("Issued Date");
  IssuedDate := FORMAT("Item Certificate"."Issued Date",0,9);
ExpirationDate :=
  FORMAT(ItemCertificateMgt.GetCertificateExpirationDate(
  "Item Certificate"."No."),0,9);
```

11. This code sample calls a function from the codeunit **Item Certificate Mgt**. To access it, declare a variable:

Name	Data Type	Subtype
`ItemCertificateMgt`	Codeunit	Item Certificate Mgt.

12. Save the object and run it from the object designer. Specify export direction, click **OK**, choose to open the file and review the result.

How it works...

The following is an example of the XML document generated by the XMLPort:

```xml
<?xml version="1.0" encoding="UTF-16" standalone="no"?>
<ItemCertificates>
  <Certificate>
    <CertificateNo>IC9276561093</CertificateNo>
    <IssuedDate>2016-01-25</IssuedDate>
    <ExpirationDate>2017-12-15</ExpirationDate>
    <Item ItemNo="1928-S" ItemDescription="AMSTERDAM Lamp" />
  </Certificate>
  <Certificate>
  ...
  </Certificate>
</ItemCertificates>
```

First element in the document structure exported by the XMLPort is the root element `ItemCertificates`. It serves the purpose of wrapping all other elements into one document. It does not have a value or attributes, so requires no property configuration.

Under the root element come certificates – one entry per table record. Table element will be repeated in the exported document as many times as there are records in the table. The number of exported entries can be limited by filtering the data source. Filters can be applied in the object designer, the property **SourceTableView**. Users can also apply filters in the XMLPort request page when running the export.

Each certificate has a related item that we want to see in the XML document as well. To export related records, a child table element **Item** is created in step 6. Properties **LinkTable** and **LinkFields** identify the parent element and the linking rule.

One more property of the child element configured in Step 7 is **SourceTableView**. This property defines the filtering and sorting order of the exported data. In this case, it does not influence the resulting recordset, since a certificate can have only one related item. We enable sorting to hide the filtering pane in the child element.

This is how the filtering pane looks with the **SourceTableView** property undefined:

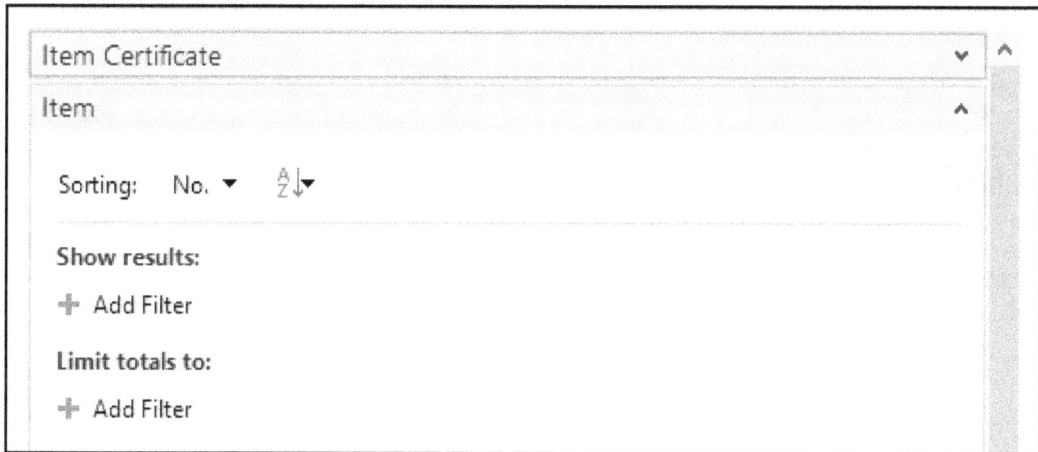

Filtering is enabled on both data source items: **Item Certificate** and **Item**, which dos not make sense – only one item must be exported inside each certificate element.

When the **SourceTableView** is defined, the sorting tab on the **Item** element disappears:

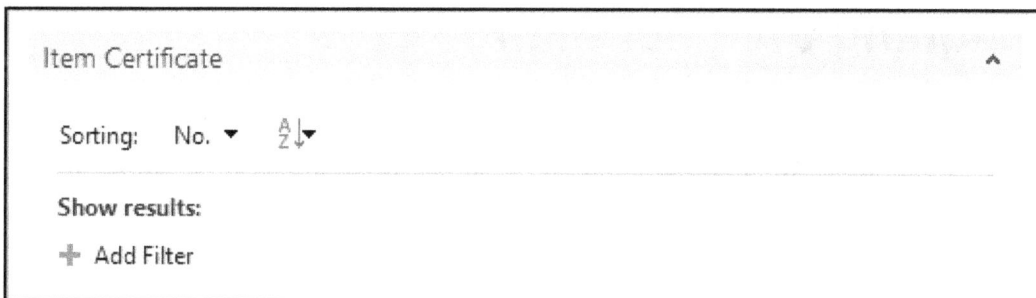

In Step 9 through Step 11, elements that cannot be mapped directly to table fields, are exported. In order to export such elements, variables are declared and the values that are to be exported are assigned to variables in the `OnAfterGetRecord` trigger.

> Variables exported in the XMLPort don't have to be declared explicitly in C/AL Globals. It is sufficient to declare a data element and assign the value to it.

The value of expiration date must be calculated by a C/AL function, it is not stored in the table – this is obvious that we have to use a C/AL function to obtain the value. It may be not quite clear why the certificate issue date has to be treated the same way if it can be exported as a table field.

The field is exported through an intermediate variable because before the export it must be properly formatted. The field value is not assigned to the variable directly, but through the `FORMAT` function:

```
IssuedDate := FORMAT("Item Certificate"."Issued Date",0,9);
```

The last parameter `9` in the function invocation is the format number that specifies which of the predefined formats will be used to export the value. `FORMAT 9` is used specifically for XML data. Dates in this format will be stored as *YYYY-MM-DD*. If you omit this formatting and setup the date to be exported as a table field, formatting will be defined by the system locale, and can be incompatible with the application importing the XML file.

Designing the user menu

It is fine for an application developer to run objects directly from the object designer while working on code. System users do not work with object designer, and access to application functions must be arranged in the user menu.

How to do it...

Now we will build a user menu for the custom solution.

1. To create a new menu suite, select **MenuSuite** in the object designer and click
   New. You will be requested to select a menu design level. Available design levels
   depend on your license. If you have a license of a certified Microsoft Partner,
   select **Dept – Partner** level. If your license is a customer's license with object
   designer access, use the menu **Dept – Company** level:

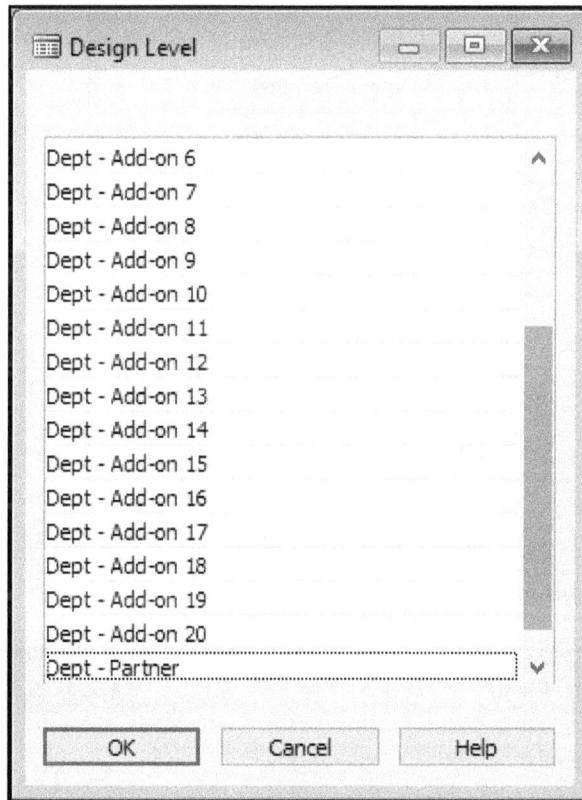

2. In the menu pane, you will see a list of menus available in all menu suites existing in the application. Right-click on any menu and choose **Create Menu** from the drop-down menu:

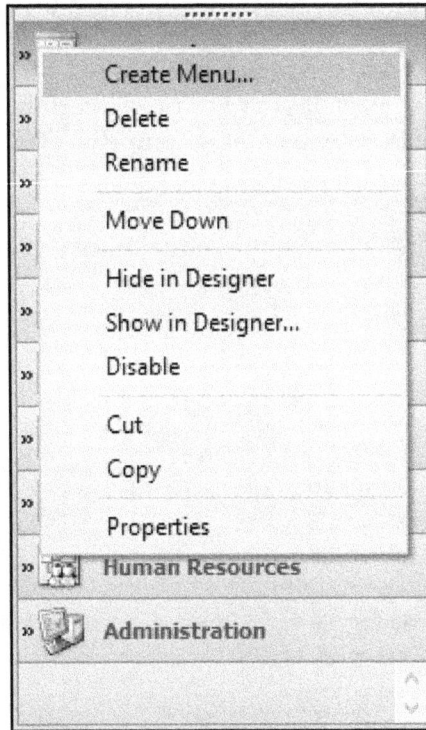

3. Enter the menu name when requested. You can also change the default bitmap:

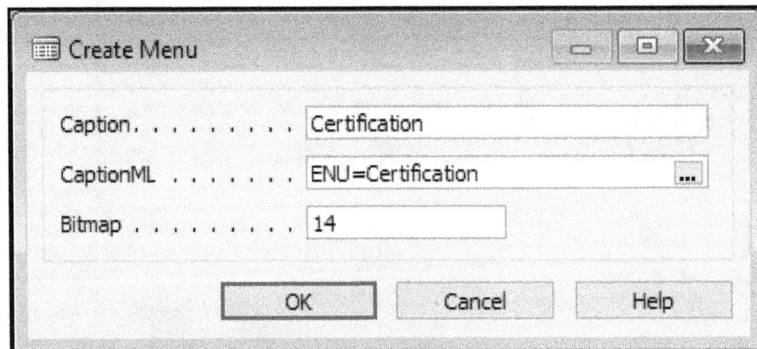

4. Click **OK**. A new empty menu will be created. The next level in the menu hierarchy that can be created is the menu group. Right-click on the **[Empty Menu]** item and choose **Create Group** from the drop-down menu:

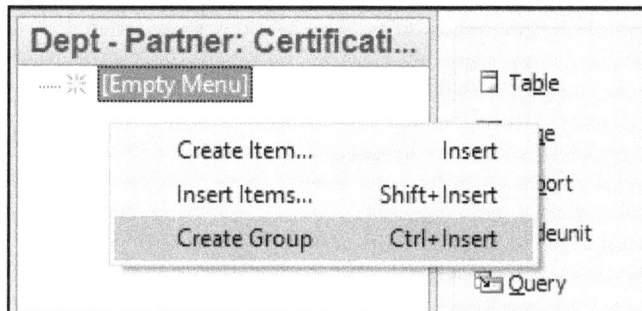

5. Name the new group **Item Certificates**.
6. Expand the **Item Certificates** group and right-click on the **[Empty Group]** item. Select **Create Item** from the drop-down menu. In the **Create Item** dialog select the **Object Type Page**, then enter page number 50013 or name it `Certificates List` in the **Object ID** field. Values for **Caption** and **Caption ML** will be copied from the page metadata. You can change them or leave the default values.
7. Select **Department Lists** and click **OK**.
8. Press *Ctrl + S* to save the page and close the menu suite designer.

How it works...

Restart the NAV client after completing the menu design – the new menu will be available in the application menu suite, in the **Departments** navigation pane:

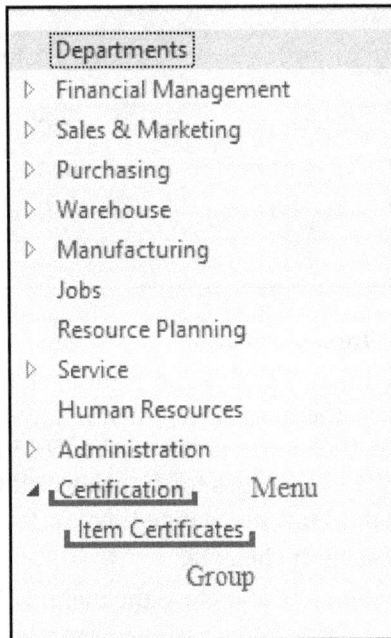

With the root menu item **Departments** selected, department menus with underlying menu groups will also be displayed in the **Departments** menu. This where you will see the bitmap customized in Step 3:

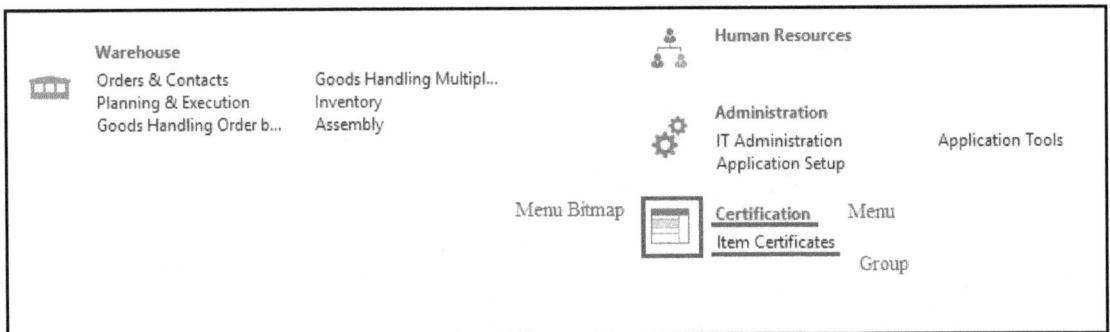

When you click your menu button either in the **Navigation** pane, or in the **Departments** menu, you are redirected to menu items, grouped by department or by category:

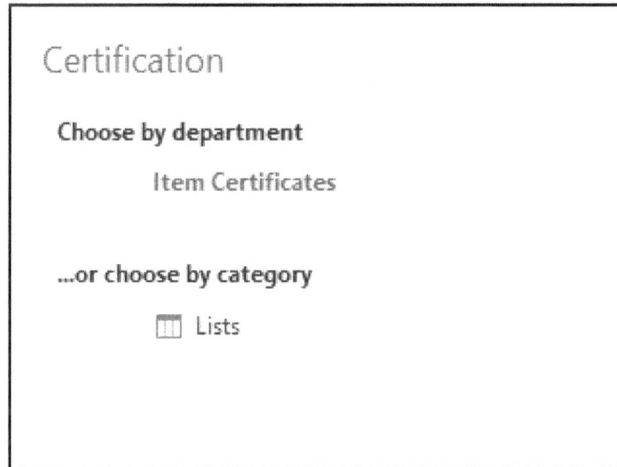

Certification

Choose by department

Item Certificates

...or choose by category

⊞ Lists

Referencing records and fields via RecordRef and FieldRef

The NAV datatype `Record` provides an interface to tables in the database. A certain limitation of the Record type is that a declaration of a `Record` variable is fixed in design time. Each variable must be linked to a table in the object design, and the link cannot be changed dynamically.

An alternative to static linking is the `RecordRef` datatype. A variable of `RecordRef` type is assigned to a specific table at runtime, but dynamics linking leads to higher complexity of code.

How to do it…

The `RecordRef` and `FieldRef` datatypes will be used to write a function comparing two records from the same table.

1. Create a codeunit in the object designer and declare a local function `CompareRecords` in the codeunit. This is the function that will do the comparison. Set the function's return type to `Boolean`.

2. Access the C/AL Locals in the function `CompareRecords`, declare a parameter `RecRef` of type `RecordRef`. After that, open the parameter properties and set **Dimensions = 2** to turn the parameter into an array with two elements. Close the parameters window.

3. Switch to the function's local variables and declare two variables:

Name	DataType
FieldRef	FieldRef
I	Integer

The **FieldRef** variable should be an array of two elements, so change its **Dimensions** property the same way, as for the `RecRef`.

4. The following function code will compare two records passed into it:

```
FOR I := 2 TO RecRef[1].FIELDCOUNT DO BEGIN
  FieldRef[1] := RecRef[1].FIELDINDEX(I);
  FieldRef[2] := RecRef[2].FIELDINDEX(I);

IF UPPERCASE(FORMAT(FieldRef[1].CLASS)) = 'NORMAL' THEN
IF FieldRef[1].VALUE <> FieldRef[2].VALUE THEN
  EXIT(FALSE);
END;
EXIT(TRUE);
```

5. Trigger `OnRun` of the codeunit will invoke the function. Two local variables must be declared in the trigger:

Name	DataType	Subtype
Customer	Record	Customer
RecRef	RecordRef	

RecRef is the array that will be passed to the function CompareRecords, so in its properties set **Dimensions = 2**.

6. In this example, we are comparing records from the **Customer** table. Records to be compared must be retrieved from the database first to get references. This code in the OnRun trigger will do that:

```
Customer.GET('10000');
RecRef[1].GETTABLE(Customer);
Customer.GET('20000');
RecRef[2].GETTABLE(Customer);

MESSAGE(FORMAT(CompareRecords(RecRef)));
```

7. Save the codeunit as 50011 **Compare Records** and close the code editor. Run the codeunit from the object designer and review the result. A message box will pop up informing you that customer records are not equal.

8. Now open the Dynamics NAV role-tailored client, navigate to /Departments/Financial Management/Receivables/Customers and create a customer record. By default, it is assigned the number C00010. Do not modify it. Create a second customer record and set **Invoice Disc. Code = C00010**. Now we have two customer records, identical in all fields except the primary key value.

9. In the OnRun trigger of the codeunit 50011, change the customer IDs from 10000 and 20000 to C00010 and C00020 respectively. Run the codeunit again. Now the function will return a positive result, confirming that customers are identical.

How it works...

Code execution starts from the invocation of the OnRun trigger when the codeunit is run. Here, the record reference is initialized and positioned on a database record. The most straightforward way to do so is to get the value from a Record variable. Although this method imposes limitations on the code flexibility, in many cases it is justified by the simplicity of the code.

After assigning record references, trigger code calls the CompareRecords function with the array of RecordRef in parameters.

The invoked function will iterated on the list of record fields in a `FOR` loop, starting from the field number 2. The first field is skipped, since this is the primary key value and cannot be equal in two different records. Number of loop iteration is defined by the function `FIELDCOUNT` that returns the number of fields in a table.

To access each particular field inside the loop we use the `FIELDINDEX` function. The function returns the reference to a field identified by its sequential number.

Before comparing two values, we ensure that the field has the `Normal` class and skip `FlowFields` and `FlowFilters`, comparing only fields actually stored in the database.

The `FieldRef.VALUE` function returns the actual value of the record field that can be compared or assigned to another variable.

Working with single instance codeunits

A single instance codeunit is an implementation of the singleton design pattern, an object that can be instantiated only once; all application objects referring to the singleton will reuse the same instance throughout the application.

Typically single instance codeunits are used to store an instance of an external dotNet component that cannot be instantiated twice, such as the Outlook application. Another example of a singleton object is a storage of user settings data, received from an external source.

How to do it...

In this recipe we will use a single instance codeunit to store user configuration read from an XML file. Configuration will include default date range for the **Item Profit** page used to report profits per item. This page is described in detail in the *Simplifying data access with queries* recipe.

1. Create a table in the object designer. The table will be used as temporary data source and won't store anything in the database.

2. Create tree fields in the table:

Field No.	Field Name	Data Type	Length
1	Primary Key	Code	10
2	From Date Formula	DateFormula	
3	To Date Formula	DateFormula	

3. Save the table. Assign the ID `50014` and name it `User Settings`.

4. Create a new XMLPort that will import data into a temporary table:

   Node: **Node Name = UserSettings, Node Type = Element, Source Type = Table, Data Source** – choose the table 50014 **User Settings**.

5. Open node properties and set **Temporary = Yes, MaxOccurs = Once**.

   New node: **NodeName = FromDate. Node Type = Element, Source Type = Field, Data Source** – choose the field **From Date Formula**.

   New node: **NodeName = ToDate. Node Type = Element, Source Type = Field, Data Source** – choose the field **To Date Formula**.

6. Open the code editor and declare a function `GetUserConfig`. This function should be accessible from external code, so open the function's properties and set **Local = No**.

7. Declare the function's parameter: `UserSettings. Record User Settings`. Set the checkmark in the **Var** field.

8. Write the following function code:

```
"User Settings".FINDFIRST;
UserSettings := "User Settings";
UserSettings.INSERT;
```

9. That's it. Save the XMLPort as 50011 **Import User Settings**.

10. Create a new codeunit. Open its properties and set **SingleInstance = Yes**.

11. Declare a global function `GetUserSettings`. The function must be accessed from other objects, so change its property `Local` to `No`.

12. Parameter `UserSettings` : **Record User Settings**. Check the **Var** field. Open properties and set **Temporary** to **Yes**:

```
GetUserSettings(VAR UserSettings : TEMPORARY Record "User
    Settings")
```

13. Declare a global variable in the codeunit:

Name	DataType	Subtype
GlobalUserSettings	Record	User Settings

In the variable's properties, set **Temporary** to **Yes**.

14. In the function `GetUserSettings`, insert local variables:

Name	DataType	Subtype
FileManagement	Codeunit	File Management
ImportUserSettings	XMLport	Import User Settings
SettingsFile	File	
XmlStream	InStream	
FileName	Text	

15. The function code is as follows:

```
UserSettings.RESET;
UserSettings.DELETEALL;

IF NOT GlobalUserSettings.FINDFIRST THEN BEGIN
IF FILE.UPLOADINTOSTREAM(
  'Specify the file to upload',
  'C:\NAV','Xml files (*.xml)|*.xml',FileName,XmlStream)
THEN BEGIN
  ImportUserSettings.SETSOURCE(XmlStream);
  ImportUserSettings.IMPORT;
  ImportUserSettings.GetUserConfig(GlobalUserSettings);
END;
END;

IF GlobalUserSettings.FINDFIRST THEN BEGIN
  UserSettings := GlobalUserSettings;
  UserSettings.INSERT;
END;
```

16. Let's add an action button to page 50018 **Item Profit** to load the default date formulas from the XML file. Open the page in page editor and switch to action designer.

17. Add an action container with one item:

Type	Subtype	Name
ActionContainer	ActionItems	Settings
Action		ApplyDefaultDateFomula

18. Select the **Action** item, open its code, and declare local variables used in the function:

Name	DataType	Subtype
UserSettings	Record	User Settings
ImportUserSettings	Codeunit	Import User Settings

19. Write the code of the OnAction trigger. Notice that the trigger code calls the function GetItems that will not be described in this recipe. For details refer to the *Simplifying data access with queries* recipe:

```
ImportUserSettings.GetUserSettings(UserSettings);
IF UserSettings.FINDFIRST THEN BEGIN
  FromDate :=
    CALCDATE(UserSettings."From Date Formula",WORKDATE);
  ToDate := CALCDATE(
    UserSettings."To Date Formula",WORKDATE);
END;

GetItems;
```

20. Save the page.

21. We are done with NAV objects. Now run a text editor and create a new text file. Insert the XML data that will be imported by the XMLPort and save the file:

```
<?xml version="1.0" standalone="no"?>
<UserSettings>
  <FromDate>-1M</FromDate>
  <ToDate>+1M</ToDate>
</UserSerttings>
```

22. Run the page 50018 **Item Profit** from the object designer. By default, entries accounted in the report, are filtered by the workdate.

23. Click the action button **Apply Default Date Formula** in the **Actions** tab. You will be requested to select the settings file. Select the XML file you created earlier. Date formulas will be imported from the file and applied to the date range.

24. Close the page, then run it again and execute the action **Apply Default Date Formula**. Now the date range is filtered immediately without file upload request.

25. Restart the NAV application and run the same page 50018 **Item Profit**, When you apply the default date range this time, file location will be requested once again.

How it works...

The following UML diagram explains the dependencies between objects in the example:

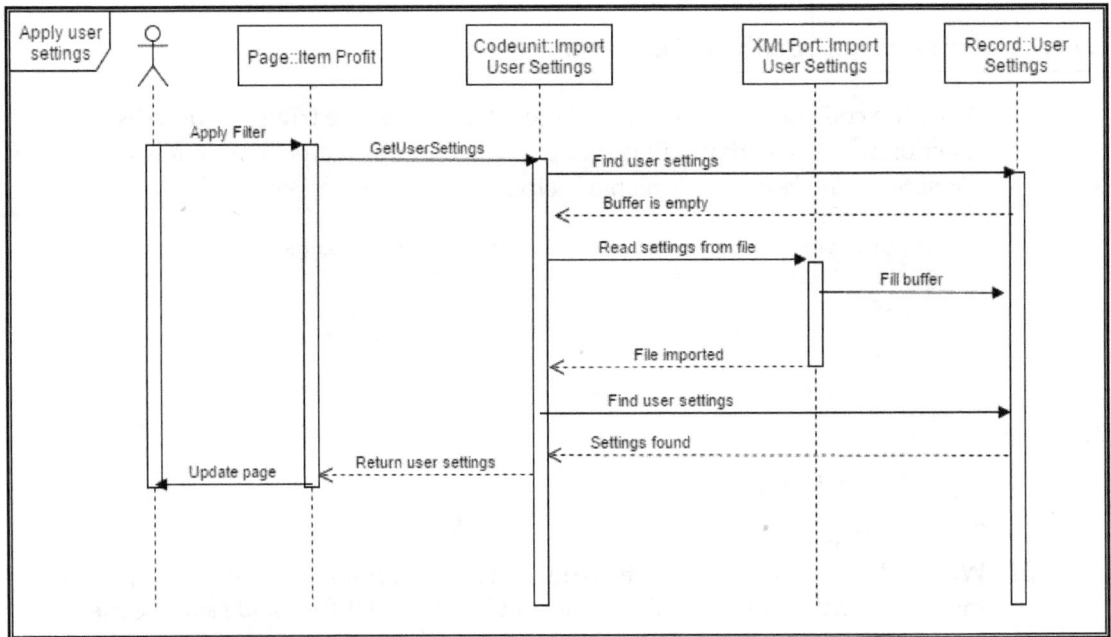

When the **Apply Default Date Formula** action is activated, the codeunit **Import User Settings** is instantiated. The codeunit keeps an instance of User Settings record in its global data. First request to User Settings after initialization returns an empty set, therefore the codeunit executes the XMLPort to import data from a file. The user is requested to choose a file name for upload.

After data is imported from a file, the global settings buffer in the single instance codeunit is initialized. Second request to the buffer returns settings received from the file, and the page is updated.

Now even if the page is closed and reopened, the instance of the codeunit and its data buffer still resides in the user session data. Next the user activates the action **Apply Default Date Formula** and filter values are retrieved from the buffer without a request to upload file.

All record variables in this example are temporary, no database queries from C/AL.

Running tasks in background sessions

When you execute long-running tasks, such as generating a large report or posting many documents in one batch, this blocks the user interface, forcing the user to wait until the task completes. Such extensive tasks can be run as background sessions, while the UI remains responsive.

How to do it...

This recipe shows how to run a batch job in a background session. The code in the recipe starts a session that posts sales and purchase invoices:

1. Create a codeunit 50019 **Post Invoices**.
2. In the OnRun trigger, declare the following local variables:

Name	DataType	Subtype
SalesHeader	Record	Sales Header
PurchaseHeader	Record	Purchase Header
SalesPost	Codeunit	Sales-Post
PurchPost	Codeunit	Purch.-Post

3. Enter the OnRun trigger code as follows:

```
WITH PurchaseHeader DO BEGIN
  SETRANGE("Document Type","Document Type"::Invoice);
IF FINDSET THEN
  REPEAT
```

```
      Receive := TRUE;
      Invoice := TRUE;
      PurchPost.RUN(PurchaseHeader);
    UNTIL NEXT = 0;
  END;

  WITH SalesHeader DO BEGIN
    SETRANGE("Document Type","Document Type"::Invoice);
  IF FINDSET THEN
    REPEAT
      Ship := TRUE;
      Invoice := TRUE;
      SalesPost.RUN(SalesHeader);
    UNTIL NEXT = 0;
  END;
```

4. Close the code editor to return back to the object designer, switch to the page designer, and create a page.

5. Open the page **Action Designer**. Add an action, **Post Invoices**.

6. Open the C/AL code editor. Declare a global variable `PostingSessionId` of `Integer` type.

7. In the `OnAction` trigger write a line of code that will start the background session and run the codeunit **Post Invoices** in that session:

```
STARTSESSION(PostingSessionId,CODEUNIT::"Post Invoices");
```

8. Create another action in the page. This is the actions that will probe the background session's execution result, `Check Result` is a good name for it. Declare a local variable in the `OnAction` trigger:

Name	DataType	Subtype
SessionEvent	Record	Session Event

9. In the `OnAction` trigger write the following C/AL code:

```
IF PostingSessionId = 0 THEN
  ERROR('Session was not started');

  SessionEvent.SETRANGE("User ID",USERID);
  SessionEvent.SETRANGE("Session ID",PostingSessionId);
  SessionEvent.SETRANGE(
    "Event Type",SessionEvent."Event Type"::Logoff);
IF SessionEvent.FINDLAST THEN
  MESSAGE(SessionEvent.Comment);
```

10. To see how the background posting works, create several purchase and sales orders, then run the page 50019 and execute the action **Post Invoices**.

How it works...

First four steps create a codeunit that, when run, finds and posts all open purchase and sales invoices. This is a simple loop – first on the table **Purchase Header**, then on **Sales Header**.

On each record, posting of an invoice and a corresponding inventory operation (a receipt for purchases, and shipment for sales) is enabled, then a posting codeunit is executed.

If you simply run this codeunit from the object designer, it will run the posting in the current user session. To delegate this task to another session, the STARTSESSION function is called in Step 7. The function takes two parameters, the second being the ID of the codeunit that should be executed in the background session. And the first one is a variable that will be assigned the session ID of the started session.

The value returned in the variable SessionID can be further used to analyze session status and execution result.

See also

To receive notifications when a document is posted, instead of refreshing the page manually, you can subscribe to integration events OnAfterPostSalesDoc and OnAfterPostPurchaseDoc declared in codeunits 80 and 90, respectively.

See the recipe, *Subscribing to business and integration events*, in Chapter 9, *Events and Extension Packages*, for details on event subscription.

3
Reporting and Data Analysis

In this chapter we will cover the following recipes:

- Designing reports in Visual Studio
- Developing Word layout for RDLC reports
- Writing C/AL code in a report
- Designing the report request page
- Writing RDLC code in a report
- Using built-in expressions in the report layout designer
- Including user interaction in reports
- Updating NAV data with the Excel add-in
- Retrieving data from NAV with Power Query
- Creating pivot tables with Power Query
- Analyzing data with Power BI
- Data hierarchies in Power BI reports
- Statistical data analysis in Power BI with R
- Sales forecast in Power BI with R
- Designing server-side reports in SQL Server Reporting Studio

Introduction

The key role of an enterprise resource management system is to collect transactional data. But the data itself makes little sense without reporting and analysis capabilities. Corporate information systems today store terabytes of data, and the more this number grows, the greater is the market demand for fast and flexible analytical tools.

Dynamics NAV has a set of built-in reporting tools, and there are also a wide variety of external tools that can be used to extend reporting capabilities.

Designing reports in Visual Studio

For an introductory example, we will create a simple client-side report presenting data in a NAV Report object. External reporting tools can provide more extensive functionality and flexibility in data manipulation, but client-side reports are a foundation of the NAV reporting toolbox. Its certain advantage is full integration with Role-Tailored Client, including the security system and the ability to execute C/AL code.

The object developed in the recipe is available in the source files (`REP50010_ItemSales.txt`).

How to do it...

In the following example, we will design a report to calculate the amount of income, cost, and profit for each sold item.

1. Switch to the report designer and press **New** to create a new `Report` object.
2. First set up the dataset. Insert one line in the **Dataset Designer: Data Type = DataItem, Data Source = Item**.
3. Under the data item, insert report fields:

Data type	Data source	Name
DataItem	Item	Item
Column	"No."	No
Column	Description	Name
Column	"COGS (LCY)"	COGSAmount
Column	"Sales (LCY)"	SalesAmount
Column	"Sales (LCY)"-"COGS (LCY)"	ProfitAmount

4. Select the first column in the report dataset, **No**, open its properties and change the value of the property **IncludeCaption** from **No** to **Yes**.

5. Do the same for the other table fields. The captions for the **No**, **Name**, **COGSAmount**, and **SalesAmount** fields will be derived from the table fields.

6. Access the **View** menu and open **Labels**. Create two labels – one for the report header, and one for the last column of the report, which is not derived directly from a table field and does not have a linked caption:

Name	Caption
SalesByItemsCap	Sales by Items
ProfitCap	Profit Amount

7. Select **Layout** in the **View** menu. This will run Visual Studio and open the report layout designer. An empty RDLC project will be created, and the blank canvas for the report layout displayed:

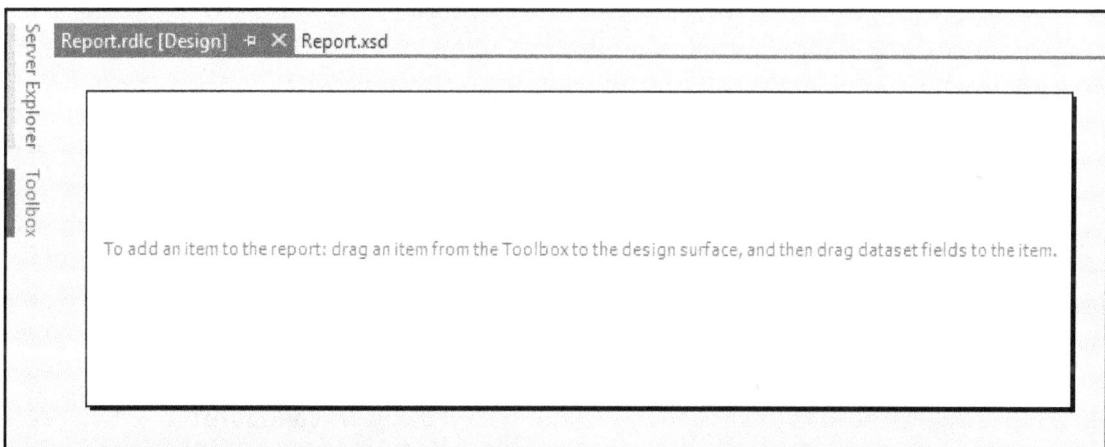

8. Click on the **Toolbox** tab on the left or select **Toolbox** in the **View** menu to unfold a list of graphical elements available in the report designer.

9. Choose the **Table** element from the toolbox and drag-and-drop it to the report canvas:

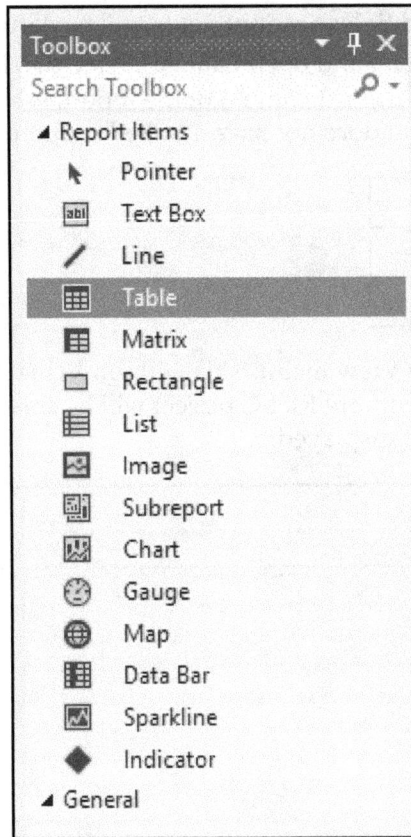

10. Now we need to link the report layout with the dataset configured in NAV.

    Select the **table** control, right-click on the **table** frame, and select **Tablix Properties...** from the drop-down menu:

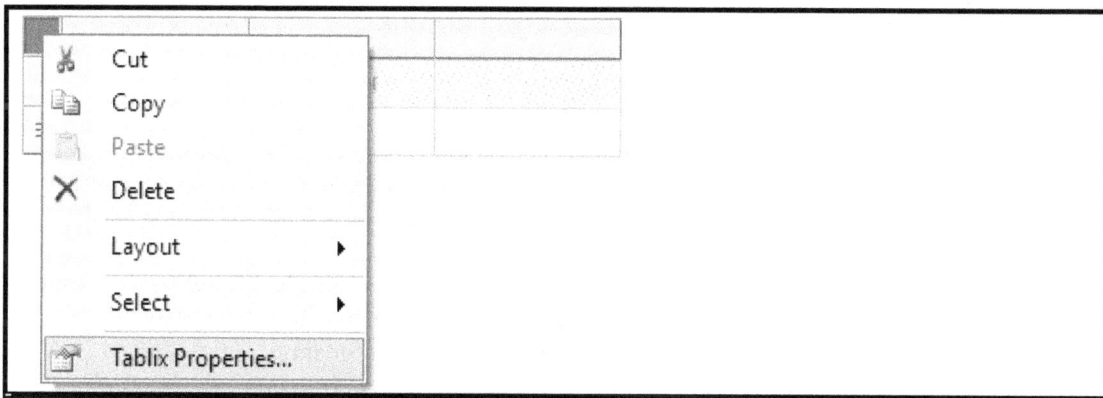

11. In the **properties** dialog, select the **General** tab, locate the field **Dataset name** and select **DataSet_Result** from the drop-down list. Click **OK** to confirm the settings:

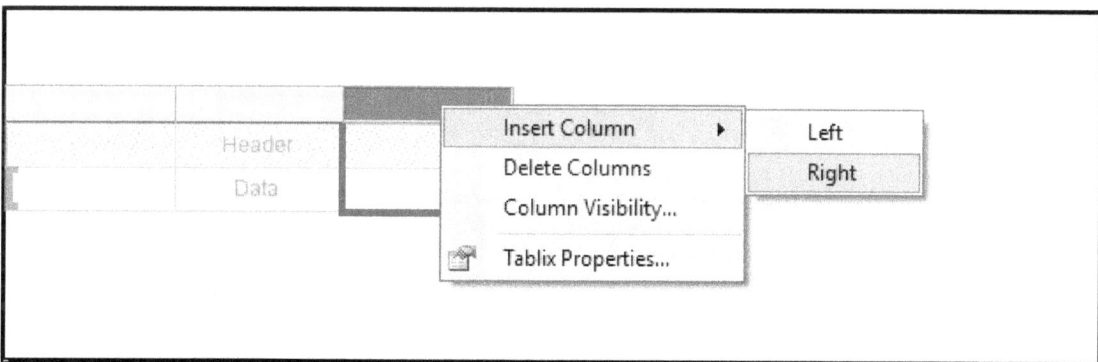

12. The default table control has three columns, but the prepared NAV dataset contains five fields. To extend the table, right-click on a column header and choose **Insert Column**, either on the left or on the right of the selected column. Repeat this step twice to increase the number of columns to five.

13. The table is now prepared and associated with the dataset, and we can link the dataset fields with table cells. To bind a value to a cell you need to set up the source expression. The table element has two lines in the design view. Select the bottom line with **Data** written in it. Right-click on the first text box in the column and choose **Expression** from the drop-down menu.

14. The expression editor window is divided into four parts. The top text box contains the source expression itself. You can enter it manually, but it is much easier to build the expression using the list of the following values.

First, choose the value **Category** in the left editor window. Report fields are located in the category **Fields (DataSet_Result)**. There is only one item in this category – **All** (the item window in the middle).

Finally, in the **Values** list on the right, select the field **No**. Double-click on the value. The field expression, =Fields!No.Value, will be copied into the Expression editor as shown in the following screenshot:

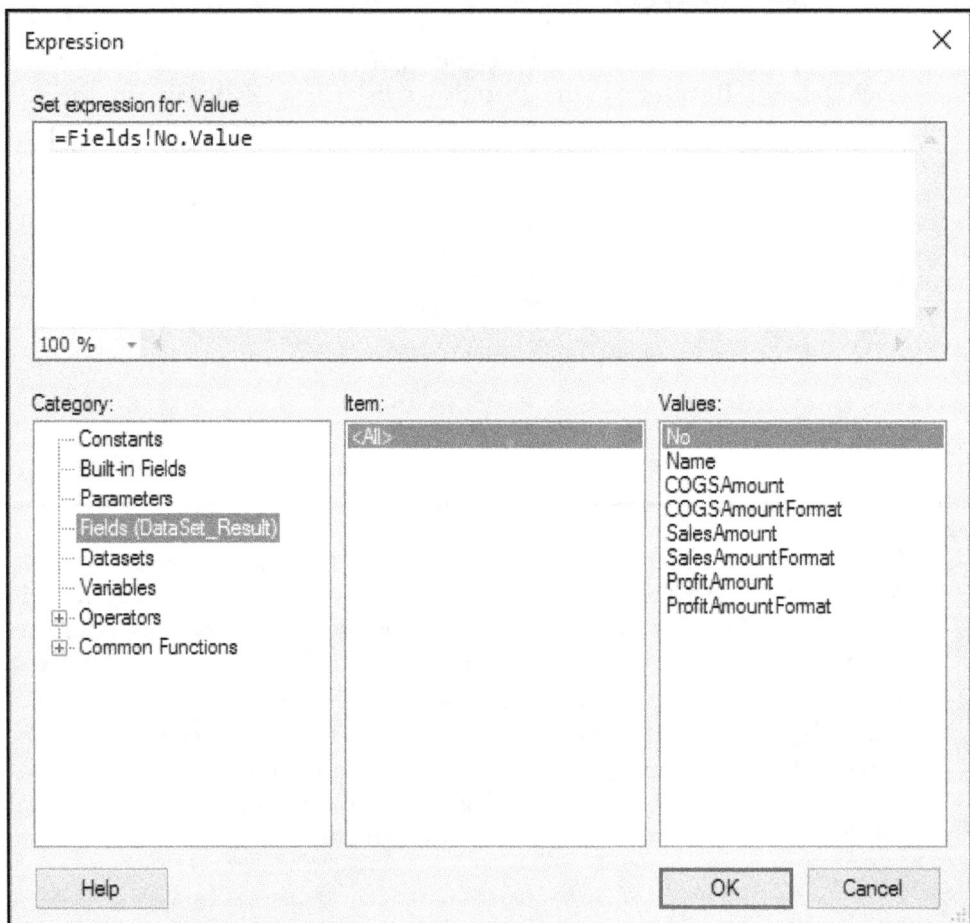

15. Click **OK** to close the expression editor and repeat the previous step for all five table columns, consecutively selecting **Name**, **COGSAmount**, **SalesAmount**, and **ProfitAmount** for fields source.

16. Now let's set up column headers. Choose the top line of the table element (the one with the `Header` text). Right-click and select **Expression**. This is the same expression editor as for the table data, but for captions we will build another expression. In **Category**, **Item**, and **Values** fields, select **Parameters** | **<All>** | **NoCaption**, respectively:

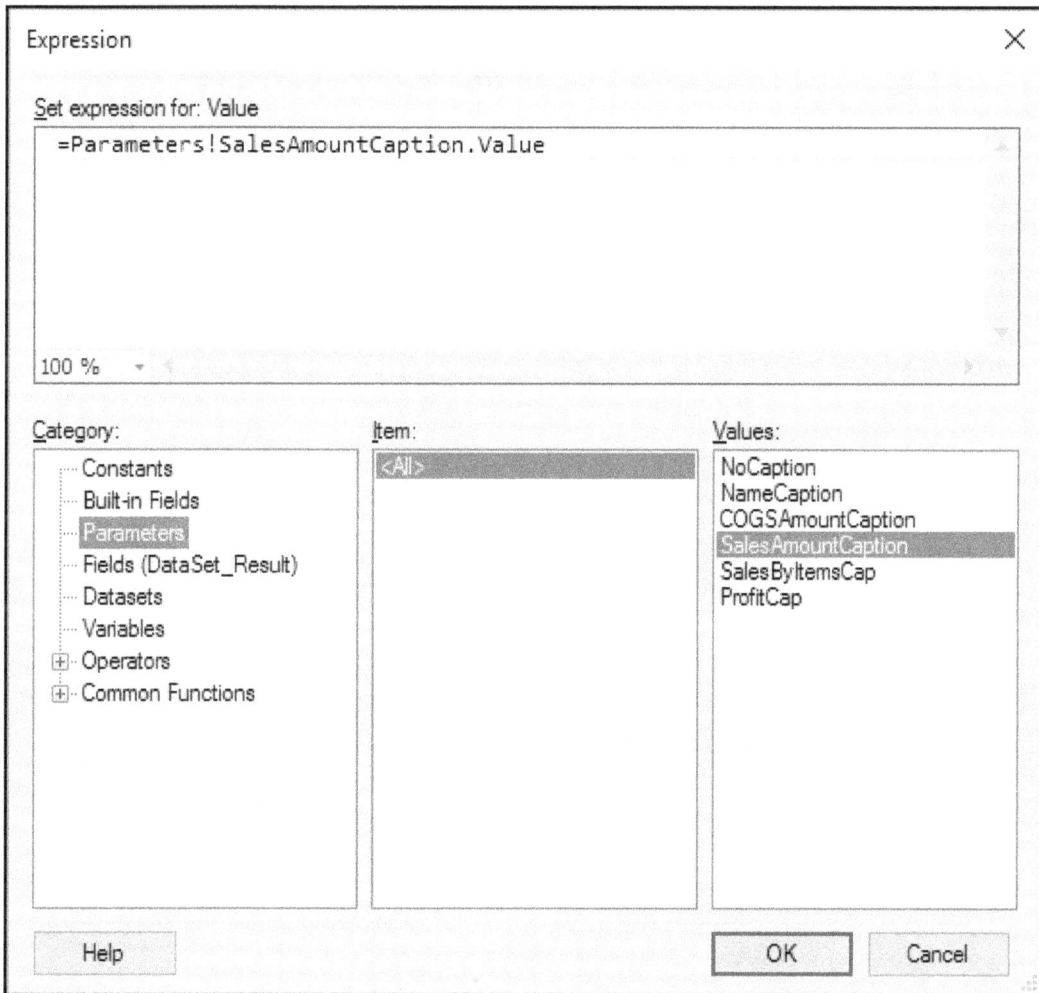

17. The table captions are in place, and now we will create the report's header, which will show its title. The label text **SalesByItemsCap** was exported from NAV exactly for this purpose. Unfold the **Toolbox**, choose the **Text Box** control, and drag-and-drop it to the canvas.

18. Position the text box as you find appropriate, right-click on it and open its source expression. Select the **SalesByItemsCap** parameter the same way you did for column headers.

19. The last thing to do in the report layout is to set up text styles. Right-click on the report caption, choose **Text Box Properties**, and switch to the **Font** tab. Select size **11pt** and check the **Bold** style option:

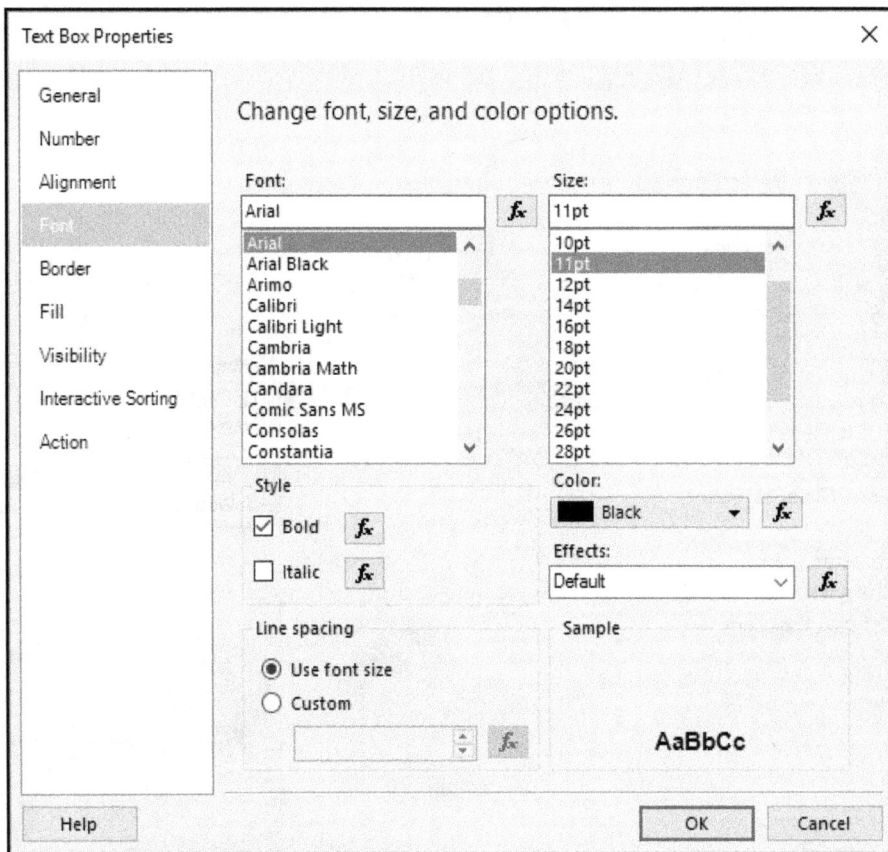

20. Do the same set up for column headers, but set the font size to **11pt**.
21. Close Visual Studio and confirm the request to save changes in the report layout project.
22. In the NAV report dataset designer, select **Item** and access its properties. Click the assist button in the **ReqFilterFields** property. In the field list, add two fields: **No.** and **Date Filter**.
23. Save the report with ID 50010 and name it `Item Sales`, then run it. You will see the report filtering request with two fields: **No.** and **Date Filter**, configured in the previous step:

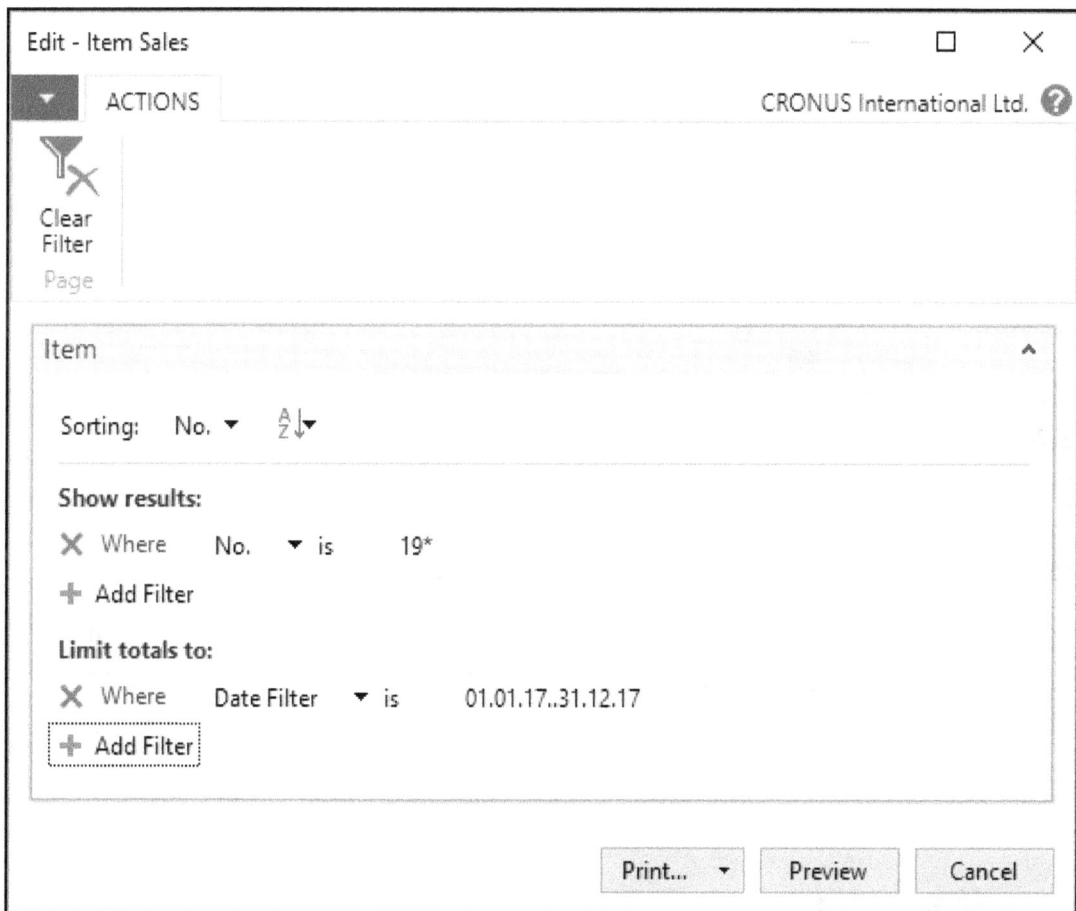

24. Limit the dataset by applying filters on the item no. and entry posting date, or just click **Preview** without filters and review the report data:

No.	Description	COGS (LCY)	Sales (LCY)	Profit Amount
1900	Frame	0,00	0,00	0,00
1900-S	PARIS Guest Chair, black	585,00	750,60	165,60
1906-S	ATHENS Mobile Pedestal	219,50	281,40	61,90
1908-S	LONDON Swivel Chair, blue	0,00	0,00	0,00
1920-S	ANTWERP Conference Table	656,00	840,80	184,80
1924-W	CHAMONIX Base Storage Unit	0,00	0,00	0,00
1928-S	AMSTERDAM Lamp	583,80	742,27	158,47
1928-W	ST.MORITZ Storage Unit/Drawers	191,90	290,78	98,88
1936-S	BERLIN Guest Chair, yellow	0,00	0,00	0,00
1952-W	OSLO Storage Unit/Shelf	93,60	134,73	41,13
1960-S	ROME Guest Chair, green	780,00	994,55	214,55
1964-S	TOKYO Guest Chair, blue	0,00	0,00	0,00
1964-W	INNSBRUCK Storage Unit/G.Door	2 056,80	3 416,40	1 359,60
1968-S	MEXICO Swivel Chair, black	1 057,10	1 337,80	280,70
1968-W	GRENOBLE Whiteboard, red	1 417,20	1 657,16	239,96
1972-S	MUNICH Swivel Chair, yellow	672,70	863,10	190,40
1972-W	SAPPORO Whiteboard, black	0,00	0,00	0,00

Sales by Items

(Report viewer toolbar: 1 of 1 | 100% | Find | Next)

How it works...

The report configuration defined in NAV Report Designer is only a dataset setup, the actual data presentation is done by external tools. In this recipe we use Visual Studio to draw the report layout.

Step 2 and Step 3 define the table used as the report data source and the table fields that will be included in the report data. We put item identification, no. and description, into the dataset, and extend it with numeric data, such as the cost of goods sold and sales amount. Both these fields are FlowFields; their values will be automatically calculated when the report is run.

The last field in the dataset is the difference between the income and expense amounts. It is not bound to any field in the table, but calculated from the values of two other table fields. Such simple expressions can be stated directly in the report element's **SourceExpr** property.

Next, in Step 4, we include field captions in the report dataset to use them as column captions in the layout. The only field without explicit table binding, **ProfitAmount**, has no associated field caption. Therefore, a **Label** is declared for this field in Step 6. All other columns will inherit captions directly for the **Item** table.

After the dataset is ready we run the Visual Studio report designer, which we will use to prepare the report layout. The NAV dataset is bound to an RDLC table as its data source, then each table cell can be associated with a field in the dataset.

The last flourish we add to the report in Step 21 is a list of fields that will be automatically presented in the filter request whenever the report is run. The filtering possibilities will not be limited to these two fields – the user can always add any fields they want into the filtering pane. But these two, as those most commonly used, will be shown in the default prompt.

Developing Word layout for RDLC reports

Besides an RDLC layout, a report can have a layout designed in MS Word specifically for the task of exporting the report into a Word document. A NAV report object can have two built-in layouts: one RDLC, and one Word layout.

Getting ready

The file name in the source files is REP50070_ItemSalesWordLayout.txt.

The Word layout for the report is in Report50070Layout.docx.

How to do it...

Now we will add a Word layout to the report created in the previous recipe.

1. Open report `50010` in the Report Designer, then save it as a new report `50070 Item Sales Word Layout`.

2. Create the built-in Word layout for the report: in the main menu, click **Tools | Word Layout | New**.

3. Export the layout into a Word file: click **Tools | Word Layout | Export**, then choose a file name for the layout file.

4. Open the file you saved in Step 3 in Microsoft Word.

5. To edit the Word report template, you will need access to the **Developer** ribbon tab. By default, it is hidden, so you'll need to show it. Right-click on the **ribbon** and choose the menu option **Customize the Ribbon**. The **Developer** tab should be listed in the **Main Tabs** option, but unchecked. Set the checkmark and click **OK**.

6. Switch to the **Insert** ribbon tab and insert a table with five columns and two rows into the document. We will need one row for the header, and another one for a repeater control representing report data.

7. Choose the **Developer** tab, then click on **XML Mapping Pane** to show report elements available for mapping:

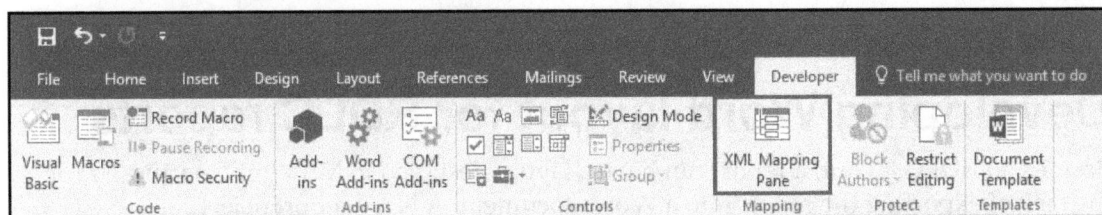

8. The mapping pane will be displayed. In the list of custom XML parts in the mapping pane; choose the namespace `urn:microsoft-dynamics-nav/reports/Item_Sales_Word/50070/`. Note the report name and ID:

XML Mapping ▼ ✕

Custom XML Part:

| urn:microsoft-dynamics-nav/reports/Item_... ▼ |

▲ NavWordReportXmlPart
   ▲ Labels
      COGSAmountCaption
      NameCaption
      NoCaption
      ProfitCap
      SalesAmountCaption
      SalesByItemsCap
   ▲ Item
      COGSAmount
      Name
      No
      ProfitAmount
      SalesAmount

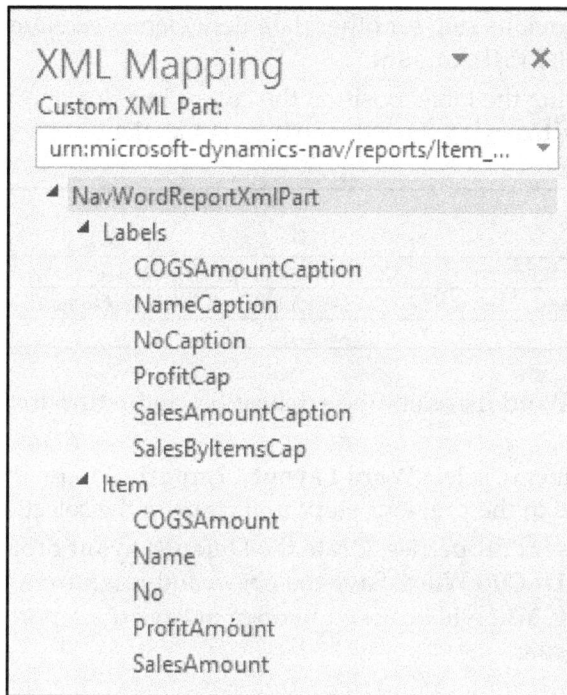

9. Position the cursor in the left top cell of the table, then select the **NoCaption** label in the **XML Mapping** pane. Right-click on **label**, choose to **Insert Content Control**, then select the **Plain Text** control.

10. Insert **NameCaption**, **COGSAmountCaption**, **SalesAmountCaption**, and **ProfitCap** in the remaining four header cells.

11. Select the entire second row of the table. In the **XML Mapping** pane, right-click on the **Item** data item, select **Insert Content Control**, then choose **Repeating**. This control will repeat the table row for each row in the dataset.

12. Position the cursor in the leftmost cell of the data row, select the **No** element of the **Item** data item. Right-click on the element and choose to **Insert Content Control/Plain Text**.

13. Repeat the previous step for other data item elements: **Name, COGSAmount, SalesAmount, ProfitAmount**:

14. After formatting the table, position the cursor in a line above it and insert the label **SalesByItemsCap** from the XML part **Labels**:

SalesByItemsCap

NoCaption	NameCaption	COGSAmountCaption	SalesAmountCaption	ProfitCap
No	Name	COGSAmount	SalesAmount	ProfitAmount

15. Save the MS Word file, close the application, and return to the NAV report designer.

16. In the **Tools** menu, select **Word Layout | Import**. Choose the file containing the layout created in the previous steps and confirm the selection.

17. Access the report properties, locate the **DefaultLayout** property, and change the value from **RDLC** to **Word**. Save the object and run it from the object designer. Click **Preview**. You will be asked to open or save the report file. Open it and review the result:

No.	Description	COGS (LCY)	Sales (LCY)	Profit Amount
1500	Lamp	10,40	0,00	-10,40
1900-S	PARIS Guest Chair, black	585,00	750,60	165,60
1906-S	ATHENS Mobile Pedestal	219,50	281,40	61,90
1920-S	ANTWERP Conference Table	656,00	840,80	184,80
1924-W	CHAMONIX Base Storage Unit	81,70	136,40	54,70
1928-S	AMSTERDAM Lamp	583,80	742,27	158,47

How it works...

A Word layout is edited in MS Word, outside the NAV report editor, but it should be created in NAV designer. As in the case of the RDLC layout, dataset elements must be declared before creating the layout in the external application, since all data items are exported in XML format to the external editor. While the RDLC report description gets synchronized between NAV and Visual Studio on each modification on both sides, the Word layout is synchronized via a Word document exported into a file.

After editing the layout in MS Word, the resulting file is imported back in NAV, and can now be used to generate reports.

There's more...

The default layout altered in the last step of the recipe can be changed by the user in the UI, without modifying the object.

To select the default layout for the report **50070**:

- In NAV client, run the page **Report Layout Selection** located in the section **Departments** | **Administration** | **IT Administration** | **Reports**.
- Find the report **50070 Item Sales Word** in the list.
- The **Selected Layout** field is now Word (built-in). Change it to RDLC (built-in) and close the page.

When you run the report next time, it will be printed with the RDLC layout instead of the Word option defined in the object designer.

Writing C/AL code in a report

The report designed in the previous example retrieved data from a database table and presented the result without extra manipulation. It is as simple as that, when the data the users require does not have to be transformed.

Getting ready

The file name in the source files is `REP50020_SalesByCustomerItem.txt`.

How to do it...

Now we will create a report that collects aggregated data into a temporary record to calculate values that cannot be retrieved from a table directly. Aggregated values are computed by C/AL code executed in report triggers.

1. Create a report object in NAV Object Designer.
2. Declare a global variable TempValueEntry of Record type and SubType = Value Entry. This is a temporary buffer where aggregated report amounts will be stored. Open its properties and set Temporary to Yes.
3. Create a data item with the Customer table as the data source.
4. Under the Customer data item, add another one and set the data source to Item Ledger Entry. Open data item properties and set up the data item view and link:

   The following table shows the DataItemView property setup:

Field	Type	Value
Source Type	CONST	Customer
Entry Type	CONST	Sale

   When configured, the property value is evaluated in a text string:

   ```
   WHERE(Source Type=CONST(Customer),Entry Type=CONST(Sale))
   ```

   The following table shows the DataItemLink property setup:

Field	Reference Field
Source No.	No.

   The DataItemLink text value is Source No.=FIELD(No.).

5. Next data item is Source = Integer. A new data item is added as a child of the one over it. Unindent the Integer item. It should be a child of Item, Item Ledger Entry. No data item link configuration is required for the Integer element, it will be filtered by C/AL code.

6. Below the `Integer` data item, insert the dataset columns that will be exported to the report. The dataset configuration will be the following:

Data Type	Data Source	Name
DataItem	Customer	Customer
DataItem	Item Ledger Entry	Item Ledger Entry
DataItem	Integer	Integer
Column	Customer.No.	CustomerNo
Column	Customer.Name	CustomerName
Column	TempValueEntry.Item No.	ItemNo
Column	TempValueEntry.Description	Description
Column	-TempValueEntry.Item Ledger Entry Quantity	Quantity
Column	-TempValueEntry.Cost Amount (Actual)	CostAmount
Column	TempValueEntry.Sales Amount (Actual)	SalesAmount

Note the – symbol in the `Quantity` and `CostAmount` expressions. `Quantity` and `CostAmount` are negative in sales transactions, so the sign must be reverted in the report.

As you can see, all amounts are exported from the temporary record `TempValueEntry`. This table is now empty, and we must fill it in with the report triggers before being able to export it.

7. To include column captions in the report dataset, open the list of report lablels (**View** | **Labels**) and fill in the name and caption field for all seven report columns:

Name	Caption
CustNoCap	Customer No.
CustNameCap	Customer Name

The `Name` field will be used by Visual Studio report designer to refer to the label. `Caption` is the text that will be displayed in the report layout. Fill these values for all columns listed in Step 6.

8. Open report C/AL code (*F9*) and declare another global variable: `EntryNo` of `Integer` type. This will be used as an identifier of aggregated entries in the temp buffer.

9. Locate the trigger `Item Ledger Entry - OnPreDataItem` and insert the initialization of global variables in it:

```
TempValueEntry.RESET;
TempValueEntry.DELETEALL;
EntryNo := 0;
```

10. Declare a function, `InitTempValueEntry`. This will do the primary initialization of the temporary record buffer before inserting a record. The function accepts one parameter:

Name	DataType	Length
ItemNo	Code	20

11. The return value of the function is a named Boolean value. Switch to the **Return Value** tab in the function's local declaration and set **Name** to **EntryExists**, and **Return Type** to **Boolean**.

12. Copy and paste or type the following function code:

```
TempValueEntry.INIT;
TempValueEntry.SETRANGE("Item No.",ItemNo);
EntryExists := TempValueEntry.FINDFIRST;

IF NOT EntryExists THEN BEGIN
  EntryNo += 1;
  TempValueEntry."Entry No." := EntryNo;
END;
```

13. Declare one more function in C/AL Globals: `UpdateTempValueEntry`. A local variable should be declared in the function:

Name	Type	Subtype
Item	Record	Item

Besides, the function takes one record parameter:

Name	Type	Subtype
ItemLedgerEntry	Record	Item Ledger Entry

As the name of the function implies, it will update the amounts in the record buffer with the amounts received in the parameter:

```
Item.GET(ItemLedgerEntry."Item No.");
TempValueEntry."Source No." := ItemLedgerEntry."Source No.";
TempValueEntry."Item No." := ItemLedgerEntry."Item No.";
TempValueEntry.Description := Item.Description;
TempValueEntry."Item Ledger Entry Quantity" +=
  ItemLedgerEntry.Quantity;
TempValueEntry."Cost Amount (Actual)" +=
  ItemLedgerEntry."Cost Amount (Actual)";
TempValueEntry."Sales Amount (Actual)" +=
  ItemLedgerEntry."Sales Amount (Actual)";
```

14. The data item trigger, Item Ledger Entry - OnAfterGetRecord, will stick all theses actions together. Declare two local variables in the trigger:

Name	DataType	Subtype
Item	Record	Item
EntryExists	Boolean	

15. Then write down the trigger code that will calculate the values of the FlowFields and update the amounts in the temporary record:

```
CALCFIELDS("Cost Amount (Actual)","Sales Amount (Actual)");
IF ("Cost Amount (Actual)" = 0) AND
   ("Sales Amount (Actual)" = 0)
THEN
  CurrReport.SKIP;

EntryExists := InitTempValueEntry("Item No.");
UpdateTempValueEntry("Item Ledger Entry");

IF EntryExists THEN
  TempValueEntry.MODIFY
ELSE
  TempValueEntry.INSERT;
```

16. The next function does not have local variables. Locate the trigger `Integer –` `OnPreDataItem` and write down the code:

```
TempValueEntry.RESET;
SETRANGE(Number,1,TempValueEntry.COUNT);
```

17. The final piece of code in the report resides in `Integer – OnAfterGetRecord` trigger. This is just one line:

```
TempValueEntry.GET(Number);
```

18. Configure the data items' default filtering fields. For the **Customer** data item, select the **field No.** in the **ReqFilterFields** property. Then select the data item **Item Ledger Entry** and choose two fields: **Item No.** and **Posting Date**.

    Select the last data item – **Integer**. Open the table view setup and enter **Number** in the **Key** field. This setup will suppress the filtering request for the temporary buffer.

19. Open the report layout in Visual Studio. Drag and drop the table control to the report canvas. Assign the dataset **DataSet_Result** to the table.

20. Below the report layout canvas, there is a list of report groups. In a new report, there is only one group, **Details**. Right-click on the group name and choose **Add Group**, then **Parent Group**:

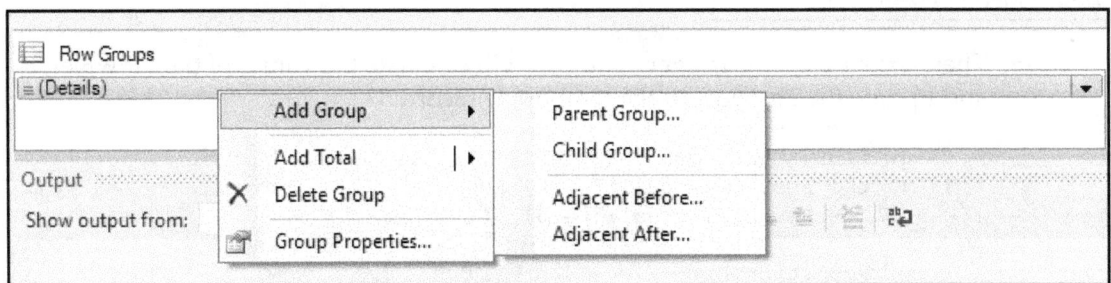

21. You will be asked to specify a field by which the dataset record will be grouped. Open the expression editor from the dialog box and select the field **CustomerNo** in the **Fields (DataSet_Result)** category.

22. You can specify only one field in the **New Group** dialog. But we also want to add customer names to the group. To insert other fields in the group, select the column **Customer No** in the report layout, right-click on it, then select **Insert Column, Inside Group – Right**:

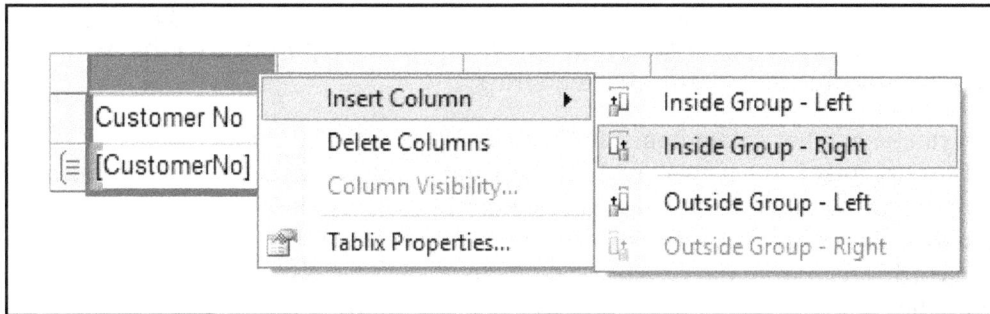

Customer No	Insert Column ▶	📥	Inside Group - Left
≡ [CustomerNo]	Delete Columns	📥	Inside Group - Right
	Column Visibility...	📥	Outside Group - Left
	📄 Tablix Properties...	📥	Outside Group - Right

Right-click on the new text box, open **Expression**, then select the field **CustomerName** from the **DataSet_Result** in the source expression.

23. There are five fields outside the group. Add two more report columns on the right side of the table and assign data source expressions. Pick fields from the dataset result: **ItemNo**, **Description**, **Quantity**, **CostAmount**, and **SalesAmount**.

24. Now the report table has seven columns. Set up captions for all fields. Pick caption texts from the **Parameters** category in the expression builder.

25. Save the report – it is now ready and can be executed:

Customer No.	Customer Name	Item No.	Description	Quantity	Cost Amount	Sales Amount
10000	The Cannon Group PLC	1968-S	MEXICO Swivel Chair, black	3	288,3	351,40
		1996-S	ATLANTA Whiteboard, base	7	4950,4	6029,56
		1964-W	INNSBRUCK Storage Unit/G.Door	10	1714	2920
		70011	Glass Door	5	184,5	361,5

How it works...

C/AL code in reports is placed in **DataItem triggers**. A **DataItem** element is a report element mapped to a table – the data source for the report. We start configuring report data items in Step 3 by creating a **Customer DataItem** element and linking it to its namesake table. When a report is executed, it retrieves records from the data source table, one by one, runs them through C/AL processing, and appends in to the report dataset that will be passed to Microsoft Report Viewer for rendering.

A report can have several data items that may be aligned in a consequential series of elements or organized in a hierarchy. In the current example, we create a hierarchical structure consisting of the data item **Customer** and a linked data item **Item Ledger Entry**, nested under **Customer**. Data elements structured this way will be run in a nested loop. First, a record is read from the **Customer** table, then all records from the Item Ledger Entry satisfying the combination of the **DataItemLink** and **DataItemView** properties are retrieved one by one. Then the sequence is repeated for the next customer record.

Each data item, as well as every table record, initiates a series of C/AL triggers in the report. This is where we place the code intended to preprocess database records before they are inserted into the report dataset. In the current example, all processing is done in two triggers of the `Item Ledger Entry` data item. The **OnPreDataItem** trigger is called before any record is read from the table and is used for initialization – global variables used in subsequent triggers are cleared here.

Item Ledger Entry – OnAfterGetRecord is triggered on each record after it is retrieved from the database. We use this trigger to fill a temporary buffer variable **TempValueEntry** where the total amounts summarized by item are aggregated.

After processing all item ledger entries for a customer, **TempValueEntry** holds sales amounts for this customer, sliced by item code. The next data item **Integer** will send the buffer data to the dataset. The table **Integer** itself is a so-called virtual table – it is not stored anywhere in the database, but represents a set of integer numbers wrapped into a table interface. Its primary job in the application is to act as an iteration counter in reports based on temporary tables. The report data item must be bound to a table in the database, there is no straight way to make it pick records from a temporary table. Still, many NAV reports rely on temporary tables to store intermediate calculation results. A standard trick is to create a data item mapped to the Integer virtual table and use it to control the report execution.

The usual data item triggers are called on the `Integer` element. In the **OnPreDataItem** trigger, the virtual table is filtered:

```
TempValueEntry.RESET;
SETRANGE(Number,1,TempValueEntry.COUNT);
```

By applying a filter on the Integer data item, we set the number of iterations to be equal to the count of records in the **TempValueEntry** buffer. If the number of records in the buffer is 10, then the trigger **Integer – OnAfterGetRecord** will be executed exactly 10 times. And the **OnAfterGetRecord** on the **Integer** data item retrieves the next record from **TempValueEntry** on each iteration. The field `Number` is the primary key of the virtual table `Integer`, and we use a simple `GET` to retrieve the record:

```
TempValueEntry.GET(Number);
```

Dataset columns, which are fields of **TempValueEntry**, are now updated on each iteration of the **Integer** data item.

Designing the report request page

The `Sales By Customer/Item` report from the previous recipe shows only the actual cost amounts. This means that goods shipped, but not yet invoiced, will not be covered in the report.

Getting ready

The following steps will be based on material presented earlier in this chapter. To be able to complete this recipe, you will need to carry out the walkthrough from the previous recipe *Writing C/AL code in the report*, or import the `REP50020_SalesByCustomerItem.txt` file from the source files.

The filename in source files is, `REP50030_ReportRequestPage.txt`.

How to do it...

Now we will use a request page to add an option to the report parameters that will enable the user to choose whether expected cost amounts should be detailed.

1. Open the report **50020 Sales By Customer/Item** in the NAV report designer. Do not open the code editor. The menu item **Request Page** required in Step 2, is available only from the report data items designer.
2. From the **View** menu, access the **Request Page** item to open the request page editor. Creating a report request page is very much similar to editing a regular NAV page object. A request page is in fact, a page object displayed before executing the report.
3. Declare a global Boolean variable **IncludeExpected** in addition to the two already defined variables. This Boolean value will be bound to a checkbox control and will store the user's selection.
4. In the request page designer, insert a **ContentArea** container with a **Group** in it. The **Group** item, in its turn, contains one **Field** element:

Type	SubType	SourceExpr	Name	Caption
Container	ContentArea		OptionsContainer	\<OptionsContainer\>
Group	Group		Options	Options
Field		IncludeExpected	IncludeExpected	Include Expected

The caption of the **Container** element does not show on the request page, so you can keep the default value for it. Captions for **Group** and **Field** will be displayed.

5. Close the request page designer, return to the report dataset designer, then open the C/AL editor.
6. The first operator in the **Item Ledger Entry – OnAfterGetRecord** trigger calculates FlowField **Cost Amount (Actual)** and **Sales Amount (Actual)**. Now we want to add the expected amounts. Replace the line with the following:

```
CALCFIELDS(
  "Cost Amount (Actual)","Sales Amount (Actual)",
  "Cost Amount (Expected)","Sales Amount (Expected)");
```

7. The next condition in the same trigger skips the entry if the actual amounts are 0. Modify this condition:

```
IF ("Cost Amount (Actual)" = 0) AND
   ("Sales Amount (Actual)" = 0) AND
   NOT IncludeExpected
THEN
   CurrReport.SKIP;
```

8. Amounts in the record buffer should be updated as well. The UpdateTempValueEntry function contains the following code:

```
Item.GET(ItemLedgerEntry."Item No.");

TempValueEntry."Source No." := ItemLedgerEntry."Source No.";
TempValueEntry."Item No." := ItemLedgerEntry."Item No.";
TempValueEntry.Description := Item.Description;
TempValueEntry."Item Ledger Entry Quantity" +=
   ItemLedgerEntry.Quantity;
TempValueEntry."Cost Amount (Actual)" +=
   ItemLedgerEntry."Cost Amount (Actual)";
TempValueEntry."Sales Amount (Actual)" +=
   ItemLedgerEntry."Sales Amount (Actual)";

IF IncludeExpected THEN BEGIN
   TempValueEntry."Cost Amount (Actual)" +=
      ItemLedgerEntry."Cost Amount (Expected)";
   TempValueEntry."Sales Amount (Actual)" +=
      ItemLedgerEntry."Sales Amount (Expected)";
END;
```

9. Save the report with a new ID and name. The report layout will not be changed.

10. Run the report. Now the request page includes, besides the standard filtering pane, an **Options** pane with the new option **Include Expected**. Enable the option and preview the report:

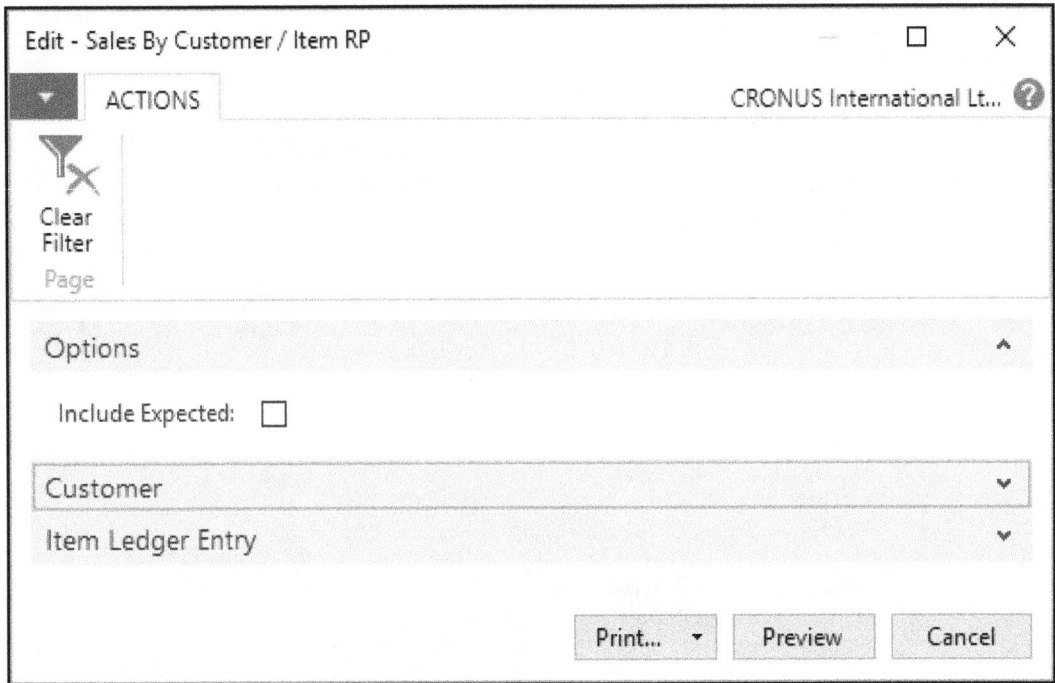

How it works...

A report request page is no different from a usual Page object. It is configured in the same Page Designer. The top-level item in the page must be a Container, which can include groups and controls. It is recommended that you insert a group under the root container, and supplement the group with control items instead of inserting controls directly into the container. This way, controls will be wrapped into a tab separated from the page filters.

Global report variables are associated with visual controls in the page, and can be accessed in the report code to determine the user's choice.

Writing RDLC code in a report

In the following recipe, we will develop a scenario similar to the earlier *Designing the report request page* recipe. Based on the report **50020 Sales By Customer/Item**, we will create a new version including expected amounts, but instead of requesting the user to select the representation mode, we will highlight the amounts awaiting invoicing, using RDLC formatting tools.

The filename in source files is, `REP50040_RDLCCode`.

Getting ready

The current walk-through is based on an object designed and developed in the recipe *Writing C/AL code in a report*. Before starting the following example, complete the prerequisites or import the report **50020 Sales By Customer/Item** from the source files.

How to do it...

1. Open the report **50020 Sales By Customer/Item** in the NAV Report Designer.
2. The expected cost and expected sales amounts will be exported to the report separately from the actual amounts, and later analyzed in the RDLC code. In the list of columns of the **Integer** data item, add two more lines:

Data Type	Data Source	Name
Column	-TempValueEntry."Cost Amount (Expected)"	CostAmountExpected
Column	TempValueEntry."Sales Amount (Expected)"	SalesAmountExpected

3. Two other columns `CostAmount` and `SalesAmount` should be renamed. The new report exports both expected and actual amounts, and these columns will display already invoiced amounts. Change the name of the `CostAmount` column to `CostAmountActual`, then rename `SalesAmount` to `SalesAmountActual`.
4. Select the **Quantity** column and display its properties. In the **DecimalPlaces** property, set the value to **2:2**. This value will later be bound to an RDLC expression to format data in the report output.

5. Open the C/AL code editor and use the **Item Ledger Entry – OnAfterGetRecord** trigger, which does all the work filling temporary buffer. In the current report, we do not skip any records, so remove the calls of CALCFIELDS and CurrReport.SKIP. The following is all the code that should be left in the **OnAfterGetRecord** trigger:

```
EntryExists := InitTempValueEntry("Item No.");
UpdateTempValueEntry("Item Ledger Entry");

IF EntryExists THEN
  TempValueEntry.MODIFY
ELSE
  TempValueEntry.INSERT;
```

6. Function InitTempValueEntry is not changed compared to report 50020, but UpdateTempValueEntry is slightly different. It should now calculate and update the expected cost amount, as well as the actual amount:

```
Item.GET(ItemLedgerEntry."Item No.");
"Item Ledger Entry".CALCFIELDS(
  "Cost Amount (Actual)","Sales Amount (Actual)",
  "Cost Amount (Expected)","Sales Amount (Expected)");

TempValueEntry."Source No." :=
  ItemLedgerEntry."Source No.";
TempValueEntry."Item No." :=
  ItemLedgerEntry."Item No.";
TempValueEntry.Description :=
  Item.Description;
TempValueEntry."Item Ledger Entry Quantity" +=
  ItemLedgerEntry.Quantity;
TempValueEntry."Cost Amount (Actual)" +=
  ItemLedgerEntry."Cost Amount (Actual)";
TempValueEntry."Sales Amount (Actual)" +=
  ItemLedgerEntry."Sales Amount (Actual)";
TempValueEntry."Cost Amount (Expected)" +=
  ItemLedgerEntry."Cost Amount (Expected)";
TempValueEntry."Sales Amount (Expected)" +=
  ItemLedgerEntry."Sales Amount (Expected)";
```

7. Open the report RDLC layout in Visual Studio.

8. The fields **CostAmount** and **SalesAmount** will change source expression. Right-click on the **CostAmount** text box and choose the **Expression** menu option.

9. Write the field's source expression:

```
=Fields!CostAmountActual.Value +
    Fields!CostAmountExpected.Value
```

Now, the cost amount consists of two parts – the expected amount and the actual amount, and the total value is calculated while the report is rendered.

10. Change the source for SalesAmount the same way:

```
=Fields!SalesAmountActual.Value +
    Fields!SalesAmountExpected.Value
```

11. Besides the total cost and sales amounts, we will add a column for the profit percent that will be calculated in the report. Add a new column to the report layout (see the recipe *Designing reports in Visual Studio* for detailed instructions on how to do it).

12. Open the source expression for the new column's header and name it Profit %.

13. In the source expression for the data item, enter the following code:

```
=Code.ProfitPct(
  Fields!CostAmountActual.Value,
  Fields!CostAmountExpected.Value,
  Fields!SalesAmountActual.Value,
  Fields!SalesAmountExpected.Value)
```

14. The preceding RDLC code will call a function, `ProfitPct`, that is undefined as yet. To define the function, close the source expression, right-click on the free space outside the report canvas and choose the option **Report Properties**:

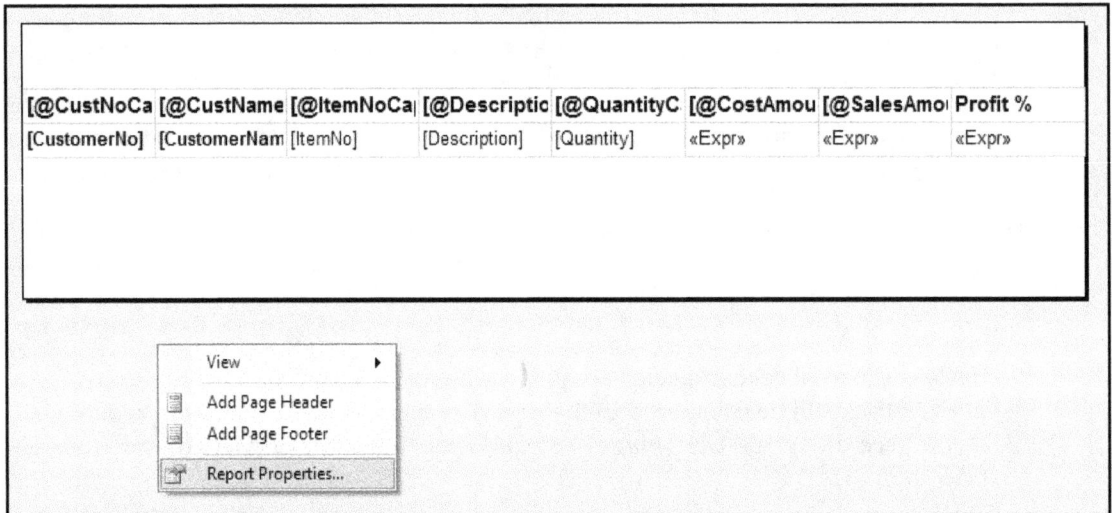

[@CustNoCa	[@CustName	[@ItemNoCa	[@Descriptio	[@QuantityC	[@CostAmou	[@SalesAmo	Profit %
[CustomerNo]	[CustomerNam	[ItemNo]	[Description]	[Quantity]	«Expr»	«Expr»	«Expr»

View ▸

Add Page Header

Add Page Footer

Report Properties...

15. In the report properties, choose the **Code** tab. This tab contains several predefined functions created by the NAV report designer. Insert the `ProfitPct` function here:

```
Public Function ProfitPct(
  ByVal CostAmtAct As Decimal, ByVal CostAmtExp As Decimal,
  ByVal SalesAmtAct As Decimal, ByVal SalesAmtExp As Decimal
  ) As Decimal

Dim CostAmtTotal As Decimal
Dim SalesAmtTotal As Decimal

CostAmtTotal = CostAmtAct + CostAmtExp
SalesAmtTotal = SalesAmtAct + SalesAmtExp

if CostAmtTotal = 0 then
  Return 0
end if

Return (SalesAmtTotal - CostAmtTotal) / CostAmtTotal
End Function
```

16. Now we will write expressions that will dynamically update formatting for sums containing un-invoiced amounts. Right-click on the **CostAmount** text box (the data item, not the header). Select **Text Box Properties** in the drop-down menu.

17. Select the **Font** tab in the **Text Box Properties** dialog. Each of the font parameters can be defined statically, as we did in previous walk-throughs. But it is possible to assign an expression to any of the style variables to update it dynamically in the runtime. To bind an expression to the font color, click on a button located to the right of the color setup text box (framed in the square in the following screenshot):

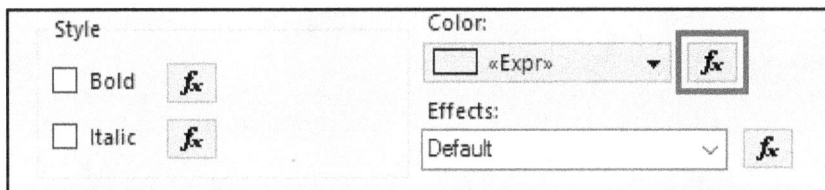

18. Write the source expression for the font color:

```
=iif(Fields!CostAmountExpected.Value = 0, "Black", "Red")
```

19. Let's add another expression to control number formatting in the text box. Still in the **Text Box Properties** dialog, switch to the **Number** tab. Choose the **Custom** category in the list of possible formatting styles. Click on the expression editor button. In the expression editor, choose the **Fields (DataSet_Result)** category, then **CostAmountActualFormat** for the value. The expression should return the value of the format string passed from NAV:

```
=Fields!CostAmountActualFormat.Value
```

20. Open the color expression in the **SalesAmount** field and write its code:

```
=iif(Fields!SalesAmountExpected.Value = 0, "Black", "Red")
```

Set up formatting for the sales amount the way you did in the **CostAmount** field.

21. Repeat Step 16 to Step 18 for the **Profit %** field. This field is not defined in the NAV report dataset and does not have a linked formatting string. Formatting for the profit column should be configured separately. In the **Number** tab of the **Text Box Properties** dialog, choose the **Percentage** category, then change the value of **Decimal places** to 1.

22. That's it for the RDLC part. Save and close the report layout, then save the report object in the object designer. Run and preview the report. All invoiced amounts will now be displayed in neutral black, and amounts not yet invoiced will be highlighted in red.

How it works...

Report code can be written directly in the RDLC report definition, although the recommended coding style is to keep the code in C/AL and move it to RDLC only when absolutely necessary. The RDLC script editor is a very basic tool. Client report code is hard to debug and prone to errors.

Still, despite the drawbacks of the editor, the report definition language allows unrivaled flexibility in report formatting.

Data formatting, defined in the NAV report dataset designer, is passed to the RDLC report and can be assigned to a format expression to control text output. We do this assignment in Step 19, connecting the NAV format properties with the RDLC expression. More elaborate formatting, such as dynamic updates of text styles, background and text color, drawing table borders, and much more, can be done by RDCL code and cannot be managed from the C/AL application.

Using built-in expressions in the report layout designer

We will create a totaling section in the report described in the previous recipe.

Getting ready

Before beginning this recipe, complete the walk-throughs *Writing C/AL code in a report* and *Writing RDLC code in a report*. Instead of performing all the steps manually, you can import the base object from the file REP50040_RDLCCode.txt.

File name in source files: REP50050_BuiltInExpressions.txt.

How to do it...

1. All changes explained further will be made in the RDLC project – the NAV dataset and C/AL code will be left unchanged. To begin working with the designer, open the report layout in Visual Studio.

2. In the **Row Groups** part, select the **Details** group, right-click and choose **Add Total/After**:

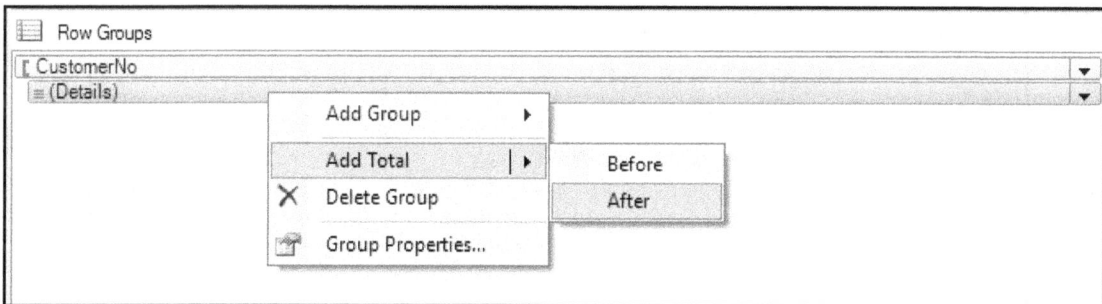

This action will create a totaling row inside the group. All columns except the totaling column **CustomerNo** and the linked **CustomerName** will be included in the totaling section.

3. Select the first two columns in the totaling row (cells located under the fields **ItemNo** and **Description**), right-click and choose the **Merge Cells** menu option. Now, when this is a single cell, right-click on it again and change its source expression to **Group Total**:

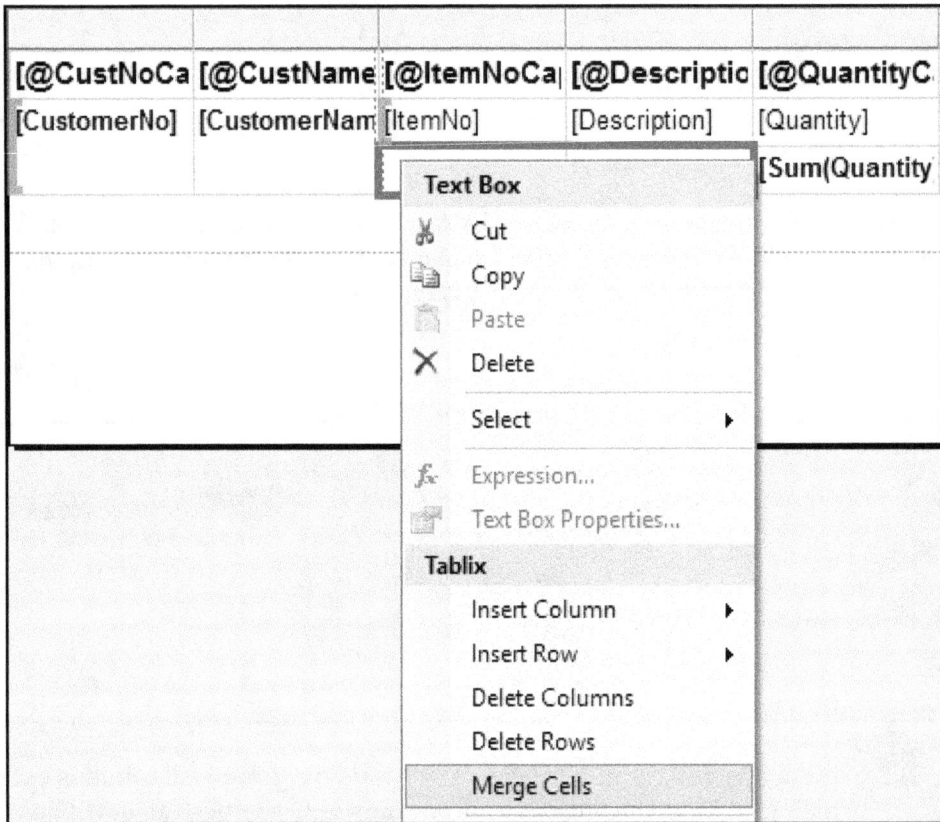

4. Select the next cell, located under the **Quantity** field, and open its source expression. In the **Category** section, unfold **Common Functions** and select **Aggregate**. In the **Item** list, select the **Sum** function. Double-click on the function name to copy it to the editor window. Do not close the editor yet. Select the dataset fields, category **Fields (DataSet_Result)**, select **Quantity** in the values, and double-click on the field name. To complete the expression, enter the closing bracket.

Alternatively, the expression can be entered manually:

```
=Sum(Fields!Quantity.Value)
```

5. Close the expression editor, select the next field, **CostAmount**, and repeat the totaling setup steps, replacing the field **Quantity** in the expression with **CostAmount**. Then do the same for **SalesAmount**.

6. Right-click in the designer area, outside the report canvas. In the context menu, select **Add Page Header**. Click again, and this time select **AddPage Footer**.

7. In the report header, we will show the date when the report was generated. Drag-and-drop a text box control from the toolbox to the page header. Open the text box source expression and write the expression value that will return the current date:

```
="Report date: " & DateString()
```

8. Another text box in the footer will display the current report page and the total page count. Drop a text box on the footer, and in its source expression, write code (including the = sign at the beginning of the line):

```
="Page " & Globals!OverallPageNumber & " of " &
    Globals!OverallTotalPages
```

9. The final report layout will be as shown in the following screenshot:

						«Expr»	
[@CustNoCa	[@CustName	[@ItemNoCa|	[@Descriptic	[@QuantityC	[@CostAmou	[@SalesAmoı	Profit %
[CustomerNo]	[CustomerNam	[ItemNo]	[Description]	[Quantity]	«Expr»	«Expr»	«Expr»
		Group Total		[Sum(Quantity	«Expr»	«Expr»	
						«Expr»	

10. Save the report and run it. The result for one customer is shown next. As in the previous recipe, this report will display a customer ID and name on the left side of the page, and detail each sold item on the right, denoting the cost and sales amounts for each item, along with the profitability of the item.

Besides that, the new version of the report will tally the total sold quantity, cost amount and sales amount per customer:

Customer No.	Customer Name	Item No.	Description	Quantity	Cost Amount	Sales Amount	Profit %
01445544	Progressive Home Furnishings	1928-S	AMSTERDAM Lamp	14,00	389,20	498,41	28,1%
		1988-W	CALGARY Whiteboard, yellow	1,00	708,60	877,32	23,8%
		1972-S	MUNICH Swivel Chair, yellow	1,00	96,10	123,30	28,3%
		Group Total		16,00	1 193,90	1 499,03	

How it works...

The RDLC report editor provides a set of functions to obtain aggregated values from the report dataset, access system information such as current data and time, and so on. We make use of several of these functions in the current recipe. In Step 4 and 5, we create totaling fields and assign aggregating functions to these fields to calculate total values within the group. The **SUM** function keeps total count of the field given to it in the parameter. When all rows in the group are rendered, the total value will be appended in the bottom line. Its functionality is not limited to inserting bottom lines – it is possible to insert the totaling section before the details group and display the total amounts first, providing details after.

Another common function used in Step 7 is `DateString`. This returns the current system date as a string formatted according to the system locale setup.

The last two functions we use are `OverallPageNumber` and `OverallTotalPages`. The first returns the current page number, and the second the total number of pages in the report. Both these functions can be used only in the page header or footer.

Including user interaction in reports

So far, the reports we have created have presented a static picture. Now let's take a step further and create an interactive report with dynamic dataset sorting and drill down to the underlying data.

Getting ready

File name in source files: `REP50060_UserInteraction.txt`.

How to do it...

1. Open report **50010 Item Sales** in NAV Report Designer. This report has no C/AL code, and it will not be required for interactive sorting and drill down, all work will be done outside the NAV reporting. Open the report layout in Visual Studio.
2. We will enable sorting on all columns of the report, one by one. Let's start from the leftmost one – **Item No**. Select the field header (not the data row), right-click on it, and open **Text Box Properties**.

3. In the **Text Box Properties** dialog, select the tab **Interactive Sorting** and check **Enable interactive sorting on this text box**. Below this option, pick the **Detail rows** radio button. In the **Sort by** box, choose the field **[No]** from the drop-down list:

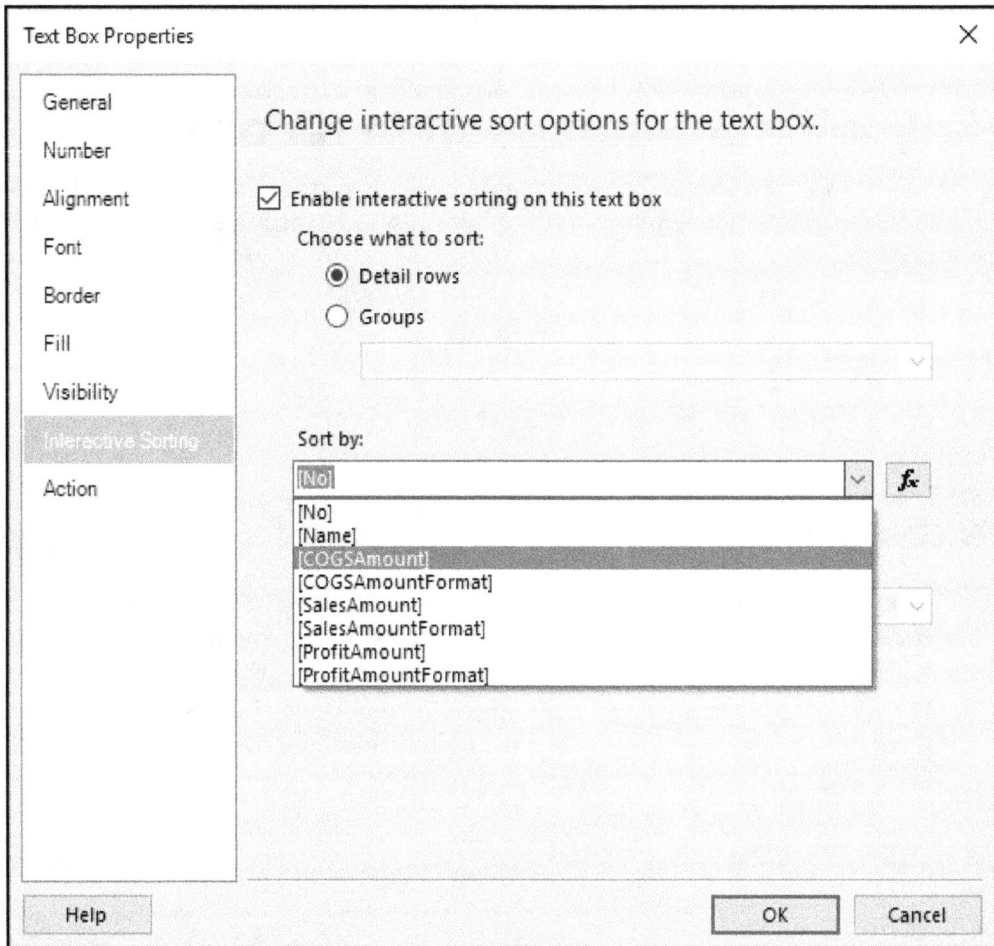

Text Box Properties ✕

General
Number
Alignment
Font
Border
Fill
Visibility
Interactive Sorting
Action

Change interactive sort options for the text box.

☑ Enable interactive sorting on this text box

Choose what to sort:

◉ Detail rows

○ Groups

Sort by:

[No]

[No]
[Name]
[COGSAmount]
[COGSAmountFormat]
[SalesAmount]
[SalesAmountFormat]
[ProfitAmount]
[ProfitAmountFormat]

Help   OK   Cancel

---

4. Click **OK** to confirm the setup. This is generally all you need to do to enable dynamic data sorting in an RDLC report. Repeat the same setup on all fields, selecting each column header and binding it to the corresponding dataset field.

5. Now let's configure a drill down to the report data source from the **COGS Amount** field. To enable the drill down action, select the data field **COGSAmount** and open the **text box** properties.

> Interactive sorting should be configured on the column header, and drill down in the data field.

6. Select the **Action** tab in the text box properties, pick the action **Go to URL**, and click on the expression editor button as follows:

Text Box Properties		✕
General	Change action options.	
Number		
Alignment	Enable as an action:	
Font	○ None	
Border	○ Go to report	
Fill	○ Go to bookmark	
Visibility	◉ Go to URL	
Interactive Sorting	Select URL:	
Action	«Expr» ⌄ *fx*	
Help	OK Cancel	

7. Configuring the URL for the drill down action is the trickiest part of the setup. It requires a careful and sometimes counter-intuitive editing of the hyperlink expression. For the sake of simplicity, we will filter records only by the item no. and entry type, then we will scrutinize the structure of the hyperlink to find out how to extend it and include other filters.

> In the hyperlink expression, enter the following URL (don't miss the = sign at the beginning):

```
="dynamicsnav://localhost:7046/dynamicsnav90/CRONUS
    International Ltd./runpage?page=5802&$filter='Value
    Entry'.'Item No.' IS " & Fields!No.Value & " AND 'Value
    Entry'.'Item Ledger Entry Type' IS Sale&mode=View"
```

8. Close the hyperlink editor, confirm the action setup, and close Visual Studio to return to the NAV report designer.

9. The only thing we need to do in the NAV designer is allow hyperlinks in the report. Open report properties and change the value of **EnableHyperlinks** to **Yes**.

10. That's it. Save the report and run it. Each column header now has a sorting button. Click on the **COGS (LCY)** header to sort the data according to the cost amount in ascending order. A second click on the same field will change the sorting order to descending. If you click in the data field in the **COGS (LCY)** column, page 5802 **Value Entries** will open with the list of entries comprising the field value:

Sales by Items

No.	Description	COGS (LCY)	Sales (LCY)	Profit Amount
1976-W	INNSBRUCK Storage Unit/W.Door	16 637,55	25 314,62	8 677,07

How it works...

While configuration of a dynamic string is quite intuitive, the hyperlink setup for drill down may look like magic at first sight. Let's see where the hyperlink comes from and how to interpret it.

All we want to do, when the user clicks on a hyperlink field, is open a certain page with a set of filters. And here we can use a trick – we will ask NAV server to generate the hyperlink for us instead of typing it manually.

To obtain the link, run the NAV client, press *Ctrl + F3*, and type the page caption `Value Entries` in the search box.

In the **Value Entries** page, show the **Filtering** tab and add two filters that we want to apply to the drill down page:

- Item Ledger Entry Type = Sale
- Item No. = 1968-S

Filter values don't really matter here, we only want to understand the principle of how the filters are passed in a page hyperlink.

After applying the filters, click **Page** | **Copy Link to Page** in the main application menu:

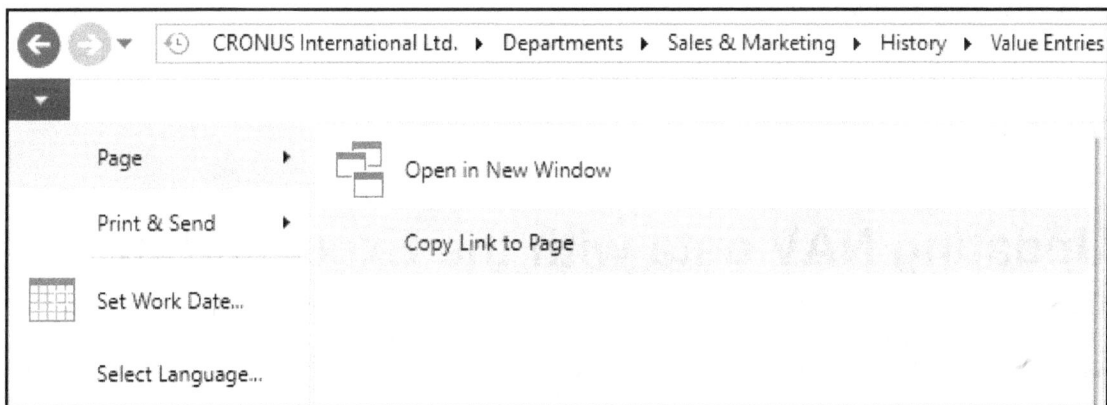

This action will copy the hyperlink into the clipboard. Run any text editor and paste the clipboard contents. The copied hyperlink contains URL-encoded characters and some optional parameters. For readability, we can replace encoding sequences %20 and %27 with a white space and an apostrophe symbol, respectively. We will also leave only the required parameters to get to the gist:

```
dynamicsnav://localhost:7046/dynamicsnav90/CRONUS  International
Ltd./runpage?page=5802&$filter='Value  Entry'.'Item Ledger Entry Type' IS
'1' AND 'Value  Entry'.'Item No.' IS '1968-S'&mode=View
```

The hyperlink can be split into the following key parts:

```
<protocol name>://<server name>:<NAV service port>/<NAV service
name>/<company name>/<command>?
```

The command (runpage in the preceding hyperlink) is followed by a list of command parameters, the first of which is the page ID. Parameter page=5802 means that the hyperlink will open the page 5802 Value Entries.

The next important parameter is $filter – record filter, which will be applied to the page data. The filter has a simple structure: '<Table Name>'.'<Field Name>' IS '<Filter Value>'. Several filters can be combined with the keyword AND.

This said, the filter string received in the example can be interpreted as a combination of filters on two fields: Item No. and Item Ledger Entry Type.

Filter values copied from the page are constant values, and we want to filter data dynamically, depending on the selected item. To achieve this, we replace the text constant with a dataset variable. The ampersand symbol (&) in RDLC means a concatenation of two strings:

```
"$filter='Value Entry'.'Item No.' IS " & Fields!No.Value & " AND  'Value
Entry'.'Item Ledger Entry Type' IS Sale"
```

Updating NAV data with the Excel add-in

The Microsoft Office Excel add-in enables the user to establish a persistent link between the Dynamics NAV server and an Excel worksheet. This connection makes it possible to update records exported from NAV inside an Excel worksheet.

Getting ready

Microsoft Office Excel add-in is a prerequisite for this recipe. The Excel add-in is provided in Dynamics NAV installation media and must be installed on the client computer on which this walk-through is going to be executed. For details, refer to the recipe *Installing NAV Development Environment* in Chapter 1, *Writing Basic C/AL Code*.

How to do it...

In this recipe, we will build a pivot table based on NAV data, and use the Excel add-in to refresh data from the Excel worksheet.

1. Run the Microsoft Dynamics NAV client, and open the page **Item Ledger Entries**. Make sure the following fields are displayed in the page:
   - Posting Date
   - Item No.
   - Invoiced Quantity
   - Cost Amount (Actual)
   - Sales Amount (Actual)

   If any of these fields are not visible, right-click on a column header, select Choose **Columns**, and move hidden columns to the list of visible columns.

2. Choose **Print & Send** in the application menu, then select the **Microsoft Excel** option:

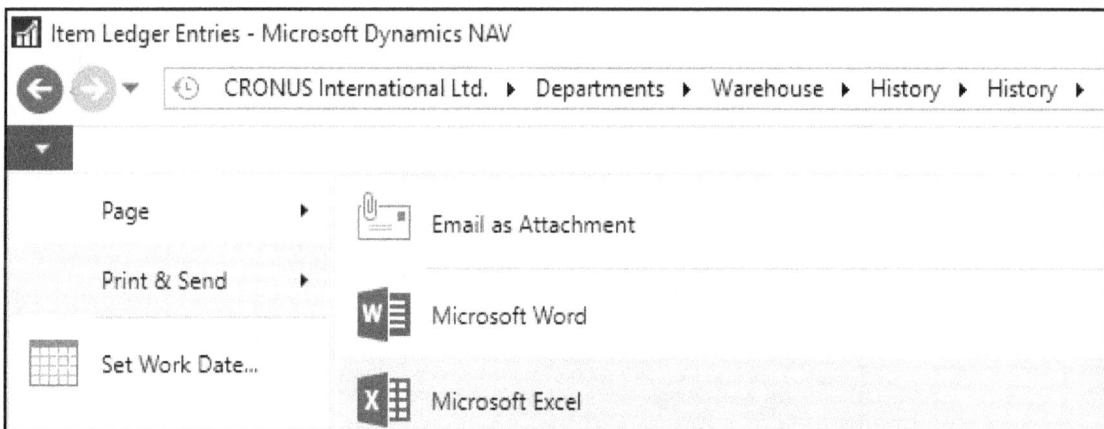

An Excel worksheet containing the NAV data will be created.

Only table fields will be exported to Excel. If there is a page field with a C/AL variable as a data source, it will be skipped during export.

3. This is going to be a worksheet containing raw data, on which the pivot table will be based. Create another worksheet for the pivot table itself. Select the **Insert** ribbon tab, and click the **PivotTable** action.

4. Select the rows imported from NAV to be the data source for the new pivot table.

   When selecting rows, skip the top two lines containing auxiliary information. Start the selection from the column headers in line 3:

	Posting Date ▼	Entry Type ▼	Document Type ▼	Document No. ▼	Item No. ▼
2	Item Ledger Entries : 8/28/2016 8:13:35 PM				
4	19.01.2018	Sale	Sales Shipment	102045	1928-S
5	18.01.2018	Sale	Sales Shipment	102044	1500
6	18.11.2017	Sale	Sales Shipment	102043	1924-W
7	15.01.2018	Sale	Sales Shipment	102042	8924-W
8	15.01.2018	Sale	Sales Shipment	102042	8908-W
9	03.12.2017	Sale	Sales Shipment	102041	8924-W

5. In the **PivotTable Fields** pane, select the **Posting Date, Item No., Sales Amount (Actual)**, and **Cost Amount (Actual) fields**. These fields will be automatically arranged between the pivot table areas **Columns, Rows**, and **Values**. For the current example, we will also need a filter field. Drag the field **Item No.** to the **Filters** area. The final layout should look as follows:

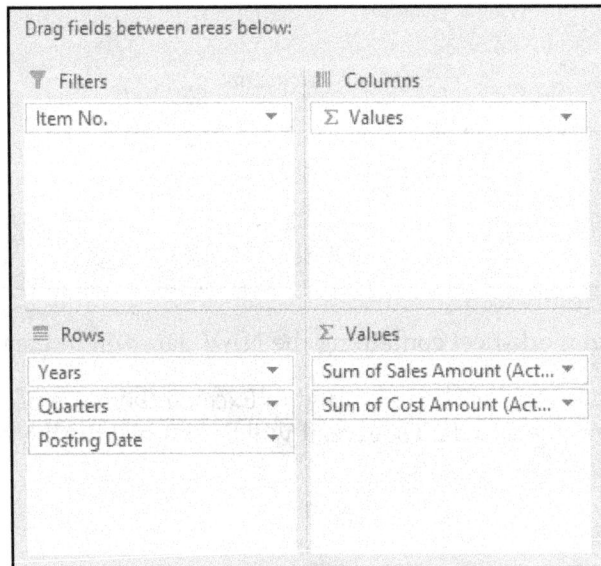

Drag fields between areas below:

▼ Filters	▦ Columns
Item No. ▼	Σ Values ▼

▦ Rows	Σ Values
Years ▼	Sum of Sales Amount (Act... ▼
Quarters ▼	Sum of Cost Amount (Act... ▼
Posting Date ▼	

6. Switch to the pivot table data and filter the data by the item no. To do so, click on the filter and select two items: **1976-W** and **1964-W**. Note the updated cost and sales amounts for year 2017:

   - Sales Amount (Actual) = 28 218,82
   - Cost Amount (Actual) = -8 623,35

7. Open the sales order 101009 in the NAV client and post it as invoiced.

8. Return to the Excel worksheet containing the data exported from NAV. In the **Dynamics NAV** ribbon tab, push the action button **Refresh**:

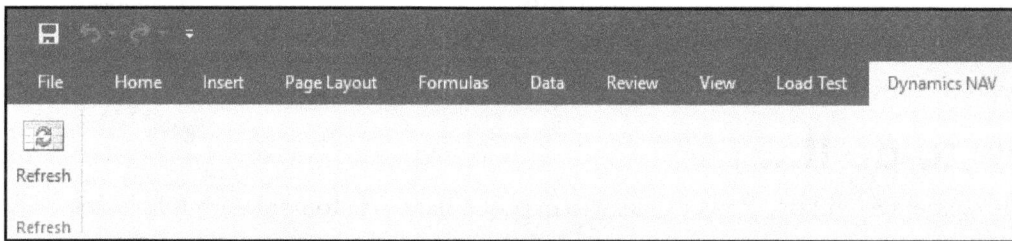

9. Select the worksheet containing the pivot table. Right-click on the table and select the action **Refresh**. Compare the new amounts with the old ones. Updated cost and sales amounts include the invoice just posted.

How it works...

An evident advantage of the NAV Excel add-in is its careful handling of page filters. If any filters are applied to the page, an Excel table will be generated with respect to those filters. Moreover, subsequent updates on the Excel side will preserve filtering and will retrieve only records satisfying records' filters.

Any NAV page can be sent to Excel, but only pages of type List, ListPlus, or Worksheet will retain the link through the Excel add-in.

Retrieving data from NAV with Power Query

Power Query is a tool for retrieving data from various data sources, which enables the user to transform, purify, and merge data with ease. Power Query is used to load data into analytical tools, such as Power BI. Data analysis in Power BI is the topic of several recipes to follow, and now we will configure a query to import data into Excel.

Getting ready

If your Microsoft Office version is 2016, Power Query is already a part of the standard setup, no additional steps are required.

For earlier versions of Office, Power Query must be installed separately. It is available for downloading on microsoft.com.

> Note that examples in the current and subsequent recipes are based on Office 2016. The Power Query Excel add-in is accessed in the **Data** ribbon tab in this version. In Excel 2010 and 2013, Power Query actions are located in the ribbon in the **Power Query** tab.

How to do it...

In this recipe, we will use Power Query to export a list of customers with total sales amounts to Excel.

1. Run Microsoft Excel and create a new workbook. In the **Data** tab, select **New Query**, then choose an option **From SQL Server Database**:

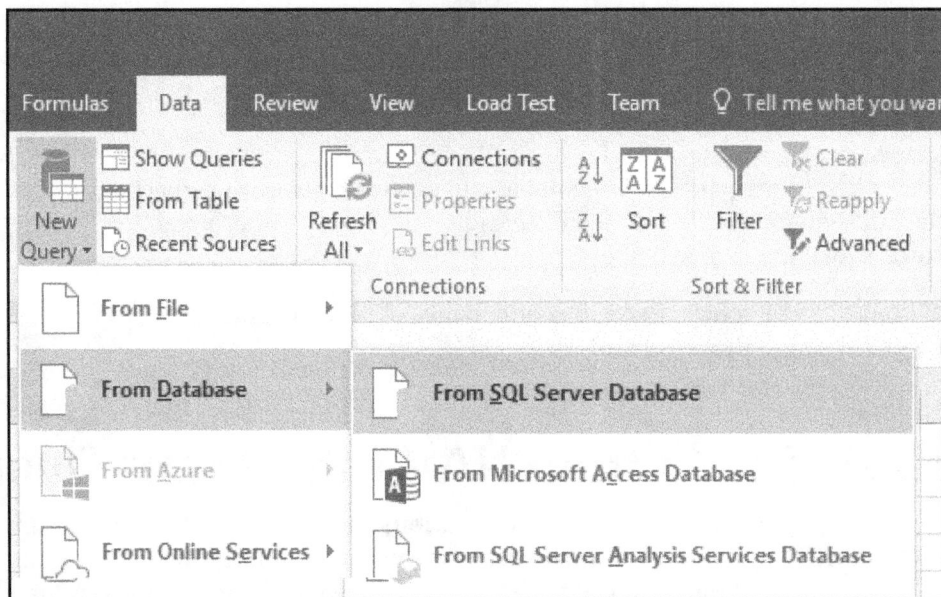

2. You will be asked to enter the server name that you want to retrieve data from. If you accepted the default installation wizard settings when installing NAV, the SQL server name is `localhost\NAVDEMO`. Otherwise, enter your server name here.

3. You can optionally enter the NAV database name in the same request window, but this is not required. If you leave the `Database` field blank, you can select the database in the next step.

4. If you entered a database name in the previous step of the wizard, now you will see the list of tables in this database. Otherwise, a list of databases will be presented. Unfold the contents of the database `Demo Database NAV (9-0)`.

5. To simplify navigation in the long list of tables, enter a part of the table name you want to select in the filtering text box. Since we are looking for the Customer table, enter `cust`. The tables list will be shrunk to a list of names containing the entered letters:

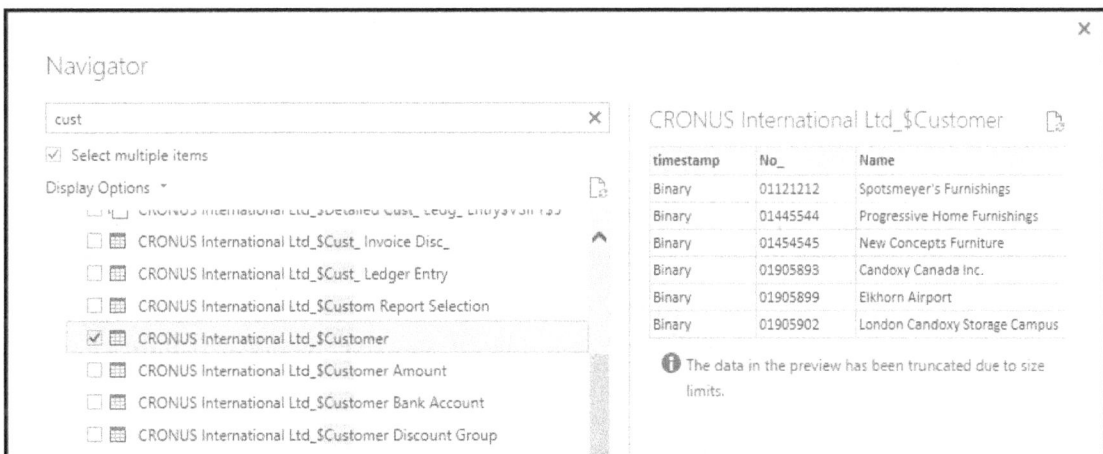

6. Tick the checkmark **Select multiple items**, then locate the **CRONUS International Ltd_$Customer**, and **CRONUS InternationalLtd_$Detailed Cust_ Ledg_ Entry** tables and set ticks against these tables. After selecting the tables, click **Edit** to fine-tune the query.

7. At first, Power Query creates a separate query for each of the selected tables and displays them in a list in the query editor. In the query editor, choose the first query named **CRONUS International Ltd_$Customer** from the list of queries. In the **Home** tab, click **Choose Columns**, remove all selections (click on **Select all columns** to remove all with one click), and select columns **No_** and **Name**. Power Query will remove all other columns from the query, as well as from the data preview:

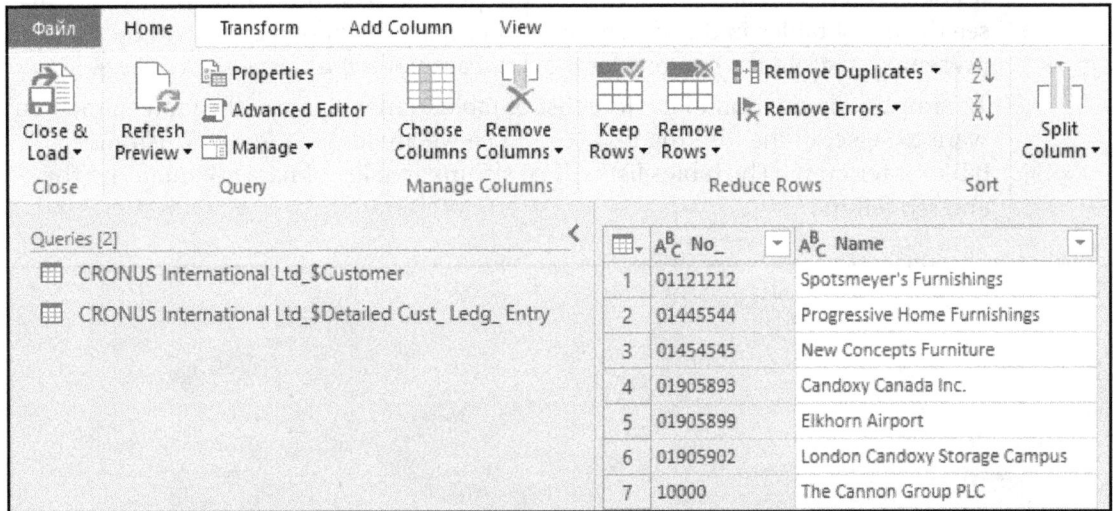

Файл	Home	Transform	Add Column	View

Properties
Advanced Editor
Manage ▾

Close & Load ▾   Refresh Preview ▾

Choose Columns   Remove Columns ▾

Keep Rows ▾   Remove Rows ▾

Remove Duplicates ▾
Remove Errors ▾

Split Column ▾

Close | Query | Manage Columns | Reduce Rows | Sort

Queries [2]

| | CRONUS International Ltd_$Customer |
| | CRONUS International Ltd_$Detailed Cust_ Ledg_ Entry |

	A^B_C No_	A^B_C Name
1	01121212	Spotsmeyer's Furnishings
2	01445544	Progressive Home Furnishings
3	01454545	New Concepts Furniture
4	01905893	Candoxy Canada Inc.
5	01905899	Elkhorn Airport
6	01905902	London Candoxy Storage Campus
7	10000	The Cannon Group PLC

8. Select the second query **CRONUS International Ltd_$Detailed Cust_ Ledg_ Entry**, then click **Choose Columns** and leave only five: **Amount, Amount (LCY), Customer No_, Currency Code**, and **Posting Date**.

9. We have configured two separate queries, retrieving the required data from two tables, and now we need to join them into one query. To set up a join on the two queries, run the **Merge Queries** action in the **Combine** group.

10. In the **Merge** operation, the selected query **CRONUS International Ltd_$Customer** is already activated. Choose the second query for the join pair. After that, select the pair of fields on which the join operation will be performed. In the **Customer** table, this field is **No_**. Its counterpart in the **Detailed Cust_ Ledg_ Entry** is **Customer No_**. In the **Join Kind** field, select **Inner (only matching rows)**:

Merge

Select a table and matching columns to create a merged table.

CRONUS International Ltd_$Customer

No_	Name
01121212	Spotsmeyer's Furnishings
01445544	Progressive Home Furnishings
01454545	New Concepts Furniture
01905893	Candoxy Canada Inc.
01905899	Elkhorn Airport

CRONUS International Ltd_$Detailed... ▾

Posting Date	Amount	Amount (LCY)	Customer No_	Currency Code
31.12.2017 0:00:00	25389,25	25389,25	10000	
31.12.2017 0:00:00	76167,75	76167,75	30000	
31.12.2017 0:00:00	63473,13	63473,13	10000	
31.12.2017 0:00:00	55010,04	55010,04	20000	
31.12.2017 0:00:00	80399,29	80399,29	30000	

Join Kind

Inner (only matching rows) ▾

11. Confirm the join setup. Appended columns derived from customer ledger entries will be shown under a header **NewColumn**. Click **Expand** in the **NewColumn** header. Remove the selection from the **Use original column name as prefix** option and click **OK**.

12. The NAV data type `Date` is actually stored in SQL as a datetime. As a result, every date record has a zero-time suffix that is automatically cut by the NAV platform when displayed inside NAV, but shows up in external reporting tools. To remove it in the Power Query dataset, select the column **Posting Date**, click on the **format** button in its header, then choose **Date**. The **Datetime** field will be transformed into a simple date by cutting the time part:

	A^B_C No_	A^B_C Name	Posting Date	1.2 Amount	1.2 Amount (LCY)
1	10000	The Cannon Group PLC	1.2 Decimal Number	25389,25	25389,25
2	30000	John Haddock Insurance Co.	$ Currency	76167,75	76167,75
3	10000	The Cannon Group PLC	1²₃ Whole Number	63473,13	63473,13
4	20000	Selangorian Ltd.	Date/Time	55010,04	55010,04
5	30000	John Haddock Insurance Co.		80399,29	80399,29
6	20000	Selangorian Ltd.	Date	38083,88	38083,88
7	30000	John Haddock Insurance Co.	Time	76167,75	76167,75
8	10000	The Cannon Group PLC	Date/Time/Timezone	33852,35	33852,35
9	01454545	New Concepts Furniture	Duration	42529,44	222241,32
10	20000	Selangorian Ltd.	A^B_C Text	42315,42	42315,42
11	10000	The Cannon Group PLC	True/False	50778,5	50778,5
12	30000	John Haddock Insurance Co.		33852,33	33852,33
13	20000	Selangorian Ltd.	Binary	25389,25	25389,25

13. We still have two duplicated fields in the resulting set – **No_** and **Customer No_**. They were required to build the merged query, but now one of them can be dropped from the dataset. Select the column **Customer No_**, right-click on the column header, and select **Remove** from the menu.

14. Click **Close and Load**. Now you have your data in the Excel worksheet.

How it works...

Note the names of the tables you selected for analysis in Step 7. These are our NAV table objects, but their names do not exactly match the representation in the SQL Server database. Naming SQL Server tables follows several conventions to allow multi-company functionality and compensate for quite loose NAV naming standards, which are unsupported in SQL.

First of all, it is normal for a NAV object name to include characters such as dots, slashes, brackets – you can see lots of them in NAV. SQL Server naming rules do now permit these symbols, therefore they have to be replaced with characters supported by SQL. By default, all unsupported symbols are substituted with an underscore _. So, the name **Detailed Cust. Ledg.** Entry will transformed into **Detailed Cust_ Ledg_ Entry**, and **G/L Account** will become **G_L Account**.

Besides that, a single NAV database can store the data from several companies, which must be separated from each other. To ensure strict segregation of data, SQL server creates a separate table per company, per NAV table. In the process, each SQL table receives a name starting from the name of a company, followed by the dollar sign, completed with the NAV table name.

Thus, the table Customer that stores the data of the company CRONUS International Ltd., viewed in the SQL Server will be named `CRONUS International Ltd_$Customer`. If we had another company called `MyCompany` in the same database, we'd have a second copy of the `Customer` table, this one called `My Company$Customer`.

Creating pivot tables with Power Query

Microsoft Excel is a powerful tool for data analysis – you can import data from many sources and build intricate analytic functions. But as the volume of data grows, it becomes harder to manipulate Excel sheets. Entry tables in NAV can contain millions of records, and importing this huge amount of data into an Excel workbook is a tedious work.

With Power Query, you can employ the Excel analytical toolbox, while keeping your data on the server. Data requests can be directed to the data provider without loading raw data into Excel.

Getting ready

The query used in the current example is the one created in the previous recipe. The walk-through in the *Retrieving data from NAV with Power Query* recipe must be completed before starting the next demonstration.

How to do it...

In the current recipe, we are creating a pivot table presenting sales amounts by customers, with Power Query.

1. A list of workbook queries should be displayed in your current workbook. If it is not, open the **Data** tab in the ribbon and click **Show Queries**.

2. In the Workbook Queries list, select the query **CRONUS International Ltd_$Customer**, right-click on the query name and select the **Load To** action:

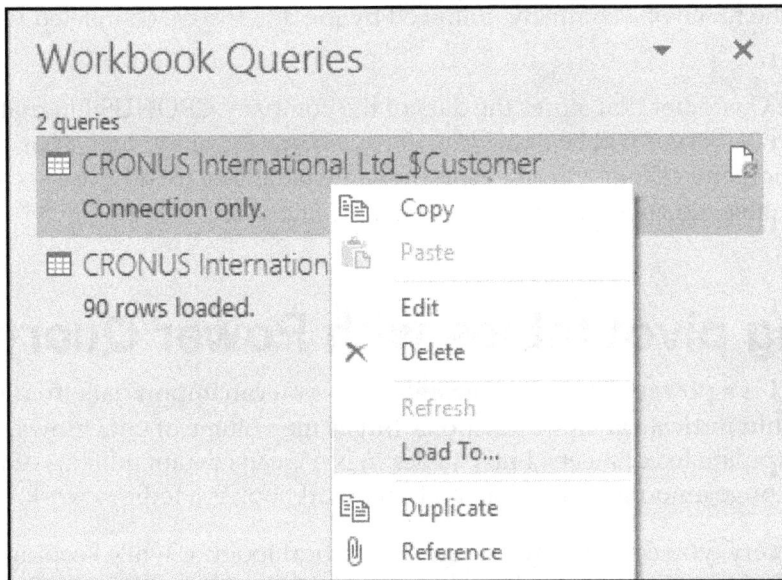

3. Now the query dataset is loaded into the current Excel workbook. To change it, select **Only create connection** in the **Load To** dialog. Click **Load**. You will be warned that all data will be removed from the worksheet. Confirm the selection.

4. Open the **Insert** tab and click **Pivot Table**. In the **Create Pivot Table** dialog, choose the **Use an external data source** option, then click **Choose Connection**:

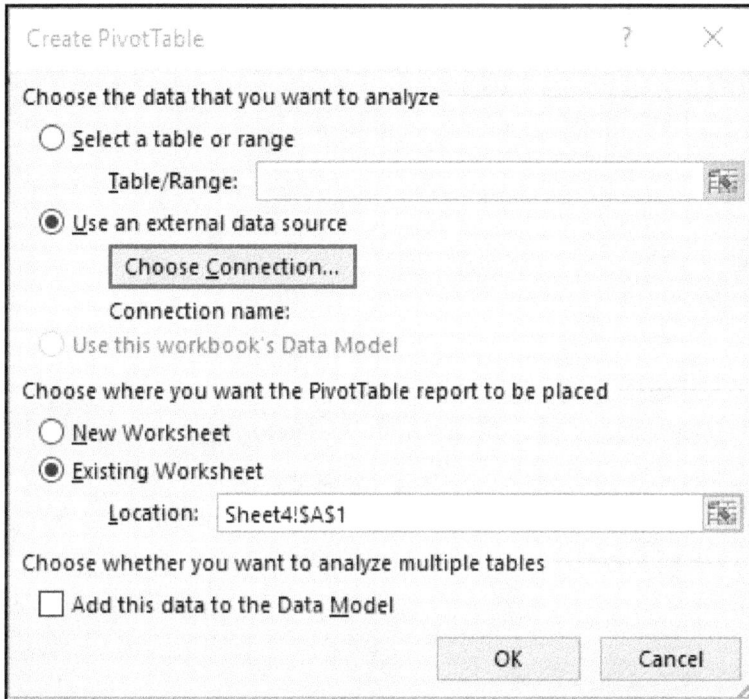

5. A list of workbook queries will be presented. Choose the query **CRONUS International Ltd_$Customer** and click **Open**. Back in the **Create Pivot Table** dialog, click **OK**. A pivot table will be created in the Excel worksheet, but the dataset will not be loaded into the Excel workbook. Instead, Excel will query the SQL server when updating the table.

6. Organize pivot table fields to get the aggregated data. The **PivotTable** fields list should be displayed automatically when the pivot table is created. If you can't see the list, open the **Analyze** tab and click the **Fields List** action button. Drag fields from the list to the pivot table areas as shown in the following screenshot:

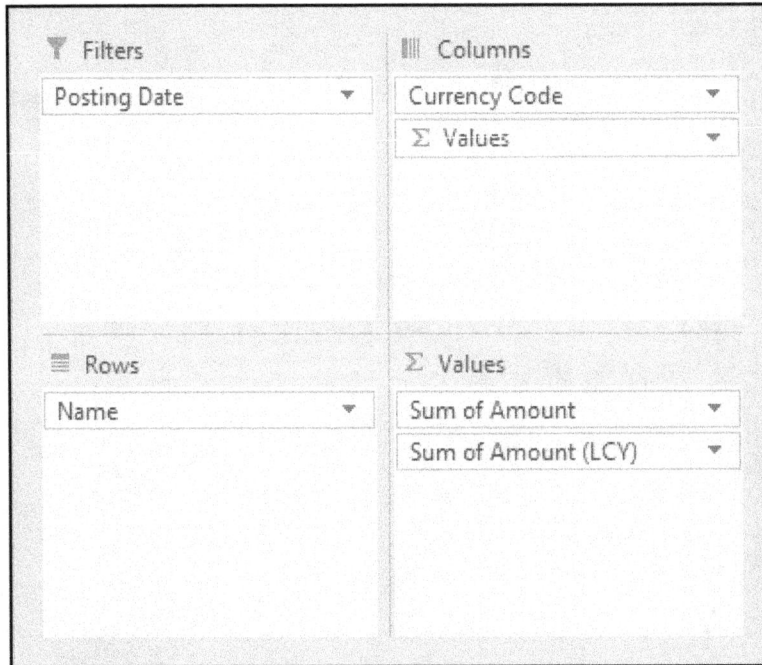

PivotTable data is updated immediately after changing the configuration.

Analyzing data with Power BI

Power BI is an analytics solution for various kinds of data study, evaluation, and presentation. With Power BI, it is possible to generate a wide variety of reports from a simple table view or bar chart to complex statistical data analysis.

Getting ready

Power BI must be installed to complete the following scenario. It is available to download from powerbi.microsoft.com.

How to do it...

Now we will build a report in Power BI presenting the sales report in a bar chart, with a simple hierarchy for periods.

1. Run the Power BI application.
2. In the **Home** tab of the ribbon, click **Get Data**, then choose **SQL Server**.
3. In the connection setting dialog, enter the name of your SQL Server where the NAV database resides. By default, when installing NAV in Developer configuration, a new SQL instance is installed on `locahost\NAVDEMO`.
4. Enter the database name. The default name for the demo database is **Demo Database NAV (9-0)**. The database name is optional in this step, and can be selected later. Click **OK**.
5. Choose to connect to the database with your current credentials and click **Connect**.
6. If you entered the database name in Step 4, you will see the list of database tables. Otherwise, select the NAV database you want to retrieve data from and unfold the list of tables.
7. In the filter box of the **Navigator** window, enter **Sales Invoice**. The list of tables will be filtered to show only table names containing this text. Select the table **CRONUS International Ltd_$Sales Invoice Header**, then click **Edit**.
8. In the **Manage Columns** group, execute the action **Choose Columns**. Remove all columns except two: **No_** and **Posting Date**.
9. Change the data type of the **Posting Date** column to **Date**, then click **Close & Apply**.

10. Choose the stacked column chart in the **Visualizations** menu:

11. As soon as you choose a chart type, the applicable report parameters appear in the chart field groups. Drag the fields from the query into the report field groups. The **No_** field should be placed in the **Value** group, and **Posting Date** settles in the **Axis** group:

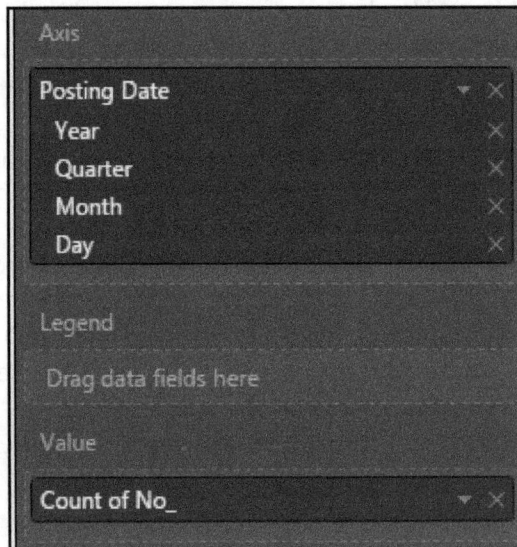

12. Note the automatic transformation of the fields. No_ turns into **Count of No_**. This field will show an aggregated value – count of sales invoices. The posting date is automatically augmented with a hierarchical set of period types from year to day. If you don't want to see low-level details, any of the aggregation levels can be removed. To do so, click on the cross in front of the period title.

13. Power BI automatically builds a date hierarchy based on date values. To switch between hierarchy levels in the chart, click on one of the arrow buttons located in the top left corner of the chart:

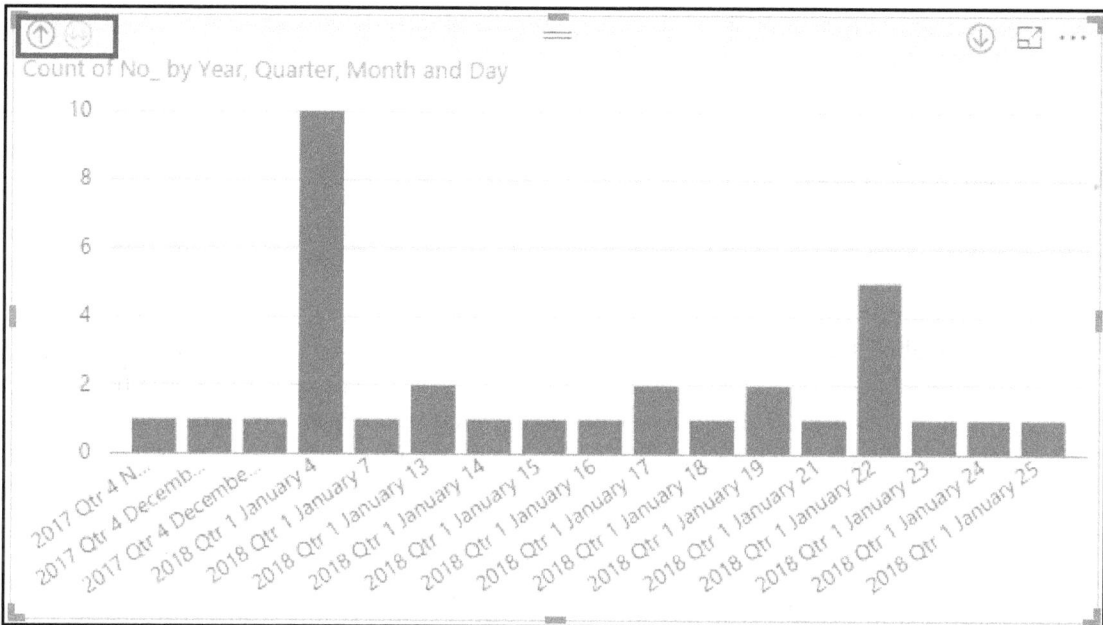

How it works...

Power BI uses the Power Query engine to retrieve data from the database and transform the dataset. Step 1 to Step 9 describe the configuration of a query that provides the dataset for the chart.

In Step 10, we select the chart type that Power BI will render based on the dataset. The type can be changed later, although other chart types may require additional data provided by the query.

Power BI shows the list of fields required for the selected visualization in the **Visualizations** area. To include query fields in the plot, drag and drop them from the **Fields** area to the **Visualizations** setup.

Data hierarchies in Power BI reports

In the previous recipe we saw how Power BI creates hierarchies based on date fields, collecting aggregated data on several levels from year to day. Date is not the only possible way to build a scalable report. It is possible to build a hierarchy based on any data, as long as you can provide a link from one level to the next.

How to do it...

In the next recipe, we will create a hierarchy based on geographical data from customer information.

1. Unfold the list of tables in the database `Demo Database NAV (9-0)`, and select two tables from the list: `CRONUS International Ltd_$Customer` and `CRONUS International Ltd_$Detailed Cust_ Ledg_ Entry`. After selecting the tables, click **Edit**. Table queries will be opened in the query editor.

2. Enter the SQL Server name where the NAV database is located (the default name is `localhost\navdemo`), then click **OK**.

3. Run Power BI, select the **Get Data** action in the **External Data** ribbon group, and choose SQL Server as the data provider type.

4. Select the **Customer** query, click **Choose Columns**, and remove all columns from the query except the following three:
   - No_
   - City
   - Country_Region Code

5. Select the second query , and choose the two following columns for the report: **Customer No_** and **Amount (LCY)**.

6. Select the **Customer** query and click **Merge Queries** from the **Combine** group. **Table Customer** will be selected as the primary table for the join operation. Select **Detailed Cust_ Ledg_ Entry** as the secondary source for the join. Select a pair of fields for mapping: **No_** in the **Customer** table, and **Customer No_** in **Detailed Cust_ Ledg_ Entry**.

7. Click **OK**, then expand the new column in the query editor. Double-click on the header of the column **NewColumn.Amount (LCY)** and remove the **NewColumn** part. This field caption will be presented in the report, and we don't want the meaningless text to be shown in the report header.

8. Close and apply the query.

9. In the **Visualizations** pane, select a map for the chart type:

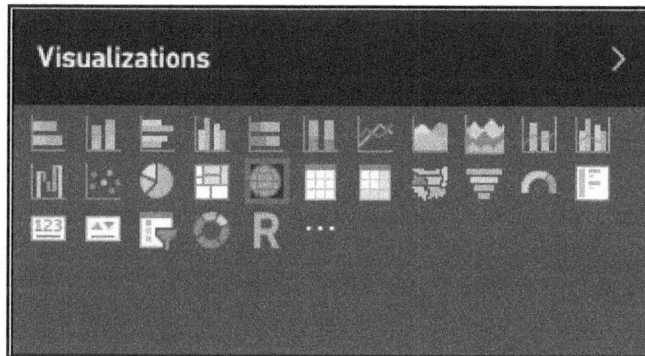

10. Drag the field **Country_Region Code** from the **Fields** pane to **Visualizations** and place it in the **Location** section. Then drag the field **City** and place it in the location below **Country_Region Code**. Place the **Amount (LCY)** field in the **Size** section.

11. And that's all you need to do to build a report based on the customer's location. The new report will show a world map with the distribution of sales by countries. The size of each circle denotes the amount relative to other locations:

Amount (LCY) by Country_Region Code

12. Click on the drill down button in the top left corner above the map to see the distribution by cities:

Now we can see that the greater part of the sales amount received by the Cronus demo company comes from Manchester.

Statistical data analysis in Power BI with R

R is a software environment for data mining, statistical analysis, and data presentation. It is widely used in statistical applications for sophisticated modeling and data mining solutions. R scripts can be executed in Power BI with the NAV database as the data source for computations.

Getting ready

The R environment must be installed for this demo. Download and install R from https://cran.r-project.org.

For a detailed description of how to connect to the Dynamics NAV database with Power Query, remove the columns from the dataset and change the column data type, refer to the recipe *Retrieving data from NAV with Power Query*.

How to do it...

In this recipe, we will use R to build a box plot based on expenses statistics.

1. Run Power BI and connect to your Dynamics NAV database. Select the **CRONUS International Ltd_$Detailed Vendor Ledg_ Entry** table for the data source and edit the query.
2. In the query editor, click **Choose Columns** and select three columns for the dataset, **Amount (LCY), Document Type, and Posting Date**. Change the data type of the column **Posting Date** from **Date/Time** to **Date**.

3. In the same column, click the arrow button in the column header. In the **Date Filters** menu, choose the option **After...** In the **Filter Rows** dialog, choose the filtering option **is after or equal to** and enter the earliest entry date that should be included in the report, 01.01.2017:

4. We are only interested in amounts from posted invoices; other document types will be ignored in the resulting dataset. This is why we need the **Document Type** field – it is not used in the data analysis, but is required for filtering. To apply the filter, select the column **Document Type**, and click the arrow button in the column header. In a filtering window, you will see the list of all unique values in the column. In the demo database, these are numbers 1, 2, 3, and 6. Remove marks from all values, leaving only 2.

5. Because we are now analyzing expense amounts, all records in the preview window have a negative sum. In the report output, though, we want to reverse the sign. We can do this by applying a transformation step that will multiply all values in the column by -1. Select the column **Amount (LCY)**, and open the **Transform** ribbon tab. Click on the **Standard** action group and select the **Multiply** action. Enter −1 in the request dialog.

6. Return to the **Home** tab and click **Close & Apply** to apply the transformation to the query.

7. After loading the data, choose the visualization type from the **Visualizations** pane. Select the R script visual:

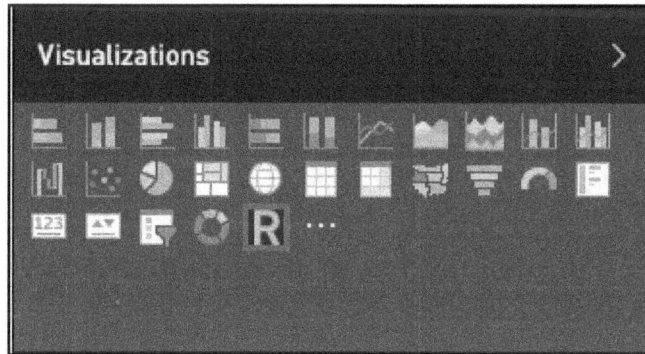

When you run this action for the first time, you will see a request to enable script visuals. Click **Enable** to confirm the request.

8. Drag two fields, **Amount (ACY)** and **Posting Date**, from the **Fields** pane to **Visualizations**. Place them in the **Values** section. The posting date is automatically split into a hierarchical list of periods. For this demo, we need it to be a date value, in one piece. To prevent the date field from being divided, right-click on the arrow button in the **Posting Date** field and in the drop-down menu, and change the selection from **Date Hierarchy** to **Posting Date**:

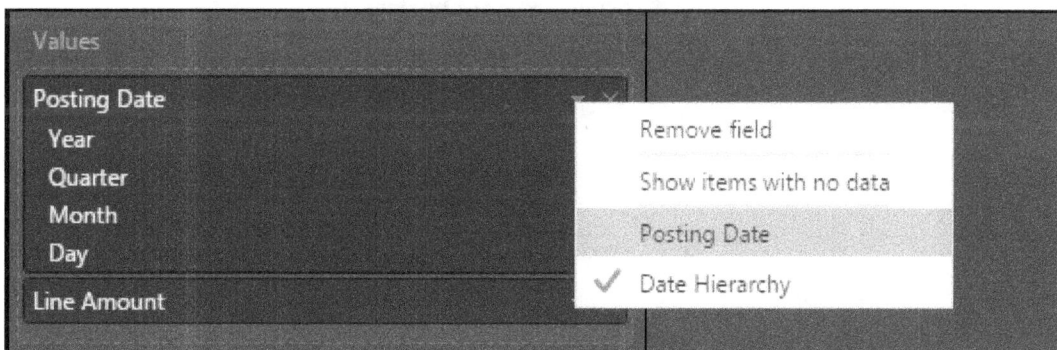

9. Click on the report visualization area. Type or copy and paste the script code in the R script editor:

```
par(las = 2)
dataset$Date <- as.Date(dataset$`Posting Date`)
boxplot(`Amount (LCY)` ~ Date, data = dataset)
title("Expenses amount by date")
par(las = 0)
mtext("Invoice date", side = 3, line = 0)
mtext("Amount", side = 4, line = 1)
```

10. To execute the script, press the run button on the top of the script editor:

11. The script execution result will be displayed in the chart area:

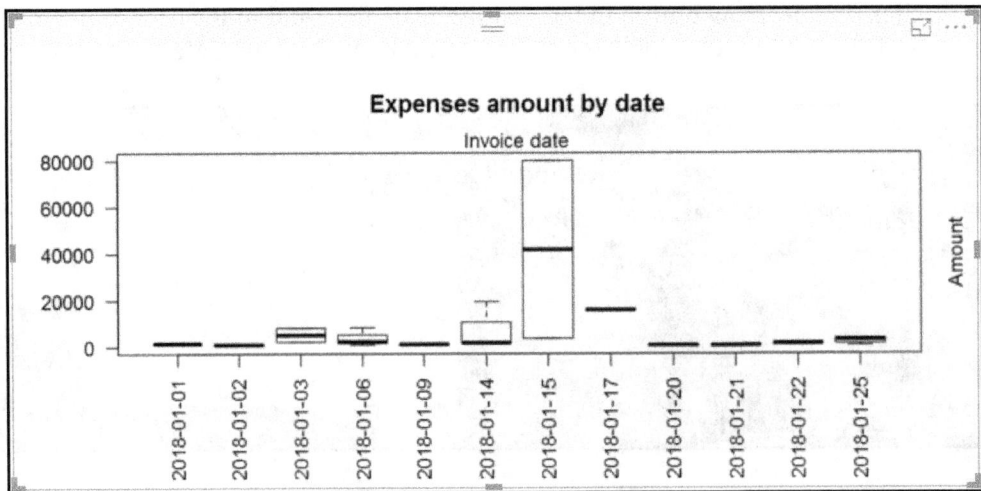

How it works...

The first steps in the recipe are familiar from previous demos – the data source for an R script is configured the same way, via Power Query. The only new configuration option is added in Step 3. Here, we remove all entries posted before 1st January 2017. This step is necessary to clean up the data, since all records before this data in the demo setup are opening balances that do not reflect the actual distribution of entries in time. A bunch of entries piled up on a single date will spoil the most accurate data mining algorithm – this is the reason why the data preparation step is so crucial for reliable statistical analysis.

Step 4 filters the dataset by source document type, leaving only invoices in the resulting query. In NAV, Document Type is an option with the following list of values: **Payment, Invoice, Credit Memo, Finance Charge Memo, Reminder, Refund**. The first space before the **Payment** option is an option value too, implying an absence of the document. In SQL Server, this data type is represented as an Integer with numbers corresponding to option values, starting from 0. Thus, a blank document type becomes **0, Payment** corresponds to **1**, and **Invoice** is represented in SQL Server as **2**. That's why we choose **2** in the list of document types when we need to select the **Invoice** document.

Records retrieved by Power Query are automatically loaded into an R dataset when the R script visual is selected in the Visualizations pane. The data hierarchy created by Power BI can be loaded into the R dataset, but we don't need hierarchies in this example and such a multi-level presentation is difficult to manipulate when all you need to do is group data on a calendar date. To load dates into the dataset as atomic values and avoid splitting them, we remove date aggregation in Step 8.

R scripts are written in R script editor, which is built into Power BI.

The script, rendering a box plot, begins with parameter initialization. The `par` function sets global graphical parameters. The only option changed in our case is `las`, which controls chart label orientation. `las = 2` means that all labels will be perpendicular to the axis.

Date values are imported into the R dataset from Power Query as `DateTime` with zero time part, and have to be transformed into the `Date` type. This is what the next statement does:
`dataset$Date <- as.Date(dataset$`Posting Date`).`

This line will create a new column named **Date** in the dataset and fill it with values from the column **Posting Date**, changing their data type to **Date** in the process. Note the backquote symbols around the column name: **Posting Date**. These are required to refer to a column with a white space in its name.

The `boxplot` function will draw the chart representing the expenses amount grouped by date. The formula is defined by the first parameter: `` `Amount (LCY)` ~ Date``. Calculations will be based on the dataset given in the second parameter: `data = dataset`. The chart rendered by the `boxplot` function is one of the most widely used graphics in statistics. We can see upper and lower quartiles, as well as the maximum and minimum values of the expenses per date.

The last four lines of the script add a chart title and axis labels.

Sales forecast in Power BI with R

R scripts can do more than simply render statistical plots. They are able, for example, to analyze time series and build a time series prediction based on various models.

Getting ready

Install R from `https://cran.r-project.org`.

You will also need the forecast R package. To install it, run your R scripting environment (for example, RStudio) and run the following command:

```
install.packages("forecast")
```

How to do it…

For a brief introduction to R prediction capabilities, we will generate a sales forecast from NAV demo data.

1. Run **Power BI** and connect to the SQL Server hosting the Dynamics NAV database. Select the table `CRONUS International Ltd_$Detailed Cust_ Ledg_ Entry` in the **Navigator** window and choose to edit the query.
2. In the query editor, click **Choose Columns** and select three columns for the dataset: **Amount (LCY)**, **Document Type**, and **Posting Date**. Select the field **Posting Date** and change the data type of the column **Date/Time** to **Date**.

3. Apply a filter on the **Posting Date** field – include only entries posted on 01.01.2017 or later.

4. We will rely on posted invoices for sales data analysis and exclude all document types except **Invoice**. To apply a column filter, select the column **Document Type**, click the arrow button in the column header, and select **2** from the list of values, removing all other marks:

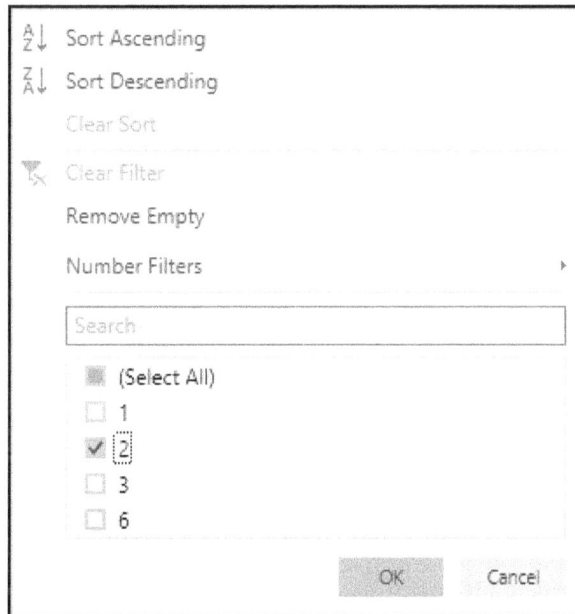

A↓Z	Sort Ascending
Z↓A	Sort Descending
	Clear Sort
▼	Clear Filter
	Remove Empty
	Number Filters ▸

```
Search
```

☐ (Select All)
☐ 1
☑ 2
☐ 3
☐ 6

OK   Cancel

5. Click **Close & Apply** to retrieve and transform data.

6. In the **Visualizations** pane, choose **R script visual**, and drag-and-drop the **Amount (LCY)** and **Posting Date** fields from the **Fields** pane to **Visualizations**.

7. Select the chart object and paste or type the following script in the R script editor:

```
library(forecast)
dataset$Date <- as.Date(dataset$`Posting Date`)
dataset <- aggregate(`Amount (LCY)` ~ Date, data = dataset,
  FUN = sum)
timeSeries <- ts(dataset$`Amount (LCY)`, frequency = 7)
decomposition <- stl(timeSeries, s.window = "periodic")
forecastSeries <- forecast(decomposition, h = 14)
plot(forecastSeries)
```

8. Run the script. It will plot the sales forecast based on the data imported from the NAV sales data:

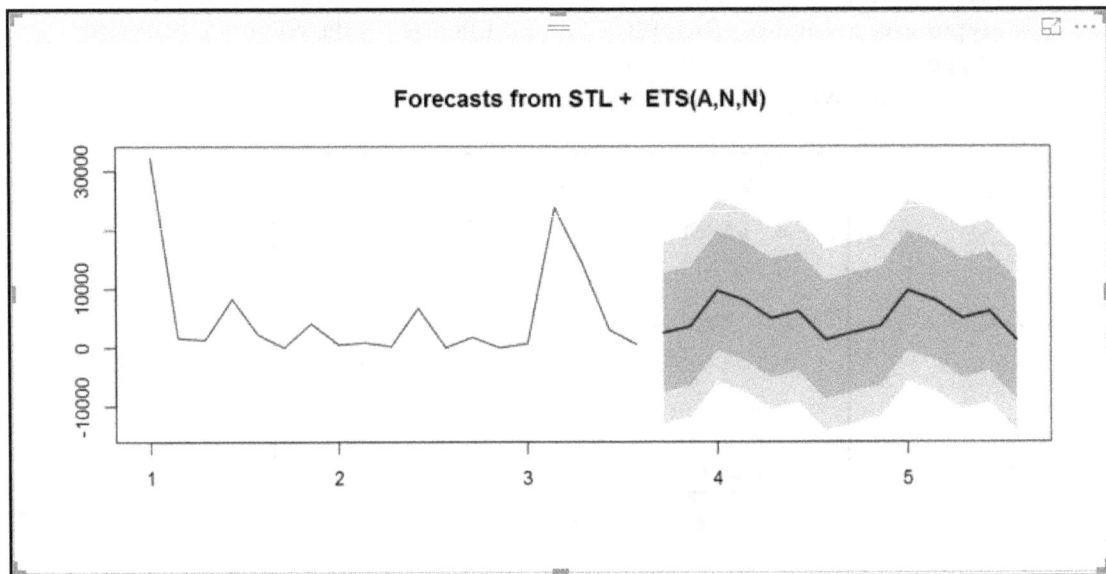

How it works...

The data preparation steps are identical to those in the recipe *Statistical data analysis in Power BI with R*. The current example is based on customer ledger entries instead of vendor entries, but is does not change the principle – both tables have a very similar structure. The same data cleanup steps are applied in this case.

The R script in the current example begins with a statement importing a package `forecast` that implements time series forecasting models.

After that, a new column **Date** is created in the dataset. It is filled with values copied from the **Posting Date** column, transformed into the **Date** data type.

The `aggregate` function collects aggregated data by applying the aggregation function passed in the parameters to the given dataset. The line aggregate (`Amount (LCY)` ~ Date, **data = dataset, FUN = sum)** can be read as **Apply SUM function to dataset to calculate aggregated Amount (LCY) by Date**.

Aggregated data is passed to the `ts` function to create a time series object from the transformed dataset. Each aggregated value in the dataset characterizes one observation for the time series. Parameter frequency defines a number of observations per period. Since our data is sampled daily, we set a period to be a week, hence the value of frequency 7.

The next step after collecting the times series is to decompose it to trend, regular factors, and irregular components. In real-life applications, operating with huge volumes of data, regular parts are usually represented by seasonal demand changes. In the demo database, with one month of data, we cannot observe seasonal fluctuations and have to limit the decomposition in the example to weekly variations.

forecast(decomposition, h = 14) generates a forecast based on the decomposed time series for the next 14 days.

Finally, **plot(forecastSeries)** plots the the graphic for the sales forecast generated in the previous step.

Designing server-side reports in SQL Server Reporting Studio

In the next recipe we will create a report based on NAV data, but not connected to the NAV server or client in any way. Server-side reports, as the name implies, are rendered on the server and published on a web portal through IIS server. Users can access these reports simply in a web browser from any computer connected to the corporate network.

The process of developing a server-side report is very similar to creating a client-side one, except that the source dataset is provided by an SQL query instead of a NAV server instance.

In source files: folder `NAV Report`, Visual Studio solution `NAVReport.sln`.

Getting ready

Download and install SQL Server Data Tools for your version of Visual Studio. The SSDT package is available on MSDN.

Internet Information Services must be installed and running on the computer that the report is going to be deployed on.

How to do it...

The report developed in the recipe shows the top 5 customers generating the highest income.

1. Start Microsoft Visual Studio. Run the application with administrator privileges.
2. Start a new project – select the **New** option in the **File** menu, then choose **Project**.
3. In the list of installed templates, select the **Business Intelligence** group, then choose the **Reporting Services** subgroup. Select the **Report Server ProjectWizard** template. Enter the name of the project, **NAV Report**, and select the **Create directory for solution** option.
4. The first step of the report wizard will ask you to configure the datasource connection. Leave the datasource type default (Microsoft SQL Server) and click the **Edit** button to set up the connection string.
5. In the **Connection Properties** window, enter the database server name: `localhost\navdemo`. In the `logon` parameters, leave the default option **Use Windows Authentication**. Select the database name from the drop-down list: `Demo Database NAV (9-0)`. Click **OK** – the connection string will be constructed based on the entered parameters.
6. In the next step, you will be prompted to enter the SQL query that will retrieve data for the report. You can either enter the query text manually or construct it using the query builder. The following is the query text on which the recipe is based:

```
SELECT TOP 5
  cust.No_ as "No.",
  cust.Name as Name,
  SUM(dle.[Amount (LCY)]) as Amount
  FROM [CRONUS International Ltd_$Customer] cust
  JOIN
  [CRONUS International Ltd_$Detailed Cust_ Ledg_ Entry] dle
  ON dle.[Customer No_] = cust.No_
  GROUP BY cust.No_, cust.Name
  ORDER BY SUM(dle.[Amount (LCY)]) DESC, cust.Name ASC
```

7. Move to the next step – report type selection. Choose the tabular presentation form.
8. In the next wizard step, you can choose how the fields are going to be grouped. Move all three available fields, **No_, Name**, and **Amount**, to the **Details** part. This report is a simple table without groups.
9. Move to the selection of the report style. This part is left completely to your taste. The report color scheme can be changed here.

10. Other configuration parameters will retain their default values, so just click Next to skip to the **Completing the Wizard** step. Enter the report name, here, **Top Customers**, and finish the report wizard. A report layout will be created. You can edit it manually before deploying it to the report server if you are not satisfied with the look:

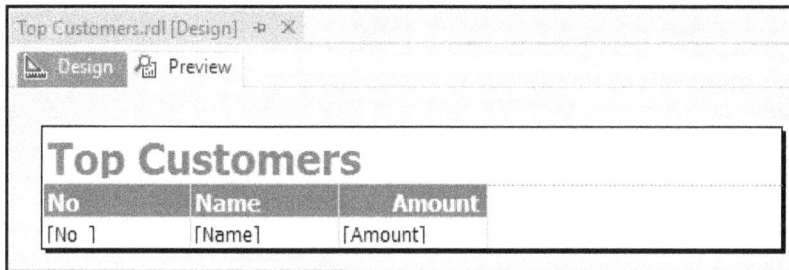

11. Right-click on the text box that refers to the **Amount** field. Select **Text Box Properties** from the drop-down menu, choose the **Number** tab, and select **Number** in the **Category** list.

12. In the main menu, select the **Build** group and run `Deploy NAV Report`.

> Remember that Visual Studio must be started with administrator privileges, otherwise report deployment will fail.

13. Run your web browser under administrator privileges and open the address `http://localhost/Reports`:

14. Enter the NAV Report folder. There is one report now located in this folder – **Top Customers**. Click on the report name to run it:

Home > NAV Report > Top Customers		

| ⏮ ◁ 1 | of 1 ▷ ⏭ | 100% ⌄ | | Find \| Next |

Top Customers

No	Name	Amount
30000	John Haddock Insurance Co.	349615.40
01454545	New Concepts Furniture	222241.32
10000	The Cannon Group PLC	168364.41
20000	Selangorian Ltd.	96049.99
49858585	Hotel Pferdesee	14395.75

How it works...

When we developed client-side reports in the previous recipes of this chapter, the first steps always included running the NAV development environment and configuring the report dataset there. Now the report is based on an SQL query that feeds data to the reporting services.

Writing a query for a report requires a deeper knowledge of the SQL language. If you are not familiar with SQL queries, just copy and paste the query text from Step 6 into the **Query string** window. After copying the text, you can push the **Edit** button and view the result. Table relations and aggregations will be reverse-engineered from the query. Simple queries can be designed in a visual interface of the query builder, although more complex queries still have to be written manually.

After the initial configuration is completed, the report wizard generates a layout for the report that can be further fine-tuned manually. Editing the layout of a server-side report is identical to the development of a client-side report. To add controls to the layout, open the **Toolbox** from the **View** menu and drag and drop report elements to the editor area.

Server-side reports can be previewed at any time during the development. Click the **Preview** button located above the report designer to see what it's going to look like.

The final step in the development part (Step 13 of the walk-through) is the deployment of the report. The default catalog for the report server location is `localhost/ReportServer`. You can view and modify these settings in the project properties. To access properties, open **NAV Report Properties** from **Project** menu.

There's more...

To learn more about report layout development in Visual Studio, see the recipe *Designing reports in Visual Studio* in this chapter.

4
.NET Interoperability in C/AL

In this chapter, we will cover the following recipes:

- Using .NET assemblies in C/AL
- Understanding static classes and methods
- Developing server-side extensions
- Developing client-side extensions
- Working with generics in C/AL
- Working with interfaces
- Accessing collections with the FOREACH statement
- Working .NET strings and arrays in C/AL
- Invoking .NET methods via reflection
- Handling exceptions with try functions
- Handling .NET events in C/AL
- Developing your own .NET class
- Starting processes in separate threads

Introduction

Application code in dynamics NAV is based on C/AL–a domain-specific language for data manipulation. The language suits perfectly well for the set of tasks it is intended to solve and it covers most of the user demands, but problems beyond the capabilities of C/AL do arise in practice from time to time. In such cases, when the capacity of C/AL is insufficient, .NET languages, such as C#, C++ .NET, or VB.NET, can come to the rescue. Assemblies developed in .NET languages can be seamlessly integrated in NAV application code and extend functionality beyond the reaches of pure C/AL.

Using .NET assemblies in C/AL

As an introduction to .NET assemblies in C/AL, we will develop a function to export the contents of any table to an XML file. The *Exchanging data with XMLPort objects* recipe in `Chapter 2`, *Advanced C/AL Development*, covered a similar topic of XML export with the `XMLPort` objects. While XMLPorts win in terms of simplicity, .NET objects are victorious in flexibility. The development of an object based on .NET interoperability requires more effort, but the result is applicable to any table, while XMLPorts are bound to a fixed table.

How to do it...

The object developed in this recipe, allows us to select any table and export its contents into an XML file.

1. First, create a page that will list all tables where the user can select a table to be exported. **Create a List type** page and select the **AllObj** table for the page data source. In the **List** page wizard, select two fields, **Object ID** and **Object Name**, to be displayed on the page.

2. Finish the wizard and open the page properties. In the `SourceTableView` property, click the assist button to set up the table view, and then click **Table Filter**. Configure the filter fields as follows:

Field	Type	Value
Object Type	CONST	Table Data

Click **OK** to close the table filter configuration window, then click **OK** again and return to the page properties. Verify the value of the `SourceTableView`. It should have updated after the filter configuration is completed:

```
WHERE(Object Type=CONST(TableData))
```

3. This page should be read-only, so set the value of the `Editable` property to **No**.

4. In C/AL Globals, declare an `ExportTable` function that will do the main job of generating an XML document from table data.

5. The XML document itself is a local variable of the `DotNet` type. To declare a DotNet variable, open the **C/AL Locals** window in the function `ExportTable` and insert a variable. Enter `XmlDoc` in the **Name** field, then select **DotNet** in DataType. A DotNet variable must refer to a .NET datatype, which is specified in the **Subtype** field. Click on the assist button in the **Subtype** field to see the list of .NET types.

6. The **.NET Type List** form is empty when it is run. To see the list of available types, select an assembly in which the desired class is compiled. Click on the assist button in the **Assembly** field to select an assembly.

7. Open the **.NET** tab and choose `System.Xml` from the list of assemblies:

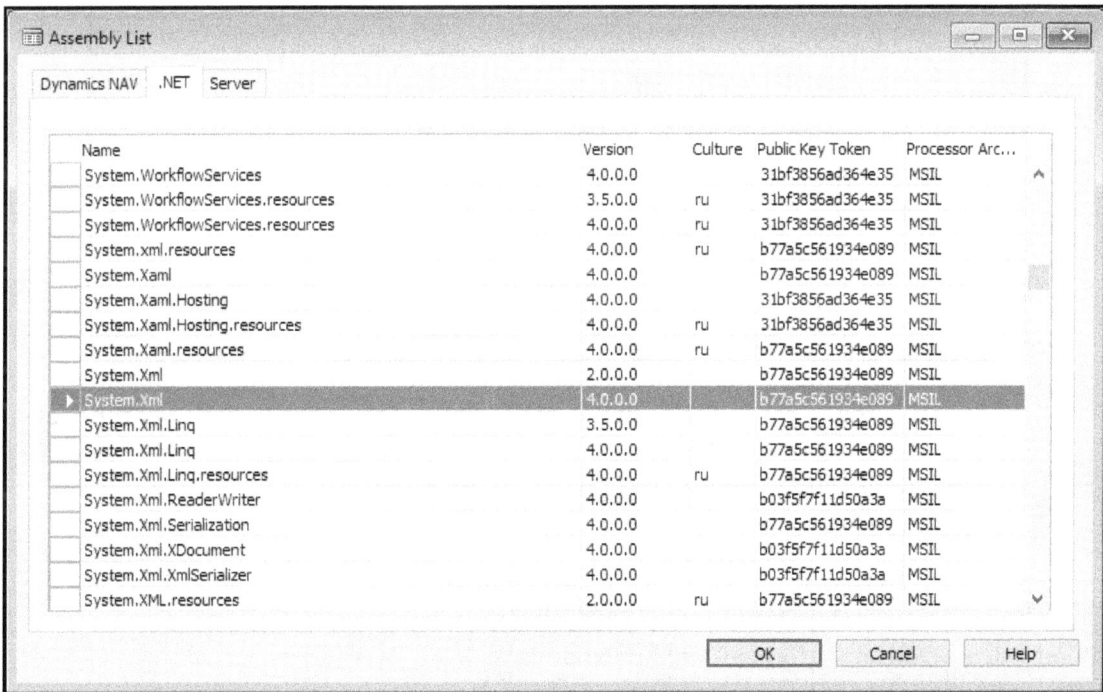

Name	Version	Culture	Public Key Token	Processor Arc...
System.WorkflowServices	4.0.0.0		31bf3856ad364e35	MSIL
System.WorkflowServices.resources	3.5.0.0	ru	31bf3856ad364e35	MSIL
System.WorkflowServices.resources	4.0.0.0	ru	31bf3856ad364e35	MSIL
System.xml.resources	4.0.0.0	ru	b77a5c561934e089	MSIL
System.Xaml	4.0.0.0		b77a5c561934e089	MSIL
System.Xaml.Hosting	4.0.0.0		31bf3856ad364e35	MSIL
System.Xaml.Hosting.resources	4.0.0.0	ru	31bf3856ad364e35	MSIL
System.Xaml.resources	4.0.0.0	ru	b77a5c561934e089	MSIL
System.Xml	2.0.0.0		b77a5c561934e089	MSIL
System.Xml	4.0.0.0		b77a5c561934e089	MSIL
System.Xml.Linq	3.5.0.0		b77a5c561934e089	MSIL
System.Xml.Linq	4.0.0.0		b77a5c561934e089	MSIL
System.Xml.Linq.resources	4.0.0.0	ru	b77a5c561934e089	MSIL
System.Xml.ReaderWriter	4.0.0.0		b03f5f7f11d50a3a	MSIL
System.Xml.Serialization	4.0.0.0		b77a5c561934e089	MSIL
System.Xml.XDocument	4.0.0.0		b03f5f7f11d50a3a	MSIL
System.Xml.XmlSerializer	4.0.0.0		b03f5f7f11d50a3a	MSIL
System.XML.resources	2.0.0.0	ru	b77a5c561934e089	MSIL

Assembly List

Dynamics NAV .NET Server

OK   Cancel   Help

8. Now the **.NET Type List** window displays all public types in the selected assembly. Choose **System.Xml.XmlDocument** from the list of types:

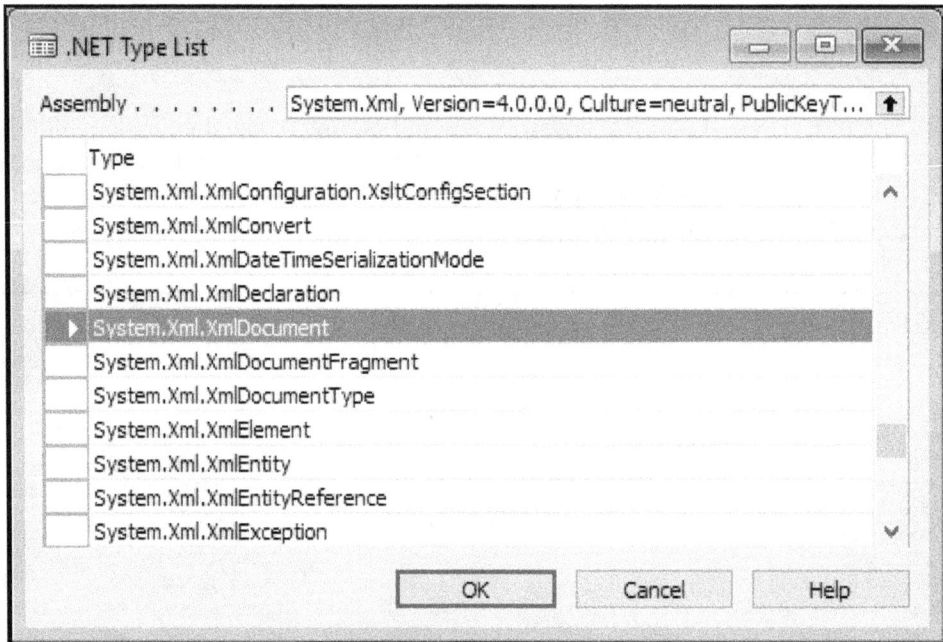

9. Declare other local variables in the `ExportTable` function. All `DotNet` types are exported in the same assembly, `System.Xml`. For the sake of readability, I will omit the assembly name in the variable types:

Name	Type	Subtype
XmlDoc	DotNet	System.Xml.XmlDocument
RootNode	DotNet	System.Xml.XmlNode
RecordNode	DotNet	System.Xml.XmlNode
RecRef	RecordRef	
FieldRef	FieldRef	
I	Integer	

10. Type or copy and paste the following function code:

```
RecRef.OPEN("Object ID");
IF RecRef.ISEMPTY THEN
  EXIT;

CreateXmlDocument(XmlDoc,RecRef);
RootNode := XmlDoc.DocumentElement;

RecRef.FINDSET;
REPEAT
  CreateXmlNode(RecordNode,XmlDoc,'Record','');
  RootNode.AppendChild(RecordNode);
  FOR I := 1 TO RecRef.FIELDCOUNT DO BEGIN
    FieldRef := RecRef.FIELDINDEX(I);
    IF UPPERCASE(FORMAT(FieldRef.CLASS)) IN
['NORMAL','FLOWFIELD'] THEN BEGIN
    IF UPPERCASE(FORMAT(FieldRef.CLASS)) = 'FLOWFIELD' THEN
      FieldRef.CALCFIELD;

    AppendChildNode(
      RecordNode,XmlDoc,FieldRef.NAME,FORMAT(FieldRef.VALUE));
    END;
  END;
UNTIL RecRef.NEXT = 0;

SaveToFile(XmlDoc);
```

11. The function code won't compile yet. We are still missing the helper functions called in the main loop. The first one is `CreateXmlDocument`. Declare this function in **C/AL Globals** and open its parameters. Insert the following parameters:

Var	Name	Type	Subtype
True	XmlDoc	DotNet	System.Xml.XmlDocument
	RecRef	RecordRef	

12. Besides, insert local variables in **C/AL Locals**:

Name	DataType	Subtype
XmlDeclaration	DotNet	System.Xml.XmlDeclaration
ReportNode	DotNet	System.Xml.XmlNode.'System.Xml

13. In this function, we are creating the XML document and its root element:

```
XmlDoc := XmlDoc.XmlDocument;
XmlDeclaration :=
XmlDoc.CreateXmlDeclaration('1.0','UTF-8','yes');
XmlDoc.AppendChild(XmlDeclaration);

CreateTableElement(ReportNode,XmlDoc,RecRef);
```

14. The next function, `CreateXmlNode`, creates an XML element with a text value. It returns a `Boolean` value and takes four parameters:

Var	Name	Type	Subtype
True	ChildNode	DotNet	System.Xml.XmlNode
	XmlDoc	DotNet	System.Xml.XmlDocument
	NodeName	Text	
	NodeValue	Text	

15. One local variable should be declared in the function:

Name	Type	Subtype
TextNode	DotNet	System.Xml.XmlNode

16. The C/AL code is then executed in the function:

```
IF NodeName = '' THEN
  EXIT(FALSE);

ChildNode := XmlDoc.CreateElement(NodeName);
TextNode := XmlDoc.CreateTextNode(NodeValue);
ChildNode.AppendChild(TextNode);

EXIT(TRUE);
```

17. Declare a `AppendChildNode` function in **C/AL Globals**.

18. The main function, `ExportTable`, does not take any parameters–it works on the global variable `Rec`. `AppendChildNode` has a number of parameters:

Var	Name	Type	Subtype
True	ParentNode	DotNet	System.Xml.XmlNode
True	XmlDoc	DotNet	System.Xml.XmlDocument
	NodeName	Text	
	NodeValue	Text	

19. The function code converts the node name received in the arguments, to remove characters invalid in XML node names, then the function creates a child node and appends it to the parent:

```
IF CreateXmlNode(
ChildNode,XmlDoc,CONVERTSTR(
   NodeName,' &<>''"%/\()[]{}^','_____'),NodeValue)
THEN
   ParentNode.AppendChild(ChildNode);
```

20. The function creating an XML node for each table is `CreateTableElement`. There are three parameters in the function, listed in the table:

Name	DataType	Subtype
TableNode	DotNet	System.Xml.XmlNode
XmlDoc	DotNet	System.Xml.XmlDocument
RecRef	RecRef	

21. After declaring the parameters, write the function code:

```
TableNode := XmlDoc.CreateElement('Table');
XmlDoc.AppendChild(TableNode);

CreateXmlAttribute(
   TableNode,XmlDoc,'ID',FORMAT(RecRef.NUMBER));
CreateXmlAttribute(
   TableNode,XmlDoc,'Name',FORMAT(RecRef.NAME));
```

22. XML attributes representing the table ID and name are inserted in the `CreateXmlAttribute` function. Create the function and add the following parameters:

Var	Name	Type	Subtype
True	XmlNode	DotNet	System.Xml.XmlNode
True	XmlDoc	DotNet	System.Xml.XmlDocument
	AttributeName	Text	
	AttributeValue	Text	

23. Then type the following function code:

```
XmlAttribute :=
    XmlDoc.CreateAttribute('',AttributeName,'');
XmlAttribute.Value := AttributeValue;
XmlNode.Attributes.Append(XmlAttribute);
```

24. Finally, the resulting document is exported into a file in the `SaveToFile` function. Its single parameter and code is as follows:

Name	DataType	Subtype
XmlDoc	DotNet	System.Xml.XmlDocument

```
FilePath := FileManagement.SaveFileDialog(
    'Save xml document','','xml files|*.xml');
XmlDoc.Save(FilePath);
```

25. Save the page with ID 50200 and name it `Data Export To Xml`. Compile and run the page. A list of all NAV tables will be displayed. Choose any table and push the action button, **Export Table**, to export its data into an XML file.

How it works...

A .NET object must declared as a local or global variable in a C/SIDE object, just like any other variable. In the list of variables accessed through C/AL Locals or the **C/AL Globals** menu options, you assign a variable name and select the **DotNet** option from the list of variable types.

What is different in declaring variables of the DotNet type is that these must refer to a .NET class compiled into a .NET assembly. A DotNet variable is bound to an assembly via its **Subtype** property. In Step 5 of the preceding example we begin configuring a DotNet reference, and Step 7 demonstrates a list of available assemblies.

The list is grouped in three separate parts presented in three different tab pages of the **Assembly List** form:

- **Dynamics NAV**: Client-side components
- **Server**: Server-side components
- **.NET**: Components registered in the **Global Assembly Cache** (**GAC**) of the development computer

When you refer to one of the .NET Framework system assemblies, GAC (.NET tab) is the place to look for it, while custom assemblies are usually placed in one of the two remaining tabs. We will cover the difference between server-side and client-side components later in this chapter.

When the assembly is selected, you see the list of all public classes available in the assembly (Step 8). After selecting the class, the declaration of the .NET variable is completed. Still, the declaration of a DotNet variable does not mean it can be immediately used. Unlike native C/AL datatypes, .NET classes, if they are not static, must be explicitly instantiated. Actually, any C/AL type is a .NET class, but the implementation is hidden from C/SIDE, and instantiation is handled by the NAV platform. With the DotNet type things are different.

The first function called in the recipe code is `CreateXmlDocument`, which in turn instantiates an XML document by calling its constructor:

```
XmlDoc := XmlDoc.XmlDocument;
```

In object-oriented programming, a constructor is a method that returns a class instance, a concept that is quite usual in languages such as C++, C#, or Java, but applicable only to external .NET classes in C/AL. Constructors always have the same name as the class they belong to, hence the `XmlDocument` class is instantiated by calling the `XmlDocument` constructor.

Explicit constructor calls are not always required to instantiate a class. The XML declaration node in Step 12, and child document nodes in subsequent steps are created via calls to different methods of the `XmlDocument` class:

```
XmlDeclaration := XmlDoc.CreateXmlDeclaration('1.0','UTF-  8','yes');
```

Understanding static classes and methods

All DotNet variables used in the previous recipe had to be instantiated before they could be used, which means that methods called on such variables are executed on a particular instance of that class. Static methods belong to the class itself and can be called without instantiating the variable.

The whole class can be declared as static. In this case, the class does not implement any constructor and all its methods have to be also static. An example of a static class is `File`–a .NET class encapsulating file operations.

A non-static class can implement both instance and static methods. `RegEx` is an example of a class that has both static and instance methods. `RegEx` is a .NET implementation of regular expressions.

How to do it...

In the following recipe, we will see how to use static classes to search for patterns in text lines with regular expressions and save the results in a file.

1. Create a worksheet page in the C/SIDE page designer, select the **Item** table as the data source, and choose two table fields to be displayed in the page: **No.** and **Description**.
2. In the page properties, set the value of **SourceTableTemporary** to **Yes**.
3. Declare a global `Text` variable, `SearchExpression`. This variable will store the regular expression entered by the user when searching.
4. In the page designer, insert a group under the **ContentArea** container. Under the new group, insert a field and set the variable **SearchExpression** in the field's source expression:

Page 50201 ItemRegEx - Page Designer

E.. Type	SubType	SourceExpr	Name	Caption
⊟ Container	ContentArea		RegExContainer	<RegExContainer>
⊟ Group	Group		RegExFilter	RegEx Filter
Field		SearchExpression	SearchExpression	Search Expression
⊟ Group	Repeater		Group	<Group>
Field		"No."	<No.>	<No.>
Field		Description	<Description>	<Description>

← → ↑ ↓　Preview　Help

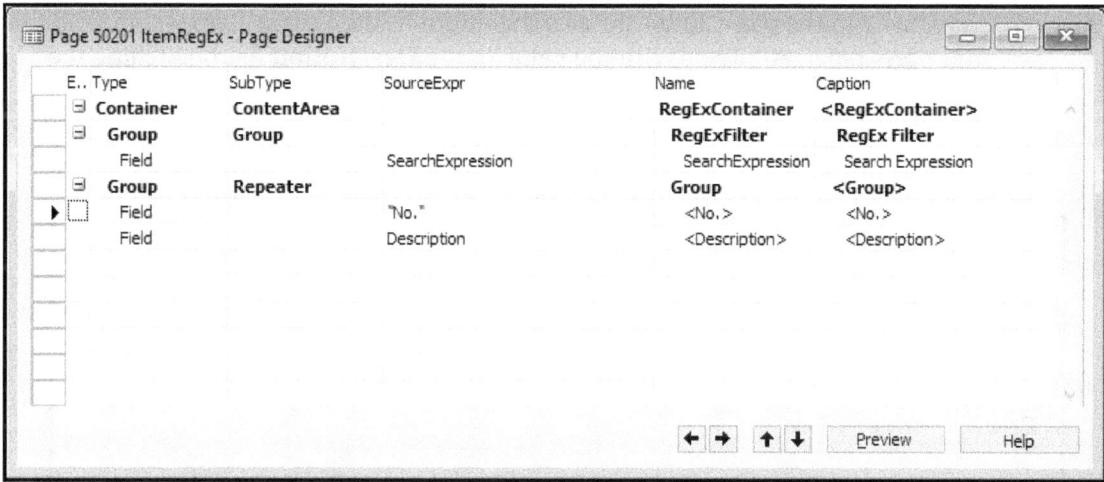

5. Select the **SearchExpression** field and open the C/AL code. This action will open C/AL triggers for the selected field. In the `OnValidate` trigger, open local C/AL declarations and insert two variables:

Name	Type	Subtype
Item	Record	Item
RegEx	DotNet	System.Text.RegularExpressions.Regex

The `RegEx` class is located in the `System` assembly. To declare a variable of the `RegEx` type, select **System** from the list of assemblies, and then choose the **System.Text.RegularExpressions.Regex** type name.

6. Paste or type the trigger code:

```
RESET;
DELETEALL;
IF Item.FINDSET THEN
  REPEAT
    IF RegEx.IsMatch(Item.Description,SearchExpression)
    THEN BEGIN
      "No." := Item."No.";
      Description := Item.Description;
      INSERT;
    END;
  UNTIL Item.NEXT = 0;
```

7. Save and run the page. Enter the search pattern in the **Search Expression** field and press *Enter*. All items with the value of the **Description** field matching the pattern will be shown in the page. For example, the following screenshot shows the result of search with a regular `speaker.*100` expression. The result contains all 100-watt speakers:

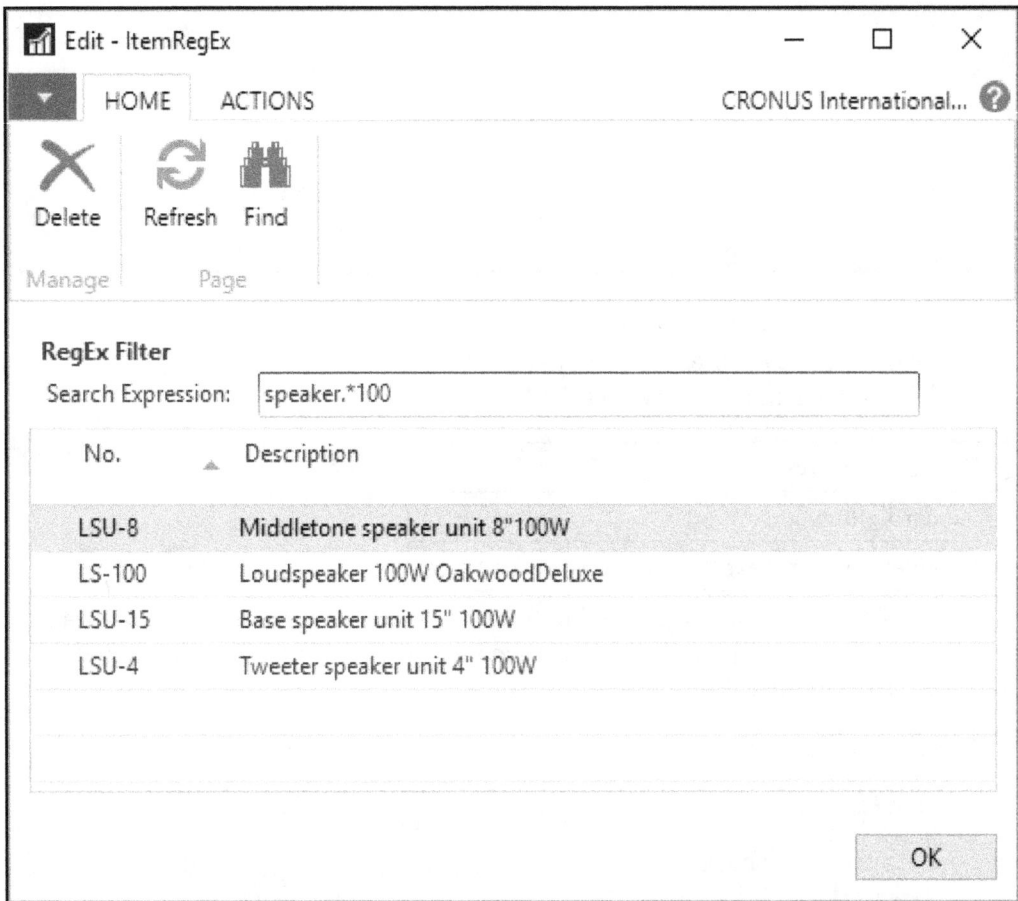

> This is a simple expression that can be easily replaced with a standard NAV filter. But regular expressions are more flexible and allow more complicated search patterns. If we wanted to find all monitors with a display size from 17 to 19 inches, we would use a `1[7-9]"` expression.

The expression for finding all CD-ROM drives in the database would look as follows: `\d?\dx`

8. Now let's return to the designer and add an action that will save found items in a file. Open the page in the page designer and switch to the action designer.

9. The default action container is created with a `NewDocumentItems` subtype. Change the subtype to `ActionItems` and insert a `Save to File` action in the container.

10. Declare local variables in the `OnAction` trigger:

Name	Type	Subtype
FileManagement	Codeunit	File Management
File	DotNet	System.IO.File
Lines	Text	
NewLine	Char	
CR	Char	
FilePath	Text	

12. Implement the function:

```
IF FINDSET THEN BEGIN
  NewLine := 13;
  CR := 10;

  REPEAT
    Lines :=
      Lines + "No." + ' ' + Description +
      FORMAT(NewLine) + FORMAT(CR);
  UNTIL NEXT = 0;

  FilePath :=
    FileManagement.SaveFileDialog('','','Text files|*.txt');
  IF FilePath <> '' THEN
    File.WriteAllText(FilePath,Lines);
END;
```

How it works...

A .NET class can have both instance and static methods. Instance methods can be called only after instantiating the class, as we did in the previous example with the XmlDocument class. The invocation of static methods does not require an instance–it is sufficient to declare a variable.

An example of such a class is RegEx. In Step 4, a variable is created and linked to the RegEx class from the System.Text.RegularExpressions namespace. Unlike the XmlDocument class, RegEx does not require any special actions to begin using the variable. The RegEx.IsMatch method in the code sample is called statically. But if you try to call, for example, the GetType method on the same RegEx variable, this will result in a runtime error, because GetType is an instance method, and the class still has to be instantiated to call instance methods.

To find out if a method you are going to use is a static or an instance method, open **C/AL Symbol Menu** and select the method in question. Static methods are marked with the static keyword:

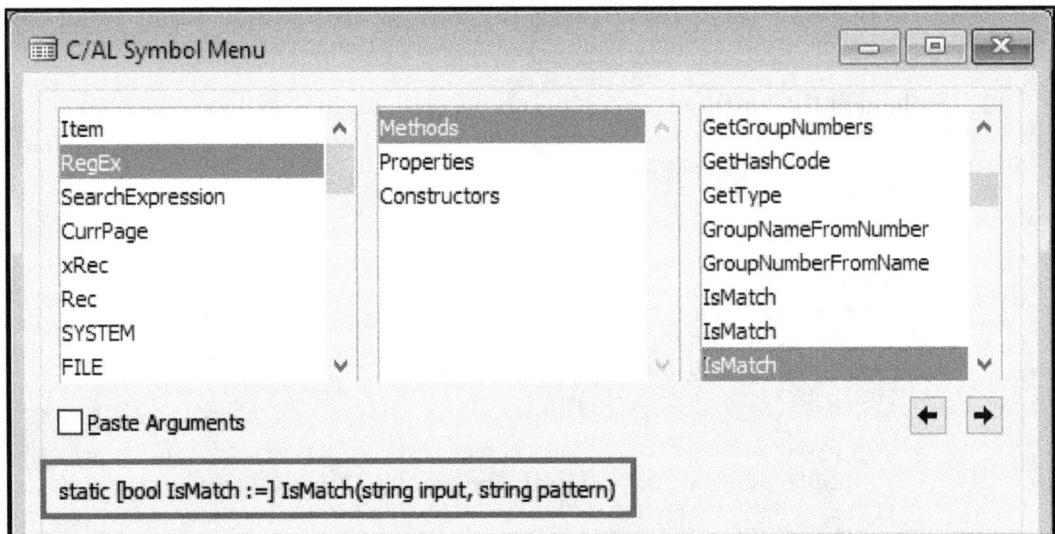

A class itself can be declared as static. A static class cannot have instance methods–all its methods must also be static.

The declaration of a DotNet variable referring to a static class is not different from what we did in the *Using .NET assemblies in C/AL* recipe in the current chapter for an instance class. The most common example of a static class in .NET Framework is `File`. As with other DotNet variables, we link the variable to a class. This time it is the `File` class from the `System.IO` namespace, in the `mscorlib` library. If you review the variable in C/AL symbols, you will see that its list of constructors is empty, and all methods are declared as static.

Developing server-side extensions

Code in .NET components integrated in NAV applications can be executed either on the server or on the client-side. The `RunOnClient` variable property is an instruction for NAV specifying which side the component should run on. Most of the .NETt code is executed in server-side components, client-side variables being a special case.

Code running on client is the topic of the next recipe, and now we will walk through creating a page that will connect to the NASDAQ website to read news in the RSS feed.

How to do it...

The page object created here, reads the RSS feed from `articlefeeds.nasdaq.com`, parses the result, and displays the news text.

1. Create a new page in the page designer. Choose to create a blank page without the wizard and leave the source table blank.
2. Open C/AL Globals and create the following variables:

Name	Type	Subtype
XmlDoc	DotNet	System.Xml.XmlDocument
XmlNodeList	DotNet	System.Xml.XmlNodeList
Title	Text	
Description	Text	
CurrNode	Integer	
NextButtonEnabled	Boolean	
PreviousButtonEnabled	Boolean	

3. In a new blank page, a default **ContentArea** container is created automatically. Insert two fields under the container:

Type	Subtype	SourceExpr	Name
Container	ContentArea		RSS Reader
Field		Title	Title
Field		Description	Description

4. Open the action designer. The default action container has a `NewDocumentItems` subtype. Change it to `ActionItems` and insert three action buttons in the container:

Type	SubType	Name
ActionContainer	ActionItems	RSS
Action		Get Feed
Action		Previous
Action		Next

5. In the action designer, open C/AL code from the **View** menu. In the `Get Feed – OnAction` trigger, write the code that will retrieve the latest RSS item from the NASDAQ RSS feed:

```
CLEAR(XmlDoc);
CLEAR(XmlNodeList);
CurrNode := 0;

XmlDoc := XmlDoc.XmlDocument;
XmlDoc.Load(
'http://articlefeeds.nasdaq.com/nasdaq/categories?
  category=Basics&format=xml');

XmlNodeList := XmlDoc.SelectNodes('/rss/channel/item');

ShowRSSItem;
SetButtonsActive;
```

6. The `ShowRSSItem` function called from the action trigger parses the active item in the node list and displays the RSS article:

```
Title :=
   XmlNodeList.Item(CurrNode).
   SelectSingleNode('./title').InnerText;
Description :=
   XmlNodeList.Item(CurrNode).
   SelectSingleNode('./description').InnerText;
```

7. The two remaining actions, `Previous` and `Next`, move the position of the active XML item and invoke the same `ShowRSSItem` function to refresh the page content. In the `Next – OnAction` trigger, write the C/AL code that will move the active RSS item forward:

```
IF CurrNode < XmlNodeList.Count - 1 THEN
   CurrNode += 1;
ShowRSSItem;
```

8. The `Previous – OnAction` trigger is almost identical to the `Next – OnAction` trigger. It moves the position of the active item back to the beginning of the list:

```
IF CurrNode > 0 THEN
   CurrNode -= 1;
ShowRSSItem;
```

How it works...

Two variables of DotNet types declared in the beginning of the example, receive the default value of the `RunOnClient` property. The property is initialized with the value `No`, which means that the variables are instantiated and executed in the server thread.

The contents of the RSS feed are loaded into an `XmlDocument` object in step 5. The `Load` function of the `XmlDocument` class can import data from a `Stream` or `StreamReader` object, or import an XML string directly from a URL.

The `SelectNodes` function in the next line runs a `XPath` query on the XML document containing the list of articles. The query `/rss/channel/item` selects all article items located under the `rss/channel` node. The initial slash in the query tells the XML parser to start looking for requested elements from the document root node.

Each item contains two lower-level elements: title and description. These are selected with two separate calls to `SelectSingleNode` on each of the XML elements retrieved by the `SelectNodes` function. The argument of the function is a `Xpath` query to be executed on the document. The `./description` query selects a node with the name description that is a direct descendant of the current node.

Developing client-side extensions

Client-side .NET components are executed on the client computer. Usually, these are components for user interaction, user interface, or parts of the application interacting with the software installed on the client computer.

How to do it...

In the following example, we will develop a document storage where the user can upload Word documents and open files to edit from the storage. MS Word is installed on the client computer and is controlled by a client-side .NET components.

1. A new table serving document storage is required for this example. Create a table in the C/SIDE table designer. Insert three fields in the new table:

Field No.	Field Name	Data Type	Length
1	ID	Integer	
2	File Name	Text	250
3	Document	BLOB	

2. Save the object as table **50202 File Storage**. The first field in the list automatically becomes the primary key, this is exactly what we want for the walk-through, so leave the default primary key.
3. Massive inserts into the file storage table are not expected; hence the primary key value can be auto-incremented on insert. To enable auto-increment, open the properties of the **ID** field and set **AutoIncrement** to **Yes**.
4. Create a new page in the page designer. Select the **50202** table created in the previous step as the source for the page and choose the **List** page type in the wizard.
5. Only one field, **File Name**, should be visible in the page. Select this field and complete the wizard.

6. We will load and edit Word documents outside NAV, and the filenames in the table should be read-only. To protect filenames from being modified in the page, open the page properties and change the value of the `Editable` property to **No**.

7. Close the page properties and open the action designer. Change the type of the default action container from `NewDocumentItems` to `ActionItems` and insert two actions in the container: `Import` and `Edit`.

8. In C/AL Globals, declare a global variable:

Name	DataType	SubType
FileManagement	Codeunit	File Management

9. Select the **Import** action item, open the C/AL code, and declare local variables in the `Import - OnAction` trigger:

Name	DataType	SubType
FileStorage	Record	File Storage
ClientFileName	Text	
ServerFileName	Text	

10. The C/AL code in the `Import - OnAction` trigger opens a file dialog that prompts the user to choose a file to import. If the file is selected, it is uploaded to the server and saved in the **File Storage** table:

```
ClientFileName :=
  FileManagement.OpenFileDialog('File to import','',
  'MS Word documents (*.doc, *.docx)|*.doc;*.docx,');
IF ClientFileName = '' THEN
  EXIT;

ServerFileName :=
  FileManagement.UploadFileSilent(ClientFileName);

FileStorage."File Name" := ClientFileName;
FileStorage.Document.IMPORT(ServerFileName);
FileStorage.INSERT;

FileManagement.DeleteServerFile(ServerFileName);
```

11. The `Edit - OnAction` trigger performs the backward operation. The file stored on the server must be downloaded to the client and opened by the MS Word application. There should be a single local variable in the trigger, `ClientFileName` of the `Text` type:

```
IF NOT Document.HASVALUE THEN
  EXIT;

ClientFileName := BLOBExport(Rec);
ClientFileName := OpenEditWordDocument(ClientFileName);

IF CONFIRM('Do you want to import the modified document?') THEN
  BLOBImport(Rec,ClientFileName);

FileManagement.DeleteClientFile(ClientFileName);
```

12. A function where MS Word is started is `OpenEditWordDocument`. It has one `Text` type parameter, `ClientFileName`. The return type is also `Text`.

13. Declare local function variables:

Name	DataType	Subtype
WordApp	DotNet	Microsoft.Office.Interop.Word.ApplicationClass
WordHelper	DotNet	Microsoft.Dynamics.Nav.Integration.Office.Word.WordHelper
WordHandler	DotNet	Microsoft.Dynamics.Nav.Integration.Office.Word.WordHandler
WordDocument	DotNet	Microsoft.Office.Interop.Word.Document
ErrorMessage	Text	

14. Open the properties for each of the DotNet variables and change the value of the `RunOnClient` property. It must be **Yes** for all variables.

15. Write the code for the `OpenEditWordDocument`:

```
WordApp := WordHelper.GetApplication(ErrorMessage);
IF ISNULL(WordApp) THEN
  ERROR(ErrorMessage);

WordHandler := WordHandler.WordHandler;
WordDocument :=
  WordHelper.CallOpen(WordApp,ClientFileName,FALSE,FALSE);
WordDocument.ActiveWindow.Caption := "File Name";
WordDocument.Application.Visible := TRUE;
WordDocument.Activate;

EXIT(WordHandler.WaitForDocument(WordDocument));
```

How it works...

Documents are stored in the table designed in the first three steps of the recipe. But the files are edited on client computers and uploaded to the server from the client side. Here we need to take care of client-server interaction and involve client-side .NET components.

Functions for file exchange between client and server are implemented in codeunit `419File Management`. A global variable referencing this `codeunit` is declared in Step 8. We later employ this `codeunit` in Step 10 to display the file selection dialog to the user:

```
ClientFileName := FileManagement.OpenFileDialog
```

The selected file is located on the client box, now it has to be uploaded to the server where it will be imported to the storage table. This is done by the `UploadFileSilent` function in the `FileManagement` codeunit:

```
ServerFileName := FileManagement.UploadFileSilent
```

Client-side .NET activities are concentrated in the `OpenEditWordDocument` function. A document stored on the server is downloaded to the client computer and sent to the application that will open and process it. Note that all .NET variables in the function must be running on the client. If any of the interacting .NET classes are instantiated in the server process, while others are on the client side, this will result in a runtime serialization error.

Working with generics in C/AL

Generic classes and methods in .NET Framework are a powerful tool allowing more extensive code reusability, while keeping the code type-safe. Generics enable the code to defer type specification until the moment of instantiation of the generic class.

To use generics in C/AL, you can declare variables of the DotNet type and bind them to one of the classes from the System.Collections.Generic namespace.

How to do it...

In this recipe, we will use a generic List class to find an item in a collection with the closest match to a provided search pattern.

1. Create a blank page in the object designer. No page wizard is required, since the page will not present any database controls and is not bound to any table.
2. In the page designer, enter a name for the default ContentArea container and insert a Field element under the container.
3. Declare a global Text variable SearchText. Enter SearchText in the SourceExpr property of the text control.
4. Create a C/AL Search function. The function is only used locally, so leave the default access modifier. It has no parameters or return value.
5. The following are local variables of the function:

Name	DataType	Subtype
Item	Record	Item
List	DotNet	System.Collections.Generic.List`1
SearchResult	Integer	

6. The following is the function code:

```
List := List.List;

Item.FINDSET;
REPEAT
  List.Add(Item.Description);
UNTIL Item.NEXT = 0;

List.Sort;
```

```
SearchResult := List.BinarySearch(SearchText);

IF SearchResult > 0 THEN
  MESSAGE('Exact match: ' + FORMAT(List.Item(SearchResult)))
ELSE IF SearchResult = -(List.Count + 1) THEN
  MESSAGE('No match')
ELSE
  MESSAGE(
    'Closest match: ' + FORMAT(List.Item(-(SearchResult
    + 1))));
```

7. In the code editor, find the `SearchText – OnValidate` trigger that is executed when a value is entered in the `SearchText` field. Call the `Search` function from this trigger: enter the function call in the trigger body:

   ```
   Search;
   ```

8. Save and run the page. Enter an item name to find, for example, **Lamp**. The exact match is then found:

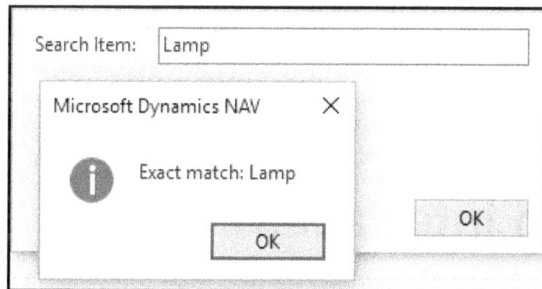

9. Now try to find `Lamb`. There is no exact match, but `Lamp` is the closest item that could be found:

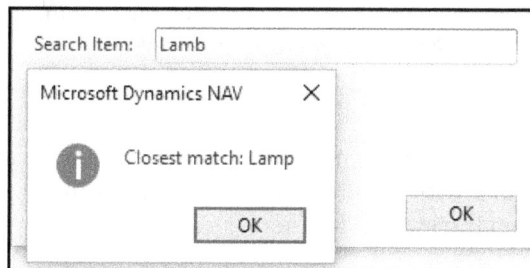

How it works...

The `List` variable in the preceding code sample is an example of a generic class. The very first line of the `Search` function creates an instance of the list by calling its default constructor: `List := List.List`.

In C/AL, you cannot explicitly specify the type name when instantiating a generic. For example, in C#, to declare a list of integers, you would write the following code:

```
List<int> list = new List<int>();
```

C/AL generics are always assigned the `System.Object` type. So, the preceding list instantiatio (`List := List.List`) corresponds to a C# statement:

```
List<Object> list = new List<Object>();
```

If your code requires precise type control, you can write your own .NET component to implement generic instantiation and type cast in the .NET code. An alternative is to make use of the `System.Activator` class.

Using custom .NET components in C/AL code is a topic in the *Developing your own .NET class* recipe. Initialization through the `Activator` class is covered in the next recipe, *Working with interfaces*.

Working with interfaces

In the next recipe, we will see how to call .NET methods that expect interfaces in the arguments.

As an example, we will consider a `Sort` method of the generic `List<T>`. The `Sort` method can be called without arguments – in this case, a default comparer for the `<T>` type will be used. But there is an overload of Sort accepting an alternative comparer passed through a reference to a class implementing the `IComparer` interface:

```
public void Sort(IComparer<T> comparer)
```

We will see how to declare a class implementing a generic interface and pass it to the method. These manipulations with an alternative comparer will allow us to sort with a culture that is different from the system locale.

How to do it...

In this example, a list will be sorted according to Spanish traditional sorting rules, repealing the system configuration.

1. The user interface in the example is going to be very simple – sorting of the list will be performed on a codeunit's OnRun trigger. Create a new codeunit in the C/SIDE object designer and move to its OnRun trigger.

2. The code for the function is relatively simple, but it involves a number of DotNet variables. Open the C/AL Locals in the OnRun trigger and declare the following variables:

Name	DataType	Subtype
List	DotNet	System.Collections.Generic.List`1
CultureInfo	DotNet	System.Globalization.CultureInfo
StringComparer	DotNet	System.StringComparer
Type	DotNet	System.Type
Activator	DotNet	System.Activator
IComparer	DotNet	System.Collections.Generic.IComparer`1

All classes are located in the mscorlib assembly.

3. The first action in the function is to create an instance of the list and fill it with data to be sorted. For an illustration, add two entries that can highlight the difference between various sorting rules:

```
List :=
  Activator.CreateInstance(
  Type.GetType(
    'System.Collections.Generic.List`1[[System.String]]'));

List.Add('calle');
List.Add('calor');
```

4. Further, in the same function write code to instantiate a `CultureInfo` class and create a string comparer based on the culture:

```
CultureInfo := CultureInfo.CultureInfo('es-ES_tradnl');
StringComparer := StringComparer.Create(CultureInfo, FALSE);

IComparer := StringComparer;
List.Sort(IComparer);

ShowResult(List);
```

5. The final part of the function displays the result by calling a `ShowResult` function that is not developed yet. Declare the function in C/AL Globals.

6. A single parameter of the function is the list to be displayed:

Name	DatType	Subtype
List	DotNet	System.Collections.Generic.List`1

7. Insert local variables in the function:

Name	DatType
NewLine	Char
MsgText	Text
I	Integer

The following is the code:

```
NewLine := 13;
FOR I := 0 TO List.Count - 1 DO
  MsgText := MsgText + FORMAT(List.Item(I)) +
    FORMAT(NewLine);

MESSAGE(MsgText);
```

8. Save the `codeunit` and run it. Here is how sorting works in traditional Spanish culture:

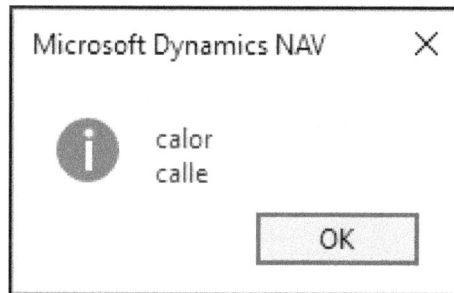

9. To see the difference, return to the code editor and change the culture name from `es-ES_tradnl` to modern Spanish `es-ES` or English `en-GB` and run the `codeunit` again. The sorting order is different now:

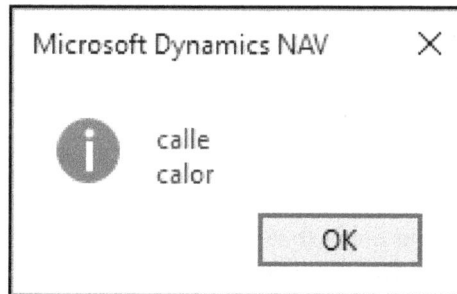

How it works...

List objects are created through the `Activator.CreateInstance` function. Invocation of the default constructor in a `List := List.List` statement will not work in this case. It will create a list of elements that have the `Object` type, and reflection requires precision when it comes to datatypes. `List.Add` inserts new string elements to the list.

In Step 4, a string comparer class instance is created to be assigned to the `IComparer` interface variable. The last variable in the declaration list in Step 2 is an interface that is expected in the arguments of `List.Sort`. The `IComparer := StringComparer` assignment is required to do the explicit type cast. After this line, `IComparer` points to the instance of the `StringComparer` class, but it is now cast to the `IComparer` type. And this is exactly what the `Sort` method expects. If we were writing this code in C#, for example, such tricks would not be nesessary. A simple `List.Sort(StringComparer)` would work just fine. But NAV cannot cast `StringComparer` to `IComparer` implicitly, and we have to give the C/AL runtime environment a hint.

Accessing collections with the FOREACH statement

The `FOREACH` statement, natural in C#, has been introduced in NAV 2016. It is commonly used in C# to iterate on instances of a structure with an enumerator, which is usually introduced by implementing the `IEnumerable` interface. In NAV 2016, you can apply the same statement to enumerable .NET objects.

How to do it...

Now we will collect a list of table fields that have relations to other tables and show them in a factbox page. Data is retrieved from object metadata in the XML format, and `FOREACH` comes in handy when iterating on lists of XML nodes:

1. The page in the following recipe consists of two parts: the main page and a `factbox` subpage. First we will create the `factbox` subpage. Create a page in the page designer, choose the `ListPart` page type, and select the virtual table `2000000041` **Field** for the data source.

2. In the page wizard, move two fields to the page, **No.** and **FieldName**, and complete the wizard.

3. In the page properties, set **Editable** to **No** and **SourceTableTemporary** to **Yes**.

4. Open the C/AL code of the page and create a new function `SetTableNo` in C/AL Globals. This function will be invoked from the main page and must be available from outside of the `factbox` page. To declare the function as global, select the function in the **C/AL Globals** window, access its properties, and set the value of the **Local** property to **No**.

5. In the C/AL Globals, switch to the **Variables** window and insert a global **TableID** variable. Select **Integer** in the **DataType** field.

6. Close global declarations, and open the **C/AL Locals** window in the **SetTableNo** function. Add an **Integer** function parameter, **NewTableID**.

7. In the C/AL editor, write the function code that initializes the global variable `TableID`:

```
TableID := NewTableID;
IF TableID > 0 THEN
  UpdateView;
```

8. The `UpdateView` function called from the preceding code is not yet declared. Return to C/AL Globals, the **Functions** tab, and add the `UpdateView` function. This one should stay local, since it will be used only inside the `factbox` page.

9. In C/AL Editor, declare local variables in the new `UpdateView` function (all DotNet type variables are located in the `System.Xml` assembly):

Name	DataType	Subtype
ObjectMetadata	Record	Object Metadata
XmlDocument	DotNet	System.Xml.XmlDocument
NamespaceMgr	DotNet	System.Xml.XmlNamespaceManager
XmlNodeList	DotNet	System.Xml.XmlNodeList
XmlNode	DotNet	System.Xml.XmlNode
Stream	InStream	

10. The function C/AL code updates the contents of the temporary `Field` table with table relation information retrieved from table metadata:

```
DELETEALL;

ObjectMetadata.GET(
  ObjectMetadata."Object Type"::Table,TableID);
ObjectMetadata.CALCFIELDS(Metadata);
ObjectMetadata.Metadata.CREATEINSTREAM(Stream);

XmlDocument := XmlDocument.XmlDocument;
XmlDocument.Load(Stream);

NamespaceMgr :=
  NamespaceMgr.XmlNamespaceManager(XmlDocument.NameTable);
```

```
NamespaceMgr.AddNamespace(
  'ns',XmlDocument.DocumentElement.NamespaceURI);
XmlNodeList :=
  XmlDocument.SelectNodes(
    '/ns:MetaTable/ns:Fields/ns:Field[ns:TableRelations]',
    NamespaceMgr);

FOREACH XmlNode IN XmlNodeList DO BEGIN
  TableNo := TableID;
  EVALUATE(
    "No.",XmlNode.Attributes.GetNamedItem('ID').Value);
  FieldName :=
    XmlNode.Attributes.GetNamedItem('Name').InnerText;
  INSERT;
END;
```

11. Save the page with the name `Table Fields Factbox` and ID 50208.

12. Create another page in the designer. This is the main page that will incorporate the factfox as a subpage. The main page has a `List` type and the `2000000001 Object` table as the data source.

13. Select two fields, **ID** and **Name**, to be shown in the page.

14. In the next step of the wizard, you can choose factboxes that you want to be presented on the page. Locate the **50208 Table Fields Factbox** page and move it to the page.

    Alternatively, you can skip this step and insert the factbox later.

15. After completing the page wizard, the C/SIDE page designer opens. Access the factbox page part properties and configure the `SubPageLink` property:

Field		Type	Value
TableNo		FIELD	ID

16. Change the value of the property **Name** to `TableFieldsFactbox`.

17. Close the subpage properties and open the properties of the list page. In the **SourceTableView** field, set up the table filter:

Field	Type	Value
Type	CONST	Table

18. The only purpose of the main is to select a table and initialize the subpage update; all work is done in the `factbox` page by the `UpdateView` function. In the new list page, open the C/AL Code designer, position in the `OnAfterGetCurrRecord` trigger, and insert a single line of code that will invoke the subpage update:

```
CurrPage.TableFieldsFactbox.PAGE.SetTableNo(ID);
```

19. Save the page with ID 50207, name it `Table Relation Info`, and run it:

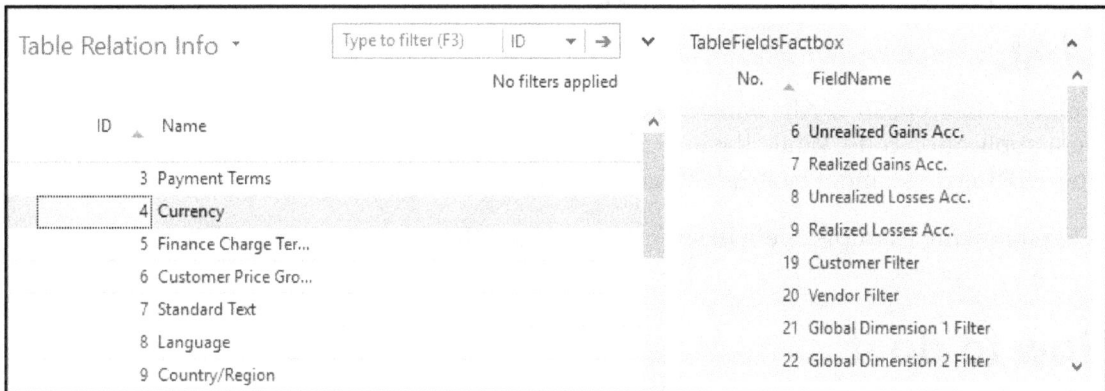

How it works...

XmlNodeList is a collection implementing the `IEnumerable` interface. The current example retrieves NAV object metadata from the `ObjectMetadata` table into an XmlDocument to extract data with Xpath queries.

The `SelectNodes` function returns an object representing the list of XML nodes matching the query criteria. The query itself (`/ns:MetaTable/ns:Fields/ns:Field[ns:TableRelations]`) can be interpreted as an instruction to the parser to select all `Field` nodes having a child node named `TableRelations`. The result is a list of nodes in the `XmlNodeList` object.

The obtained list can be traversed with the `FOREACH` statement. The syntax of the statement is: `FOREACH Object IN Collection DO`.

Here, `Collection` is the enumerable array or collection, and `Object` is a single object whose type matches that of the collection elements. Since each element of `XmlNodeList` has the `XmlNode` type, Object must have the same type. On each iteration of the loop, the next value from `XmlNodeList` is assigned to the `XmlNode` type, and the position of the active element moves to the next item. Loop execution breaks when the list reaches the last element.

Working with .NET strings and arrays in C/AL

The .NET datatype in C/AL enables developers to use .NET strings and dynamics arrays in client application code. While the `Syste.String` datatype is compatible with NAV Text type, .NET arrays cannot be directly converted to NAV arrays.

In the following example, we will see how to efficiently use these datatypes in your code.

How to do it…

Objects developed in the walk-through get stock exchange data from the Yahoo Finance website and present the result in a table. Stock indicators are published in CSV format – a list of comma-separated strings, each containing a dataset related to a separate index.

1. First of all, let's create a table where the data received from the stock information provider will be stored. Open `Table Designer` in C/SIDE and create a table.
2. Create the table fields as shown in the following table:

Field No.	Field Name	Data Type	Length
1	Symbol	Code	10
2	Trade Date	Date	
3	Name	Text	100
4	Change	Text	30
5	Volume	Decimal	
6	Price	Decimal	

3. Save the table with ID and Name, 50209 and Yahoo Stock, respectively.

4. Create a page that will provide a user interface for the stock data. In the page wizard, select the **List** page type and set table 50209 as the data source for the new page.

5. In the next wizard step, move all five table fields to the page.

6. Complete the page wizard. In the page designer, open the **Page Actions** designer and create an ActionItems action container and an action button named GetData.

7. Open the C/AL code designer and declare local variables in the GetData - OnAction trigger code:

Name	DataType	Subtype
HttpWebRequest	DotNet	System.Net.HttpWebRequest
HttpWebResponse	DotNet	System.Net.HttpWebResponse
DotNetString	DotNet	System.String
CharArray	DotNet	System.Array
Type	DotNet	System.Type
ResponseStream	InStream	
ResponseText	Text	
Separator	Char	
BytesRead	Integer	

8. Now type or paste the function code:

```
HttpWebRequest :=
HttpWebRequest.Create(
  'http://finance.yahoo.com/d/quotes.csv?s=
  MSFT+YHOO+GOOG+ORCL+AAPL&f=snl1d1cv');
HttpWebResponse := HttpWebRequest.GetResponse;
ResponseStream := HttpWebResponse.GetResponseStream;

REPEAT
  BytesRead := ResponseStream.READTEXT(ResponseText);
  IF BytesRead > 0 THEN BEGIN
    DotNetString := ResponseText;

    Type := Type.GetType('System.Char');
    CharArray := CharArray.CreateInstance(Type,1);
```

```
        Separator := ',';
        CharArray.SetValue(Separator,0);

        SaveResponseData(DotNetString.Split(CharArray));
    END;
  UNTIL BytesRead = 0;
```

9. Create a `FormatString` function that has one parameter:

Name	DataType	Subtype
String	DotNet	System.String

10. The function simply removes quotation marks enclosing the text values:

```
    EXIT(DELCHR(String,'<>','"'));
```

11. Create a `StringToDecimal` function. It has one `String` parameter of the `System.String` type, exactly as in `FormatString`. The return type of the function should be `Decimal`.

12. The two local variables are as follows:

Name	DataType	Subtype
CultureInfo	DotNet	System.Globalization
Convert	DotNet	System.Convert

13. The C/AL code of the function converts a text variable into a numeric value with regard to the number formatting:

```
    CultureInfo := CultureInfo.CultureInfo('en-US');
    EXIT(Convert.ToDecimal(String,CultureInfo));
```

14. `StringToDate` is a function similar to `StringToDecimal`. The parameter and local variables are the same as in `StringToDecimal`.

15. Its code converts text into a date value, taking formatting rules from the `CultureInfo` object:

```
    CultureInfo := CultureInfo.CultureInfo('en-US');
    EXIT(DT2DATE(Convert.ToDateTime(String,CultureInfo)));
```

16. The `FormatString` function simply removes extra quotation mark symbols from the text lines, since each value in the downloaded `.csv` file is enclosed in quotes. Declare the function, set its return type to `Text`, and insert a parameter:

Name	DataType	Subtype
String	DotNet	System.String

17. The function code makes one call to the standard C/AL function `DELCHR`, passing the `DotNet` argument to it:

```
EXIT(DELCHR(String,'<>','"'));
```

18. After inserting the parameter, open the **Return Value** tab and change the return type to `Decimal`.

19. Two local `DotNet` variables are required in this function:

Name	DataType	Subtype
CultureInfo	DotNet	System.Globalization.CultureInfo
Convert	DotNet	System.Convert

20. The following is the C/AL code that converts a string to a decimal value:

```
CultureInfo := CultureInfo.CultureInfo('en-US');
EXIT(Convert.ToDecimal(String,CultureInfo));
```

21. The next function, `StringToDate`, converts a string to the `Date` datatype. It takes one parameter – a `DotNet` string, identical to the previous function. Two local variables, `CultureInfo` and `Convert`, are also the same.

    Since the incoming string is supposed to be converted into a date, the function return type must be `Date`.

22. The function code also looks similar to the `StringToDecimal` datatype, although not exactly the same:

```
CultureInfo := CultureInfo.CultureInfo('en-US');
EXIT(DT2DATE(Convert.ToDateTime(String,CultureInfo)));
```

23. In the last function of this recipe, we are saving data received from Yahoo Finance to the table created at the very beginning of the exercise. Declare a `SaveResponseData` function. In its single parameter, the function takes an array of stock indicators:

Name	DataType	Subtype
StringArray	DotNet	System.Array

24. The table where the data will be saved, is a local variable:

Name	DataType	Subtype
YahooStock	Record	Yahoo Stock

25. Write the code to format the obtained data rows and save them in the table:

```
WITH YahooStock DO BEGIN
  INIT;
  Symbol := FormatString(StringArray.GetValue(0));
  Name := FormatString(StringArray.GetValue(1));
  Price :=
    StringToDecimal(FormatString(StringArray.GetValue(2)));
  "Trade Date" :=
    StringToDate(FormatString(StringArray.GetValue(3)));
  Change := FormatString(StringArray.GetValue(4));
  EVALUATE(Volume,StringArray.GetValue(5));
  IF NOT INSERT THEN
    MODIFY;
END;
```

26. Save the results and run the page. Click the **Get Data** action button to download the latest trading data:

How it works...

Stock data is loaded from the web source in Step 8. The work is done by the `HttpWebRequest` object that sends a request to a web resource and reads the response into an `HttpWebResponse` object. The web address where the request is directed is `http://finance.yahoo.com/d/quotes.csv`.

The following parameter string contains request details. For a detailed manual on quotes in `.csv` format you can refer to the Yahoo Finance documentation. In the preceding web request, returned data consists of the trade date, daily change, and total volume of trading operations for five companies: Microsoft, Yahoo, Google, Oracle, and Apple.

Data returned by the `HttpWebResponse` object can be read in a memory stream. The NAV objects `InStream` and `OutStream` are interchangeable with the .NET `Stream` object, so we can read the contents of the web response into a NAV `InStream` variable, `ResponseStream`.

The `READTEXT` function of the `InStream` object loads data from the stream into a text variable. This function call illustrates the fact that compatibility between the NAV Text datatype and `.Net System.String` is not complete. We have to call `READTEXT` with a `Text` type variable and make an assignment later. The `DotNetString := ResponseText` line will do the implicit type cast, while `READTEXT(DotNetString)` would fail.

The last thing that the action trigger does before saving the data, is split the comma-separated list into an array of strings: `StringArray :=`
`DotNetString.Split(CharArray)`.

The parameter of the Split function is an array of symbols that should be treated as separators. The array of substrings is returned.

Separate fields in the comma-separated line are also enclosed in quotation marks that are removed in Step 19 by the `DELCHR` function. Note that this is a native C/AL function that nevertheless accepts a .NET string.

The String array formed from the string is then passed to `SaveResponseData`, where the text lines are formatted and converted to appropriate datatypes where necessary. Step 24 through Step 26 use the `System.Convert` object along with `CultureInfo` to convert text data into a numeric value and date. Since we know that the response comes in the US English culture, we can instantiate the corresponding converter and let it take care of the formatting. Thus, a date 09-21-2016 will be interpreted correctly as the 21st of September, 2016, no matter how the date is formatted on the computer running the code. The same applies to formatting of numeric values. A number 123.45 will be treated as a decimal number even if the active system locale uses commas to separate the decimal part from the integer.

Invoking .NET methods via reflection

Reflection is the ability of a program to control its own structure and change the flow dynamically at runtime. .NET Framework provides reflection capabilities through the `System.Reflection` assembly. The key class implemented in this assembly is `Type`, which gives access to the instantiation of datatypes and allows inspecting type methods and properties.

How to do it...

The following example executes one of two functions on a List object, when the function name becomes known only in runtime.

1. Create a `Page` object in the C/SIDE page designer. This will be a container for actions executing reflected functions.
2. The code of the function is as follows:

```
Item.FINDSET;
REPEAT
   ItemList.Add(Item.Description);
UNTIL Item.NEXT = 0;
```

3. Create a function in C/AL Globals and name it `RunFunction`. It should have one text parameter, `FunctionName`.
4. Declare local variables. All classes in the list are compiled in the `mscorlib` assembly:

Name	DataType	Subtype
Activator	DotNet	System.Activator
Type	DotNet	System.Type
TypesArray	DotNet	System.Array
MethodInfo	DotNet	System.Reflection.MethodInfo
Args	DotNet	System.Collections.Generic.List`1
ItemList	DotNet	System.Collections.Generic.List`1

5. Enter function code to instantiate the `Type` class and call a dynamically bound function on the `ItemList` object:

```
ItemList := Activator.CreateInstance(
  Type.GetType(
  'System.Collections.Generic.List`1[[System.String]]'));
InitializeList(ItemList);

Type := ItemList.GetType;
TypesArray :=
  TypesArray.CreateInstance(Type.GetType('System.Type'),0);
MethodInfo := Type.GetMethod(FunctionName,TypesArray);

Args := Args.List;
MethodInfo.Invoke(ItemList, Args.ToArray);

ShowResult(ItemList);
```

6. Open the Action Designer form and create two action buttons. The first one is named `Sort`, the second is `Reverse`.

7. Open the trigger code and insert the function call. First, the `Sort` action:

```
RunFunction('Sort');
```

8. The Reverse – `OnAction` trigger calls the `RunFunction` function as well, but with another function name in the argument:

```
RunFunction('Reverse');
```

9. Two functions called in the preceding code do not exist yet. The first is `InitializeList`. Declare the function and insert a parameter:

Name	DataType	Subtype
ItemList	DotNet	System.Collections.Generic.List`1

10. Besides, `InitializeList` has one local variable:

Name	DataType	Subtype
Item	Record	Item

11. The `InitializeList` function simply initializes the list with a set of values. Write down its code:

```
IF Item.FINDSET THEN
  REPEAT
    ItemList.Add(Item.Description);
  UNTIL Item.NEXT = 0;
```

12. The last function to declare is `ShowResult`. It has one parameter as follows:

Name	DataType	Subtype
ItemList	DotNet	System.Collections.Generic.List`1

And two local variables as follows:

Name	DataType
MsgText	Text
I	Integer

13. `ShowResult` formats a very long message and displays the execution result:

```
FOR I := 0 TO ItemList.Count - 1 DO
  MsgText := MsgText + FORMAT(ItemList.Item(I)) + '';

MESSAGE(MsgText);
```

14. Run the page. Click the **Sort** action button – it will show a sorted list. Try another button – **Reverse action** reverses the order of elements in the list.

How it works...

The first thing you might have noticed is that we do not instantiate the list through its default constructor that would be called by the `ItemList := ItemList.List` statement.

Instead, the `Activator` object is used. `Activator.CreateInstance` does almost the same as a simple constructor call – it creates an instance of the given type and calls its default constructor. The difference with the first instantiation statement is that `CreateInstance` performs the type cast and returns an instance of the type specified in its argument. A direct constructor call in NAV creates a list of `Object` elements (`List<Object>`). The activator returns a list of strings (`List<String>`). And this makes all the difference in reflection – type control is crucial in this example.

After initializing the list we create an instance of the `Type` class: `Type :=` `ItemList.GetType`. This is required to retrieve the method info from the instance of the type. To find the method, `Type.GetMethodInfo` requires two parameters: the method name and an array of parameter types that the method accepts. Together, these two form a method signature unambiguously identifying the method. Since we call methods without parameters, `TypesArray` passed to the `GetMethodInfo` is empty.

After the `MethodInfo` object is prepared, the method can be called with `MethodInfo.Invoke`. It requires two parameters: an instance of a class on which the method will be executed, and an array of method arguments. Once again we pass an empty array instead of an arguments array, since both, `Sort` and `Reverse` methods, do not require any parameters.

Handling exceptions with try functions

The `TryFunction` property has been introduced to C/AL to handle exceptions thrown by .NET objects. It allows NAV application developers to catch exceptions and handle them the way the `try...catch` statement would in C#.

How to do it...

The following example explains how to declare a try function and catch exceptions from
.NET objects.

1. To illustrate why we need the `TryFunction` attribute at all, let's create a codeunit
   with a function that will fail and throw a .NET exception. Let's call the
   `GetDataFromRemoteSource` function and suppose it is intended to load data
   from some web resource:

   ```
   HttpWebRequest := HttpWebRequest.Create('http://unknown');
   HttpWebResponse := HttpWebRequest.GetResponse;
   ```

2. In the codeunit, the `OnRun` trigger will call the function:

   ```
   GetDataFromRemoteSource;
   ```

   Then save and run the codeunit. The function fails, as expected:

   > **Microsoft Dynamics NAV**   ✕
   >
   > ❌ A call to System.Net.HttpWebRequest.GetResponse failed with this
   > message: The remote name could not be resolved: 'unknown'
   >
   >   OK

3. This exception interrupts code execution and might frighten the user with
   the technical details they don't want to see. If our application can continue
   functioning and get data from a backup local source, all we want to do is inform
   the user and continue the normal code flow.

   Open the codeunit in the object designer, access the properties of the function
   `GetDataFromRemoteSource` and set `TryFunction=Yes`.

4. Create another function in the codeunit, `LoadDataFromLocalSource`. This is a dummy function that won't actually load anything. Its only purpose is to demonstrate the code flow after catching an exception. Let the function display a message:

```
MESSAGE('Getting data from local source.');
```

5. Declare a text constant that will be shown instead of the exception text:

Name	ConstValue
WebRequestFailedErr	Failed to connect to the web resource.\Message received from component:\%1

6. Modify the `GetDataFromRemoteSource` function:

```
IF NOT GetDataFromRemoteSource THEN BEGIN;
   MESSAGE(WebRequestFailedErr,GETLASTERRORTEXT);

   GetDataFromLocalSource;
END;
```

7. Compile and run the object. Now the function will display a user-friendly message and continue execution after handling the exception.

How it works...

The `TryFunction` property is a relatively new feature in C/AL, but it has already seen a lot of misuse. The only purpose of introducing the feature was to handle exceptions from external .NET components. Try functions can catch errors thrown by C/AL statements, but it is recommended not to mask C/AL errors with the `try` functions, since this can hide serious errors in code and result in data corruption.

To illustrate a possible damage to data, create a codeunit with a `InsertCustomer` function that is declared as a `TryFunction` function. Insert the following C/AL code in the function:

```
Customer.VALIDATE("No.",'TEST');
Customer.VALIDATE(Name,'Test customer');
Customer.INSERT;

Customer.VALIDATE("Customer Disc. Group",'TEST GROUP');
```

You can see that the last line called after the INSERT statement will cause a field validation error, unless you manually insert a customer discount group TEST GROUP. Normally, such an attempt of inconsistent assignment will fail and rollback the transaction, including the Customer.INSERT statement.

Let's see what happens when this code is called inside a TryFunction function. Invoke the function from the OnRun trigger:

```
IF NOT InsertCustomer THEN
    MESSAGE(GETLASTERRORTEXT);
```

Modify the code, then save and run the object. After the code is executed, review the customers list. You will see that the transaction did not roll back; the customer record is inserted despite the validation error.

> Use try functions to catch .NET exceptions only. Code that modifies data in the database should not be executed in a try function, as this may corrupt data consistency.

Handling .Net events in C/AL

.NET components embedded in a NAV object can communicate with their host object by means of events that are handled by C/AL code. Events are raised by .NET components that invoke event handlers in NAV.

How to do it...

The FileSystemWatcher component will be used to illustrate .NET events handling in C/SIDE. The component monitors changes in the filesystem and raises events in response to any file modification. These events will handled by a NAV object.

1. A new table will be required for the following demo to store data received from the FileSystemWatcher component. Open the table designer and create a table.

2. Insert four fields in the table:

Field No.	Field Name	Data Type	Length
1	ID	Integer	
2	Path	Text	250
3	Name	Text	100
4	Change Type	Option	

Select the last field **Change Type**, open its properties and assign an option string: **All, Changed, Created, Deleted, Renamed** in the **OptionString** property.

3. Save the table as a new table `50210 Filesystem Event`. Accept the default selection of the primary key – field ID.

4. Create a **Worksheet** page in the C/SIDE page designer. In the **Table** field, select the `50210` table created in Step 2 and Step 3.

5. Move the fields **Path**, **Name**, and **Change Type** to the page in the page wizard, then complete the wizard.

6. In the page designer that opens after the wizard finishes, access page properties and modify the **SourceTableTemporary** property to `Yes`. The table will be used only to display file operations, but it will not store the data.

7. Open the **C/AL Globals** window and create a global variable `DirectoryName` of type `Text`.

8. Insert a group in the content area container. Place the group before the Repeater group. In the new group, insert a field and select the **DirectoryName** variable in the **SourceExpr** column:

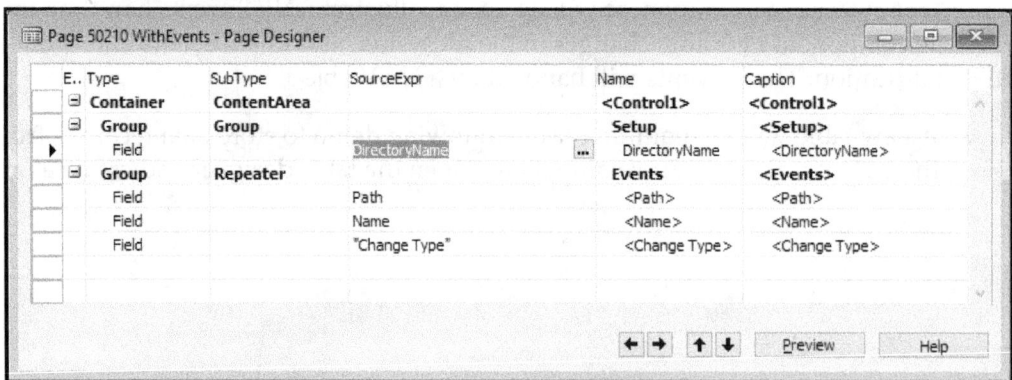

E.. Type	SubType	SourceExpr		Name	Caption
⊟ Container	ContentArea			<Control1>	<Control1>
⊟ Group	Group			Setup	<Setup>
▸ Field		DirectoryName	...	DirectoryName	<DirectoryName>
⊟ Group	Repeater			Events	<Events>
Field		Path		<Path>	<Path>
Field		Name		<Name>	<Name>
Field		"Change Type"		<Change Type>	<Change Type>

9. The **DirectoryName** field is the name of the folder where `FileSystemWatcher` will be monitoring changes. We will allow the user to enter the folder name in runtime. Write the following code in `DirectoryName - OnValidate` trigger to handle user input:

```
IF DirectoryName = '' THEN
   StopWatching
ELSE
   StartWatching;
```

10. Once again, return to the **C/AL Globals** window and declare the remaining global variables:

Name	DataType	Subtype
FileSystemWatcher	DotNet	System.IO.FileSystemWatcher
DirectoryName	Text	
LastEventID	Integer	

11. Select the `FileSystemWatcher` variable and open the **Properties** window. One of the properties of the DotNet variable is called **WithEvents**. Its default value is No, indicating that the component will not raise events. Change the value of this property to Yes.

12. From the list of global variables, tab to the functions list. Insert a `StartWatching` function that will initialize the `FileSystemWatcher` object and enable events.

13. One local variable in this function is a .NET string:

Name	DataType	Subtype
String	DotNet	System.String

14. Write function code to set up the directory to monitor and enable the watcher component:

```
IF ISNULL(FileSystemWatcher) THEN
   FileSystemWatcher := FileSystemWatcher.FileSystemWatcher;

String := DirectoryName;
String.Replace('','');
FileSystemWatcher.Path := String;
FileSystemWatcher.IncludeSubdirectories := TRUE;
FileSystemWatcher.EnableRaisingEvents := TRUE;
```

15. A function that stops the `FileSystemWatcher` object and cancels monitoring is called `StopWatching`. It does not have any local variables or parameters:

```
IF ISNULL(FileSystemWatcher) THEN
   EXIT;

FileSystemWatcher.EnableRaisingEvents := FALSE;
   CLEAR(FileSystemWatcher);
```

16. In C/AL Globals, declare a `LogChange` function that is intended to insert data received from the .NET component, into the table. A parameter of the function is an object encapsulating event information received from the event sender:

Name	DataType	Subtype
EventArgs	DotNet	System.IO.FileSystemEventArgs

17. A local `ChangeTypes` variable is required to translate `EventArgs` into the NAV `Option` type:

Name	DataType	Subtype
ChangeTypes	DotNet	System.IO.WatcherChangeTypes

18. Write the C/AL code in the `LogChange` function to interpret the change type from `EventAgrs` and insert the result into the temporary table:

```
LastEventID += 1;
ID := LastEventID;
Path := EventArgs.FullPath;
Name := EventArgs.Name;

CASE 0 OF
  EventArgs.ChangeType.CompareTo(ChangeTypes.Changed):
    "Change Type" := "Change Type"::Changed;
  EventArgs.ChangeType.CompareTo(ChangeTypes.Created):
    "Change Type" := "Change Type"::Created;
  EventArgs.ChangeType.CompareTo(ChangeTypes.Deleted):
    "Change Type" := "Change Type"::Deleted;
  EventArgs.ChangeType.CompareTo(ChangeTypes.Renamed):
    "Change Type" := "Change Type"::Renamed;
END;

INSERT(TRUE);
FINDLAST;
CurrPage.UPDATE(FALSE);
```

19. By now you might have noticed new triggers that appeared in the page with names starting with `FileSystemWatcher::`.

    These triggers are the handlers of events raised by the `FileSystemWatcher` object. Events corresponding to filesystem notifications should call the `LogChange` function.

20. Insert the function call in the following event handlers:
    - `FileSystemWatcher::Changed`
    - `FileSystemWatcher::Created`
    - `FileSystemWatcher::Deleted`
    - `FileSystemWatcher::Renamed`

    The code to insert is just one line:

```
LogChange(e);
```

21. Save the page and run it. As soon as you enter a folder name in the **Directory Name** field, the `FileSystemWatcher` component begins monitoring file changes in the entered directory and raising corresponding events:

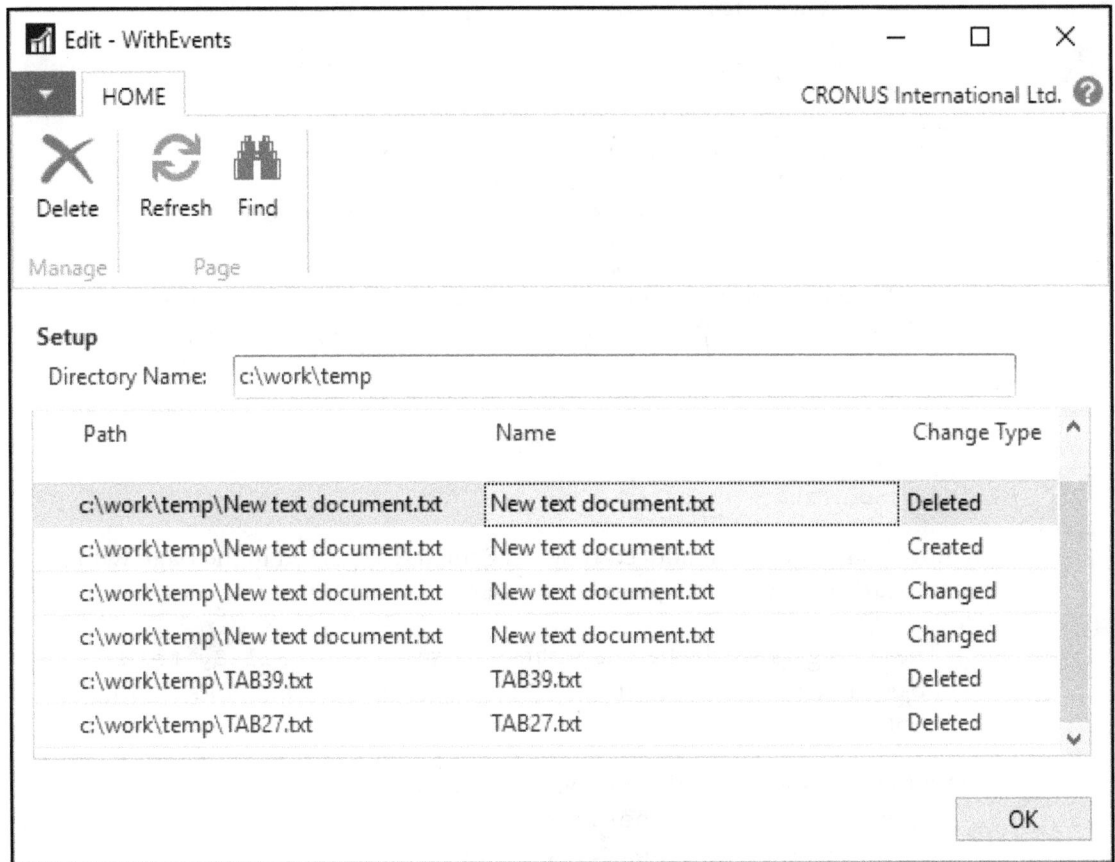

How it works...

The `FileSystemWatcher` DotNet variable declared in Step 9 is the component that is going to raise events. To enable events handling in NAV, the **WithEvents** variable property must be switched to `Yes`. Only global variables can have assigned event handlers in NAV, therefore `FileSystemWatcher` is created in global scope.

When the `WithEvents` property is enabled, you can notice new functions appearing in the code editor. The name of each function begins with the .NET component name `FileSystemWatcher`, followed by an event name (`Changed`, `Deleted`, `Created`, `Renamed`, and so on). These are event handlers called by the component when the corresponding filesystem event happens.

Developing your own .NET class

In the next recipe, we will develop a .NET assembly in C# language and export a class from it to consume the .NET functionality in a `C/SIDE Page` object.

The example is in C#, but assemblies can be developed in any .NET language, such as Visual C++ .NET, VB.NET, or F#.

How to do it...

Custom components developed in the following recipe return a list of NAV services installed in the system.

1. Run Visual Studio and create a new project (click **Project** in the **New** menu). In the **New Project** dialog window, unfold the list of installed templates, select the **Windows** application templates group, and choose the **Class Library** template.
2. Enter the project name in the **Name** field below the templates list: `NavServiceController`.

3. Select the option **Create new solution**. A solution with the same name as the project will be created:

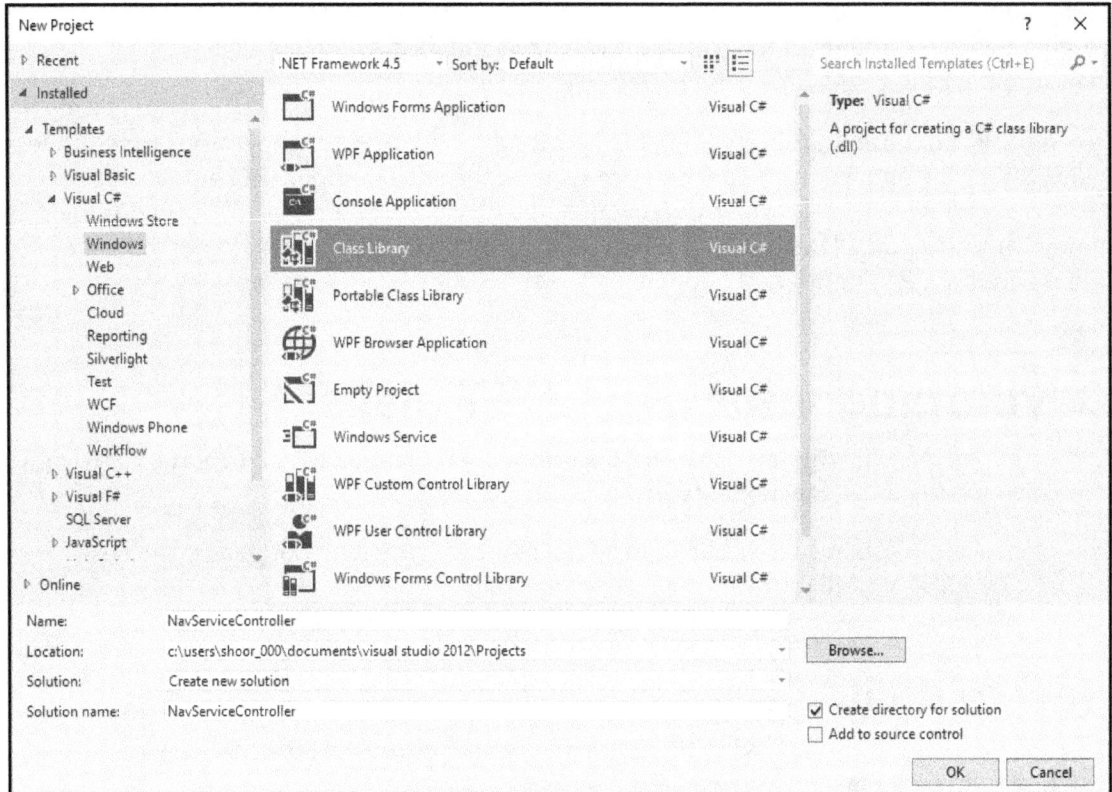

4. A field above the templates selection list specifies the target .NET Framework version. Select the **.Net Framework 4.5** option. Click **OK** – a new C# project will be created.

5. To access the list of services running in the system, a reference to an external `System.ServiceProcess.dll` library is required. Project references are managed in the **Solution Explorer** window. If the window is not available in your environment, open it from the **View** menu.

6. In the solution explorer, right-click on **References** and choose the **Add Reference** option:

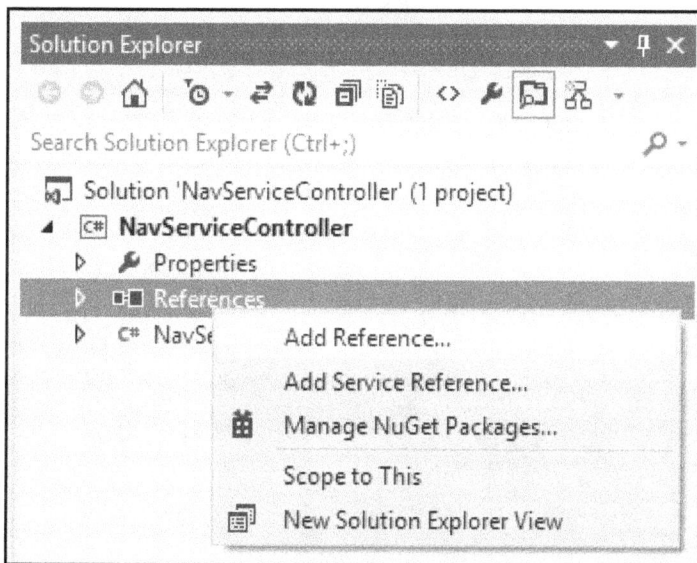

7. The **Add Reference** link opens the **Reference Manager**. Unfold the **Assemblies** tab in the manager, and then locate and select the assembly `System.ServiceProcess` (set a checkmark against the assembly name to include the reference):

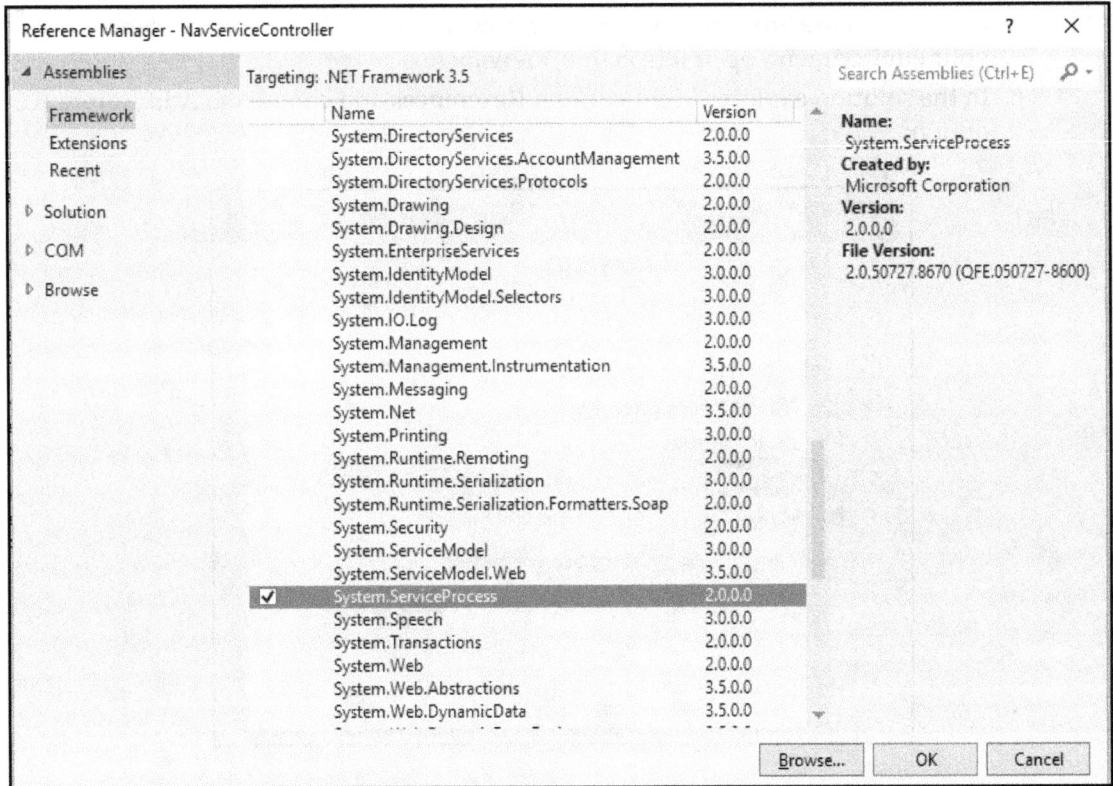

Reference Manager - NavServiceController			? ✕
▲ Assemblies	Targeting: .NET Framework 3.5		Search Assemblies (Ctrl+E) 🔍 ▾

	Name	Version	
Framework	System.DirectoryServices	2.0.0.0	**Name:**
Extensions	System.DirectoryServices.AccountManagement	3.5.0.0	System.ServiceProcess
Recent	System.DirectoryServices.Protocols	2.0.0.0	**Created by:**
▷ Solution	System.Drawing	2.0.0.0	Microsoft Corporation
	System.Drawing.Design	2.0.0.0	**Version:**
▷ COM	System.EnterpriseServices	2.0.0.0	2.0.0.0
	System.IdentityModel	3.0.0.0	**File Version:**
▷ Browse	System.IdentityModel.Selectors	3.0.0.0	2.0.50727.8670 (QFE.050727-8600)
	System.IO.Log	3.0.0.0	
	System.Management	2.0.0.0	
	System.Management.Instrumentation	3.5.0.0	
	System.Messaging	2.0.0.0	
	System.Net	3.5.0.0	
	System.Printing	3.0.0.0	
	System.Runtime.Remoting	2.0.0.0	
	System.Runtime.Serialization	3.0.0.0	
	System.Runtime.Serialization.Formatters.Soap	2.0.0.0	
	System.Security	2.0.0.0	
	System.ServiceModel	3.0.0.0	
	System.ServiceModel.Web	3.5.0.0	
☑	System.ServiceProcess	2.0.0.0	
	System.Speech	3.0.0.0	
	System.Transactions	2.0.0.0	
	System.Web	2.0.0.0	
	System.Web.Abstractions	3.5.0.0	
	System.Web.DynamicData	3.5.0.0	

Browse... | OK | Cancel

8. Click **OK** to return to the code editor. Now include the global namespaces required for the project:

```
using System.Xml;
using System.ServiceProcess;
```

Remove all other using directives inserted automatically.

9. The project namespace, `NavServiceController`, is declared by the framework. Insert a `static` class declaration inside the namespace. The name of the class is `NavServiceInfo`:

```
namespace NavServiceController
{
  public static class NavServiceInfo
  {
  }
}
```

10. The only public method of the class retrieves the list of NAV services and serializes service information into an XML document. Since the class is declared as `static`, all its methods must also be `static`:

```
public static XmlDocument GetNavServices()
{
  XmlDocument xmlDoc = new XmlDocument();
  XmlElement rootNode = xmlDoc.CreateElement("Controllers");
  xmlDoc.AppendChild(rootNode);

  ServiceController[] controllers =
    ServiceController.GetServices();
  foreach (ServiceController controller in controllers)
    if (controller.ServiceName.StartsWith(
      "MicrosoftDynamicsNavServer"))
    rootNode.AppendChild(
      CreateControllerNode(xmlDoc, controller));

  return xmlDoc;
}
```

Two other static methods called here are `CreateControllerNode` and `AppendXmlChildNode`. These methods must also be created in the class `NavServiceInfo`. You can find them in the source files.

11. Build the solution – run the `Build Solution` command in the `Build` menu. The `NavServiceController.dll` assembly file is placed in the `bin\Debug` folder under your solution directory. Copy the `.dll` file to the `Add-in` folder in your NAV Role-Tailored Client installation. The default path for client add-ins is `C:\Program Files (x86)\Microsoft Dynamics NAV\90\RoleTailored Client\Add-ins`.

12. From this step, the development process moves to NAV and C/SIDE. First of all, we need a table to store the list of services received from the .NET component. Create a table in the C/SIDE table designer. Insert four fields:

Field No.	Field Name	Data Type	Length
1	ID	Integer	
2	Display Name	Text	250
3	Service Name	Text	250
4	Status	Text	30

13. Save the table and move to the page designer where the UI part of the component will be designed. Create a `List` page based on the tables from Step 11. Run the page wizard and insert **Display Name**, **Service Name**, and **Status** fields in the page.

14. Open **page** properties and make two changes: first, switch **Editable** to **No**, then set **SourceTableTemporary** to **Yes**.

15. Create a `RefreshServicesList` function in C/AL Globals. This is the action that the user will activate to read the list of services and refresh the contents of the temporary table.

16. The `NavServiceController` object must be declared in this function. Add a reference to your new component, declare a DotNet type variable, and in the `Subtype` field look up the list of assemblies. To select the custom assembly that is not registered in the global assembly cache, open the **Dynamics NAV** tab in the **Assembly List** form.

17. A full list of local variables in the function looks as follows:

Name	DataType	Subtype
NavServiceInfo	DotNet	NavServiceController.NavServiceInfo
XmlDoc	DotNet	System.Xml.XmlDocument
XmlNode	DotNet	System.Xml.XmlNode
NextID	Integer	

18. The function sends a request to the `NavServiceInfo` component and deserializes the XML document received in the response:

```
XmlDoc := NavServiceInfo.GetNavServices;

DELETEALL;
NextID := 1;
FOREACH XmlNode IN XmlDoc.DocumentElement.ChildNodes
DO BEGIN
  ID := NextID;
  "Display Name" :=
    XmlNode.SelectSingleNode('DisplayName').InnerText;
  "Service Name" :=
    XmlNode.SelectSingleNode('ServiceName').InnerText;
  Status := XmlNode.SelectSingleNode('Status').InnerText;
  INSERT;

  NextID += 1;
END;
```

19. In the action designer, insert a `Refresh` action. `RefreshServicesList` is called from the `Refresh - OnAction` action trigger:

```
RefreshServicesList;
```

20. The `NavServiceController` .NET component is configured to run on the server side and must be deployed on the server before the object can be executed. To deploy the assembly, just copy the `NavServiceController.dll` file to the `Add-ins` folder in your NAV Server installation directory. The default installation path is `C:\Program Files\Microsoft Dynamics NAV\90\Service\Add-ins`

21. Now the page can be executed:

How it works...

Developed solutions are compiled into a .NET assembly in a `.dll` file. This should be exposed to a NAV development environment first, and after that to a NAV client or server, depending on which side the .NET code is going to be executed.

Be careful when giving names to the project and its namespaces and classes. These names will identify the .NET variable in NAV. For example, the full name of the `NavServiceInfo` component from the current example is `NavServiceController.NavServiceInfo`.

Here, the first part of the name is the object's namespace from Step 9. The part after the dot (`NavServiceInfo`) is the name of the class declared in the same Step 9.

This namespace is located in the `NavServiceController` assembly – this name is displayed in the **Assembly List** form. Step 17 in the demo is where you see this name in NAV object designer. And this name is defined in Visual Studio in Step 2 – the project name itself.

The `GetNavServices` function described in Step 10 does the main work of reading the list of installed services from the service controller and filtering the list to separate only NAV server instances – these are all services with the name starting with `MicrosoftDynamicsNavServer`.

A refined list is then wrapped in XML and returned to the caller. In Step 19, the `RefreshServicesList` NAV function invokes the .NET component, deserializes the list of services, and inserts them into a table.

Starting processes in separate threads

In the previous recipe, we developed a `NavServiceController` .NET component that is capable of retrieving information on the status of available NAV services. Now we will add control functionality to the same component. With the new version of the service controller, it will be possible to start and stop services. Control tasks will be started in background threads to avoid UI freeze on long-running processes. To report task execution status, the service controller will raise custom events handled by a NAV host object.

Getting ready

The current example is based on the `NavServiceController` assembly developed in the *Developing your own .NET class* recipe. The prerequisite walkthrough must be completed prior to starting the current exercise.

How to do it...

1. Start Visual Studio and open the `NavServiceController` solution from the previous recipe.
2. Open the **Solution Explorer** window and right-click on the **solution name**. Select **Add**, then **Class** from the drop-down menu.

3. Enter the new class name, `NavServiceStatusController`, and click **Add** to accept the suggested class template:

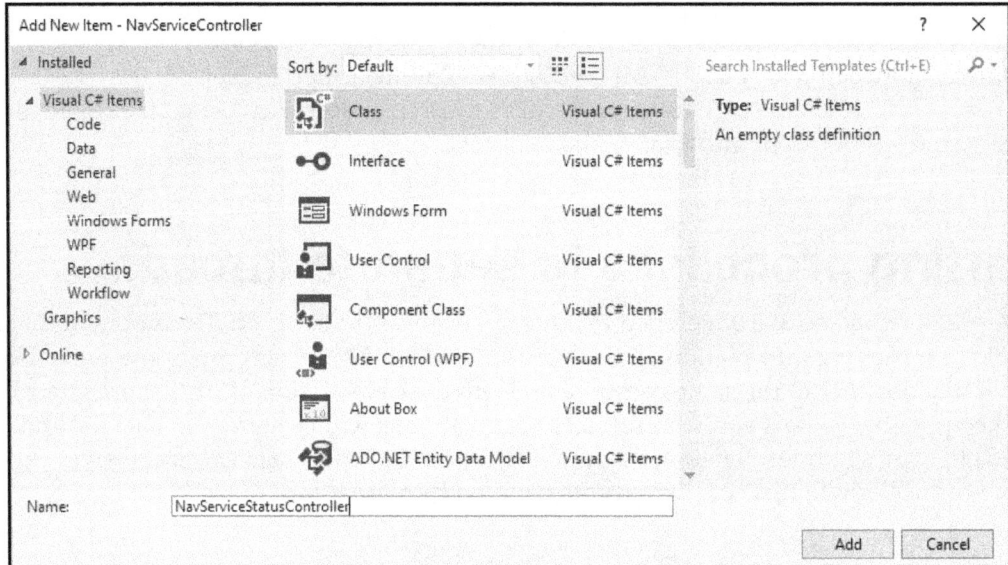

4. The first lines of the code file list the references namespaces. Remove all `using` directives suggested by the development environment and enter the following references:

```
using System;
using System.ServiceProcess;
using System.Threading.Tasks;
```

5. The `NavServiceStatusController` public class is already declared in the `NavServiceController` namespace. Insert three public event handlers in the class. Three types of event that will be sent to the host application (NAV) are: service started, service stopped, and operation failed:

```
namespace NavServiceController
{
  public class NavServiceStatusController
  {
    public event EventHandler<string> ServiceStarted;
    public event EventHandler<string> ServiceStopped;
    public event EventHandler<string> OperationFailed;
  }
}
```

6. One of the functions raising events is `OnServiceStartedEvent`:

```
protected virtual void OnServiceStartedEvent(stringserviceName)
{
  EventHandler<string> handler = ServiceStarted;
  handler(this, serviceName);
}
```

7. The other two are `OnServiceStoppedEvent` and `OnOperationFailedEvent`. They are almost identical to the first function. You can refer to the project source files to view all events declarations.

8. Events are a means of communication between the controller thread and NAV application. They will be triggered by two functions, `StartService` and `StopService`, performing corresponding tasks. The `StartService` function is listed as follows:

```
public bool StartService(string serviceName)
{
  ServiceController controller =
    new ServiceController(serviceName);
  if (controller.Status != ServiceControllerStatus.Stopped)
  return false;

  Task awaitResponse = Task.Run(() =>
  {
    controller.Start();
    controller.WaitForStatus(
      ServiceControllerStatus.Running,
      new TimeSpan(30 * TimeSpan.TicksPerSecond));
  });

  awaitResponse.ContinueWith(
    antecedent => OnServiceStartedEvent(serviceName),
    TaskContinuationOptions.OnlyOnRanToCompletion |
    TaskContinuationOptions.ExecuteSynchronously);

  awaitResponse.ContinueWith(
    antecedent => OnOperationFailedEvent(serviceName),
    TaskContinuationOptions.NotOnRanToCompletion |
    TaskContinuationOptions.ExecuteSynchronously);

  return true;
}
```

9. The `StopService` function runs a background thread the same way as `StartService` does. It is very similar to `StartService`, and is available for your reference in source files.

10. Build the solution and copy the `.dll` file to the client `Add-ins` folder. A server copy is not required, since we are going to run the component of the client.

> It may be required to close the C/SIDE environment before copying the file. If the library is being used by the development environment, copying will fail.

11. Run the NAV development environment. Create a `List` page in the page designer with the `50211 NAV Service` table as a data source. Alternatively, you can modify the `50211 NAV Services List` page created earlier – the new design is based on the older page.

12. Declare a global .NET variable referencing the newly created object:

Name	DataType	Subtype
ServiceStatusController	DotNet	NavServiceController.NavServiceStatusController

13. In the variable properties, set **RunOnClient** to **Yes**, **WithEvents** to **Yes**.

14. Close the variable declarations and open the code editor. In the function `RefreshServicesList`, add the following lines that should precede any other code in the function:

```
IF ISNULL(ServiceStatusController) THEN
    ServiceStatusController :=
    ServiceStatusController.NavServiceStatusController;
```

15. In the page action designer, add two actions buttons below the **Refresh** button that was created earlier. The new actions are `Start` and `Stop`.

16. The service name is already available in action triggers – all the preparatory work for this was done in the *Developing your own .Net class* recipe. All we need to do is call the service controller. In the `Start - OnAction` action trigger, place the following code:

```
IF "Service Name" <> '' THEN
    ServiceStatusController.StartService("Service Name");
```

17. `Stop – OnAction` makes a call the same way:

    ```
    IF "Service Name" <> '' THEN
        ServiceStatusController.StopService("Service Name");
    ```

18. The code editor now shows three empty event handlers created in the C# project in Visual Studio: `ServiceStatusController::ServiceStarted`, `ServiceStatusController::ServiceStopped`, and `ServiceStatusController::OperationFailed`.

19. Insert C/AL code displaying an appropriate message on each of the events. For the `ServiceStarted` event, the message would be:

    ```
    MESSAGE('Service started ' + e);
    ```

20. Update other event handlers respectively, then save and compile the object. Changing the status of OS services is considered an administrative task and requires elevated privileges. To test this code, run the NAV client with administrative privileges (run as administrator). To be able to run the page directly from the object designer, you must run the NAV development environment under the same elevated permission set.

How it works...

The `StartService` function shown in Step 8, and its sibling `StopService`, both initiate a background task executed on the application thread pool. A `Task` object created by the function starts a thread and runs the code received as a lambda expression in the argument to the `Run` method.

Inside the thread, a service controller sends the `Start` command to the NAV service and waits for the response. Two parameters of the `ServiceController.WaitForStatus` function are the expected service status (Running) and the timeout (30 seconds).

A new task is executed asynchronously, which means that the main application thread waits for user input immediately after starting the task. The user does not see the delay while the thread is waiting for the service to change its state.

To notify the main thread of the task result, a continuation task is scheduled by calling the `ContinueWith` task method. The first method parameter is a delegate method (or another lambda expression, as in the preceding example) that will be executed when the first task is completed. .NET Framework multithreading capabilities allow the developer to specify conditions for the continuation task. We use continuation conditions to raise different events depending on the operation outcome.

`ContinueWith` is called for the first time with the `OnlyOnRanToCompletion` option. This branch applies only to successfully completed tasks, and we call the `OnServiceStartedEvent` event to send the notification. The second branch is executed only if the task could not complete within the given timeout – this continuation option is `NotOnRanToCompletion`. The event sent in this case is `OnOperationFailedEvent`.

5

Extending C/AL with COM Components

In this chapter, we will cover the following recipes:

- Using COM type libraries in C/AL
- Mapping COM datatypes to C/AL
- Disposing of COM objects
- Working with the Variant datatype
- Sending data to the Excel automation server
- Creating a Word document using automation objects
- Creating and registering a COM component that can be used in NAV

Introduction

The **Component Object Model** (**COM**) is a platform-independent interoperability model. Each COM library is a piece of software that can be bound to a client application at runtime. NAV application code can use classes and interfaces exported by COM type libraries, although this support has certain limitations:

- COM automation objects can run only on the NAV client. Server-side automation objects are not supported.
- Automation objects cannot run on the NAV Web client.
- Only non-visual components are supported.
- Exception handling is not supported.
- In NAV 2016, C/SIDE cannot receive events from automation servers.

Using COM type libraries in C/AL

A COM type library is a binary file containing the definition of a COM component.

How to do it...

To illustrate the principles of working with OLE automation in NAV, we will create a simple codeunit that reads data from a NAV server configuration file that is stored in XML format.

1. Create a `codeunit` object in C/SIDE object designer.
2. All code will be placed in the `OnRun` trigger of the `codeunit`. Open local variables of the trigger and create a `XMLDoc` variable. In the **DataType** field, select the **Automation** option.
3. Click the **assist** button in the **Subtype** field to open a list of automation objects registered in the system. At first, the list is blank. Click on the lookup button in the **Automation Server** field to see the list of available automation servers.
4. Select **Microsoft XML, v6.0** in the **Automation Server List** form:

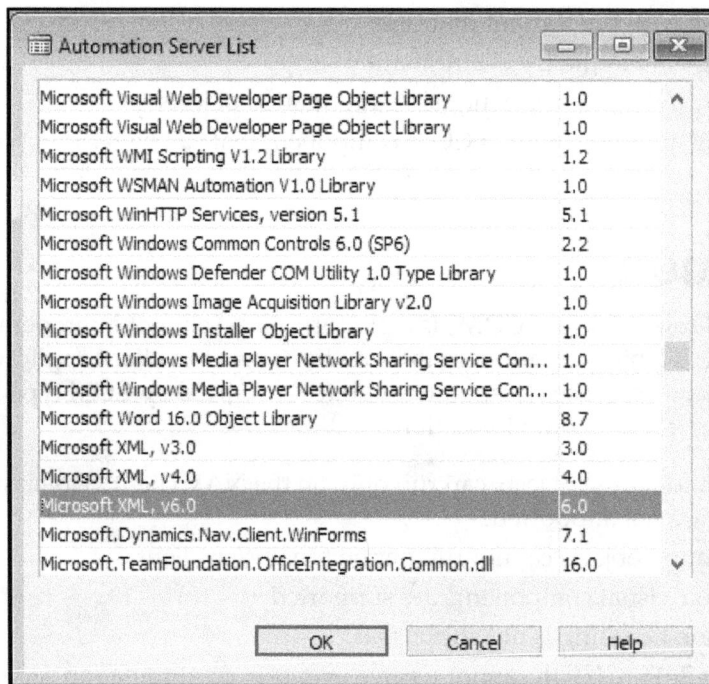

Automation Server List		
Microsoft Visual Web Developer Page Object Library	1.0	
Microsoft Visual Web Developer Page Object Library	1.0	
Microsoft WMI Scripting V1.2 Library	1.2	
Microsoft WSMAN Automation V1.0 Library	1.0	
Microsoft WinHTTP Services, version 5.1	5.1	
Microsoft Windows Common Controls 6.0 (SP6)	2.2	
Microsoft Windows Defender COM Utility 1.0 Type Library	1.0	
Microsoft Windows Image Acquisition Library v2.0	1.0	
Microsoft Windows Installer Object Library	1.0	
Microsoft Windows Media Player Network Sharing Service Con...	1.0	
Microsoft Windows Media Player Network Sharing Service Con...	1.0	
Microsoft Word 16.0 Object Library	8.7	
Microsoft XML, v3.0	3.0	
Microsoft XML, v4.0	4.0	
Microsoft XML, v6.0	6.0	
Microsoft.Dynamics.Nav.Client.WinForms	7.1	
Microsoft.TeamFoundation.OfficeIntegration.Common.dll	16.0	

OK   Cancel   Help

5. After you click **OK** and return to the previous form, the list of automation objects will show objects exported from the selected library. Select the **DOMDocument60** object and confirm the choice:

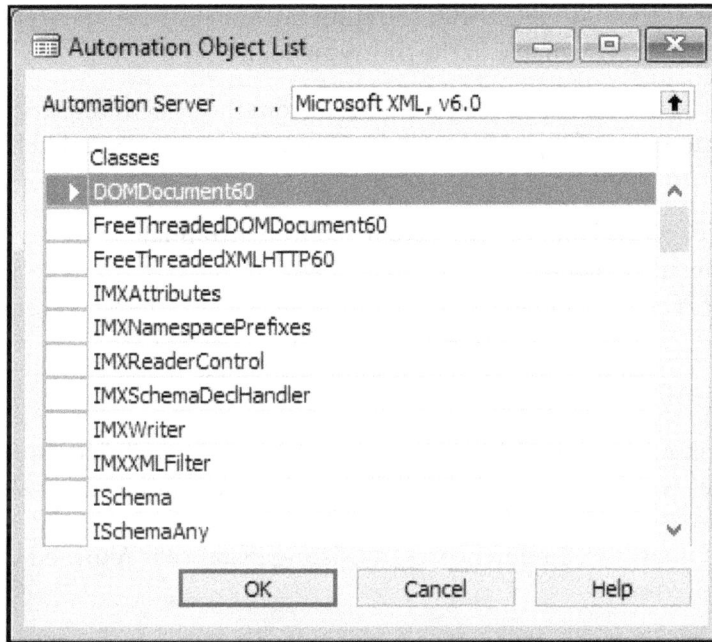

6. Create another `Automation` type variable in `OnRun` locals:

7. The trigger code is as follows:

```
CREATE(XMLDoc,FALSE,TRUE);
XMLDoc.load(
'C:\Program Files\Microsoft Dynamics
  NAV\90Service\CustomSettings.config');
XmlAttribute :=
  XMLDoc.selectSingleNode(
    '/appSettings/add[@key="DatabaseServer"]/@value');
MESSAGE(FORMAT(XmlAttribute.value));
```

8. Save and compile the `codeunit` with ID 50301 and name it `Automation Basics`, and then run it from the development environment.

How it works...

The first steps of the recipe declare a variable of the `Automation` datatype. This type is used in C/AL to refer to OLE/COM automation servers. Variable declaration is very similar to the process of creating a .NET variable. After selecting the `Automation` datatype, a list of registered type libraries is available in the **Subtype** field.

Step 4 shows a list of COM type libraries retrieved from the system registry. When a library is selected, the **Automation Object List** window contains objects exported from the selected library.

Before an `Automation` variable can be used, it must be instantiated. This is illustrated in Step 7. The first line in the code sample calls the `CREATE` function to create an instance of the automation server. The function has three parameters and returns a `boolean` operation status:

```
[Ok :=] CREATE(Automation [,NewServer] [,OnClient])
```

The first parameter, `Automation`, is the variable to be instantiated. The `NewServer` parameter specifies whether an existing instance of the automation server should be reused, if it exists. If the `NewServer` parameter is `FALSE`, a new instance is created every time `CREATE` is called. Otherwise, a reference to an existing instance is returned whenever possible.

The last parameter, `OnClient`, specifies if the instance of the automation server should be created on the client (`TRUE`) or on the server (`FALSE`).

> In NAV 2016, the `OnClient` argument must always evaluate to `TRUE`, since server-side automation components are not supported.

Mapping COM datatypes to C/AL

The component object model was developed as a platform-independent and programming language-independent object-oriented system. To avoid dependency on any language-specific type system, COM implements its own set of datatypes. When working with COM interfaces, you have to deal with the COM type system, which is seamlessly integrated with C/AL datatypes. In the next example, we will see how NAV datatypes correspond to COM types.

How to do it...

1. Create a page object in C/SIDE object designer. Create a blank page without the page wizard and source table – required page content will be configured manually.

2. Open the properties for the new page and change the value of the **PageType** property from the default value **Card** to **Worksheet**.

3. Global variables required for the walkthrough are listed in the following table:

Name	DataType
FromFileName	Text
ToFileName	Text
FileSize	Integer
FileCharset	Text
NoOfCharsToCopy	Integer

4. All of these variables serve as data sources for page fields. Create a page content area, name it `Parameters`, and insert five data fields under the content area:

Type	SubType	SourceExpr	Name
Container	ContentArea		Parameters
Field		FromFileName	FromFileName
Field		ToFileName	ToFileName
Field		FileSize	FileSize
Field		FileCharset	FileCharset
Field		NoOfCharsToCopy	BytesToCopy

5. In the **Action Designer** page, create an action container with the **ActionItems** type and insert two action buttons: **FileInfo** and **Copy**.

6. Open the C/AL editor from the action designer and declare local variables in the `FileInfo - OnAction` action trigger:

Name	DataType	Subtype
Stream	Automation	'Microsoft ActiveX Data Objects 6.1 Library'.Stream
FileContent	Text	

7. The action trigger code reads the file to retrieve the file info:

```
CREATE(Stream,FALSE,TRUE);
Stream.Open;
Stream.LoadFromFile(FromFileName);
FileSize := Stream.Size;
FileCharset := Stream.Charset;
```

8. Add the following local variables in the `Copy` action trigger:

Name	DataType	Subtype
InStream	Automation	'Microsoft ActiveX Data Objects 6.1 Library'.Stream
OutStream	Automation	'Microsoft ActiveX Data Objects 6.1 Library'.Stream
FileContent	Text	

9. And enter the trigger code as follows:

```
CREATE(InStream,FALSE,TRUE);
CREATE(OutStream,FALSE,TRUE);
InStream.Open;
InStream.LoadFromFile(FromFileName);
FileContent := InStream.ReadText(NoOfCharsToCopy);
InStream.Close;

OutStream.Open;
OutStream.WriteText(FileContent);
OutStream.SaveToFile(ToFileName);
OutStream.Close;
```

10. Compile and run the page. Enter the name of the file you want to copy. The **File Info** action will read the size and the charset of the file and fill in the corresponding fields in the page.

Enter the name of the destination file and the number of characters to copy to the new file, then click the **Copy** action button. The requested number of characters will be copied into the new file:

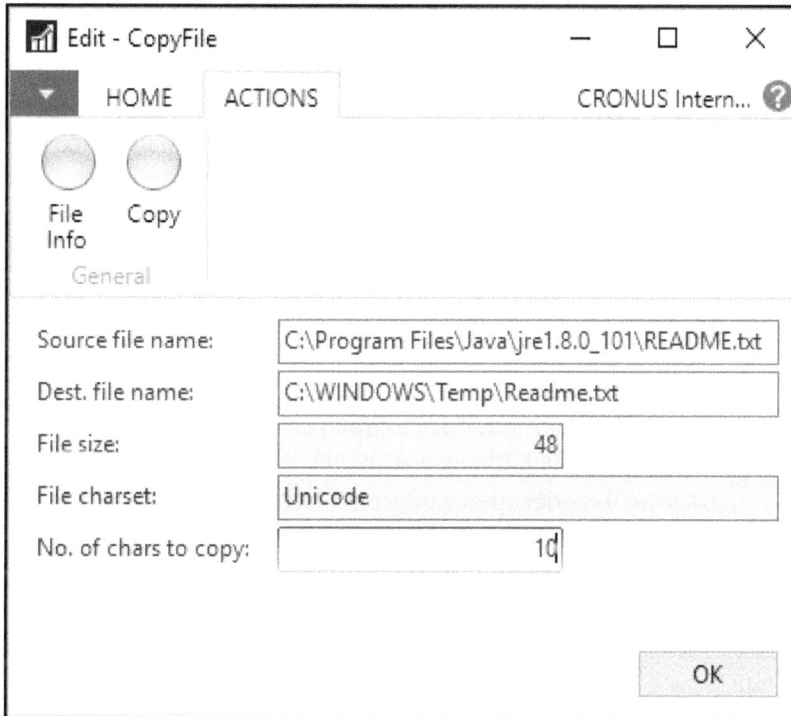

How it works...

If you review any of the functions called from automation libraries in the preceding example, you can see that most datatype names do not correspond to those in C/AL. For example, a prototype of the `ReadText` function in the C/AL Symbol menu looks as follows:

```
[BSTR ReadText :=] ReadText([LONG NumChars])
```

The return type is BSTR, and the only parameter has a LONG datatype. In the COM type system, BSTR represents text data, and LONG is a 4-byte signed integer. In Step 9 of the previous example, this function is called with a NAV Integer argument, and the return value is assigned to a Text variable.

Disposing of COM objects

A C/AL variable of the Automation type is only a reference to a COM object that is created and disposed in runtime. Object instances are created with the CREATE function, and destroyed by the Garbage Collector when the variable leaves the scope. Sometimes it is necessary to destroy an object instance explicitly or ensure that the instance does not exist before calling the CREATE function on the variable. C/AL functions disposing of automation objects will be described in the current recipe.

How to do it...

1. A new page will be required for the following example. Create a blank page in C/SIDE. This is only a container for action buttons, so choose to create a blank page without any source table or wizard.
2. Open the page actions designer and insert two action buttons: GetProcessorSpeed and GetMemorySize.
3. Open the C/AL code designer and access the list of global variables. Declare an Automation variable:

Name	DataType	Subtype
ShellControl	Automation	Microsoft Shell Controls And Automation.Shell

4. Declare a GetSystemInfo global function. Add one parameter:

Name	DataType
Name	Text

5. Type the function code as shown:

```
CREATE(ShellControl,FALSE,TRUE);
MESSAGE(FORMAT(ShellControl.GetSystemInformation(Name)));
CLEAR(ShellControl);
```

6. The `GetSystemInfo` function should be called from two action triggers. The `GetProcessorSpeed` action invokes the function to retrieve the speed of the CPU:

```
GetSystemInfo('ProcessorSpeed');
```

7. Code in the `GetMemorySize` action button reads the size of the computer's RAM:

```
GetSystemInfo('PhysicalMemoryInstalled');
```

The object is ready to run.

How it works...

In the current example, one global Automation variable, `ShellControl`, is used by two C/AL functions. Since the variable is declared in the global context, it never goes out of scope as long as the page is active. Once created, it could be used by all code within the same object without the need to recreate it again.

Sometimes the situation demands the object should be destroyed when it is not used by client code – for example, if it is rarely used, but consumes a large volume of memory. Garbage Collector cannot dispose of `ShellControl` until the page is closed. So if we want to remove it, this must be done explicitly in the C/AL code.

The `GetSystemInfo` function in Step 5, which creates the shell object, calls the `CLEAR` function after using the object, to destroy the instance. When the function is called next time, the object has to be created again.

The current state of an automation variable can be retrieved with the `ISCLEAR` function. Its return value is `FALSE` if the automation object has been instantiated, and `TRUE` otherwise.

Working with the Variant datatype

The Variant datatype is widely used in the Component Object Model to represent variables with no explicitly defined type. The datatype of the value stored in a Variant variable can be defined at runtime, when the value is assigned.

C/AL supports Variant variables and a variety of functions that help to identify the type of a variable content.

The following example runs a database query through the **ActiveX Data Objects (ADO)** library. Field values in the resulting recordset are returned as Variant data that can be interpreted by the client C/AL code.

How to do it...

1. The code for this example will be implemented in a `Page` object. Run the NAV object designer and create a page. Select the **Customer** table as a data source from the page, and then select the **List** page type in the page wizard.
2. In the **Action Designer** page, create a `Show Balance` action button. Open the action trigger code and declare local variables required in the function:

Name	DataType	Subtype
Connection	Automation	Microsoft ActiveX Data Objects 6.1 Library.Connection
Recordset	Automation	Microsoft ActiveX Data Objects 6.1 Library.Recordset
QueryString	Text	

3. Copy the function code:

```
CREATE(Connection,FALSE,TRUE);

QueryString :=
  STRSUBSTNO(
    'SELECT MAX([Posting Date]), SUM(Amount) FROM ' +
    '[CRONUS International Ltd_$Detailed Cust_ Ledg_ Entry] ' +
    'WHERE [Customer No_] = ''%1''',"No.");
Connection.Open(
  'Provider=SQLNCLI11;Server=localhost\NAVDEMO;' +
  'Database=Demo Database NAV (9-0);Trusted_Connection=yes;');
Recordset := Connection.Execute(QueryString);
```

```
MESSAGE(
  'Balance of customer %1 on %2 is %3',FormatField(Name),
  FormatField(Recordset.Fields.Item(0).Value),
  FormatField(Recordset.Fields.Item(1).Value));
Connection.Close;
```

4. The `FormatField` function deals with Variant values received from the ADO library. Declare the function in C/AL globals.

5. Open the C/AL locals window. In the **Return Value** tab, assign the `Text` return type to the function.

6. In the **Parameters** tab of the C/AL locals form, insert a function parameter:

Name	DataType
FieldValue	Variant

7. The code of the function `FormatField` is as following:

```
IF FieldValue.ISDATETIME THEN
  EXIT(FORMAT(FieldValue,0,'<Day,2>-<Month,2>-<Year4>'));

IF FieldValue.ISDECIMAL THEN
  EXIT(
    FORMAT(
      FieldValue,0,'<Sign><Integer Thousand><Decimals>'));

EXIT(FORMAT(FieldValue));
```

How it works...

To keep the example simple, the query is run against the NAV demo database, although it is not recommended to do so in a live environment.

Normally, a database connection is created to read data from external sources – any non-NAV database. When an internal C/AL function, such as `FIND`, is executed, the NAV platform runs a permission check to verify that the user running the query is authorized to access the requested data. Queries executed through ADO objects will bypass internal NAV permission configuration, but require the user to have permission to run queries on the database server.

In the first two steps of the recipe, automation variables are declared. Connection objects are instantiated in the first line of Step 3.

The next, lines prepare a query string and a connection string. The SQL query depends only on the database structure, which is the standard NAV demo database. Connection strings passed to the `Conection.Open` function can vary depending on your server configuration. The key component of the connection string that is subject to change is the data provider name: **Provider=SQLNCLI11**, which stands for **SQL Server Native Client 11.0 (SQLNC11)**. If you have another version of the SQL native client installed, look for the correct provider name in the **ODBC Data Source Administrator** in the **Control Panel**.

The table that is queried in the code in Step 3 is `CRONUS International Ltd_$Detailed Cust_ Ledg_ Entry`. Inside NAV, this table is seen as `Detailed Cust. Ledg. Enry`. But in the SQL database its name is prefixed with the name of the company. To query the table with external tools, we must use the name as it appears in SQL Server instead of the internal NAV table name. If you execute this example on a localized version of the demo database, the company name may be different. Replace `CRONUS International Ltd_` with the name of your demo company.

When the connection is ready, the query is executed by calling the `Connection.Execute` function. It returns a `Recordset` object containing the data received from the data provider. The `Recordset` object is another Automation type variable is declared at the beginning of the example. But, unlike, the `Connection` object, it does not have to be created explicitly in the client code – we do not call `CREATE` on the `recordset`. Instead, the instance is created inside the Connection automation server and returned to the Automation controller.

The `Recordset` object contains data stored in a collection of `Field` objects. Each field can be accessed by its index through the Item property. Each field is a `Variant` variable that can contain various data. To identify the actual datatype of the field and format it accordingly, the `FormatField` function is used. It is described in Step 4 through Step 7. The function accepts a `Variant` parameter and determines the actual type of the variable content via the `ISDATETIME` and `ISDECIMAL` functions. The `ISDATETIME` function returns `TRUE` if the value of the `Variant` variable, `FieldValue`, has the `DateTime` type. The `ISDECIMAL` function will yield `TRUE` for a decimal value. We do not expect any other type to be returned by the query, since the query field list is limited to the entry posting the date and amount, but C/AL provides similar functions for all supported types that can be stored in a `Variant` variable.

Finally, when the type of the field is resolved, the `FORMAT` function is applied to the field value with formatting parameters corresponding to the datatype. As you can see, `FORMAT` accepts a `Variant` argument and formats it as if it were a normal DateTime or Decimal value.

Sending data to the Excel automation server

The automation datatype in C/AL is frequently used in practice for communication with Microsoft Office applications that export their API through automation servers.

Now we will export the contents of the **Customer** table from a `codeunit` using the COM automation library.

How to do it....

1. Create a new `codeunit` in the object designer. This will be the object exporting data through an automation server.
2. Triggering `OnRun` of the `codeunit` will instantiate the automation server and iterate on records of the **Customer** table to export each of them. First declare local variables in the trigger:

Name	DataType	Subtype
Customer	Record	Customer
ExcelApp	Automation	Microsoft Excel 16.0 Object Library.Application
Workbook	Automation	Microsoft Excel 16.0 Object Library.Workbook
Worksheet	Automation	Microsoft Excel 16.0 Object Library.Worksheet
RowNo	Integer	

> The **Microsoft Excel 16 Object Library** version in variable declarations corresponds to Microsoft Office 2016. If you have another version of MS Office installed on your dev computer, the library version will differ. Choose an appropriate version in the **Automation Server List** window.

3. Type the trigger code:

```
CREATE(ExcelApp,FALSE,TRUE);
Workbook := ExcelApp.Workbooks.Add;
Worksheet := Workbook.ActiveSheet;
Worksheet.Name := 'Customers';

ExcelApp.Visible := TRUE;

FillColumnHeaders(Worksheet,Customer);
```

```
RowNo := 1;
IF Customer.FINDSET THEN BEGIN
  REPEAT
    RowNo += 1;
    ExportRecord(Worksheet,Customer,RowNo);
  UNTIL Customer.NEXT = 0;
END;
```

4. The OnRun trigger refers to several functions that do not exist yet. Declare the first of them in C/AL globals. This is a FillCellValue function. It does not return any value, but has five parameters:

Name	DataType	Subtype
Worksheet	Automation	'Microsoft Excel 16.0 Object Library'.Worksheet
ColumnNo	Integer	
RowNo	Integer	
CellValue	Text	
FontBold	Integer	

5. Besides parameters, the function needs two local variables:

Name	DataType	Subtype
Column	Automation	'Microsoft Excel 16.0 Object Library'.Range
Cell	Automation	'Microsoft Excel 16.0 Object Library'.Range

6. The function sets a value of a worksheet cell identified by the parameters ColumnNo and RowNo:

```
Column := Worksheet.Columns.Item(ColumnNo);
Cell := Column.Rows.Item(RowNo);
Cell.Value := CellValue;
Cell.Font.Bold := FontBold;
```

7. The `FillColumnHeaders` function goes through the list of table fields to create column headers in the worksheet. Parameters of the function are as follows:

Name	DataType	Subtype
Worksheet	Automation	'Microsoft Excel 16.0 Object Library'.Worksheet
Customer	Record	Customer

8. Do not leave the function's local declaration. Insert the following local variables:

Name	DataType
RecRef	RecordRef
FieldRef	FieldRef
ColNo	Integer

9. The function code is as follows:

```
RecRef.OPEN(DATABASE::Customer);
FOR ColNo := 1 TO RecRef.FIELDCOUNT DO BEGIN
   FieldRef := RecRef.FIELDINDEX(ColNo);
   IF UPPERCASE(FORMAT(FieldRef.CLASS)) IN
      ['NORMAL','FLOWFIELD'] THEN
      FillCellValue(Worksheet,ColNo,1,FieldRef.CAPTION,1);
END;
```

10. The last function to declare is `ExportRecord`. Declare its parameters:

Name	DataType	Subtype
Worksheet	Automation	'Microsoft Excel 16.0 Object Library'.Worksheet
Customer	Record	Customer
RowNo	Integer	

11. Insert local variables in the function:

Name	DataType
RecRef	RecordRef
FieldRef	FieldRef
FieldClass	Text
ColNo	Integer

12. The function code is as follows:

```
RecRef.GETTABLE(Customer);
FOR ColNo := 1 TO RecRef.FIELDCOUNT DO BEGIN
  FieldRef := RecRef.FIELDINDEX(ColNo);
  FieldClass := UPPERCASE(FORMAT(FieldRef.CLASS));
  IF FieldClass IN ['NORMAL','FLOWFIELD'] THEN BEGIN
    IF FieldClass = 'FLOWFIELD' THEN
      FieldRef.CALCFIELD;

    FillCellValue(
        Worksheet,ColNo,RowNo,FORMAT(FieldRef.VALUE),0);
  END;
END;
```

How it works...

The code sample starts with the declaration of automation variables and the instantiation of the Excel automation server in Step 1 to Step 3. The `ExcelApp` variable contains a link to the running instance of the Excel application, and this is the only automation variable that has to be created by calling the `CREATE` function. All other objects are managed by the Excel application itself. A new workbook is created by calling the `Add` method on the Workbooks collection of the Excel instance: `Workbook := ExcelApp.Workbooks.Add`. This will add a default workbook that already contains a blank worksheet, which automatically becomes active and can be selected by calling `Workbook.ActiveSheet`.

The following line `ExcelApp.Visible := TRUE` shows the running application (before that it was hidden from the user). It can be done at any point after creating the application instance. We do it rather early, before any data is generated, because exporting through an automation server is a slow process. When the application is visible throughout the export, the user won't have the impression that the application freezes.

Loop in Step 3 will iterate on records in the **Cutomer** table. In each iteration, an `ExportRecord` function receives an active Excel worksheet and the current record to be exported, along with the row number where they will be inserted.

Step 6 illustrates how a value is inserted into a cell. Usually, rows in an Excel worksheet are numbered, while columns are marked with letters. And the simplest way to access a worksheet cell is to use the same reference style. For example, cell `A1` would be `Worksheet.Range.Item('A1')`. In the current example, we don't have a fixed set of columns, but rather refer to them via indexes as well. This is why the approach used in Step 6 is a bit tricky – first a column is selected by its index, then a particular cell from the found column.

Creating a Word document using automation objects

Microsoft Word exposes its object model through COM automation the same way as Excel. The following example demonstrates how to export a dataset into a Word document via Automation variables. We will create a document containing a table and export a list of items in the Where-used report into the table.

The Where-used report is a list of assembled items, which includes the given item as a component in their bill of materials.

How to do it...

1. Open C/SIDE page designer and create a list page. In the **Table** field, select the **Item** table. Run the page wizard and include two table fields in the page: **No.** and **Description**.
2. After completing the wizard, open the page action designer and insert an `Export` action button that will be used to trigger document creation. In the `Export` – `OnAction` C/AL trigger insert one line of code:

    ```
    CreateWordDocument("No.");
    ```

3. In C/AL globals, declare the `CreateWordDocument` function just referenced in Step 2. One parameter on the function is `ItemNo` of type `Code[20]`.

4. Declare local variables in `CreateWordDocument` function:

Name	DataType	Subtype
Item	Record	Item
WordApp	Automation	'Microsoft Word 16.0 Object Library'.Application
Document	Automation	'Microsoft Word 16.0 Object Library'.Document

5. This function performs initial automation server instantiation to pass it further:

```
CREATE(WordApp,FALSE,TRUE);
Document := WordApp.Documents.Add;
InsertParagraph(Document,'Where used',1,16);

Item.GET(ItemNo);
ExportWhereUsedList(Document,Item);

WordApp.Visible := TRUE;
```

6. Declare a `InsertParagraph` function, which inserts a text paragraph into a Word document. Its parameters are listed in the following table:

Name	DataType	Subtype
Document	Automation	'Microsoft Word 16.0 Object Library'.Document
ParagraphText	Text	
FontBold	Integer	
FontSize	Integer	

7. One local variable is required in the function:

Name	DataType	Subtype
Paragraph	Automation	'Microsoft Word 16.0 Object Library'.Paragraph

8. Now code the function:

```
Paragraph := Document.Content.Paragraphs.Add;
Paragraph.Range.Text := ParagraphText;
Paragraph.Range.Font.Bold := FontBold;
Paragraph.Range.Font.Size := FontSize;
Paragraph.Range.InsertParagraphAfter;
```

9. The last function, `ExportWhereUsedList`, collects assembly bills of materials where the item is used and exports them into a table in the document. Declare the function, then its two parameters:

Name	DataType	Subtype
Document	Automation	'Microsoft Word 16.0 Object Library'.Document
ComponentItem	Record	Item

10. Create a list of the function's local variables:

Name	DataType	Subtype
BOMComponent	Record	BOM Component
ParentItem	Record	Item
Table	Automation	'Microsoft Word 16.0 Object Library'.Table
Range	Automation	'Microsoft Word 16.0 Object Library'.Range
Paragraph	Automation	'Microsoft Word 16.0 Object Library'.Paragraph
EndOfDocBookmark	Variant	
I	Integer	

11. Type the function code:

```
BOMComponent.SETRANGE(Type,BOMComponent.Type::Item);
BOMComponent.SETRANGE("No.",ComponentItem."No.");
IF BOMComponent.FINDSET THEN BEGIN
  InsertParagraph(
 Document,'Component item: ' + ComponentItem."No." + ' '
 + ComponentItem.Description,1,12);

  EndOfDocBookmark := '\endofdoc';
  Range := Document.Bookmarks.Item(EndOfDocBookmark).Range;
  Paragraph := Document.Content.Paragraphs.Add;
```

```
Table := Document.Tables.Add(Range,BOMComponent.COUNT,3);

REPEAT
  I += 1;
  ParentItem.GET(BOMComponent."Parent Item No.");
  Table.Cell(I,1).Range.Text := ParentItem."No.";
  Table.Cell(I,2).Range.Text := ParentItem.Description;
  Table.Cell(I,3).Range.Text :=
    FORMAT(BOMComponent."Quantity per");
  Table.Rows.Item(I).Range.Font.Bold := 0;
UNTIL BOMComponent.NEXT = 0;

Table.Columns.Item(1).AutoFit;
Table.Columns.Item(2).AutoFit;
END;
```

How it works...

The first two steps create a page object where the code will reside. In Steps 3 and 4, automation variables required to access Word object models are declared. As in the *Sending data to the Excel automation server* recipe, only the automation server controlling the WordApp Word application must be instantiated explicitly in the client code. The WordApp object will create all dependencies. For example, a new document is created by calling the Add function on the collection of documents: Document := WordApp.Documents.Add.

Text inside a document is structured in paragraphs. A paragraph must be created in order to insert any text data into a document. This is done in the InsertParagraph function in Step 6. Note that simply creating a paragraph is insufficient to show it. The paragraph must be assigned to a specific position in the document after it is created and formatted. Hence the last statement in the function is Paragraph.Range.InsertParagraphAfter, which inserts the paragraph in the last position in the document, after all other content.

The last function, ExportWhereUsedList, in Step 9 to Step 11 creates a table containing the list of items. Like any other document content, the table is created in its separate paragraph. To identify the position of the table paragraph, we refer to it via a predefined document constant \endofdoc, which refers to the end of the document content.

After identifying the location of the table, we call the Add function on the collection of document tables to create the object:

```
Table := Document.Tables.Add(Range,BOMComponent.COUNT,3)
```

The first argument, `Range`, is the position of the new table; the remaining two are the number of rows and columns, respectively.

Inside a loop on the `BOMComponent` table, cells are filled with data and formatted. In the last statement of Step 11, `ExportWhereUsedList` invokes `AutoFit` on table columns to adjust the column width to the content.

Finally, the application is displayed on the screen: `WordApp.Visible := TRUE`.

Creating and registering a COM component that can be used in NAV

We will implement a simple custom COM component that exposes an interface to multiply two decimal numbers.

How to do it...

1. Start Visual Studio and create a new project. The initial steps repeat those from the *Developing your own .NET class* recipe from `Chapter 4`, *.NET Interoperability in C/AL* – you need to create a project based on a Class Library template. Name the project `NAVAutomationServer` and choose to create a new solution for the project.

2. In the new project, remove all automatically generated using directives and insert one instead:

   ```
   using System.Runtime.InteropServices;
   ```

3. The following is code of the exported class:

   ```
   namespace NavAutomationServer
   {
     [ComVisible(true)]
     public interface IMultiplication
     {
       int Multiply(int x, int y);
     }


     [ComVisible(true)]
     [ProgId("My.TestClass")]
   ```

```
public class Multiplication : IMultiplication
{
  public int Multiply(int x, int y)
  {
    return x * y;
  }
}
}
```

4. Each COM class or interface is registered in the system registry and identified by its **Globally Unique IDentifier** (**GUID**). To generate a GUID for COM declaration, run a Visual Studio tool **Create GUID** from the **Tools** menu.

5. The generated identifier can be presented in different forms for different purposes. For our COM interface, we need an attribute presentation **[Guid(...)]**. Choose the required form in the list and click **Copy**:

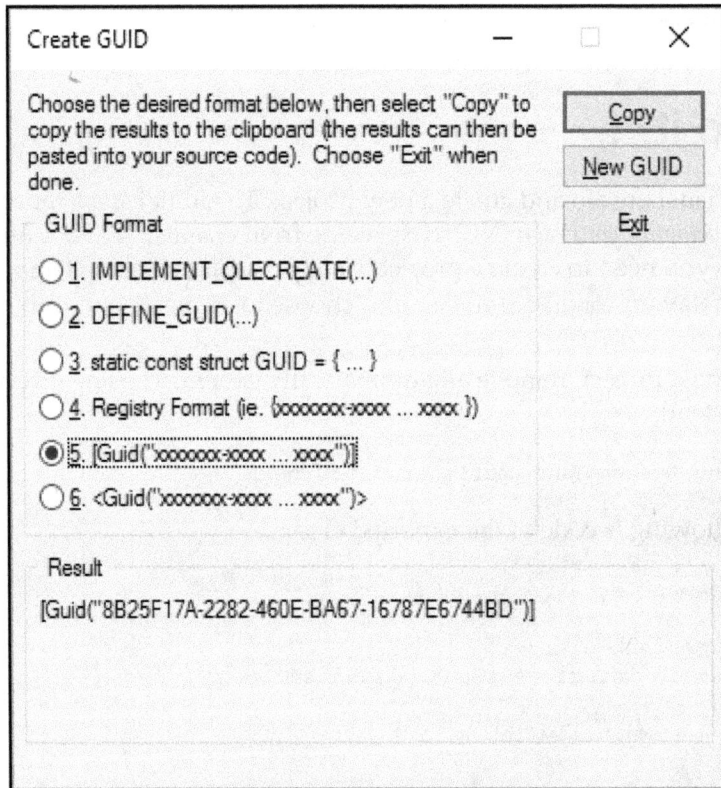

6. The new GUID is copied into the clipboard. Return to the code editor and insert it before the `interface` keyword. The complete interface declaration should look as follows:

```
[Guid("F74FD5F7-B5FA-4939-892C-A4F222DFBF1D")]
[ComVisible(true)]
public interface ITestInterface
{
    int Multiply(int x, int y);
}
```

7. Click **New GUID** in form **Create GUID** to generate a new identifier for the `Multiplication` class, implementing the `IMultiplication` interface.

8. Open project properties from the **Project** menu. In the **Build** tab, make sure that the **Platform** target is **x64**. If your build is targeting another platform, change it to **x64**.

9. In the same tab, enable the **Register for COM interop** option.

> Visual Studio must be run with administrator credentials to register a COM component in the system registry.

10. Close the properties and build the project. A library will be generated and automatically registered.

11. In NAV C/SIDE, create a codeunit to test the new automation server.

12. In the `OnRun` trigger, open C/AL locals and declare two variables exported from the COM type library:

Name	DataType	Subtype
Multiplication	Automation	'NAVAutomationServer'. Multiplication
IMultiplication	Automation	'NAVAutomationServer'.IMultiplication

```
CREATE(Multiplication,FALSE,TRUE);
IMultiplication := Multiplication;
MESSAGE(FORMAT(IMultiplication.Multiply(2,8)));
```

How it works...

The .NET implementation of COM interfaces hides technical details from the developer. The development of a COM component without the .NET framework requires the definition of interfaces in **Interface Definition Language** (**IDL**) and its implementation. With the .NET framework, it is sufficient to declare an interface and a class implementing this interface with the `ComVisible` attribute.

Each COM interop library, class, and interface is identified with a GUID that must be registered in the system registry. Step 4 through Step 6 describe how to generate a GUID and assign it to COM declarations.

All that is required to register the library is to enable the **Register for COM interop** option in the project properties, as shown in Step 9.

After the library is registered, it can be used in C/AL as an Automation type variable – this is done in Step 12. Here, we create an instance of the `Multiplication` class and perform an explicit type cast by assigning the class variable to an interface variable:

```
IMultiplication := Multiplication;
```

6
SharePoint Integration

In this chapter, we will cover the following recipes:

- Creating a developer SharePoint site
- Developing NAV apps for SharePoint
- Embedding NAV page objects in site pages
- Publishing NAV reports in SharePoint
- Deploying applications on SharePoint
- Configuring authentication and user permissions

Introduction

Microsoft SharePoint is a collection of corporate tools for team collaboration and enterprise content management.

The product can be installed on-premises within your corporate infrastructure or deployed in the cloud with a SharePoint online subscription.

Regardless of the solution architecture, you can publish data and applications on a SharePoint site that is accessible to authorized company employees. You can easily publish documents created in Microsoft Office products on a team portal. With an Azure account, SharePoint can be integrated with your Office 365 subscription.

Microsoft Dynamics NAV can also be published as a SharePoint application. You can control access to NAV by exposing either the default web server page or limiting it to a single object.

A prerequisite for this chapter is a configured and running NAV web server. To learn how to set up a web server, refer to the *Configuring web server* recipe from `Chapter 1`, *Writing Basic C/AL Code*. You must have access to an on-premises installation of SharePoint Server or have a SharePoint Online subscription supporting a developer site.

The following examples are based on SharePoint Online 2013.

Creating a developer SharePoint site

Before publishing any content on SharePoint, you must create and setup a site. To make deployment and development easier, create a developer site where you will have access to the SharePoint development tools.

To find out if your SharePoint subscription supports creating developer sites, refer to MSDN. The first recipe describes setting up of a site that will be used throughout the chapter, so this walkthrough is a prerequisite for all subsequent recipes.

How to do it...

1. Sign-in to your Office 365 account as a SharePoint administrator.
2. Click the app launch button in the top left corner of the panel and select the **Admin** tile:

3. Expand **Admin centers** and click **SharePoint** to open the SharePoint admin center:

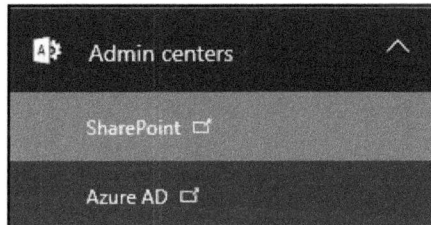

4. Select **Site Collections** from the navigation panel on the left. In the **Site Collections** tab, click **New**, then **Private Site Collection**:

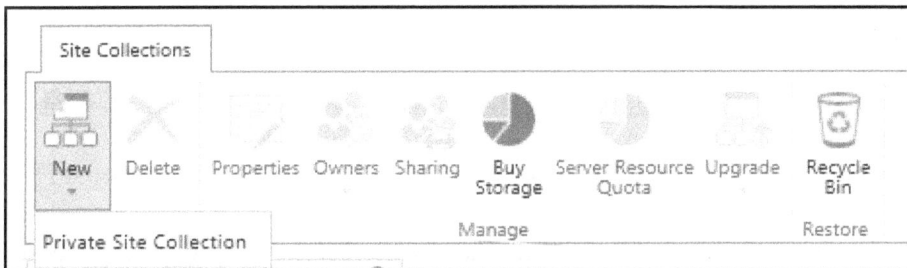

5. Fill in the site configuration parameters:
   - **Title**: Dynamics NAV integration testing
   - **Web site address**: Choose your domain name from the list, choose **/sites/** for the site URL, and type the site collection name: `NavAppTest`
   - **Template**: Select the **Developer Site** template from a list
   - **Administrator**: Enter your login name. You can use the **Check Names** button on the right of this field to verify the user name

6. Click **OK**. A new developer site will be added to the list of site collections in the SharePoint **Admin center**. The new site will have the following URL:

```
https://<Your SharePoint account
name>.sharepoint.com/sites/NavAppTest.
```

Type or copy this URL into the browser address bar to access your developer site.

Developing NAV apps for SharePoint

In the first recipe, we will publish Dynamics NAV as an app for SharePoint or SharePoint Add-in–the name depends on the version of SharePoint you are using. After completing the following walkthrough, you will be able to access the NAV application from the list of applications on the SharePoint portal.

Getting ready

To complete this recipe, the **Office Developer Tools** add-in for Visual Studio is required. You can download the package from `https://www.visualstudio.com/vs/office-tools/`.

How to do it...

1. Access your SharePoint site created in the previous recipe and open the app registration page, `AppRegNew.aspx`:
   `http://<SharePointWebsite>/_layouts/15/AppRegNew.aspx`. Here, `<SharePointWebsite>` is the name of your site.

2. Click the **Generate** button located under the **Client Id** field, then generate a **Client Secret** by pressing the corresponding **Generate** button:

   Client Id:

   | cd23b820-187d-4ccf-8fe0-b93c0f1fb4ee | Generate |

   Client Secret:

   | V2uejJBYX6Bf/CVbNHObwn7LXCwE2iN+W8zKr | Generate |

   Title:

   | Microsoft Dynamics Nav |

   App Domain:

   | localhost:8080 |

   Example: "www.contoso.com"

   Redirect URI:

   | http://localhost:8080/DynamicsNAV | × |

   You must specify a value for this required field.
   Example: "https://www.contoso.com/default.aspx"

Save the generated **Client Id** and **Client Secret** values, they will be required later.

3. In the **Title** field, enter the app title that will be shown to the SharePoint users.
4. In a local development environment, **App Domain** is `localhost:8080`, and **Redirect URL** should be set to the URL of your NAV web service: `http://localhost:8080/DynamicsNAV`.
5. Click **Create**–SharePoint will inform you when the app identifier is successfully created.
6. Run Visual Studio and create a new project. Select **App for SharePoint** from the list of templates. Enter the name for the solution, `NavSharePointApp`:

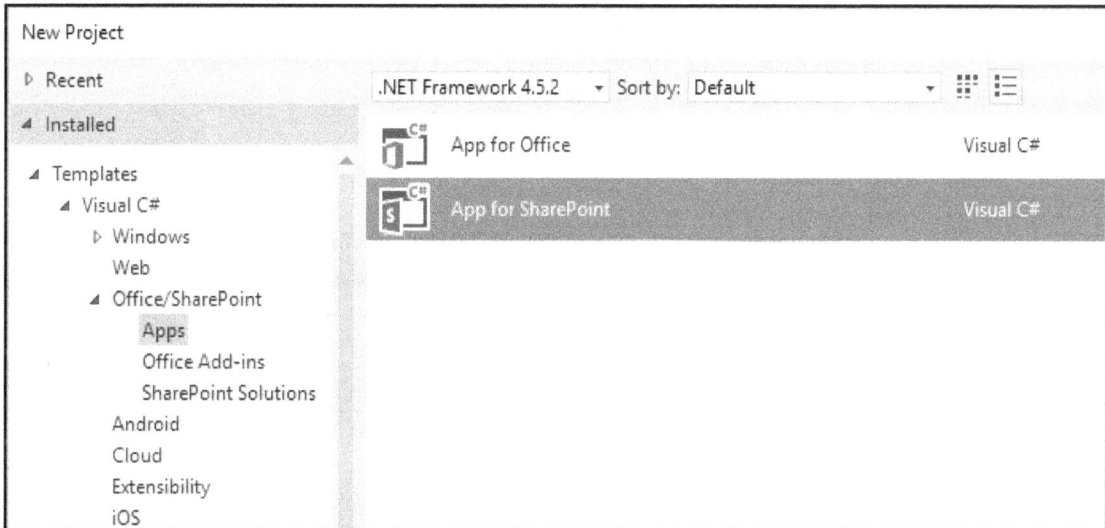

If you are developing your application in Visual Studio version 2015 or higher, you should select the **SharePoint Add-in** template instead of **App for SharePoint**.

7. Choose **Provider-hosted** and enter the name of your SharePoint site:

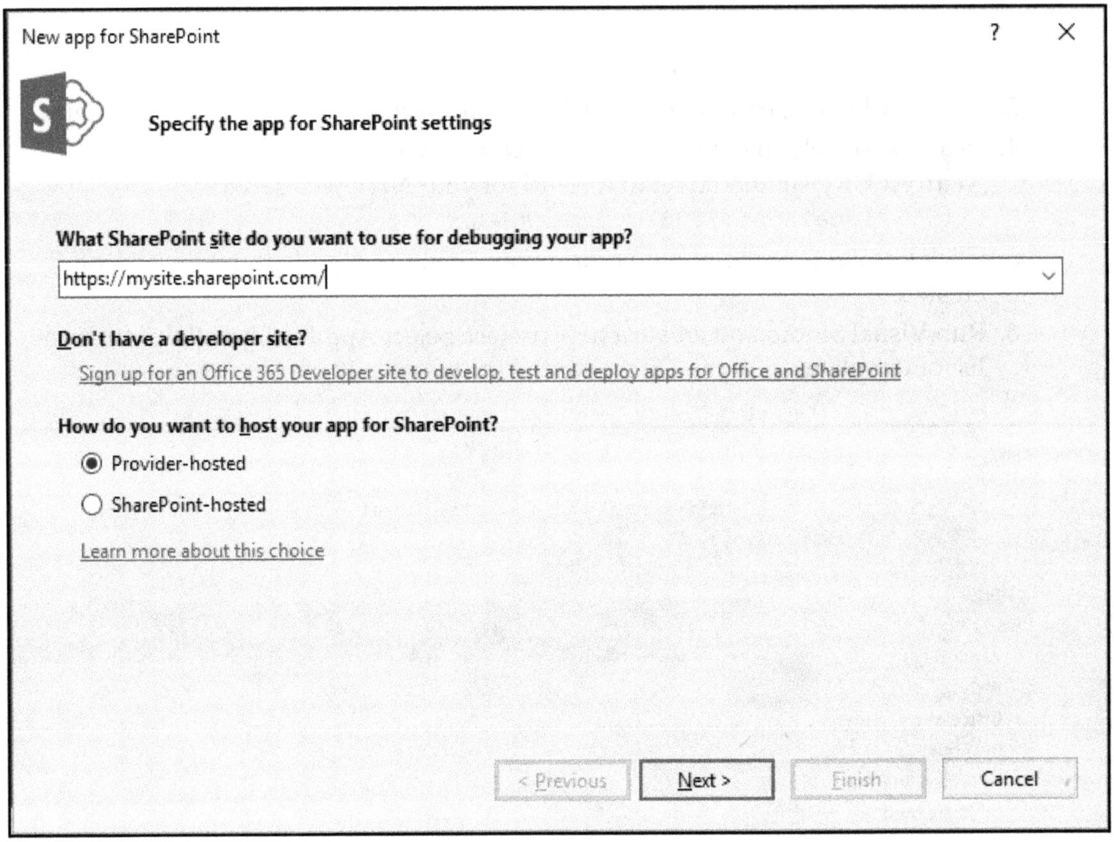

New app for SharePoint   ?   ✕

Specify the app for SharePoint settings

What SharePoint site do you want to use for debugging your app?

https://mysite.sharepoint.com/

Don't have a developer site?

Sign up for an Office 365 Developer site to develop, test and deploy apps for Office and SharePoint

How do you want to host your app for SharePoint?

◉ Provider-hosted

○ SharePoint-hosted

Learn more about this choice

< Previous   Next >   Finish   Cancel

8. Click **Next**. You will be asked to authenticate on the site you entered. After confirming the authentication details, choose which version of SharePoint the application will target. In this example, we will target **SharePoint Online**, although the same app should work with an on-premises installation:

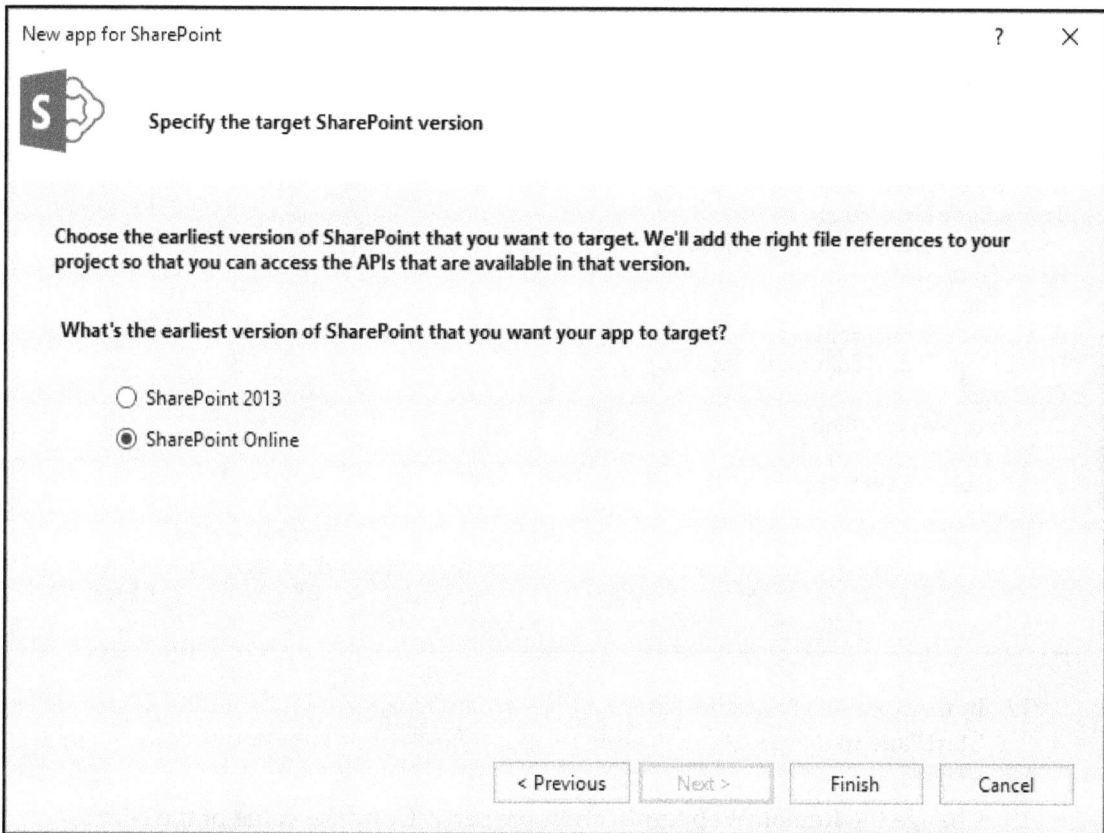

New app for SharePoint   ?   ✕

Specify the target SharePoint version

Choose the earliest version of SharePoint that you want to target. We'll add the right file references to your project so that you can access the APIs that are available in that version.

What's the earliest version of SharePoint that you want your app to target?

○ SharePoint 2013

◉ SharePoint Online

                < Previous   Next >   Finish   Cancel

---

9. Created solutions contain two projects: `NavSharePointApp` and `NavSharePointAppWeb`. The `NavSharePointAppWeb` project includes ASP.NET pages and is not required to build an app that uses Microsoft Dynamics NAV data. Therefore, you can safely delete this project.

10. Modify `AppManifest.xml`. Right-click on `AppManifest.xml` and choose **Open With…**.

11. Select **XML (Text) Editor** from the suggested list as shown:

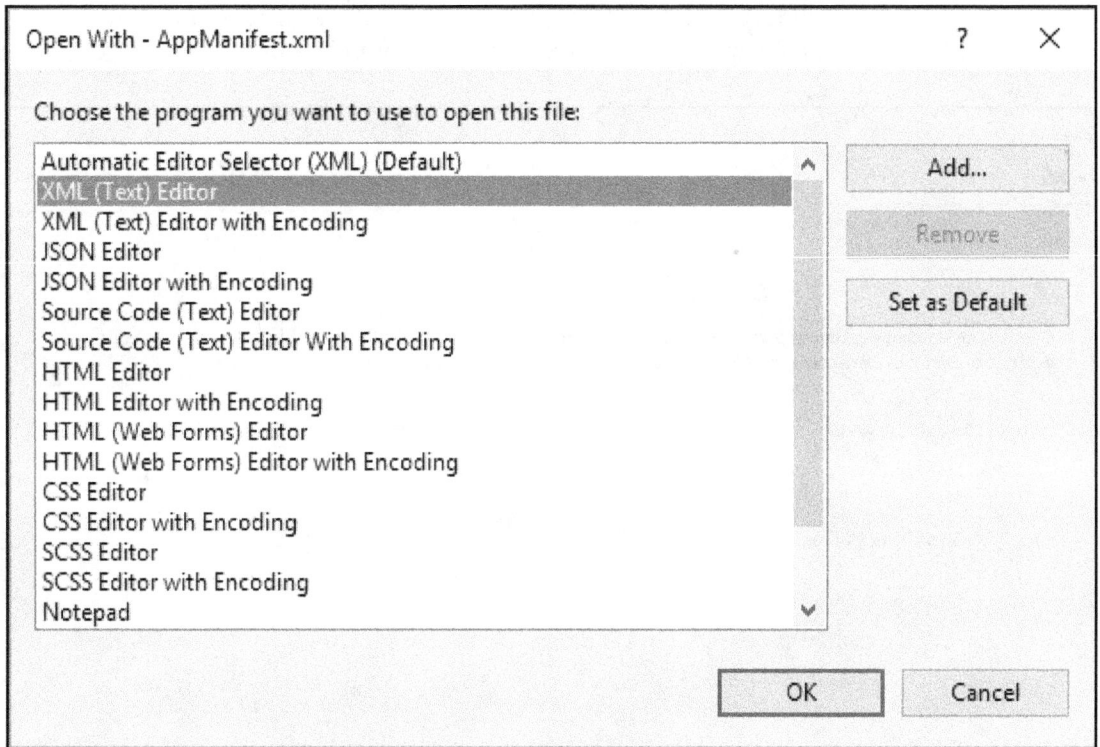

12. In the `AppManifest` file, set
    StartPage to `http://localhost:8080/DynamicsNAV90/WebClient/?{Stand ardTokens}`.

13. Change the **RemoteWebApplication** property. Copy the value of the client ID obtained in Step 2.

14. After all modifications, the contents of the `AppManifest.xml` file should be as follows:

```xml
<?xml version="1.0" encoding="utf-8" ?>
<App xmlns=
  "http://schemas.microsoft.com/sharepoint/2012/app/manifest"
    Name="NavSharepointApp"
  ProductID="{20ec7e1f-62ad-486d-bd7c-bad951d9e124}"
  Version="1.0.0.0"
  SharePointMinVersion="16.0.0.0">
  <Properties>
    <Title>Nav SharePoint App</Title>
```

```
<StartPage>http://localhost:8080/DynamicsNAV90/WebClient//?
  {StandardTokens}?{StandardTokens}?{StandardTokens}
  </StartPage>
</Properties>

<AppPrincipal>
  <RemoteWebApplication ClientId=
    "cd23b820-187d-4ccf-8fe0-b93c0f1fb4ee" />
</AppPrincipal>
</App>
```

15. Build the application. The application is automatically deployed to the SharePoint site. Wait for the installation to complete.
16. The web page will open. Confirm that you trust the application–you will be redirected to NAV Web Client. Users can now access NAV from the SharePoint apps list (or apps in Testing, if you are deploying on a developer site).

How it works...

After completing the previously described configuration, you will see Dynamics NAV registered as a SharePoint application accessible through the **Applications** list. Users will receive an access point to NAV from the SharePoint portal, while all requests are redirected to the NAV web server.

Embedding NAV page objects in site pages

In the next recipe, we will see how to publish NAV pages on a SharePoint site as web parts–web site construction blocks. Published through a web part, a NAV page object can be embedded into a page and combined with other visual elements in one page.

Getting ready

To complete this recipe, the **Office Developer Tools** add-in for Visual Studio is required. You can download the package from https://www.visualstudio.com/vs/office-tools/.

The current example is based on the project created in the *Developing NAV apps for SharePoint* recipe. Complete it first before starting the following recipe.

How to do it…

1. Open the **NavSharePointApp** project created in the first recipe, right-click on the project name, and choose the **New Item** option.
2. Select the **Client Web Part (Host Web)** option located under the **Office/SharePoint** tab:

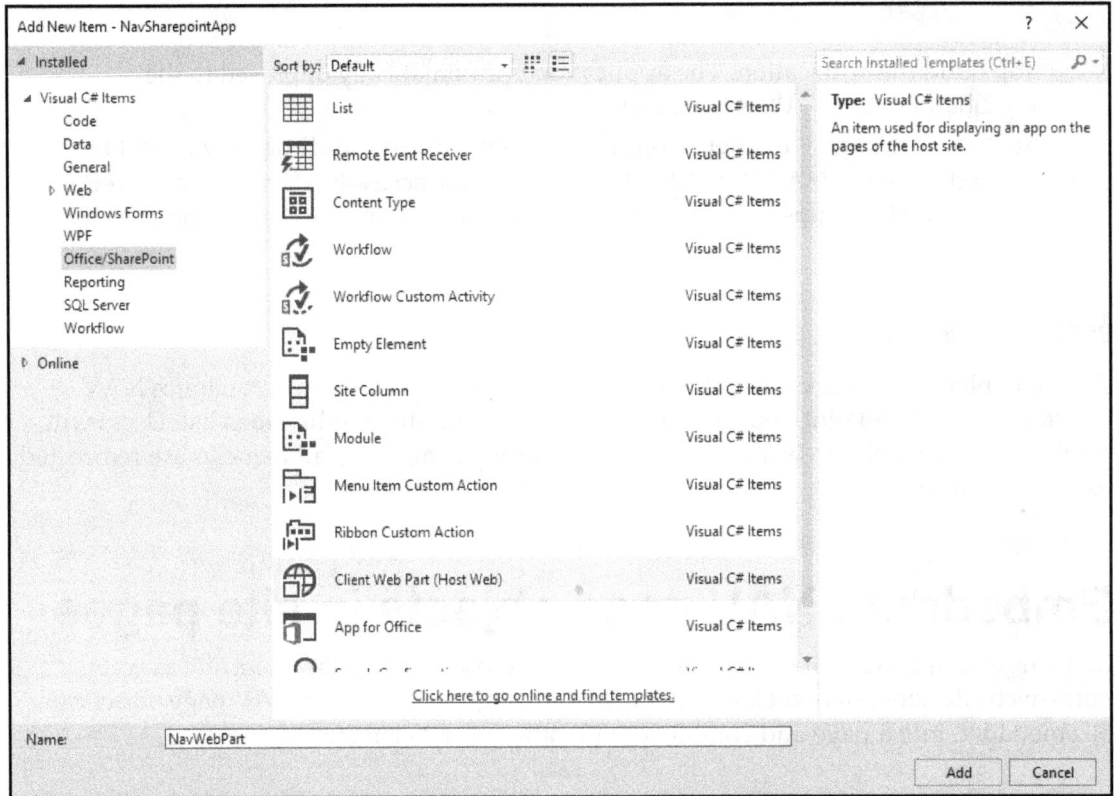

3. Click **Add**, and then choose the **Select or enter the URL of an existing web page for the client web part content** option. Enter the following URL in the text field:

```
http://localhost:8080/DynamicsNAV90/WebClient/default.aspx?mode=View&amp;isembedded=1&amp;page=_PageID_&amp;shownavigation=0&amp;showribbon=0&amp;showuiparts=0&amp;pagesize=7&amp;SPHostUrl={HostUrl}:
```

Create Client Web Part	? X

Specify the client web part page

Client web parts display the contents of a specified web page on the host web where the app is installed. Select the option to create a new web page or specify an existing web page.

○ **Create a new app web page for the client web part content**
A new page is created in the app for SharePoint project.

Page name:
```
NavWebPart
```

◉ **Select or enter the URL of an existing web page for the client web part content**
```
https://localhost/DynamicsNAV/WebClient/default.aspx?mode=View&isembedded=1&page=42&shownaviga ∨
```

< Previous	Next >	Finish	Cancel

Note the **page =_PageID_** parameter. It will be replaced with a parameter value in SharePoint.

4. Click **Finish**–a new web part page is created.

5. To declare a web part property, edit the `Elements.xml` file. Choose the text editor to open it, the same way as in steps 10 – 11 of the previous recipe.

6. Insert a `Property` node:

```
<Properties>
  <Property
    Name="PageID"
    Type="int"
    RequiresDesignerPermission="false"
    DefaultValue="9305"
    WebCategory="Microsoft Dynamics NAV"
    WebDisplayName="Page ID">
  </Property>
</Properties>
```

7. In the `ClientWebPart` node, set the title and change the default web part size:
   ```
   <ClientWebPart Name="NavWebPart" Title="Sales Orders List"
   Description="NavWebPart Description" DefaultWidth="500"
   DefaultHeight="200">.
   ```

8. Build the project. The web part is automatically deployed to the SharePoint site.

9. Open the SharePoint site, access the **Site contents** page, then click the **Pages** link. Create a new page and choose the **Web Part** page type.

10. Enter the page name and choose (**Full Page, Vertical**) layout template. Click **Create**:

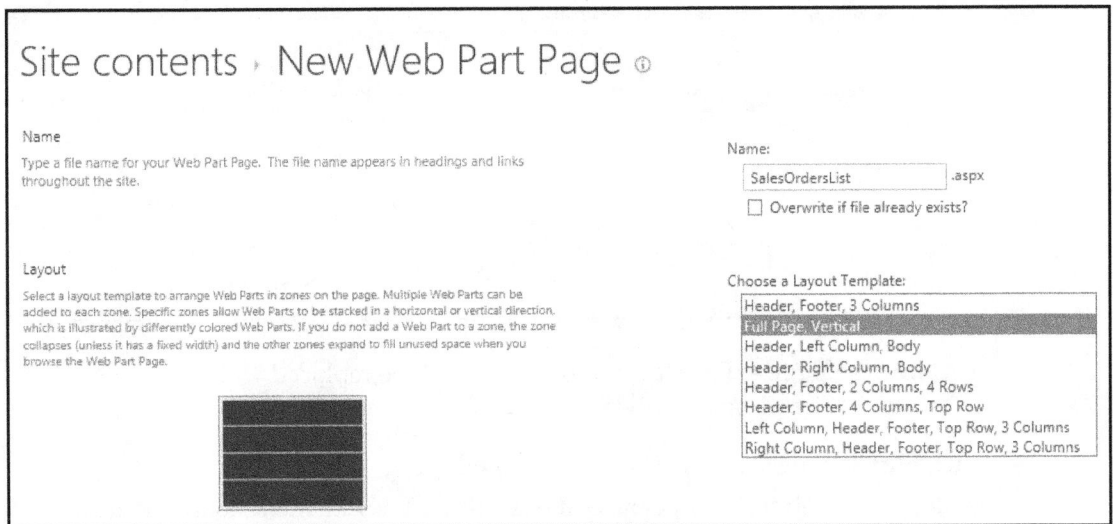

Site contents › New Web Part Page ⓘ

Name

Type a file name for your Web Part Page. The file name appears in headings and links throughout the site.

Name:

| SalesOrdersList | .aspx |

☐ Overwrite if file already exists?

Layout

Select a layout template to arrange Web Parts in zones on the page. Multiple Web Parts can be added to each zone. Specific zones allow Web Parts to be stacked in a horizontal or vertical direction, which is illustrated by differently colored Web Parts. If you do not add a Web Part to a zone, the zone collapses (unless it has a fixed width) and the other zones expand to fill unused space when you browse the Web Part Page.

Choose a Layout Template:

```
Header, Footer, 3 Columns
Full Page, Vertical
Header, Left Column, Body
Header, Right Column, Body
Header, Footer, 2 Columns, 4 Rows
Header, Footer, 4 Columns, Top Row
Left Column, Header, Footer, Top Row, 3 Columns
Right Column, Header, Footer, Top Row, 3 Columns
```

11. When the page is created, click **Add a Web Part**.

12. Select the **Apps** category, choose the **Sales Orders List** part in the **Parts** list, and click **Add** as shown in the following screenshot:

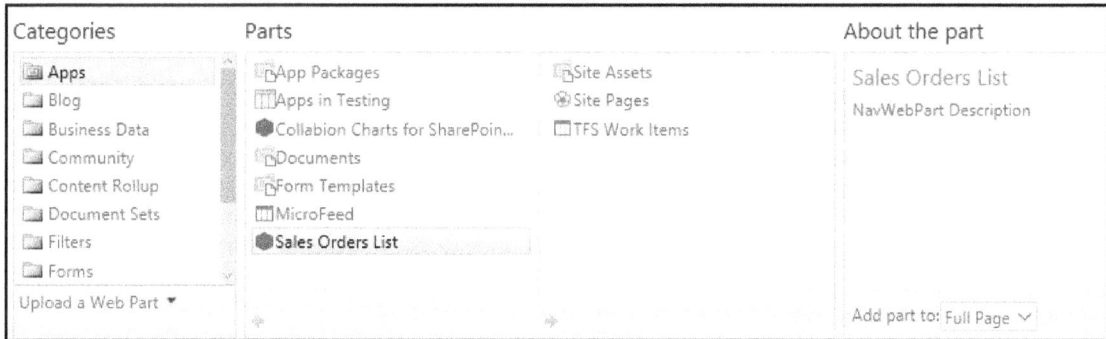

Categories	Parts		About the part
🖼 Apps	🗋App Packages	🗋Site Assets	Sales Orders List
📁 Blog	🎬Apps in Testing	⚙Site Pages	NavWebPart Description
📁 Business Data	●Collabion Charts for SharePoin...	🗋TFS Work Items	
📁 Community	🗋Documents		
📁 Content Rollup	🗋Form Templates		
📁 Document Sets	🎬MicroFeed		
📁 Filters	●Sales Orders List		
📁 Forms			
Upload a Web Part ▼			Add part to: Full Page ∨

13. Select the web part and click **Web Part Properties** in the main menu as shown in the following screenshot:

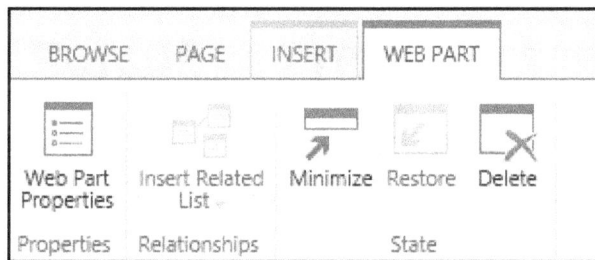

BROWSE	PAGE	INSERT	WEB PART
Web Part Properties	Insert Related List	Minimize Restore Delete	
Properties	Relationships	State	

14. The **Page ID** property declared in the Visual Studio project is available in the **Properties** section, under the **Microsoft Dynamics NAV** tab as shown:

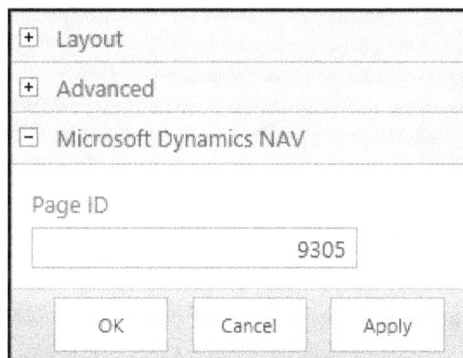

⊞ Layout
⊞ Advanced
⊟ Microsoft Dynamics NAV
Page ID
9305
OK   Cancel   Apply

15. You can leave the default value 9305, or enter the number of another page you want to display. Click **Stop editing and open the new page**. Now you can see a list of sales orders embedded in a SharePoint page.

How it works...

Web requests from SharePoint are redirected to the NAV web server, as we did in the first recipe. But instead of redirecting the user to the home page of the NAV web application, a particular page specified in the request parameters is displayed. The ID of the page that will be shown in a web part is defined by the `PageID` parameter in Step 3. Note the two underscore symbols around the parameter name in the URL: `_PageID_`.

Step 6 maps the request parameter to a parameter of the web part configurable in SharePoint designer. It receives a default value 9305 (page **Sales Order List**), which can be changed in the **Web Part Properties** setup (Step 13 through Step 15).

Publishing NAV reports in SharePoint

NAV page objects can be published on a SharePoint site as SharePoint apps or web parts that will be embedded into site pages. Reports are not so flexible–there is no option to set a report in a page as a web part. NAV reports can only be presented as an application.

Now we will develop a SharePoint app that will expose a NAV report in the site apps list. This recipe is very similar to the *Developing NAV apps for SharePoint* recipe. Steps overlapping in these two recipes will be outlined here. If you need a detailed description, refer to the aforementioned recipe.

How to do it...

1. Open your developer site on SharePoint, access the application registration page located on the URL `http://<SharePointWebsite>/_layouts/15/AppRegNew.aspx`, and register a new app, as described in *Developing NAV apps for SharePoint* recipe, Step 1 through Step 5.

2. Run Visual Studio and create a new project. Select the application template **App for SharePoint**.

3. Type a name for the project. Name it `NavSharePointReport` and click **OK**.

4. Visual Studio will request the type of the application–either **SharePoint-hosted** or **Provider-hosted**. Choose **Provider-hosted**, enter the URL of your SharePoint site, then click **Next**.

5. Select the version of SharePoint that you want to target your application at. Choose a version appropriate for your setup, then click **Finish**.

6. Two reports are generated in the solution: `NavSharePointReport` and `NavSharePointReportWeb`. The `NavSharePointReportWeb` web project containing ASP.NET pages will not be used in this example and can be deleted.

7. In the **Solution Explorer** window, expand the list of project files and right-click on `Manifest.xml`. Choose **Open With...** and select **XML (Text) Editor**.

8. Set the value of the **StartPage** property:
`http://localhost:8080/DynamicsNAV90/WebClient/?report=309.`

9. In the `RemoteWebApplication` property, set the value obtained from SharePoint in Step 1.

10. In the **Title** property, set the report title that will be displayed on the site. Finally, the contents of `Manifest.xml` should be as follows (note that values of `ProductID` and `ClientID` will be generated individually for each application, and `SharePointMinVersion` depends on the version of the software installed on your server):

```xml
<?xml version="1.0" encoding="utf-8" ?>
<App xmlns=
  "http://schemas.microsoft.com/sharepoint/2012/app/manifest"
  Name="PurchListReport"
  ProductID="{a2fd7d81-3cf4-401c-a222-37afd808b468}"
  Version="1.0.0.0"
  SharePointMinVersion="16.0.0.0">
  <Properties>
    <Title>Vendor - Purchase List</Title>
    <StartPage>http://localhost:8080/DynamicsNAV90/WebClient/?
      report=309</StartPage>
  </Properties>

  <AppPrincipal>
    <RemoteWebApplication ClientId=
      "e9942529-c528-47cf-aad3-05119ce55141" />
  </AppPrincipal>
</App>
```

11. Save the project and build it. The SharePoint app will be deployed to the site.

12. To run the report, open the SharePoint site and locate the application in the **Apps in Testing** list:

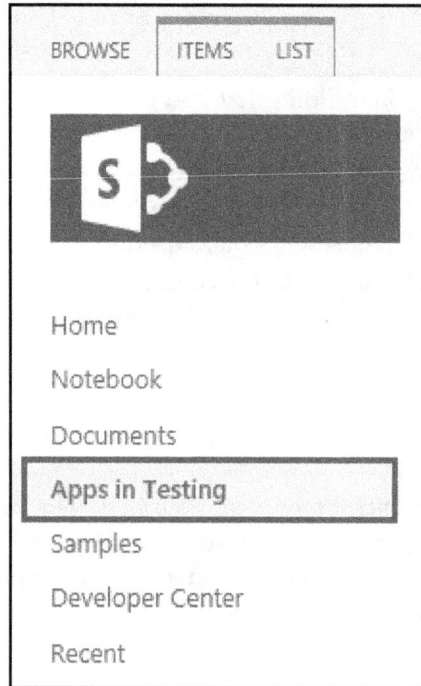

13. When the application is run, a report request page is displayed. To see the report data, fill in the request parameters, click the **Send** to button, and select a report format (**PDF / Word / Excel**):

Edit - Vendor - Purchase List ☐ ✕

Options

Amounts (LCY) Greater Than   0.00

Hide Address Detail   ☐

Vendor

Show results:

Where: No.   ⌄   is: 01254796   …

Limit totals to:

Where: Date Filter   ⌄   is: 01/01/16..31/12/16

Deploying applications on SharePoint

While developing an application, you can deploy it from Visual Studio. This is very handy when working with a test site, while in a production environment other deployment methods are used.

In the current recipe, we will deploy a compiled SharePoint application on a web portal.

How to do it...

1. Access your SharePoint site, and open the **Apps in Testing** page, then open the **List** ribbon tab and click **Deploy App**:

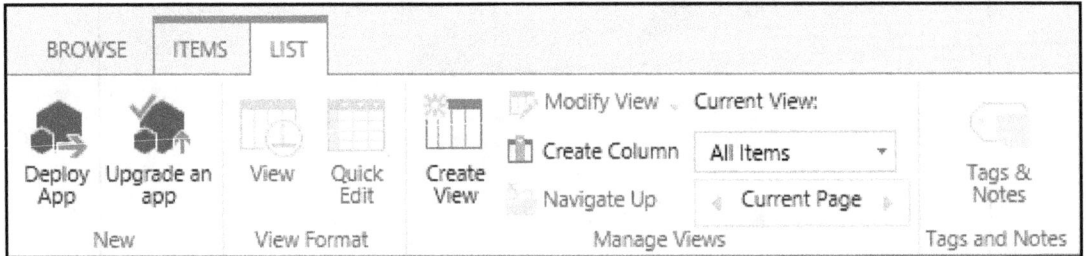

BROWSE	ITEMS	LIST					
Deploy App	Upgrade an app	View	Quick Edit	Create View	Modify View — Current View: Create Column — All Items ▼ Navigate Up — Current Page ▸		Tags & Notes
New		View Format			Manage Views		Tags and Notes

2. In the **Deploy App** page, click the **upload it** link to upload your application to the site:

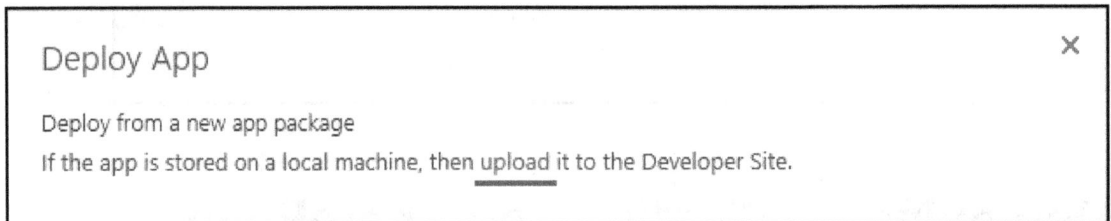

Deploy App   ✕

Deploy from a new app package

If the app is stored on a local machine, then upload it to the Developer Site.

---

3. The default path to the SharePoint application assembly is under the `Projects` folder of your Visual Studio installation:
    `\NavSharepointApp\NavSharepointApp\bin\Debug\app.publish\1.0.0.0\ NavSharepointApp.app`.

    Open the **upload** dialog and select the app package.

4. After uploading the application to SharePoint, enter the name of the site where you want your application to be deployed, and click **Deploy**:

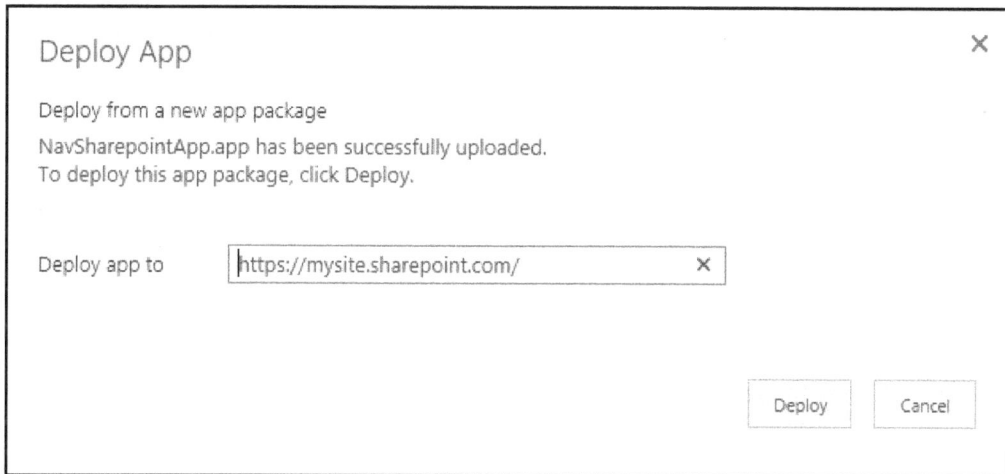

Deploy App   ✕

Deploy from a new app package

NavSharepointApp.app has been successfully uploaded.
To deploy this app package, click Deploy.

Deploy app to | https://mysite.sharepoint.com/   ✕ |

                                                        [Deploy]   [Cancel]

---

5. The `NavSharePointApp` project is added to the list of applications. To run it, open the **Apps in Testing** list and click on the application name.

How it works...

When deployment is completed, SharePoint will ask you to confirm that you trust the application. If the request is confirmed, the application is added to the list of trusted applications that can be managed on **Site App Permissions,** page available from the **Site Settings** menu:

Site Settings ▸ Site App Permissions ⓘ

App Display Name↑

✕   Collabion Charts for SharePoint Online

✕   Microsoft Dynamics Nav

✕   Microsoft.SharePoint

To remove an application from the list, access the **Apps in Testing** list, check the application that you want to delete, expand the actions list, as shown in the following screenshot, and choose **Remove**:

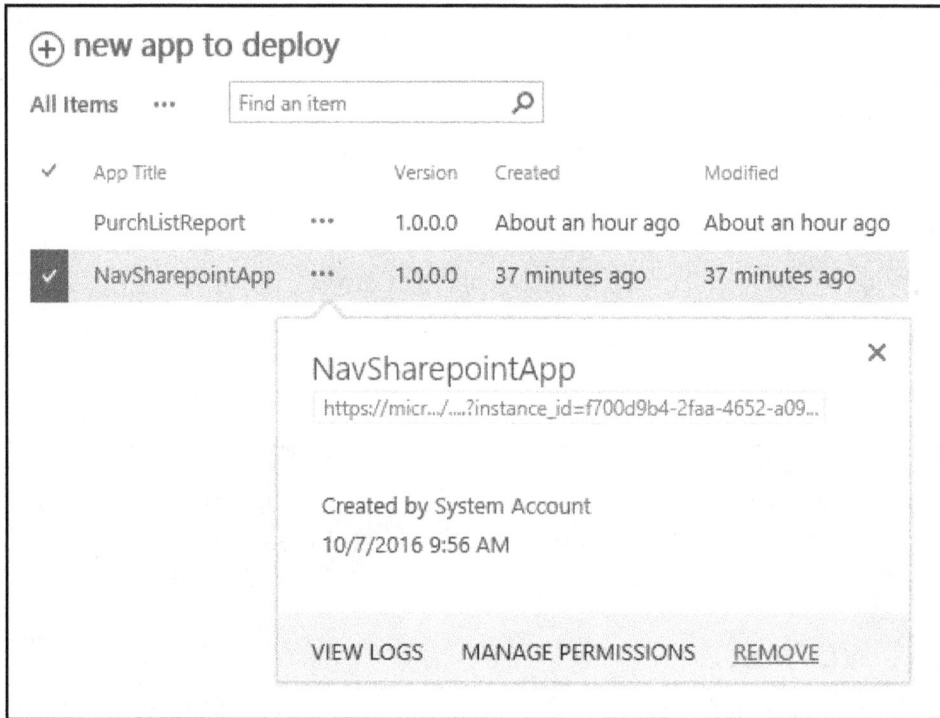

Configuring user permissions

User authentication in NAV is performed by the NAV server, no matter whether the application is accessed from a role-tailored client, web client, or if it is published on a SharePoint site. SharePoint can control user access to its content–read applications, and list and execute an application, while NAV authentication requests will be redirected to the NAV server.

In this recipe, we will set up a user account that will be able to run NAV applications published on a SharePoint portal.

How to do it...

1. Open the **Settings** menu and click **Site Settings**. On the **Site Settings** page, open **Site permissions** as shown:

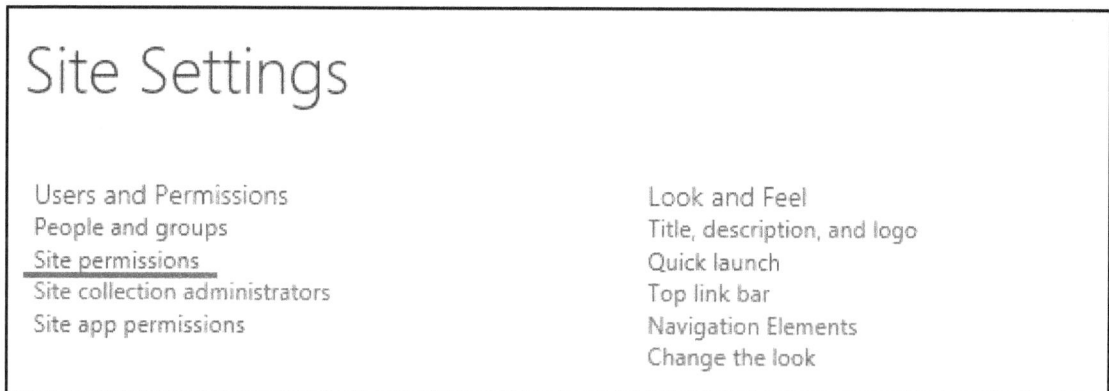

2. To create a permission level, click **Permission Levels** in the **PERMISSIONS** menu:

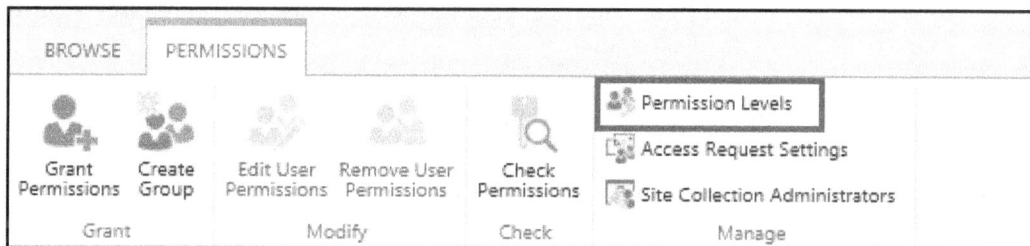

3. SharePoint comes with a set of predefined permission levels that are listed in this page. To create a custom permission level, click **Add a Permission Level**:

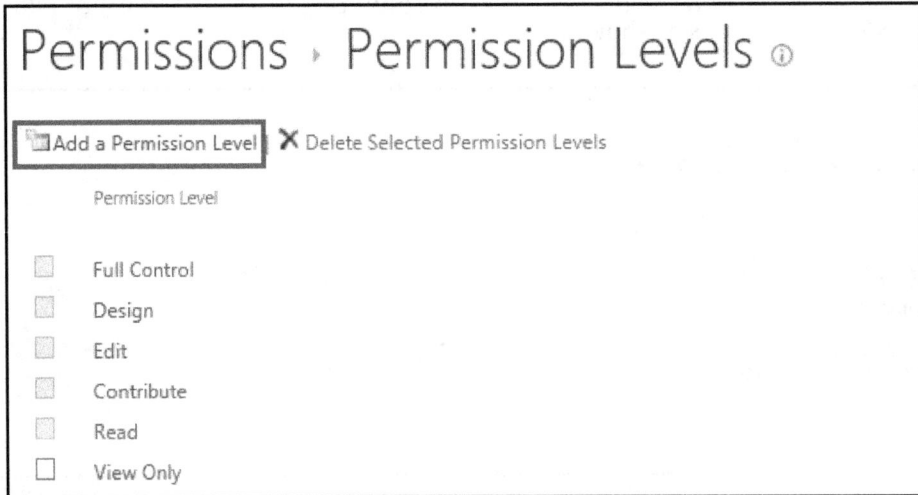

4. Enter the name of the new permission level (AppUsers) and a description. In the list of permissions, check the **View Application Pages** permission option. The related permission, **Open**, will be checked automatically. Click the **Create** button to save the new permission level.

5. The **AppUsers** permission level must be assigned to one of the user groups. Return to the **Site Settings** page and click the **People and Groups** link to access the group management interface.

6. Click the **Create Group** button in the **Permissions** menu and enter a name for the new group: NAVAppUsers. After filling in the group name and description, click **Create**:

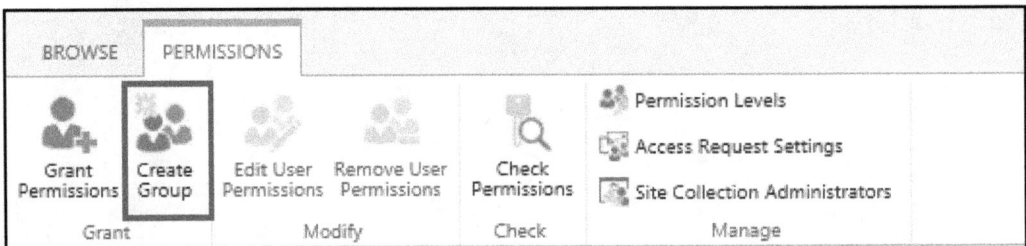

7. Return to the list of groups and select the **NAVAppUsers** group.
8. In the **New** menu, select the **Add Users** option:

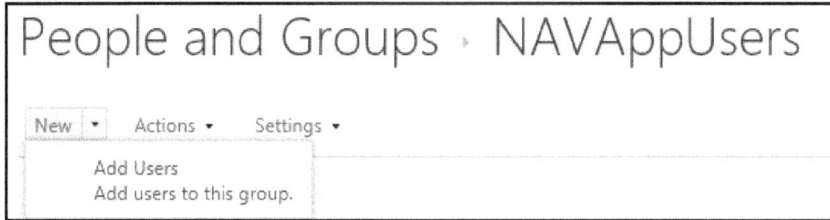

People and Groups ▸ NAVAppUsers

New ▾   Actions ▾   Settings ▾

Add Users
Add users to this group.

9. Enter the name of the user that you want to add to the group, and then click **Share**.
10. Once again, click on **Site Settings**, then select **Site permissions** to see the list of user groups.
11. Tick the checkbox in front of the **NAVAppUsers** group, and then click the **Edit User Permissions** button in the **Permissions** menu:

	Name	Type
☐	Excel Services Viewers	SharePoint Group
☑	NAVAppUsers	SharePoint Group

12. A list of permission levels opens. Select the **AppUsers** level from the list (tick the checkbox) and click **OK**.

How it works...

Access to SharePoint resources is defined by permission levels assigned to groups. User accounts must then be included in appropriate groups to obtain access to site pages and applications.

In Step 1 through Step 4 we created a custom permission level that will give read access to applications published on the SharePoint site.

Step 5 to Step 7 create a group that will receive the permission level created before. Finally, when user accounts are added to the new group, users will receive e-mail notifications and will be able to access the site and run applications.

7
Control Add-ins

In this chapter, we will cover the following recipes:

- Developing a control add-in
- Signing the control add-in assembly
- Registering and embedding a control add-in
- JavaScript in web, phone, and tablet clients
- Installing and using JavaScript control add-ins
- Sending events from add-ins to NAV server
- Linking add-ins with the database
- Exchanging data with add-ins

Introduction

Microsoft Dynamics NAV provides a software developer with a variety of options for extending application functionality via .NET assemblies, COM components, and many other tools. Extension possibilities covered so far in this book gave you a way to enrich NAV functional capabilities, but they did not allow you to modify UI elements.

This chapter will walk the reader through creating a custom user interface extension that can be embedded in native NAV pages and make data presentation highly customizable. We will see how to use the NAV UI Extensibility Framework to create **WinForms** controls compatible with the NAV user interface. A separate recipe is dedicated to developing control elements in JavaScript language. Client controls based on the UI Extensibility Framework are developed in .NET languages and run in the .NET environment, which limits their application to NAV Windows clients only. JavaScript controls follow the Dynamics NAV Universal App concept and can be used on any type of client.

In the *Linking add-ins with the database* recipe, we will bind a textbox control to a table field in the NAV database, so that all modifications made in the textbox content will be automatically reflected in the associated table field.

The *Sending events from add-ins to NAV server* recipe will demonstrate how to maintain communication between a control add-in and the NAV server by raising events in a control and handling them in NAV applications.

Developing a control add-in

The first recipe covers the basics of developing a control add-in. We will walk through developing a web browser control that can be embedded in a NAV page, allowing a user to open web pages directly in NAV applications without switching to external software.

How to do it...

The current recipe covers the .NET library project in Visual Studio, while subsequent recipes *Signing the control add-in assembly* and *Registering and embedding a control add-in* will continue the discussion and demonstrate how to assign a strong name to the assembly and embed the control to the NAV user interface.

1. Run Visual Studio and start a new project. In the **New Project** dialog, select the **Class Library** template located under the **Windows** templates collection.

2. Type a name for the new project. Name it `NavBrowserControl`. Select a location for the project and choose to create a new solution:

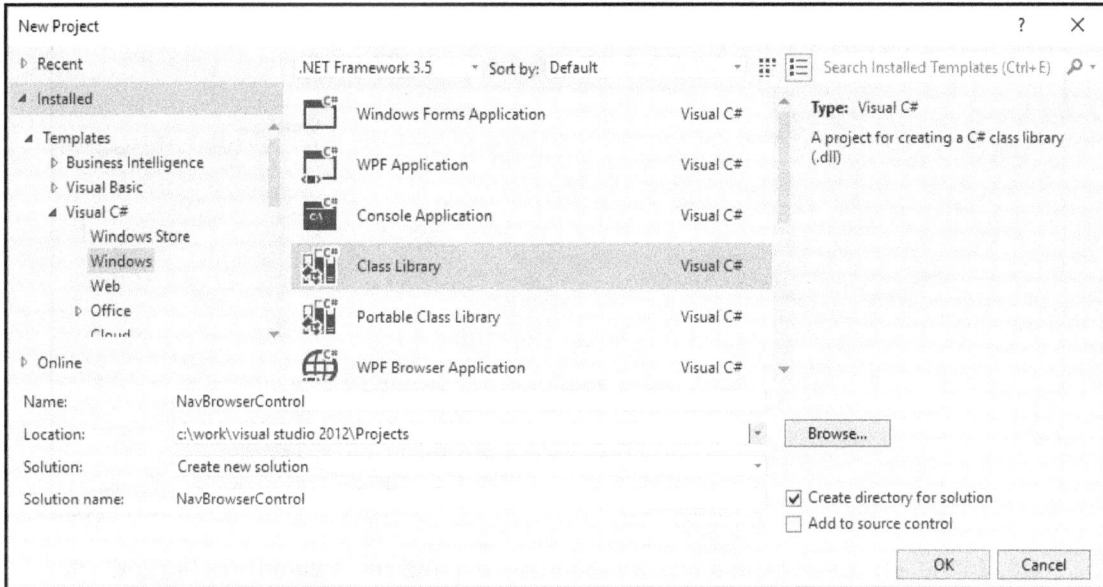

3. Click **OK**. A project containing one class named **Class1** is created. In the **Solution Explorer** window, right-click on the filename `Class1.cs` and choose the **Rename** menu option. Rename the file to `NavWebBrowser.cs`. Confirm renaming of the code references when asked.

4. Right-click on **References** in **Solution Explorer** and choose **Add Reference**.

5. The **Reference Manager** window will open. Click **Browse** and navigate to the folder where NAV role-tailored client is installed. The default installation path is `C:\Program Files (x86)\Microsoft Dynamics NAV\90\RoleTailored Client`.

6. Select the **Microsoft.Dynamics.Framework.UI.Extensibility.dll** library and click the **Add** button.

7. Mark the library in the reference manager, but do not close it yet – we still need another reference:

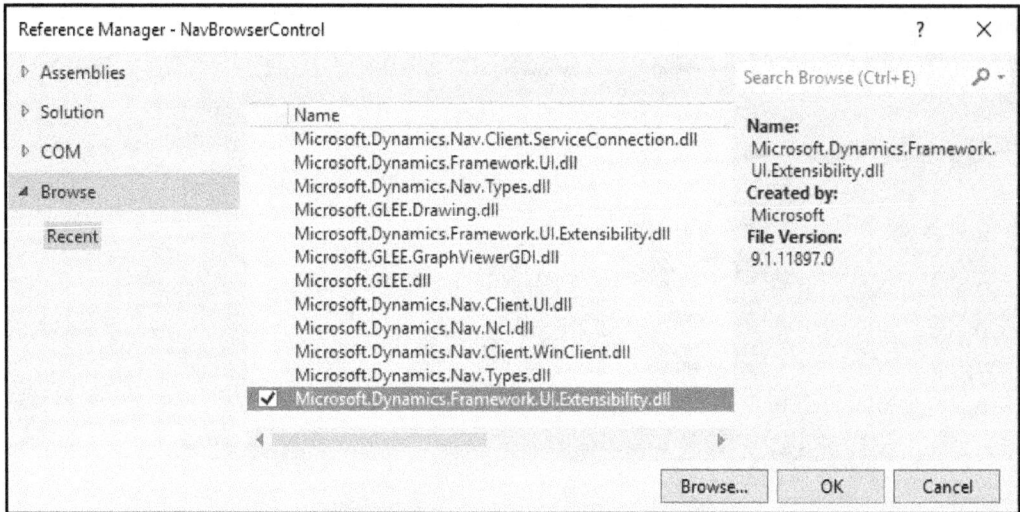

8. In the left pane of the reference manager, expand the **Assemblies** list and select the **Framework** assembly group. In the list of assemblies, locate and mark **System.Windows.Forms**:

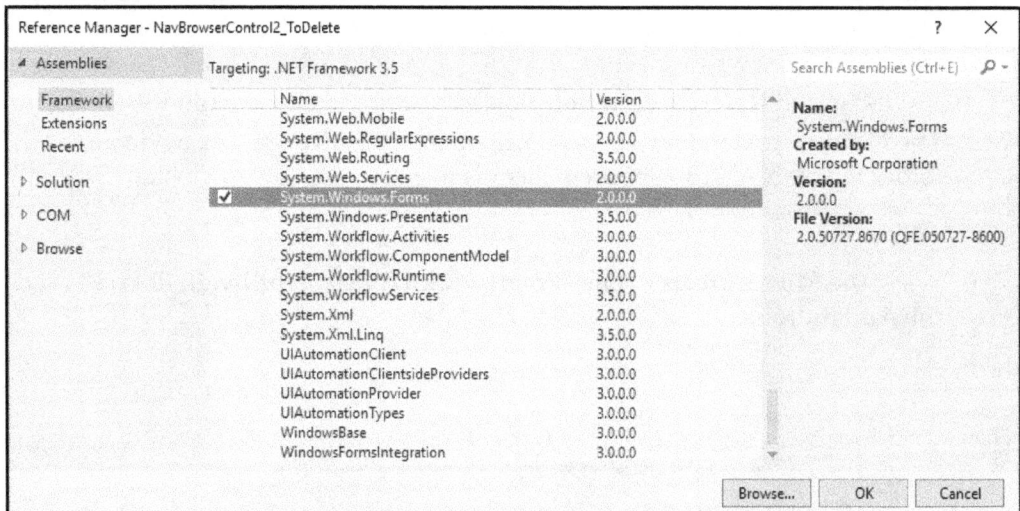

9. Click **OK**. Two references to the selected libraries will be added to the project.

10. In the code editor, remove using statements inserted automatically by Visual Studio.

11. Insert the following statements instead of deleted ones:

```
using Microsoft.Dynamics.Framework.UI.Extensibility;
using Microsoft.Dynamics.Framework.UI.Extensibility.WinForms;
using System.Windows.Forms;
```

12. After renaming the class `Class1` to `NavWebBrowser` in Step 3, the `NavWebBrowser.cs` source file contains a namespace declaration with a class name in it:

```
namespace NavBrowserControl
{
  public class NavWebBrowser
  {
  }
}
```

13. Change the class declaration to the following:

```
[ControlAddInExport("NavWebBrowserControl")]
public class NavWebBrowser : WinFormsControlAddInBase
{
}
```

14. Inside the class definition, declare a private property:

```
private WebBrowser browser;
```

15. Insert a method that will create the control and return a reference to the calling code:

```
protected override Control CreateControl()
{
  browser = new WebBrowser();
  browser.Dock = DockStyle.Fill;

  return browser;
}
```

16. The next method is `Navigate`, which follows `CreateControl` in the source code:

```
[ApplicationVisible]
public void Navigate(string url)
{
  browser.Navigate(url);
}
```

How it works...

NAV control add-in is built as a .NET assembly compiled in a `.dll` library, therefore the recipe starts from creating a class library project. First steps are identical to creating a .NET or a COM component. In `Chapter 4`, *.NET Interoperability in C/AL* we also added references to external libraries, as we do here in step 4. What's special in developing a UI control is that a control add-in library must always include a reference to the UI extensibility assembly `Microsoft.Dynamics.Framework.UI.Extensibility.dll`. Besides, the `System.Windows.Forms` assembly is also required in most cases. This namespace includes a rich variety of Windows UI features that can be included in your application.

Steps 10 and 11 replace default namespace references defined by the template, with those required in NAV UI control project. The first one `Microsoft.Dynamics.Framework.UI.Extensibility` contains definition of the `IObjectControlAddInDefinition` interface, which we will implement in one of the recipes in this chapter. But what's important for this walkthrough, is that the `ControlAddInExportAttribute` and `ApplicationVisibleAttribute` attributes are also declared in this namespace. These two attributes will be required in any class implementing a UI control.

The `WinFormsControlAddInBase` class, the base class for `NavWebBrowser`, is declared in the `Microsoft.Dynamics.Framework.UI.Extensibility.WinForms` namespace that is also included in the project.

The last using directive required for the control project is the `using System.Windows.Forms.WebBrowser` control, which will be displayed on a NAV page, is declared in this namespace.

In Step 13, the class declaration is expanded with a
`[ControlAddInExport("NavWebBrowserControl")]` attribute. This attribute is required
for the class to be recognized as a control add-in by the NAV Windows client. Text constant
`NavWebBrowserControl` is the name of the control. This name in combination with the
public key token will be used to identify the add-in.

The private `WebBrowser` browser private property, declared in Step 14, is the WinForms
control that will be displayed on a page. We do not allow direct access to the control from
other classes by declaring it as a private property. Instead, a reference to the control will be
returned to the caller by the `CreateControl` method described in Step 15. `CreateControl`
method is an abstract method declared in the `WinFormsControlAddInBase` base class and
it must be implemented in a derived class. Its purpose is to instantiate the control and
return the reference to the NAV client that calls the method.

Signing the control add-in assembly

An application using a developed assembly (Dynamics NAV in our case) must be able to
identify it. For this purpose, an add-in assembly must be signed with a strong name, which
is used to refer to the assembly by a unique identifier. The strong name consists of a human-
readable text name and a public key token generated with the **SHA-1 Algorithm**.

How to do it...

In this recipe, you will learn how sign the control add-in assembly.

1. In the **Project** menu, select **NavBrowserControl Properties** and open the **Signing**
   tab.
2. Set the checkmark in the **Sign the assembly** field.

3. In the following drop-down box, select the **<New>** option for the strong name key file:

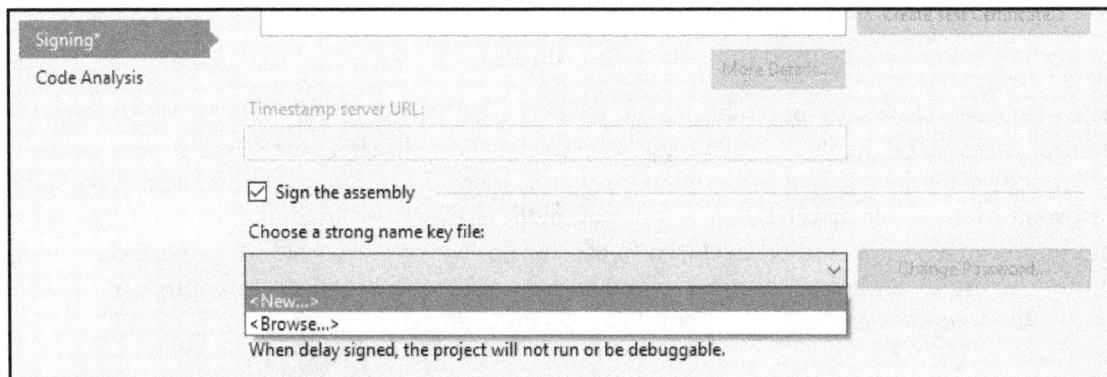

4. The **Create Strong Name Key** dialog will now open. Enter the name of the key file and the password and click **OK**:

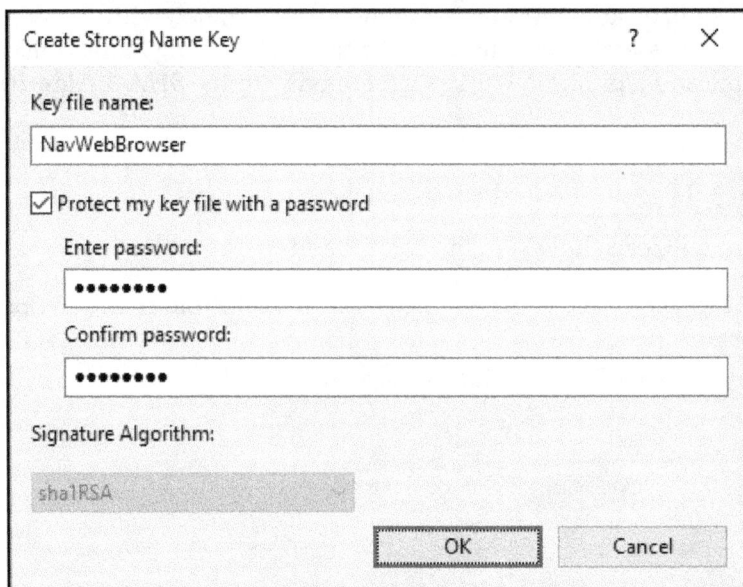

5. Save and build the solution.
6. To register a control add-in, you need to obtain a public key token assigned to the library during signing. In the **Tools** menu, choose **External Tools** to access the list of configured tools.

7. Click **Add** to set up a new tool and fill the form fields:
   - **Title:** `Get Public Key`
   - **Command:** `C:\Program Files (x86)\Microsoft SDKs\Windows\v8.0A\bin\NETFX 4.0 Tools\sn.exe`
   - **Arguments:** `-Tp $(TargetPath)`

The path in the Command field depends on the version of Windows SDK installed on your computer. In the example above, `v8.0A` is the version number. Replace it with the version you have installed.

Set the checkmark in the **Use Output Window** field.

Configuration of the tool in illustrated in the following screenshot:

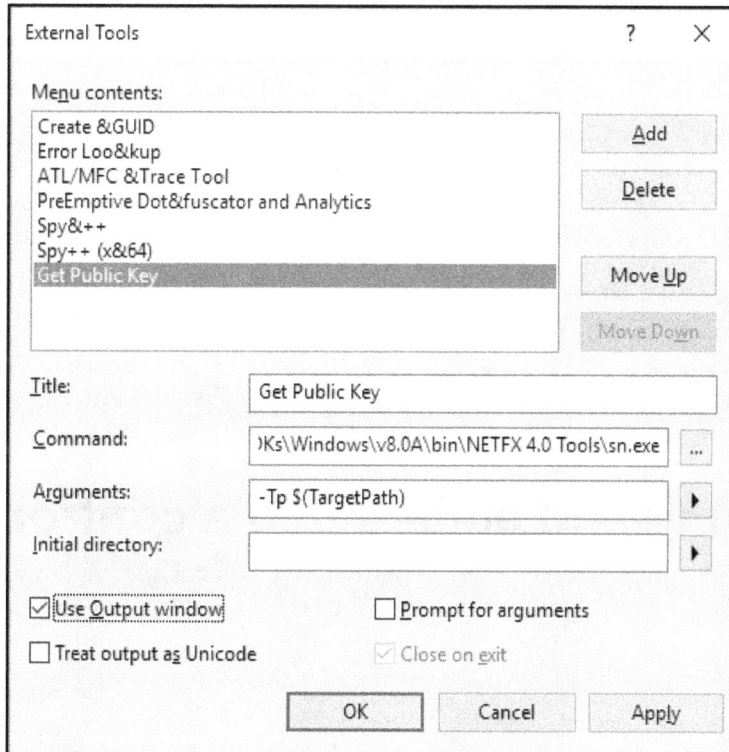

8. Click **OK**. Now a new **Get Public Key** option is available in the **Tools** menu. Select this menu option–public key token will be shown in the **Output** window:

```
Output
Show output from:  Get Public Key                                    ▾  🔍  ≡  ≡  ⩲  ᵃᵇ

Public key (hash algorithm: sha1):
00240000048000009400000006020000002400005253413100040000010001003510383896beb2b4
5ed2b47c9f5e5094492c46917bb09033a883092b942c2688f616265e02de121134fe559b0e718f
29cf713a6f98fc2918bf8e3e5d39d939c90ebe37d747875c872d45441770f80fca0cae16e2feea
83da3ae0a169241dd0f4e1c922db5e668fb83866b034e8709aefb50d5ddaaefa63b0340c8eb837
282e02a3

Public key token is e1c495ba8bddd8b7
```

How it works...

Step 1 through Step 5 describe a standard process of assembly signing in Visual Studio with built-in tools. Steps from 6 till the end of the recipe represent an alternative way of reading the public key from a signed assembly. A simple utility Sn.exe (**strong name tool**) included in the .NET SDK package is used to sign a .NET assembly and manage keys.

> **TIP**
>
> Normally, when you need to retrieve a public key from a signed assembly, you can run the utility from the command line. This becomes inconvenient if the tool must be used regularly. In this case, we can use the possibility of extending the standard toolset provided by Visual Studio.

Registering and embedding a control add-in

After building and signing the assembly containing the control add-in, it must be registered in the NAV database. After registering the add-in can be used in NAV development environment.

How to do it...

This recipe describes the process of registering the control and integrating it into a NAV client user interface.

1. Navigate to your projects' build output directory. Copy the `NavBrowserControl.dll` library to the client add-ins folder, `Add-ins`, located under the role-tailored client installation path. The default location of the folder is `C:\Program Files (x86)\Microsoft Dynamics NAV\90\RoleTailored Client\Add-ins`.

2. Run the NAV role-tailored client and open the **Control Add-ins** page located under `/Departments/Administration/IT Administration/General`.

3. Click **New** and fill the page fields:

   - **Add-in Name**: `NavWebBrowserControl`
   - **Public Key Token**: Refer to the *Signing the control add-in assembly* recipe to learn how to sign the assembly and obtain the public key token
   - **Category**: Choose **DotNet Control Add-in**:

Control Add-ins ▾		Type to filter (F3)	Add-in Name ▾ →	
				No filters applied
Add-in Name ▲	Public Key Token ▲	Category	Description	
Microsoft.Dynamics.Nav.Client.PingPo...	31bf3856ad364e35	DotNet Control Add-in	Microsoft Dynamics PingPong cont	
Microsoft.Dynamics.Nav.Client.SocialLi...	31bf3856ad364e35	JavaScript Control Add-in	Microsoft Social Listening control a	
Microsoft.Dynamics.Nav.Client.Timelin...	31bf3856ad364e35	DotNet Control Add-in	Interactive visualizion for a timeline	
Microsoft.Dynamics.Nav.Client.VideoPl...	31bf3856ad364e35	JavaScript Control Add-in	Microsoft Dynamics VideoPlayer co	
Microsoft.Dynamics.Nav.Client.WebPa...	31bf3856ad364e35	JavaScript Control Add-in	Microsoft Web Page Viewer control	
NavWebBrowserControl	e1c495ba8bddd8b7	DotNet Control Add-in	Web browser control	

4. Start NAV Development Environment and create a page object in page designer. Choose to create a blank page, no wizard is required.

5. Open **C/AL Globals** and declare a global variable `Address` of type `Text`.

6. Close the variable declaration window and insert a **Container** element of the `ContentArea` type in the page designer. Insert two `Field` elements under the container: `Address` and `WebBrowser`. In the **Address** field, type `Address` in the `SourceExpr` field to bind the global variable to the field.

7. In the same container, insert another field, `WebBrowser`. The field structure should be as follows:

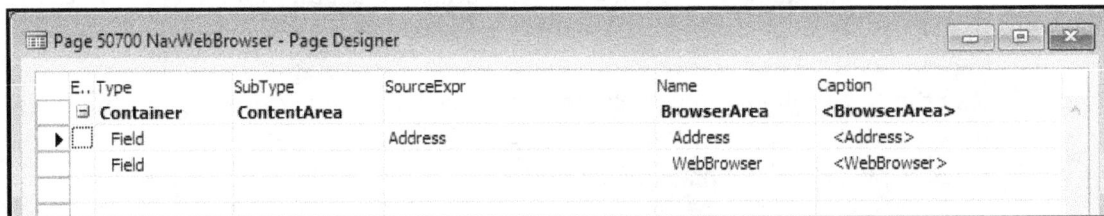

E.. Type	SubType	SourceExpr	Name	Caption
⊟ **Container**	**ContentArea**		**BrowserArea**	**<BrowserArea>**
▶ ⬚ Field		Address	Address	<Address>
Field			WebBrowser	<WebBrowser>

Page 50700 NavWebBrowser - Page Designer

8. Open properties of the **WebBrowser** field, locate the **ControlAddIn** property and click the lookup button. In the **Client Add-in** form, select the **NavWebBrowserControl** add-in, and click **OK**.

9. Set the value of the **ShowCaption** property to **No** and close the field properties.

10. In **C/AL Globals**, declare a `NavigateToAddress` function. Type the function code:

```
CurrPage.WebBrowser.Navigate(Address);
```

11. In the `Address - OnValidate()` trigger, insert the invocation of the function:

```
NavigateToAddress;
```

12. Save and compile the page, then run it from the object designer. In the **Address** field, type the URL you want to open (for example, `http://www.bing.com/`) and press *Enter*. The web page will open inside the NAV interface.

How it works...

Generated assembly file, `NavBrowserControl.dll`, must be placed in the client `add-ins` folder of the development computer, as shown in the first step of the recipe. Next, Step 2 and Step 3 register the extensibility component in the database. To register a control add-in, provide its name and the public key token. The add-in name is defined when developing the component–this is the value of the `ControlAddInExport` attribute. This attribute is declared in Step 13 of the *Developing control add-ins* recipe as `[ControlAddInExport("NavWebBrowserControl")]`. `NavWebBrowserControl` is the name of the control add-in that must be entered in the **Add-in Name** field when registering a new add-in.

The value of the **Public Key Token** field is the identification of the assembly received after the strong name signing. This process is described in detail in the *Signing the control add-in assembly* recipe.

When the control is registered, it is ready to be used in a development environment. You assign a control add-in to a page field by setting the field's property `ControlAddIn`, as shown in Step 7 and Step 8. The final steps of the recipe demonstrate the usage of the attribute `[ApplicationVisible]`. The `Navigate` method marked with this attribute becomes available in the NAV code editor and can be called from the application.

JavaScript in web, phone, and tablet clients

.NET control add-ins are a powerful tool to customize the user interface of NAV Windows clients, but these controls have a significant limitation – they can be used on role-tailored clients only. NAV clients running on web and mobile devices cannot execute client-side .NET code. As an alternative way to customize UI on devices and web, UI elements can be created in JavaScript. The following recipe demonstrates how to create a custom table control based on popular libraries jQuery and jqWidgets. An advantage of the resulting JavaScript control is that it can be executed on any type of NAV client.

Getting ready

This example uses two third-party libraries that should be downloaded from developers' websites prior to beginning work on the recipe.

Download jQuery library from `https://jquery.com/download/`.

Download jqWidgets library from `http://www.jqwidgets.com/download/`.

> jqWidjets library is free for personal use, but an appropriate license must be obtained if you want to use it in a commercial project.

How to do it...

Now we will develop a control add-in that can be embedded in a NAV page and shown in any type of client. Installation of the add-in and development of user interface with the control will be covered in the next recipe.

1. Start a new `Class Library` project in Visual Studio. Choose a **Create new solution** option and enter the name of the project: `NavCustomTable`.

2. Rename the `Class1` class to `CustomTableControl` in the solution explorer and confirm the request to rename related code references.

3. From the solution explorer, add a reference to the `Microsoft.Dynamics.Framework.UI.Extensibility.dll` assembly.

4. Replace all default using directives with one:

   ```
   using Microsoft.Dynamics.Framework.UI.Extensibility;
   ```

5. The `CustomTableControl` assembly should export only an interface definition, all implementation is carried out in JavaScript files and C/AL code. Remove the class declaration and replace it with the following interface:

   ```
   namespace NavCustomTable
   {
     [ControlAddInExport("CustomTableControl")]
     public interface ICustomTableControl
     {
       [ApplicationVisible]
       event ApplicationEventHandler ControlAddInReady;
       [ApplicationVisible]
   ```

```
            void UpdateDataTable(string jsonString);
        }
    }
```

6. Sign the assembly as described in the *Signing the control add-in assembly* recipe, then build the solution.

7. In your favorite code editor, type the JavaScript function that will be called to convert a JSON string into a `jqxDataTable` table object by one of the `jqWidgets` scripts:

```
function UpdateDataTable(jsonString)
{
    var data = JSON.parse(jsonString);

    var source =
    {
        dataType: 'json',
        dataFields:
            [{ name: 'No_' }, { name: 'Name' }],
            localData: data
    };
    var dataAdapter = new $.jqx.dataAdapter(source);
    $(document).ready(function () {
        $("#dataTable").jqxDataTable(
        {
            source: dataAdapter,
            altRows: true,
            sortable: true,
            columnsResize: true,
            width: 600,
            height: 400,
            columns: [
                { text: 'No.',
                dataField: 'No_', width: 100 },
                { text: 'Name',
                dataField: 'Name', width: 100 }
            ]
        });
    });
}
```

8. Copy the jQuery library `jquery-3.1.1.min.js` to the same folder (actual filename depends on the version of the downloaded library).

9. Make a `Script` folder in your working directory and copy the script file into this folder.

10. Save the JavaScript code as `navdatatable.js`.

11. Unpack the jQWidgets archive `jqwidgets-ver4.0.0.zip`. The exact filename depends on the product version you downloaded. Extract the following files from the archive and copy them to the `Script` folder:

    - `jqxcore.js`

    - `jqxdata.js`

    - `jqxbuttons.js`

    - `jqxscrollbar.js`

    - `jqxdatatable.js`

12. In your working directory, create a `StyleSheet` folder and copy a `jqx.base.css` file from the `jqWidgets` archive, located in the `jqwidgets\styles` folder.

13. In any text editor, create a new `Manifest.xml` text file. Insert the root xml element `<Manifest>`, and then fill the list of included resources in the `<Resources>` node. Block `<Script>` inside the manifest that contains executable JavaScript code:

```xml
<?xml version="1.0" encoding="utf-8"?>
<Manifest>
  <Resources>
    <Script>navdatatable.js</Script>
    <StyleSheet>jqx.base.css</StyleSheet>
    <Script>jquery-3.1.1.min.js</Script>
    <Script>jqxcore.js</Script>
    <Script>jqxdata.js</Script>
    <Script>jqxbuttons.js</Script>
    <Script>jqxscrollbar.js</Script>
    <Script>jqxdatatable.js</Script>
  </Resources>
  <Script>
    <![CDATA[
      var chartContainer = document.createElement("div");
      chartContainer.setAttribute("id","dataTable");
      chartContainer.setAttribute(
        "style","width:600px; height: 400px");
      $("#controlAddIn").get(0).appendChild(chartContainer);
      Microsoft.Dynamics.NAV.InvokeExtensibilityMethod(
        'ControlAddInReady');
    ]]>
  </Script>
</Manifest>
```

```
    <RequestedHeight>400</RequestedHeight>
    <RequestedWidth>600</RequestedWidth>
    <VerticalStretch>false</VerticalStretch>
    <HorizontalStretch>false</HorizontalStretch>
</Manifest>
```

How it works...

Step 1 through Step 6 cover the development of a .NET assembly containing the control add-in definition. But, unlike previous recipes, current example exports only an interface, not a class. All implementation is carried out in a JavaScript file presented in Step 7.

The key part of this recipe is the `Manifest.xml` file defined in Step 13. The Manifest file wraps together all resources included in the project. The list of included resource files, such as scripts, style sheets, or image files, must be presented in the `<Resources>` section of the file. Each filename is presented as a separate XML node. The node name for a script file is `<Script>`, **CSS** style sheets go under `<StyleSheet>` nodes, and a node name `<Image>` is reserved for image resources.

The resource description block is followed by the `<Script>` section that includes actual executable JavaScript code that must be placed inside a `<![CDATA[]]>` tag. Code inside this block is executed when the control add-in is initialized and includes any additional custom configuration. In this case, we create a div element that will be transformed into a data table widget.

To append the element to the document DOM structure, we use the following jQuery request:

```
$("#controlAddIn").get(0).appendChild(chartContainer);
```

Here, the `#controlAddIn ID` refers to the DOM element containing the whole add-in. NAV 2016 defines this add-in container as `<div id="controlAddIn"></div>`.

After all preparation work is completed, the control add-in notifies the NAV server and passes control to the extensibility method, `ControlAddInReady`, executed on the sever side. In the next recipe, we will see how this method works and how to use it to prepare data for presentation in the UI control.

Installing and using JavaScript control add-ins

The process of installing a JavaScript control mostly follows the installation of a .Net add-in, but it has its own specifics determined by the necessity of including a bunch of script files and style sheets into an installation along with the .NET assembly file.

How to do it...

The current recipe covers installation of a JavaScript control add-in and its subsequent usage in application development.

1. Copy the `NavCustomTable.dll` assembly file developed in the *JavaScript in web, phone, and tablet clients* recipe, into the NAV client add-ins folder.
2. Pack the `Manifest.xml` file along with both `Script` and `StyleSheet` folders in a `.zip` archive, `NavCustomTable.zip`. The archive should have the following structure:

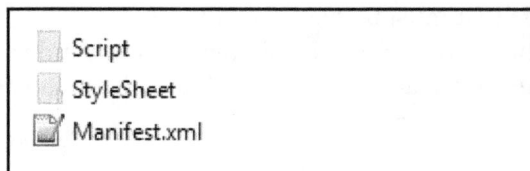

> Script
> StyleSheet
> Manifest.xml

3. Run the NAV client and open the **Control Add-ins** page located under **Departments | Administration | IT Administration | General**.
4. In the **Control Add-ins** list, click **New** and fill the control add-in parameters:
   - **Name:** `CustomTableControl`

The name of the control must match the value of the attribute `ControlAddInExport` defined in Step 5 of the recipe *JavaScript in web, phone, and tablet clients*.

   - **Public Key Token**: Enter the key token received after signing the assembly
   - **Category**: Choose the **JavaScript Control Add-in** option

5. After filling the required fields, click the **Import** action button from the **Control Add-in Resource** action group. Select the `NavCustomTable.zip` file created in Step 2, then click `Open`.

6. After the resource file is imported, the control add-in is ready for use in NAV development environment. Start NAV object designer and create a new page. As in other scenarios of this chapter, this should be a blank page, not based on any page wizard.

7. Create a **ContentArea** container in the page designer and insert a field in the container. In the field's property, `ControlAddIn`, open the list of add-ins and select the **CustomTableControl**. Change the name of the field to `CustomersTable`.

8. Open C/AL code editor. An event handler function, `CustomersTable::ControlAddInReady`, is available in the editor after configuring the control add-in. Declare local variables in this function:

Name	DataType	Subtype
Customer	Record	Customer
JsonString	Text	
IsLastRecord	Boolean	

9. Code in the trigger `CustomersTable::ControlAddInReady`:

```
IF Customer.FINDSET THEN BEGIN
  JsonString := '[';
  REPEAT
    JsonString := JsonString + '{';
    JsonString := JsonString + '"No_":"' +
      Customer."No." + '",';
    JsonString :=
      JsonString + '"Name":"' +
        ConvertString(Customer.Name) + '"';
    JsonString := JsonString + '}';
    IsLastRecord := Customer.NEXT = 0;
    IF NOT IsLastRecord THEN
      JsonString := JsonString + ',';
  UNTIL IsLastRecord;
    JsonString := JsonString + ']';
END;
CurrPage.CustomersTable.UpdateDataTable(JsonString);
```

10. Declare a `ConvertString` function called from the event handler. In C/AL Locals, set the function return type to `Text`. The function takes one parameter `String` of type `Text`.

11. In C/AL Locals, declare two local variables:

Name	DataType
I	Integer
ConvertedString	Text

12. Type the following function code:

```
FOR I := 1 TO STRLEN(String) DO
  CASE String[I] OF
    '"' :
      ConvertedString := ConvertedString + '"';
    ELSE
      ConvertedString := ConvertedString + FORMAT(String[I]);
  END;
EXIT(ConvertedString);
```

13. Save and run the new page. It shows the list of customers in a table generated by JavaScript:

JavaScript Table

No.	Name
01905902	London Candoxy Storage Campus
10000	The Cannon Group PLC
20000	Selangorian Ltd.
20309920	Metatorad Malaysia Sdn Bhd
20312912	Highlights Electronics Sdn Bhd
20339921	TraxTonic Sdn Bhd
21233572	Somadis

How it works...

When installing a JavaScript add-in, you copy an assembly file into the `Add-ins` folder of the development computer; you then provide the add-in name and public key token in the **Control Add-ins** page. This part is not different from registering a .NET control. The next step, however, is unique for a JavaScript control. A `.zip` archive containing the control add-in resources must be imported into the database. We pack the resource archive in Step 2 and Step 3 to import the file in Step 4.

Registered add-ins can be used in NAV development environment to customize standard page objects. Although, in case of JavaScript controls, all work on control initialization and drawing must be done by the client script. When developing a .NET control, we always implement a `CreateControl` method in the add-in assembly. This method called by the NAV client, instantiates the control. Here, the client application will invoke the `ControlAddInReady` event handler when the page is initialized. This is where we can start drawing the table. The rest of the recipe – Step 8 through Step 13 draw the table object.

In Step 9, the C/AL handler of the `CustomersTable::ControlAddInReady` event collects the customers' data and formats the result in a **JSON (Java Script Object Notation)** string. Although, data can be passed to the client script in any convenient format and JSON is not a requirement, it is supported by many JavaScript libraries, and has become the de facto standard in communication with JavaScript client applications. Converting a JSON string into an object is very simple: `JSON.parse(jsonString)` parses the string and returns an object.

When the formatted string is prepared, we pass it to the `UpdateDataTable` JavaScript function:

```
CurrPage.CustomersTable.UpdateDataTable(JsonString);
```

Note that `UpdateDataTable` is a JavaScript function implemented in `navdatatable.js`. But since we invoke it from C/AL code, we must also declare is as a .NET method in the `ICustomTableControl` interface and mark the method as `[ApplicationVisible]`.

Sending events from add-ins to NAV server

In the next recipe, we will update the web browser control and enrich it with a custom address bar that will change the background color depending on the browser state. Browser control should implement events to communicate its current state to other components. NAV server will subscribe to events and update the address bar accordingly.

Getting ready

The current recipe is based on the project developed in the *Developing control add-ins* recipe. Complete the walkthrough or copy the source code from the source files accompanying the book.

How to do it...

1. Run Visual Studio and open the `NavBrowserControl` project created in the *Developing control add-ins* recipe.
2. For this demo, we will declare two custom event handlers. Insert the following declaration after the `ControlAddIn` event handler:

   ```
   [ApplicationVisible]
   public event ControlAddInEventHandler BrowserNavigating;
   [ApplicationVisible]
   public event ControlAddInEventHandler BrowserNavigated;
   ```

3. Insert two private methods in the `NavWebBrowser` class:

   ```
   private void Browser_Navigating(object sender, EventArgs e)
   {
     BrowserNavigating(0, String.Empty);
   }

   private void Browser_Navigated(object sender, EventArgs e)
   {
     BrowserNavigated(0, String.Empty);
   }
   ```

4. Modify the method `CreateControl`. Insert the following lines before the return statement:

```
browser.Navigating += Browser_Navigating;
browser.Navigated += Browser_Navigated;
```

5. This is all we need to do to raise events in a control add-in. Now we will create another add-in that will react to browser control events. Start a new project in Visual Studio. In the **New Project** dialog, choose **Class Library** project template and select an option **Add to solution** from the **Solution** drop-down list. In the **Name** field, type the name of the new project `NavAddressBar`.

6. From the solution explorer, add references to the following assemblies:

    - `Microsoft.Dynamics.Framework.UI.Extensibility.dll`
    - `System.Drawing`
    - `System.Windows.Forms`

7. Remove automatically created using directives and replace them with the following:

```
using System;
using Microsoft.Dynamics.Framework.UI.Extensibility;
using Microsoft.Dynamics.Framework.UI.Extensibility.WinForms;
using System.Windows.Forms;
using System.Drawing;
```

8. Rename the default class `Class1` to `AddressBarControl` using solution explorer, then modify the class definition as follows:

```
namespace NavAddressBar
{
  [ControlAddInExport("NavAddressBar")]
  public class AddressBarControl : WinFormsControlAddInBase
  {
  }
}
```

9. Declare a private `addressTextBox` class property:

```
private TextBox addressTextBox;
```

10. The `Text` property will keep the text entered by the user in the address bar:

```
[ApplicationVisible]
public string Text
{
    get { return addressTextBox.Text; }
    set { addressTextBox.Text = value; }
}
```

11. Add the method instantiating the control:

```
protected override Control CreateControl()
{
    addressTextBox = new TextBox();
    return addressTextBox;
}
```

12. Create a method that will change the background color of the address bar when called from C/AL code:

```
[ApplicationVisible]
public void SetBackgroundColor(int red, int green, int blue)
{
    addressTextBox.BackColor = Color.FromArgb(red, green, blue);
}
```

13. Sign the assembly as described in *Signing the control add-in assembly* recipe.
14. Run the **Build Solution** command from the **Build** menu. This will build both projects in the solution and generate two assemblies, `NavBrowserControl.dll` and `NavAddressBar.dll`. Copy both files to the NAV client add-ins location. The default path is `C:\Program Files (x86)\Microsoft Dynamics NAV\90\RoleTailored Client\Add-ins`.
15. Register the assemblies as described in the *Registering and embedding a control add-in* recipe.
16. Run the NAV development environment and create a page. In the page designer, configure the controls structure as in the table:

Type	SubType	Name
Container	ContentArea	BrowserArea
Field		AddressControl
Field		WebBrowser

17. Note that the **SourceExpr** property remains blank for all controls, since none of them are assigned to C/AL variables.

18. Open properties for the **AddressControl** field and click the lookup button in the **ControlAddIn** field. Select the **NavAddressBar** add-in from the list of client add-ins.

19. In the list of properties for the **WebBrowser** field, locate the `ControlAddIn` property and select **NavWebBrowserControl** from the list of add-ins.

20. Select the **Page Actions** option in the **View** menu to open the action designer. Insert an `ActionContainer` item. Choose **ActionItems** in the **SubType** field. Insert one action in the container. Type the action name: `Navigate`.

21. Open the C/AL code editor and insert a call to the web browser's `Navigate` function in the `Navigate - OnAction()` trigger:

```
CurrPage.WebBrowser.Navigate(CurrPage.AddressControl.Text);
```

22. Two event handlers associated with the `WebBrowser` controls are now available in the code editor: `WebBrowser::BrowserNavigating` and `WebBrowser::BrowserNavigated`. First, edit the `WebBrowser::BrowserNavigating` event handler. Insert a code line:

```
CurrPage.AddressControl.SetBackgroundColor(255,255,0);
```

23. In the `WebBrowser::BrowserNavigated` function, insert a line:

```
CurrPage.AddressControl.SetBackgroundColor(0,255,0);
```

24. Save and run the page. Enter a URL that you want to open in the **Address** text box, and then click the **Navigate** action button. The address textbox changes background color to yellow while the page is being loaded. As soon as the page is opened, the color changes to green.

How it works...

Step 1 to Step 12 demonstrate a solution in Visual Studio containing two projects. The first four steps are modification to a previous project, `NavBrowserControl`. Step 2 introduces events that will be raised by the browser control when it begins opening a web page (`BrowserNavigating`) and when the page is completely loaded (`BrowserNavigated`). Both events are declared with the `[ApplicationVisible]` attribute to expose them to NAV development environment.

The `NavBrowserControl` class does not actually raise its own events – the task is to catch and redirect events from the `WebBrowser` control declared as a private property browser in `NavBrowserControl` class. This is what we do in Step 4: `NavBrowserControl` subscribes to events from the browser by attaching event handlers `Browser_Navigating` and `Browser_Navigated` to corresponding events. Both handlers, when called, invoke related events from the `NavBrowserControl` class.

Step 5 through Step 13 cover the process of development of the browser's address bar responding to events. The new control is based on the same principle – this is a class inherited from `WinFormsControlAddInBase` that instantiates a textbox control in the `CreateControl` method and returns the reference to the calling code.

To handle the control from C/AL code, we include two `ApplicationVisible` class members: the `Text` property and a `SetBackgroundColor` method. The property is required to get the web address entered by the user, while the method is responsible for changing the control background color.

Step 15 of the recipe moves development to NAV page designer. A NAV page object that includes both custom controls, acts as an integration point between them. NAV subscribes to events `BrowserNavigating` and `BrowserNavigated`. Corresponding event handlers `WebBrowser::BrowserNavigating` and `WebBrowser::BrowserNavigated` are automatically created in the page object. To handle events in NAV client application, we place C/AL code to one of these functions. Event handler `WebBrowser::BrowserNavigating` is called when the user types a web address and activates the **Navigate** action button. In this handler, we change the color of the address bar to yellow by calling the `SetBackgroundColor` method on the `AddressControl` object. After the page is loaded, the `WebBrowser::BrowserNavigated` event handler is called, and the background changes color to green via the same `SetBackgroundColor` method.

Linking add-ins with the database

The current recipe will cover the topic of creating a custom textbox control bound to a database field. Such control can be linked with a table field via the standard NAV property, `SourceExpr`. Any changes made by the user in a control linked to a table field are automatically reflected in the database.

How to do it...

1. Run Visual Studio and create a **Class Library** project. Choose to create a new solution and enter `NavDatabaseFieldControl` as the name of the project.
2. Rename the class `Class1` in the solution explorer. Assign a new name, `DatabaseFieldControl`, and accept renaming all code references.
3. In the solution explorer window, add references to assemblies `Microsoft.Dynamics.Framework.UI.Extensibility.dll` and `System.Windows.Forms`.
4. Remove default using statements and replace them with the following:

```
using System;
using Microsoft.Dynamics.Framework.UI.Extensibility;
using Microsoft.Dynamics.Framework.UI.Extensibility.WinForms;
using System.Windows.Forms;
```

5. Add references to the base class and interface to the class declaration, and insert the `ControlAddInExport` attribute:

```
namespace NavDatabaseFieldControl
{
  [ControlAddInExport("NavDatabaseFieldControl")]
  public class DatabaseFieldControl : WinFormsControlAddInBase,
    IObjectControlAddInDefinition
  {
  }
}
```

6. Declare two private properties in the class:

```
private TextBox textBox;
private bool valueChanged;
```

7. After the private declarations, insert implementation of interface members inherited from `IObjectControlAddInDefinition`:

```
public event ControlAddInEventHandler ControlAddIn;
public bool HasValueChanged {
  get { return valueChanged; }
}

public object Value
{
  get { return textBox.Text; }
```

```
    set {
      textBox.Text = (string)value;
      valueChanged = false;
    }
  }
```

8. The last method declared in the interface that must be implemented in the `DatabaseFieldControl` class is `CreateControl`:

```
protected override Control CreateControl()
{
  textBox = new TextBox();
  textBox.TextChanged += TextBox_TextChanged;

  ControlAddIn(0, string.Empty);

  return textBox;
}
```

9. Insert the following code to declare a `Editable` property that will control if the user is allowed to edit the field:

```
[ApplicationVisible]
public bool Editable
{
  get { return !textBox.ReadOnly; }
  set { textBox.ReadOnly = !value; }
}
```

10. Type the code of the event handler called when the text in the `TextBox` control has changed:

```
private void TextBox_TextChanged(object sender, EventArgs e)
{
  valueChanged = true;
}
```

11. Sign the assembly (see the *Signing the control add-in assembly* recipe for details on how to do it).
12. Build the project and copy the `NavDatabaseFieldControl.dll` assembly file to the client add-ins location.
13. Run NAV client and register the control. The registration procedure is described in the *Registering and embedding a control add-in* recipe.

11. In NAV page designer, create a blank page. Open properties of the new page and set the value of the `SourceTable` property to `Customer`.

12. In the page designer, configure the following controls:

Type	SubType	SourceExpr	Name
Container	ContentArea		Customer
Field		"No."	CustomerNo
Field		Name	CustomerName

16. Access properties of the **CustomerNo** field, and in the `ControlAddIn` property open the list of client add-ins. Select **NavDatabaseFieldControl** from the list.

17. The **CustomerName** field should refer to the same control add-in, so repeat step 16 for this field.

18. Open C/AL code editor. In the `CustomerNo - OnControlAddIn` event handler type the following code:

```
CurrPage.CustomerNo.Editable := FALSE;
```

19. Save the page and run it to view and edit customer records in custom controls.

How it works...

The first four steps of this recipe add references to external libraries. In step 5, the `DatabaseFieldControl` class that will implement the database-bound control is declared. This class is inherited from `WinFormsControlAddInBase`. Besides, the control class must implement an `IObjectControlAddInDefinition` interface in order to enable the connection between the UI component and data field.

The `ControlAddIn` event and two public properties, `Value` and `HasValueChanged`, are members of `IObjectControlAddInDefinition` that must be implemented in the class. All these interface members are implemented in step 7.

The `ControlAddIn` event is raised in the `CreateControl` method to notify the calling function (in our case, this will be a C/AL function) that the control is created and ready.

Step 9 defines an additional `Editable` property that is not required by the interface definition, but will be very useful to protect a control from editing. To make the property accessible from the NAV page designer, we mark with the `[ApplicationVisible]` attribute.

Step 15 through Step 19 demonstrate how to use the developed component. Two fields from the **Customer** table are displayed in a page in a custom textbox controls instead of standard NAV fields. To assign a table field to a control add-in, we use the standard `SourceExpr` property. No additional C/AL code is required to process the data. When a record is retrieved from the table, the NAV platform updates the value of the control through the `IObjectControlAddInDefinition` interface. The same way, the new value is automatically saved by the platform when the user updates the control content.

Exchanging data with add-ins

In this chapter, we learned how to create custom visual controls, call add-in methods from NAV application code, and raise and handle control events. Almost all recipes so far covered controls that accept scalar values in parameter methods. This is good for extensions displaying a single value, but if you need to show a table control, sending values for each table cell one by one is not the best way to fill the dataset. Recipes dedicated to JavaScript controls, explain one possible solution for this problem – sending data to the control as a JSON string. JSON format is native to a JavaScript environment. In .NET controls, wrapping data in a DataTable object is a more common approach.

How to do it...

This recipe shows how to create a custom `DataGridView` control that shows a list of customers in a table. To populate the control with data, we will employ the DataTable .NET object.

1. Start a new C# project in Visual Studio based on the **Class Library** template. In the **New Project** window, type the project name `NAVDataGridView` and choose to create a new solution.

2. In the solution explorer window, right-click on the name of the file `Class1.cs` and rename it to `NAVDataGrid.cs`. Accept the request to rename code references to the `Class1` class.

3. Do not leave the solution explorer. Right-click on **References** and add references to the `Microsoft.Dynamics.Framework.UI.Extensibility.dll` and `System.Windows.Forms` assemblies.

4. Replace the using directives auto-generated by the framework, with the following:

```
using Microsoft.Dynamics.Framework.UI.Extensibility;
using Microsoft.Dynamics.Framework.UI.Extensibility.WinForms;
using System.Windows.Forms;
using System.Data;
```

5. Add the base class reference and the `ControlAddInExport` attribute to the `NavDataGrid` class:

```
namespace NAVDataGridView
{
  [ControlAddInExport("NAVDataGridView")]
  public class NAVDataGrid : WinFormsControlAddInBase
  {
  }
}
```

6. The `WinForms` control, `DataGridView`, which will be displayed in the page, is declared as a private property in `NAVDataGridView`. Insert the declaration in the class:

```
private DataGridView dataGridView;
```

7. We will need to raise an event to notify the NAV server when the control is initialized. Insert the event declaration after the `dataGridView` property:

```
[ApplicationVisible]
public event ControlAddInEventHandler ControlAddIn;
```

8. Type the `CreateControl` method that overrides the abstract method of the base class:

```
protected override Control CreateControl()
{
    dataGridView = new DataGridView();
    dataGridView.Dock = DockStyle.Fill;
    dataGridView.ReadOnly = true;

    ControlAddIn(0, string.Empty);

    return dataGridView;
}
```

9. The `UpdateView` method will be called from NAV C/AL code to update contents of the data grid control. Declare the method and mark it `[ApplicationVisible]` to expose it to NAV server:

```
[ApplicationVisible]
public void UpdateView(DataTable dataTable)
{
    dataGridView.DataSource = dataTable;
}
```

10. Sign the assembly (refer to the *Signing the control add-in assembly* recipe if you require detailed description of the signing procedure).

11. Build the project, then run NAV client and register the control add-in, as described in *Registering and embedding a control add-in*. The name of the control add-in should be `NAVDataGridView`.

12. Run NAV Development Environment and create a blank page. In the page designer, insert a `ContentArea` container and add one field to the container. Enter `Customers` in the `Name` property of the field.

13. Select the `ControlAddIn` property of the field and select the add-in registered in Step 11.

14. Open C/AL editor. Declare a local `UpdateControl` function. Declare the following local variables in the function:

Name	DataType	SubType
Customer	Record	Customer
DataTable	DotNet	System.Data.DataTable
DataColumn	DotNet	System.Data.DataColumn
DataRow	DotNet	System.Data.DataRow

15. Type or copy the function code:

```
DataTable := DataTable.DataTable;

DataColumn := DataColumn.DataColumn;
DataColumn.ColumnName := 'No.';
DataTable.Columns.Add(DataColumn);

DataColumn := DataColumn.DataColumn;
DataColumn.ColumnName := 'Name';
DataTable.Columns.Add(DataColumn);

Customer.FINDSET;
REPEAT
  DataRow := DataTable.NewRow;
  DataRow.Item(0,Customer."No.");
 DataRow.Item(1,Customer.Name);
  DataTable.Rows.Add(DataRow);
UNTIL Customer.NEXT = 0;
CurrPage.Customers.UpdateView(DataTable);
```

16. Locate the control add-in trigger `Customers - OnControlAddIn` and invoke the `UpdateControl` function from it:

```
UpdateControl;
```

17. Now the page is ready. Compile and run the object to see the list of customers in the custom `DataGridView` control.

How it works...

In the first part of the recipe, a control add-in assembly is developed and compiled in Visual Studio. Declaration of the add-in is almost identical to developing a WinForms add-in described in *Developing a control add-in*, except for a `ControlAddIn` event that must be raised when the control is created and ready to receive data. Note that the event has an `[ApplicationVisible]` attribute.

Step 8 instantiates the `DataGridView` control that will be displayed in the page by implementing the `CreateControl` abstract method inherited from `WinFormsControlAddInBase`. This is the standard method of creating an add-in instance, except for the invocation of the `ControlAddIn` event prior to returning the instance reference to the calling code:

```
ControlAddIn(0, string.Empty);
```

At this point, an instance of the `DataGridView` control is already created and ready to receive the data to be displayed. The `ControlAddIn` event is handled by a NAV client application that prepares the dataset.

The event handler that receives control is `Customers – OnControlAddIn` in Step 16. The handler simply calls the `UpdateControl` function, where each customer record is presented as a `DataRow` object. All rows are inserted into a table represented by the `DataTable` object. Finally, the formatted table is passed as a parameter to the control's `UpdateView` function.

The `UpdateView` method in Step 9 demonstrates why `DataTable` is as natural for .NET as JSON is for JavaScript. All we need to bind the data received from NAV, to the control, is assign the variable to the `DataSource` property of the control:

```
dataGridView.DataSource = dataTable;
```

.NET framework will do the rest. It takes care of parsing the data table and assigning values to individual table cells.

8
Web Services

In this chapter, we will cover the following recipes:

- Publishing a SOAP web service
- Calling object methods in SOAP web services
- Exposing and consuming OData web services
- Querying NAV OData web services with LINQ
- Updating NAV data through web services
- Securing access to web services
- Consuming a NAV web service from Java

Introduction

A web service is defined by the World Wide Web Consortium as a software system designed to support machine-to-machine interaction over a network. Web services usually provide application interfaces accessible through a communication protocol, such as HTTP. Data and functionality exposed in a web service can be consumed by another software system.

NAV 2016 allows publishing application objects in SOAP or OData web services in several clicks. Three types of objects can be published: codeunits, pages, and queries. The first recipe of the chapter guides the reader through publishing a codeunit in a SOAP web service and exposing its global functions to client applications. The next recipe gives an example of a .Net application consuming the published SOAP service and calling its methods.

After that, we will cover several topics related to OData services and data access. We will walk through publishing a service providing access to NAV data and different approaches to retrieving the exposed data. In a recipe dedicated to data modification, we will create a sales order through the web service interface.

When it comes to exposing your data in a network, security becomes the top priority. We will also cover the important topic of protecting the service endpoints and user credentials.

Publishing a SOAP web service

Simple Object Access Protocol (**SOAP**) is an XML-based network communication protocol for web services. A web service call in SOAP is represented as an XML document, consisting of an external enclosing element, called SOAP envelope, a message header, and the body.

A SOAP service provides an object-oriented access to the resource. NAV can publish pages and codeunits through SOAP services, allowing objects' methods to be called from external applications over the network.

How to do it...

The first recipe shows how to enable web services on a NAV server instance to publish a codeunit as a SOAP web service.

1. Run the Dynamics NAV 2016 Administration application. In the console root, select the server name you want to configure. The default service name is **DynamicsNAV90**.
2. Make sure that the option **Enable SOAP Services** in the **SOAP Services** tab is enabled. Open the **OData Services** tab and verify the option **Enable OData Services**:

3. If either of these options is disabled, click the **Edit** button and enable both, then click **Save** and restart the NAV server.

4. In the NAV development environment, create a codeunit that will export its methods in a web service. Create a new codeunit object 50800 `Post Code Info`. This codeunit will expose one method `GetCityByPostCode` that accepts a postal code as a parameter and returns the name of the city this code belongs to.

5. Declare the function `GetCityByPostCode` in the **C/AL Globals** section. The value of the function's property `Local` should be `No` to make it accessible from the web service. Set `Text[30]` as the function return type and insert one parameter:

Name	DataType	Length
PostCode	Code	20

6. Declare a local variable in the function:

Name	DataType	Subtype
PostCodeCatalog	Record	Post Code

7. Type the following function code:

```
PostCodeCatalog.SETRANGE(Code,PostCode);
PostCodeCatalog.FINDFIRST;
EXIT(PostCodeCatalog.City);
Now let's publish this codeunit via a web service.
Start NAV client and open the page Web Services from
Departments/Administration/IT Administration/Services.
```

8. On the **Home** tab of the ribbon, click the action button **New** to create a new web service:

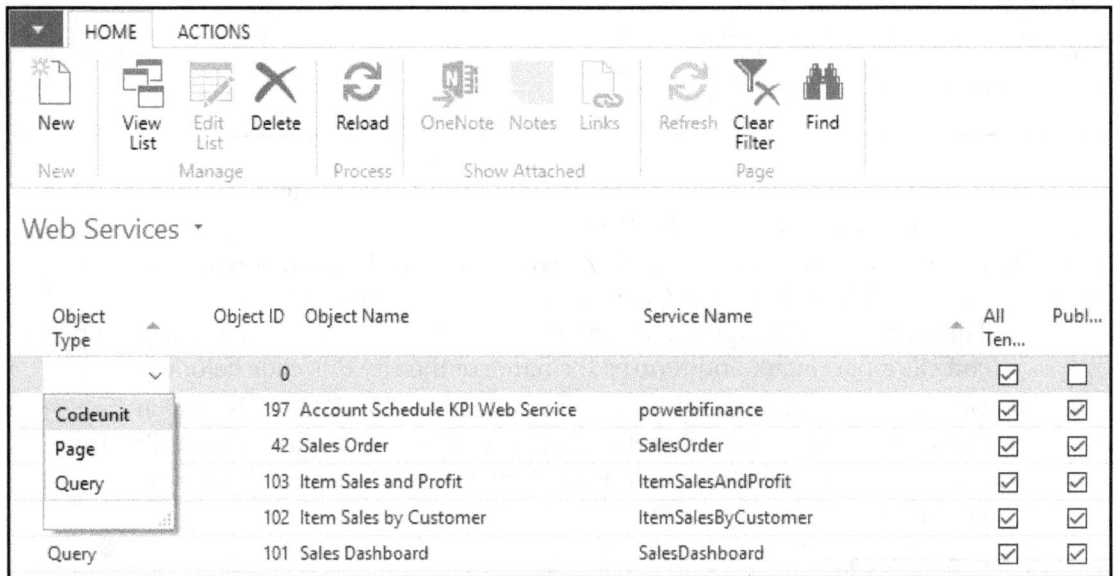

Object Type	Object ID	Object Name	Service Name	All Ten...	Publ...
⌄	0			☑	☐
Codeunit	197	Account Schedule KPI Web Service	powerbifinance	☑	☑
Page	42	Sales Order	SalesOrder	☑	☑
Query	103	Item Sales and Profit	ItemSalesAndProfit	☑	☑
	102	Item Sales by Customer	ItemSalesByCustomer	☑	☑
Query	101	Sales Dashboard	SalesDashboard	☑	☑

9. In the **Object Type** field, select the type of the object you want to publish in the web service. In this walkthrough, we will expose a codeunit object, so choose the **Codeunit** option.

10. Click the lookup button in the **Object ID** field to open the list of pages. Select the codeunit 50800 **Post Code Info** and click **OK**. This is the object that will be exposed in the web service.

11. To publish a web service, you must assign a name to it. In the field **Service Name**, enter the name `PostCodeInfo`.

12. Set the checkmark in the **Published** field. This will publish the web service. The **SOAP URL** field will be automatically filled with the address of the service. **OData URL** retains the value **Not applicable** because a codeunit web service can be accessed only via the SOAP protocol.

13. To ensure that the web service works as expected, select the web service you just created and click the link in the field **SOAP URL**. The link will open in your default web browser displaying the WSDL definition of the published web service.

Calling object methods in SOAP web services

The SOAP protocol is designed to provide access to object's methods over the TCP connection. In the previous recipe, we published a NAV object, and now we will see how to consume the service provided by the published codeunit and call its methods.

How to do it…

In this recipe, you will create a project in Visual Studio to consume a NAV web service and call a codeunit method.

1. Run Visual Studio. Create a new project based on the **Console Application** project template. In the **Name** field, enter the name of the project: `PostCodeWebServiceClient`.

2. In the **Solution Explorer** window, expand the contents of the project, right-click on the **References** section, and choose the option **Add Service Reference** from the drop-down menu:

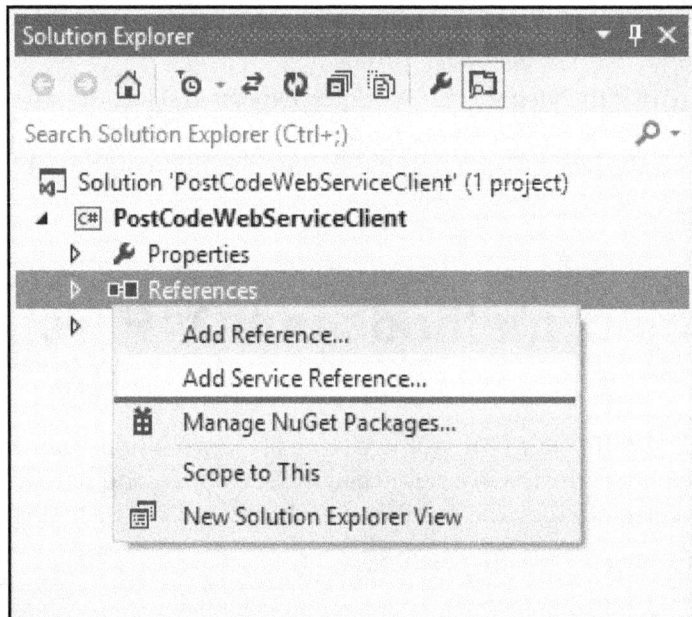

3. The **Add Service Reference** dialog opens. Click the **Advanced** button, then choose **Add Web Reference**.
4. In the **URL** field, enter the following address to access the list of published SOAP web services: `http://localhost:7047/DynamicsNAV90/WS/Services`

After entering the address, click the **Go** button located to the right of the **URL** field.

5. Find the service
`http://localhost:7047/DynamicsNAV90/WS/Codeunit/ApplicationMana`
`gement` in the list under**Discovery Page**, and click **View Service**:

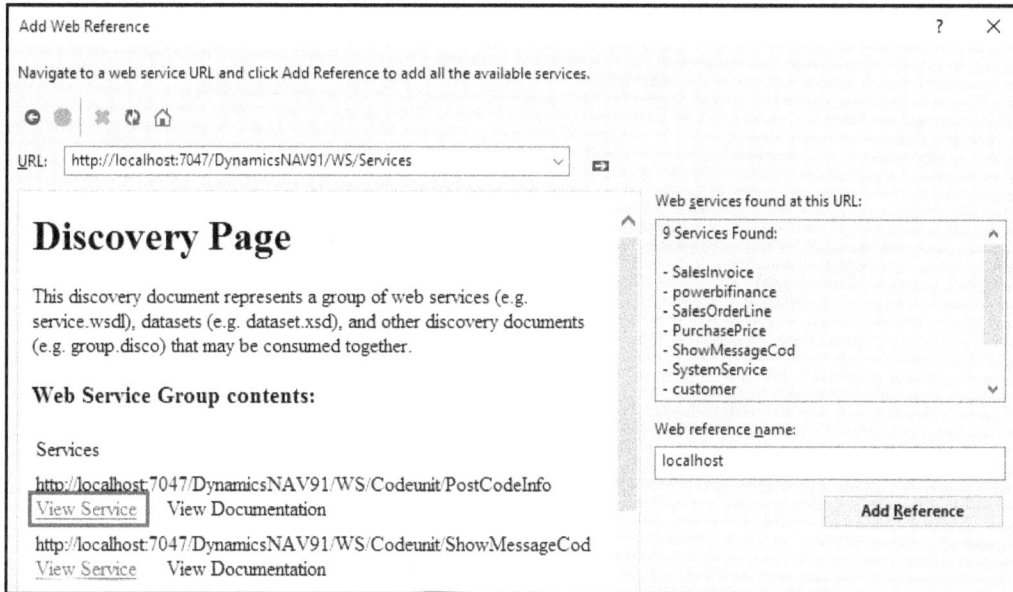

6. In the **Web reference name** field, enter `PostCodeInfoService` and click **Add Reference**:

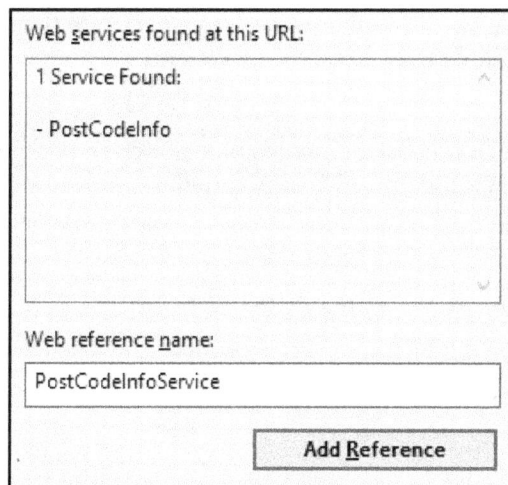

7. A new web reference is created in the project. Return to the code editor and include the web service namespace `PostCodeInfoService` in your source code. Insert the using directive inside the project namespace `PostCodeWebServiceClient`:

```
namespace PostCodeWebServiceClient
{
  using PostCodeInfoService;

  class Program
  {
```

8. Inside the `Main` function, type the code calling the web service:

```
PostCodeInfo postCodeInfo = new PostCodeInfo();
Console.WriteLine(
  postCodeInfo.GetCityByPostCode("BR 22291-040"));
Console.ReadLine();
```

9. Build and run the project. The execution result will be presented in the console window. To close the window, press *Enter*.

How it works...

To access the NAV web service, we start a .NET project in Visual Studio and add a reference to the service interface. Basically, this is all we need to do to obtain access to the web service. Step 2 through Step 7 describe how to add a service reference to the project. When these steps are done, Visual Studio will automatically generate the set of proxy classes wrapping all service communication details and provide access to the classes through the namespace `PostCodeInfoService` defined in Step 6.

The names of the classes available in the namespace match the names of web services published in NAV. The service we published is called `PostCodeInfo`, so this will be the name of the class inside the `PostCodeInfoService` namespace where the methods of codeunit 50800 `Post Code Info` are exposed.

The only thing left to do after creating the service reference, is to instantiate the class `PostCodeInfo` and call the method `GetCityByPostCode`. The execution result will be shown in the console window.

Exposing and consuming OData web services

The SOAP protocol serves well when you need a standardized interface for an object's methods. If you need to read and update table data, the **OData (Open Data)** protocol can be a better alternative. It is especially efficient in providing APIs that are open for querying.

NAV Page and Query objects can be published as OData services, providing access to underlying table data to consuming applications.

How to do it...

Now we will publish a page object as an OData web service and read the records from an external application in C#.

1. Start the NAV client and open the page **Web Services** from **Departments |
   Administration | IT Administration | Services**.
2. Click **New** to create a web service. Select **Page** in the **Object Type** field, then choose the page 7012 **Purchase Prices** in the **Object ID** field.
3. Assign a name to the web service to identify it. In the field **Service Name**, enter the name PurchasePrice.
4. Set the checkmark in the field **Published**. This will publish the web service. The **OData URL** and **SOAP URL** fields will be filled automatically. These are URL addresses to access the new web service via OData or the SOAP protocol.
5. Start a new project in Visual Studio and select the **Console Application** project template from the **Visual C# / Windows** template collection. Enter the project name NAVPurchasePricesWebService in the **Name** field.
6. Right-click on the **References** section located under the project name in the solution explorer. Select an option **Add Service Reference**.

7. Enter the URI of the web service in the **Address** field:
   `http://localhost:7048/DynamicsNAV90/OData/`.

   After filling in the **Address** field, click **Go**. Discovered OData services will be listed in the **Services** field. Choose the **NAV** service:

Add Service Reference   ?   ✕

To see a list of available services on a specific server, enter a service URL and click Go. To browse for available services, click Discover.

Address:

`http://localhost:7048/DynamicsNAV91/OData/`   ∨   [Go] | [Discover ▾]

Services: Operations:

⊙ ꞉⊕ NAV

                                 WCF Data Service: No operations found.

1 service(s) found at address 'http://localhost:7048/DynamicsNAV91/OData/'.

Namespace:

`PurchasePricesWebService`

[Advanced...]   [OK]   [Cancel]

---

8. In the **Namespace** field, enter the namespace that will be generated in the project: PurchasePricesWebService, then click **OK**.

9. After generating the service reference, include the namespaces required for the project:

```
using System;
using System.Net;
using System.Data.Services.Client;
using System.Collections.Generic;
using System.Linq;
```

10. Inside the namespace NAVPurchasePricesWebService, add another namespace reference:

```
using PurchasePricesWebService;
```

11. The function Main is automatically created in the project when you select the Console template. Now insert the following code into this function:

```
static void Main(string[] args)
{
  NAV nav = new NAV(
  new Uri(
    "http://localhost:7048/DynamicsNAV90/OData"));
  nav.Credentials = CredentialCache.DefaultCredentials;

  DataServiceQuery<PurchasePrice> query =
    nav.CreateQuery<PurchasePrice>("PurchasePrice");
  List<PurchasePrice> prices =
    query.Execute().ToList<PurchasePrice>();

  foreach (PurchasePrice price in prices)
  {
    Console.WriteLine(
      "Item: {0}, Unit cost: {1}",
      price.Item_No, price.Direct_Unit_Cost);
  }

  Console.ReadLine();
}
```

12. Run the project. A list of registered purchase prices will be displayed in the console:

```
Item: 70000, Unit cost: 17,3
Item: 70001, Unit cost: 22,7
Item: 70002, Unit cost: 16,1
Item: 70003, Unit cost: 16,6
Item: 70010, Unit cost: 29,2
Item: 70011, Unit cost: 40,6
Item: 70040, Unit cost: 60,7
Item: 70041, Unit cost: 13,2
Item: 70060, Unit cost: 7,4
Item: 70100, Unit cost: 1,6
Item: 70101, Unit cost: 1,6
Item: 70102, Unit cost: 1,6
Item: 70103, Unit cost: 1,6
Item: 70104, Unit cost: 1,6
Item: 70200, Unit cost: 0,8
Item: 70201, Unit cost: 0,7
```

13. To close the console window, press *Enter*.

How it works...

Like the previous recipe, the major part of the current walkthrough is dedicated to creating a service reference to the NAV web service. The steps are very similar to the SOAP example, although we use a simple service reference instead of the web reference.

Step 1 to Step 5 walk you through publishing an OData service in NAV. The process is no different from publishing a SOAP service. All the difference is made by the object we expose in a service. Only pages and codeunits can be exposed in SOAP services, and the OData service can give access to pages and queries. Only pages can export both functionality via a SOAP service and data through an OData service. Queries and codeunits are limited each by its own service protocol.

In Step 6 to Step 9 a service reference is created in a Visual Studio project with proxy classes for the web service created behind the scenes.

The client application accesses web service functionality through the autogenerated namespace `PurchasePricesWebService` declared in Step 9. It is included in the application later in step 11.

The function `Main` in Step 12 establishes a connection to the web service. All web services published by the NAV server are available through an instance of an object `NAV` instantiated here.

Querying NAV OData web services with LINQ

Language Integrated Query (**LINQ**) is an extremely convenient interface for writing SQL queries in .NET languages. SQL-like queries are integrated in the .NET syntax, so that the developer can write application code and database queries in a unified way instead of injecting database interaction statements in text constants.

The System.Linq library allows access to different data sources, including OData service interfaces.

How to do it...

Now we will walk through receiving data from a NAV page with a LINQ query.

1. Publish page 42 **Sales Order** as a web service. Refer to the *Exposing and consuming OData web services* recipe for a step-by-step description of OData service publishing. Assign the name `SalesOrder` to the new service.

2. In Visual Studio, start a **Console Application** project: `NAVSalesOrdersWebService`.

3. Open the **Add Service Reference** dialog. Run service discovery on `http://localhost:7048/DynamicsNAV90/OData/`

4. Select the service NAV in the list of discovered services. Set the namespace name to `SalesOrdersWebService` and click **OK**.

5. After completing the service reference configuration, return to the code editor and insert references to the required namespaces:

```
using System;
using System.Net;
using System.Linq;
namespace NAVSalesOrdersWebService
{
  using SalesOrdersWebService;
  class Program
```

6. Extend the automatically created function `Main` first by inserting the code instantiating the NAV object and assigning default credentials to the connection:

```
NAV nav = new NAV(
  new Uri("http://localhost:7048/DynamicsNAV90/OData"));
nav.Credentials = CredentialCache.DefaultCredentials;
```

Still inside the `Main` function, type the LINQ query to fetch sales orders from the `SalesOrder` web service:

```
var orders = from so in nav.SalesOrder
where so.Status == "Released" ||
so.Status == "Pending Approval" ||
so.Status == "Pending Prepayment"
select so;
```

The next block of code in `Main` shows the result of the executed query in the console window:

```
foreach (SalesOrder order in orders)
{
  Console.WriteLine(
    "Order No.: {0}, Sell-to Customer: {1}, {2:d}",
    order.No, order.Sell_to_Customer_Name, order.Due_Date);
}

Console.ReadLine();
```

7. Now build and run the project. Review the result in the console window.

How it works...

Step 1 through Step 4 repeat the initial setup steps from the previous recipe with small variations in object names.

In the next step, we include the required namespaces. There are three namespaces we need to employ to run the example. `System` contains the definition of the `Uri` class that defines the location of the web service. The next one, `System.Net`, holds the `CredentialCache` class, and the namespace `System.Linq` is where the language integrated query functionality is implemented.

The code in Step 6 creates an instance of the proxy class through which we will access the web services functionality. To identify the user connecting to the service, authentication information must be passed to the server. We assign default credentials by assigning the static property `CredentialCache.DefaultCredentials` to `nav.Credentials`.

Step 7 is where the LINQ query is executed. This is not exactly a SQL query, but the syntax is designed to resemble the database query language. This is a `select` statement with a set of filtering conditions in the `where` clause that returns a set of records that match the given criteria, from the `SalesOrder` web service.

Updating NAV data through web services

The functionality of page web services in NAV is not limited to reading data from the NAV server. Data exposed through an OData web service can be updated as well. In the following recipe, we will create a sales order using the OData web service.

Getting ready

To create a sales document in NAV, we must have access to at least two tables: sales header and sales line. Each NAV web service can expose a single object, therefore, to have access to both sales header and sales lines, we need to publish two web services. If you completed the *Querying NAV OData web services with LINQ* recipe, Page 42 `Sales Order`, representing the `Sales Header` table, is already published. Otherwise, refer to the aforementioned recipe to expose the first of the pages required in the following walk-through.

How to do it...

In this recipe, we will develop a C# application that will connect to the NAV database via a web service to create a sales order.

1. In addition to page 42, publish page 46 `Sales Order Subform` in an OData web service with the name `SalesOrderLine`. This service will serve as an interface for sales order lines.

2. In Visual Studio, start a **Console Application** project, `NAVWebServiceInsertData`.

3. In the solution explorer, add a service reference to the published NAV OData services. In further steps, it is assumed that the name of the web service namespace is `SalesOrdersWebService`.

4. In the code editor, include the required system namespaces:

```
using System;
using System.Net;
using System.Linq;
```

5. Inside the project namespace, refer to the namespace of the web service:

```
namespace NAVWebServiceInsertData
{
   using SalesOrdersWebService;
}
```

6. The class `Program` with the method `Main` is automatically generated by Visual Studio. Inside the **Main** function, type the code to instantiate the web service proxy class and set up authentication:

```
NAV nav = new NAV(
   new Uri("http://localhost:7048/DynamicsNAV90/OData"));
   nav.Credentials = CredentialCache.DefaultCredentials;
```

7. After instantiating the NAV proxy class, you can create an instance of the class `SalesOrder` and initialize the sales order header:

```
SalesOrder order = new SalesOrder();
order.Document_Type = "Order";
order.No = "00001";
order.Sell_to_Customer_No = "10000";
nav.AddToSalesOrder(order);
```

8. When the header is created, initialize a sales line:

```
SalesOrderLine orderLine = new SalesOrderLine();
orderLine.Document_Type = "Order";
orderLine.Document_No = "00001";
orderLine.Type = "Item";
orderLine.No = "1001";
orderLine.Quantity = 2;
nav.AddToSalesOrderLine(orderLine);
```

9. To insert the data into the NAV tables `Sales Header` and `Sales Line`, call the function `SaveChanges` and inform the user about the operation result. To handle possible errors correctly, the call to `SaveChanges` is wrapped in a `try..catch` block:

```
try
{
  nav.SaveChanges();
  Console.WriteLine(
    "Sales order was successfully created");
}
catch (DataServiceRequestException ex)
{
  Exception innerEx = ex.InnerException;
    System.Diagnostics.Trace.WriteLine(
      ex.Message + "\n" + innerEx.Message);
    Console.WriteLine("Could not create the sales order.");
}
```

10. Return to the NAV client, open the sales orders list and find the order `00001` created via the web service.

How it works...

Creating a sales order involved at least two pages – `Sales Order` and `Sales Order Subform`, based on the database tables `Sales Header` and `Sales Line`, respectively. Both pages must be published as web services.

In Step 3, a service reference is created. If you need to refresh your experience on publishing OData services, refer to the *Exposing and consuming OData web services* recipe.

The class NAV has methods for adding records to data objects. The names of these methods are prefixed with `AddTo`, followed by an object name. We use two of these objects in the code sample above: `nav.AddToSalesOrder` and `nav.AddToSalesOrderLine`, first to create a sales order header, then to add a line to the order.

Finally, changes are committed to the database by calling the method `nav.SaveChanges`.

> When records are inserted or updated through a web service, C/AL data modification triggers are also executed. If you open sales order dimensions, you can see that all default dimensions assigned to the customer, have been transferred to the document. This is done by the C/AL trigger `Bill-to Customer No. - OnValidate`.

`Nav.SaveChanges` is called inside a `try..catch` block to help diagnose an error if the operation fails. The text of the exception that caused the failure will be printed in the Visual Studio **Output** window.

The `SaveChanges` method returns an instance of the `DataServiceResponse` class. You can assign the value to a variable to analyze the operation status:

```
DataServiceResponse res = nav.SaveChanges();
```

Securing access to web services

SOAP and OData web services provide functionality over the HTTP protocol. This is fine as long as you consume the service inside the corporate domain and your data is protected from intrusion. If a web service must be available over the web, HTTP does not provide sufficient protection to ensure the security of your data. The HTTPS protocol is preferable is this case.

In this recipe, we will create a separate instance of a NAV server accepting authentication requests over the HTTPS protocol. This instance will be a web service access point for external users.

Getting ready

To run the example in the current recipe, you will need an SSL certificate installed on your NAV server and client computers. The process of generating a self-signed certificate for testing purposes is described in the *Configuring NAV server* recipe in `Chapter 1`, *Writing Basic C/AL Code*.

How to do it...

This recipe demonstrates NAV server setup for secure user access with an SSL certificate.

1. Run **Dynamics NAV 2016 Administration** from the **Start** menu.
2. Right-click on **Microsoft Dynamics NAV** under the console root and choose **Add Instance**:

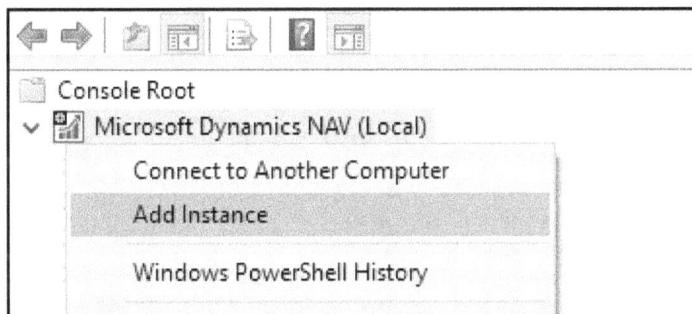

3. In the **Server Instance** window, fill in the server instance configuration:
    - **Server Instance:** NAV2016_WebService
    - **Management Services Port:** 7055
    - **Client Services Port:** 7056
    - **SOAP Services Port:** 7057
    - **OData Services Port:** 7058
    - **Account:** Network Service

4. The new web server instance NAV2016_WebService will be added to the list of servers under the console root in the left pane. Select the instance and click the **Edit** button to edit the server configuration.

5. Expand the **OData Services** tab in the middle pane and enable the **Enable SSL** option:

NAV2016_WebService - (Running)

General

Database

Client Services

SOAP Services

OData Services		
Enable OData Services:	☑	OData Base URL:
Enable SSL:	☑	Port:
Max Page Size:	1000	

6. Expand the **SOAP Services** tab and enable SSL for SOAP web services as well.
7. Click **Save**, then restart the server instance for the new configuration to take effect.
8. In the following steps, you will create a user account that will be used by web services to authenticate on the NAV server. Run Role-Tailored Client and connect to your NAV server instance.
9. In the main application menu, navigate to **Administration | IT Administration | General | Users** to open the list of user accounts and click **New**.
10. Fill in the user card. Enter the **User Name**, then click on the **assist** button in the **Password** field and enter the user **password**.
11. Expand the **Web Service Access** tab. Click the **assist** button in the **Web Service Access Key** field. You will be requested to set up the key expiration date. Check the **Key Never Expires** field and click **OK** to close the request window.
12. The web service access key is generated:

Web Service Access

Web Service Access Key:	Oc1CCKHvZabryCcK56y+II9mE1aKdryn9FB8+q/zEt8=	...

13. Start a new **Console Application** project in Visual Studio.

14. Add a service reference to the published query, in the same way as in previous recipes, but with HTTPS protocol instead of HTTP: `https://localhost:7058/NAV2016_WebService/OData/`.

15. In the code editor, type the code to include the required namespaces:

```
using System;
using System.Net;
using System.Linq;
```

16. Inside the declaration of the namespace `WebServiceAccessKeyAuth`, add a reference to the web service namespace `SalesOpportunitiesService`:

```
namespace WebServiceAccessKeyAuth
{
  using SalesOpportunitiesService;

  class Program
  {
    static void Main(string[] args)
    {
    }
  }
}
```

17. Implement the method `Main` of the `Program` class. In the network credentials, the web service access key is passed instead of the password. The key should be copied from the user account created in Step 10, and used in the parameters of the constructor of the `NetworkCredential` class:

```
NAV nav = new NAV(
  new Uri("https://localhost:7058/NAV2016_WebService/OData"));

SalesOpportunities opp = new SalesOpportunities();
CredentialCache cache = new CredentialCache();
cache.Add(
  nav.BaseUri, "Basic",
  new NetworkCredential(
    "NAVUSER",
    "Oc1CCKHvZabryCcK56y+Il9mE1aKdryn9FB8+q/zEt8="));
nav.Credentials = cache;

var salesOpp = from so in nav.SalesOpportunities select so;

foreach (var o in salesOpp)
Console.WriteLine(
```

```
       "{0}. Estimated value: {1}; Chance of success: {2}\n",
       o.Description, o.Estimated_Value_LCY, o.Chances_of_Success);

Console.ReadLine();
```

How it works...

We begin this example by creating a separate instance of the NAV server that will accept connections over the HTTPS protocol protected by SSL encryption. We enable protection with the option **Enable SSL** in the service instance configuration in Step 5.

Step 8 through Step 12 create a user account that will be used to access the web service. Since our intention is to provide access to web services from a wide area network, we want the user to use a protected connection and don't want to expose domain credentials. For this purpose, we generate a web service access key in Step 12. This is a random string that can be used instead of a password when connecting to a web service. It provides a higher security level because you cannot use the string to access the application. A login attempt with the web service access key will be accepted only when connecting to SOAP or OData services.

The application code is demonstrated in Step 17. Unlike in previous examples, in this scenario we instantiate a `CredentialCache` class to authenticate on the NAV server:

```
CredentialCache cache = new CredentialCache();
cache.Add(
  nav.BaseUri, "Basic",
  new NetworkCredential(
    "NAVUSER", "Oc1CCKHvZabryCcK56y+Il9mE1aKdryn9FB8+q/zEt8="));
nav.Credentials = cache;
```

An instance of `NetworkCredential` class is assigned to the credential cache. In the constructor of the class we pass the name of the user account created in Step 9, then provide the web service access key instead of the password in the second parameter of the constructor.

This is the only change that must be done in the code of the application consuming the service – the NAV server will authenticate the user with the service access key.

> Note that, if you try to verify the web service availability and open the service page
> `https://localhost:7058/NAV2016_WebService/OData/` in a web browser, some browsers (for example, Google Chrome or Microsoft Edge) may warn you that the site you are connecting to is unsafe. The reason for this warning is the algorithm SHA-1 that is used for signing the test certificate. Currently, this algorithm is considered weak and not providing a sufficient security level. It is recommended to use SHA-2 or SHA-3 instead.

If the NAV server and client are located on different computers, an SSL certificate must be installed on both.

Consuming the NAV web service from Java

Web service protocols such as SOAP and OData, are industry standards independent of a language or technology. They provide a high-level communication format for applications built on different platforms, allowing data exchange without the need to worry about underlying implementation details.

Due to the protocol's independence, it is possible to consume NAV data and functionality exposed through web services, from various client applications built on different technologies. In the next example, we will see how to call methods of a NAV web service from a Java application. The service used in this example is the one published earlier in the *Calling object methods in SOAP web services* recipe.

Getting ready

To be able to write and execute Java code, and to make the development process smooth, you will need some tools installed on your dev machine. The first requirement is to download and install **Java Development Kit (JDK)** from `www.oracle.com`.

It is possible to write Java code in Notepad and compile it from the command line, but a good integrated development environment saves a lot of effort while coding. The following example demonstrates development in IDE Eclipse, the Luna release. Eclipse can be freely downloaded from `https://eclipse.org`.

Besides additional development packs, you will need a running instance of a NAV server with the `NavUserAuthentication` credential type. If you completed the walkthrough in the *Securing access to web services* recipe, there should be an instance running. Otherwise, create a service instance as described in the preceding recipe.

How to do it...

The last recipe of the chapter shows how to explicitly generate proxy classes from a web service WSDL definition and consume a NAV web service from a Java application.

1. Access the **Start** menu and run **Dynamics NAV 2016 Administration**.
2. Select the server instance `NAV2016_WebService`. Click **Edit** to switch the form to edit mode. Under the **General** tab, locate the option **Use NTLM Authentication** and tick the checkmark:

NAV2016_WebService - (Running)

Enable Debugging:	☐	Services Option Text Source:	OptionC... ∨
Enable Event Logging to Windows Application Log:	☑	Session Event Table Retain Period:	3
Enable File Access by C/AL Functions:	☑	UI Elements Removal:	LicenseF... ∨
Enable Full C/AL Function Tracing:	☐	Use NTLM Authentication:	☑
Encryption Provider:	LocalKe... ∨		

3. Click **Save**, then restart the service.
4. Now you need a directory where proxy classes for web services will be generated. Create a directory where the `.java` source files will be located.
5. In your new directory, create a file with authentication information. I called the file `JWSAuth.txt` and placed it in the folder `C:\Work\JavaWS`. Further in this recipe, I will refer to this folder as `<RootFolder>`. You can give it any name you like.
6. Open the file in a text editor and insert a single line in it. Replace the placeholders `<username>` and `<password>` with the real user name and the password of the NAV user:

```
http://<username>:
  <pasword>@localhost:
  7057/NAV2016_WebService/WS/Codeunit/PostCodeInfo
```

7. Open the command prompt and change the current directory to the folder where you installed the JDK package. For example, if JDK binaries are installed in the folder `C:\Program Files\jdk1.8.0_111\bin`, then execute the following command:

```
cd C:\Program Files\jdk1.8.0_111\bin
```

8. In the command line, run the command:

```
wsimport -Xauthfile <RootFolder>\JWSAuth.txt -d <RootFolder>
-s <RootFolder>\src
http://localhost:7057/NAV2016_WebService/
WS/Codeunit/PostCodeInfo
```

9. The previous command generates a set of compiled Java bytecode files in a folder specified after the argument `-d`. The source files are located in the folder defined by the argument `-s`.

10. Run Eclipse IDE and create a new project. To start the project, choose the option **New / Java Project** in the **File** menu.

11. In the **New Java Project** dialog, enter the name of the project `NavWebServiceClient`. Leave default values in other fields. Click **Finish** to create the project.

12. In the **Package Explorer** tab, select your new project, right-click on it, and choose the **New / Package** option:

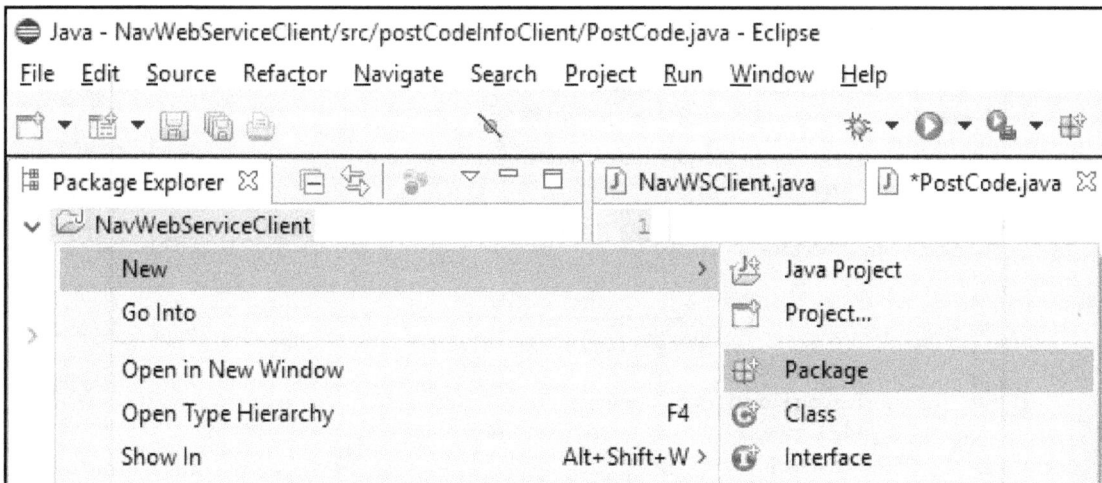

13. Keep the default value for the package source folder and enter the package name: `postCodeInfoClient`:

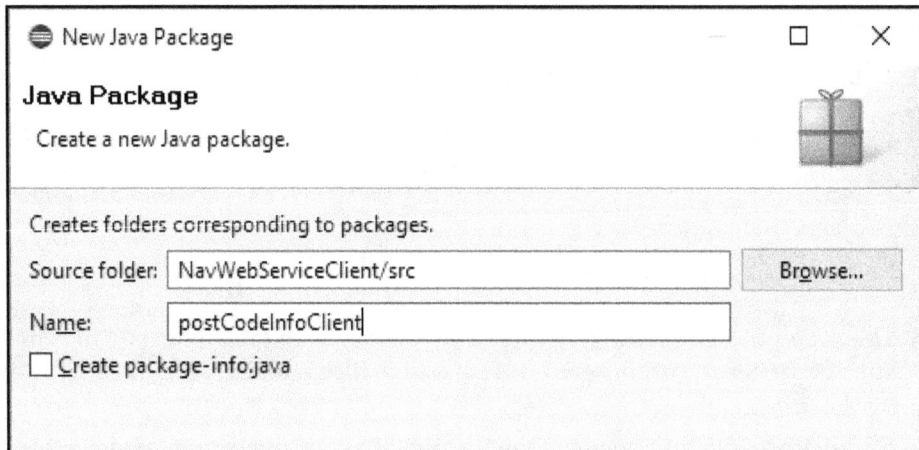

14. Create another package in the Java project. The second package must be named `schemas.dynamics.microsoft.codeunit.postcodeinfo`. In this package, we will import the web service proxy generated by Java Development Kit.

15. In the **Package Explorer** tab, select the package created in Step 12, right-click on the package, and choose the menu option**Import**. In the dialog window, choose the **File System** option to import new files into the project:

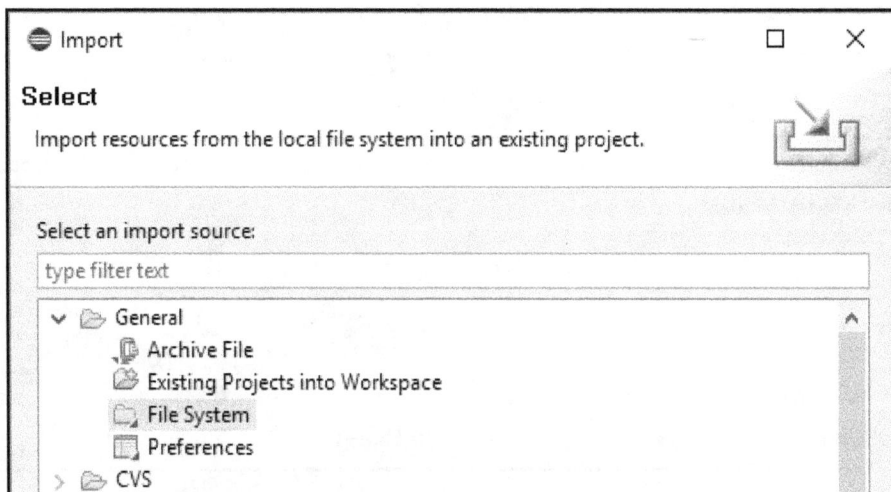

16. In the next dialog box, browse to the folder
    `<RootFolder>\src\schemas\dynamics\microsoft\codeunit\postcodein`
    `fo`. Select this directory in the **Import From** dialog box. Mark all files and click
    Finish. All classes based on web service import will be included in the package
    `schemas.dynamics.microsoft.codeunit.postcodeinfo`.

17. Select the package name `postCodeInfoClient` in the package explorer. In the
    File menu, choose **New**, then **Class**. Type the class name `PostCode`, keeping
    other fields as suggested by the template.

18. Start writing Java code in the new file `PostCode.java`. The file already contains
    the declaration of the class `PostCode`, as well as the package reference:

    ```
    package postCodeInfoClient;

    public class PostCode {
      public static void main(String[] args) {
      }
    }
    ```

19. Import the external classes required for the project. The package definition
    should be the first statement in the class file. Type the following import
    statements right after the package reference, before the class declaration:

    ```
    import java.net.*;
    import javax.xml.namespace.*;
    import schemas.dynamics.microsoft.codeunit.postcodeinfo.*;
    ```

20. To be able to authenticate on the NAV server, a Java client should implement a
    class extending the `Authenticator` class and provide user credentials inside it.
    Declare the class `MyAuthenticator` in your source code:

    ```
    class MyAuthenticator extends Authenticator {
      public PasswordAuthentication getPasswordAuthentication() {
        String userName = "<username>";
        String password = "<password>";
        return (new PasswordAuthentication(userName,
          password.toCharArray()));
      }
    }
    ```

21. Implement the `Main` method in the class `PostCode`:

```
public static void main(String[] args) {
  Authenticator.setDefault(new MyAuthenticator());

URL wsURL;
try {
  wsURL = new URL(
    "http://localhost:7057/
    NAV2016_WebService/WS/Codeunit/PostCodeInfo");
  } catch (MalformedURLException e) {
    e.printStackTrace();
    return;
  }

  QName wsQName = new QName(
    "urn:microsoft-dynamics-schemas/codeunit/PostCodeInfo",
    "PostCodeInfo");
  PostCodeInfo postCodeInfo =
    new PostCodeInfo(wsURL, wsQName);
  PostCodeInfoPort postCodeInfoPort =
    postCodeInfo.getPostCodeInfoPort();
  String city =
    postCodeInfoPort.getCityByPostCode("DK-2950");

  System.out.println("City: " + city);
}
```

22. Run the application. You will see the result in the **Console** window on the bottom of the window layout, below the code editor:

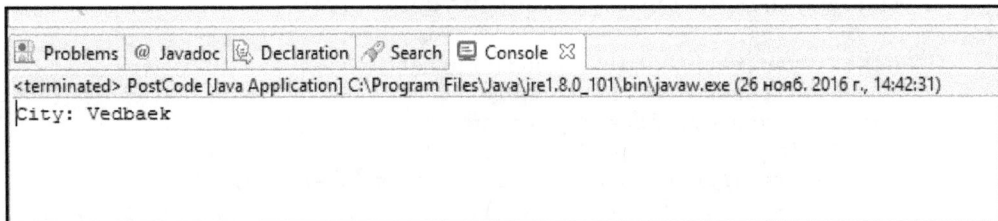

```
Problems  @ Javadoc  Declaration  Search  Console

<terminated> PostCode [Java Application] C:\Program Files\Java\jre1.8.0_101\bin\javaw.exe (26 ноя6. 2016 г., 14:42:31)
City: Vedbaek
```

How it works...

In the first step of the recipe, we enable the option allowing external application to connect to the NAV server using the NTML authentication mechanism. NTLM is supported by **Java Platform Standard Edition (Java SE)**, version 6 and higher.

A web service client communicates with the service by sending messages in XML format, wrapped in HTTP requests. The service responds in the same manner, wrapping the data in XML and sending it in HTTP packets. Therefore, it is even possible to communicate with a web service by manually creating XML documents and sending them to the web service endpoint. As long as you post the XML document formatted according to the WSDL definition, you will get the result. But normally, these implementation details are hidden from the application developer. The laborious task of wrapping a function call into an XML document is performed by the proxy class.

When you develop a web service client in Visual Studio, proxy classes are generated from the web service WSDL description when you add the service reference to the project.

For a Java project, you must generate corresponding classes from WSDL explicitly by running the utility `wsimport`. This is done in Step 4 through Step 9. The text file created in Step 5 and Step 6 must contain the user credentials of a NAV user authorized to access the web service. This file is passed to the `wsimport` command in Step 8.

The result of this command is a set of `.class` files containing compiled Java bytecode along with corresponding source files. The source `.java` files will be included in the project. These files contain all Java code required to access the web service published in NAV.

In the subsequent steps, we create a Java package and import autogenerated proxy classes into the package. To refer to proxy classes in the application code, we need to import them, which is done in Step 19.

To authenticate on the server, the application must extend the abstract class `Authenticator` and override its method `getPasswordAuthentication` to provide user credentials, which is done in Step 20.

Step 21 is where the code calling the web service method is implemented. And the very first statement in the `Main` function sets the instance of `MyAuthenticator` as the default authenticator. After that, an instance of the proxy class `PostCodeInfo` is created to call the required web service method.

Note the `try..catch` block in Step 21 that handles the exception `MalformedURLException`. This may seem excessive, since the URL is hardcoded in this example, and we are sure it is well-formed. Still, this is a requirement to handle `MalformedURLException` when instantiating the URL class. Removing this statement will cause a compilation error.

9
Events and Extension Packages

In this chapter, we will cover the following recipes:

- Subscribing to business and integration events
- Subscribing to global events
- Using database trigger events
- Extending UI with page trigger events
- Creating custom events
- Subscribing to events in runtime
- Developing an extension
- Installing an extension

Introduction

The concept of events has been introduced in NAV 2016 to simplify the customization of system functionality and isolate custom modifications in the code and the data model from the NAV application. Keeping custom modifications apart from the base application helps developers to reduce maintenance cost and simplify the upgrade process.

Event processing includes two steps. First, an event is raised by an event publisher object. Event subscribers, bound to the corresponding event, receive a notification, and execute event processing code. Different types of application events will be discussed in the beginning of the chapter. The first recipes show how custom objects subscribe to events raised by the application business login, or by the NAV platform.

In the *Creating custom events* recipe, you will learn how to raise a custom event that can be handled by other event subscribers.

The practical application of events is further developed in recipes dedicated to NAV extension packages. A NAV extension package is a file containing custom modification to NAV application code. Extensions are not allowed to modify C/AL code, and all customizations of code are done through event subscription.

Subscribing to business and integration events

Business and integration events are raised by C/AL code to notify subscribers about the execution of certain actions in application business logic. For example, these kinds of events in codeunit 90 `Purch.-Post`, are `OnBeforePostPurchaseDoc` and `OnAfterPostPurchaseDoc`. The first one is raised when a purchase document is submitted to the posting procedure, before processing, and the second event is called immediately after the document is processed.

Codeunit 22 `Item Jnl.-Post Line` raises a corresponding event when inserting a certain type of a ledger entry. Now we will see how to update an item ledger entry, filling in custom fields, by subscribing to an integration event to avoid modifying the application code in codeunit 22.

How to do it...

This recipe illustrates the steps required to create an object subscribing to an event raised by the codeunit `Item Jnl.-Post Line` when it processes a journal line.

1. In C/SIDE table designer, select the table 32 `Item Ledger Entry` and click the **Design** button to open the table in design mode.

   > Export the unchanged version of the table to a file before modifying it – the original object will be required later in the *Developing an extension* recipe.

2. Add two fields to the table design:

Field No.	Field Name	Data Type	Field Class
50000	Created Date	Date	Normal
50001	Created Time	Time	Normal

Create a codeunit in the object designer. In the new codeunit, access **C/AL Globals** and declare a function `UpdateItemLedgEntryDateTime`. This is the function that will subscribe to an event. It does not have to be global, so keep the default value of the property `Local = Yes`.

4. Access the function properties and change the value of `Event` property to `Subscriber`.

5. After the previous step, some new properties, specific to event subscriber functions, will be available in the list. We will use two of these properties now.

6. In the property `EventPublisherObject`, type `Codeunit 22`. When the value of the property is validated, it will automatically change to `Codeunit Item Jnl.-Post Line`.

7. Select the next property, `EventFunction` and click the **lookup** button in the property value field. From the list of events, choose the function `OnAfterInsertItemLedgEntry`. At this point, the system will request a confirmation that you want to change the function signature. Confirm the request.

8. Close the function properties and return to the code editor. Review the parameters of the function. Its signature was updated to match that of the event publisher and now contains two parameters:

Name	DataType	Subtype
ItemLedgerEntry	Record	Item Ledger Entry
ItemJournalLine	Record	Item Journal Line

In the function `UpdateItemLedgEntryDateTime`, type the following code:

```
ItemLedgerEntry.VALIDATE("Created Date",TODAY);
ItemLedgerEntry.VALIDATE("Created Time",TIME);
ItemLedgerEntry.MODIFY(TRUE);
```

9. Save the object as codeunit `50900 Item Ledger DateTime`. Compile it, then run the page 9510 `Event Subscriptions` to ensure that the new subscription is active:

Subs... Cod...	Subscriber Codeunit Name	Subscriber Function	Event Type	Publisher Object ...	Publis... Obje...	Publisher Object Name	Published Function
6700	Contact Sync. Implementation	SetupContactSyncJobQueue	Integration	Codeunit	2	Company-Initialize	OnCompanyInitialize
9002	Permission Manager	AddUserToAllUserGroupsOfThePl...	Trigger	Table	9005	User Plan	OnAfterInsertEvent
9002	Permission Manager	RemoveUserFromUserGroupsOfT...	Trigger	Table	9005	User Plan	OnAfterDeleteEvent
9010	Azure AD User Management	HandleBeforeCompanyOpen	Integration	Codeunit	1	ApplicationManagement	OnBeforeCompanyOpen
50900	Item Ledger DateTime	UpdateItemLedgEntryDateTime	Integration	Codeunit	22	Item Jnl.-Post Line	OnAfterInsertItemLedgEntry
130410	Sys. Warmup Test Runner	WarmUpOnAfterCompanyOpen	Integration	Codeunit	1	ApplicationManagement	OnAfterCompanyOpen

10. Post any inventory movement – either in a purchase/sales document or via item journal. Review the last posted item ledger entry and make sure that it has fields `Created Date` and `Created Time` filled.

How it works...

The current recipe begins with a step creating custom fields in the table `Item Ledger Entry` that will be filled in the event subscriber function. These fields will contain the date and time when the entry was created.

Step 3 describes a codeunit that contains the event subscriber code. The function `UpdateItemLedgEntryDateTime` is the event subscriber – it will be invoked when the event it subscribes to, is raised. To bind the subscriber to a publisher and a particular event, we configure a set of function properties in Step 4 through Step 7. First, the subscriber function must have the `Subscriber` attribute, then we can select the object and a method to which it must be subscribed.

> It is possible to publish business and integration events from any C/AL object that can contain application code. Event subscribers can be declared only in codeunits.

Records in the `Item Ledger Entry` table are inserted by the codeunit 22 `Item Jnl.-Post Line`, which raises an event `OnAfterInsertItemLedgEntry` when it inserts an entry into the table. The event subscriber must react to this event and modify the entry record that will be passed in the function parameters. The list of parameters in the subscriber function is copied from the event publisher declaration. The function `OnAfterInsertItemLedgEntry` is codeunit 22 is declared with two parameters: a record `Item Ledger Entry`, and a record `Item Journal Line`. As shown in Step 7 and Step 8, the event subscriber function will automatically receive the same set of parameters after subscribing to the event.

Static event subscription is managed by the NAV platform at compile time. As soon as the object subscribing to an event is compiled, it will receive event notifications. Step 10 shows how to review the event subscriptions to make sure that your new subscription is active.

You can run the page `Event Subscriptions` directly from the object designer or open it from the `Session List` window. To open the session list, in the NAV development environment, choose the **Tools** menu, then select the **Debugger** submenu and select **Debug Session**.

The event **Subscriptions** action is located in the **Home** tab:

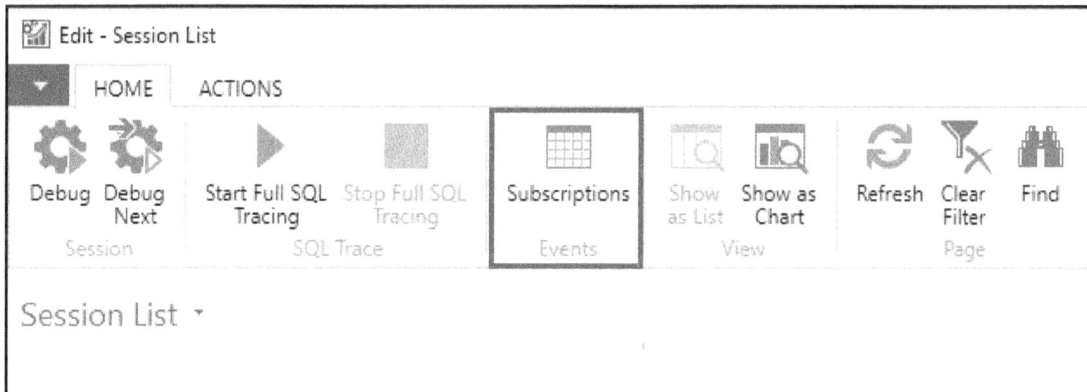

Subscribing to global events

Global events are raised by codeunit 1 `ApplicationManagement` in response to certain application-wide actions, such as opening and closing the company or opening the user's default role center.

How to do it...

The following recipe will show how to subscribe to the global events OnCompanyOpen and OnCompanyClose to log user activities in each company. Event information will be stored in a separate table.

1. Create a table in NAV table designer. Open the table properties window, from the **View** menu, select the **Properties** option, or press *Shift + F4*. Update the value of the property DataPerCompany from the default value Yes to No.

2. Create four fields, as shown in the following table:

Field No.	Field Name	Data Type	Length
1	Event ID	Integer	
2	Event Type	Option	
3	User ID	Code	50
4	Company Name	Text	50
5	Event Date	Date	
6	Event Time	Time	

3. Select the field 1 Event ID and open its properties. In the property AutoIncrement, change the value to Yes.

4. Open the properties for the field 2 Event Type. Modify the property OptionString. Add two options in the property value: Company Open, Company Close.

5. The table does not contain any trigger code. Save the new object as table 50901 Company Event.

6. Switch to the codeunit designer in C/SIDE and create a new codeunit object.

7. In **C/AL Globals**, declare a function LogEvent. Open the function parameters and add one parameter:

Name	DataType
EventType	Option

This variable will be a generic option, without option string. There is no need to modify the OptionString property.

8. Open the **Variables** tab in the **C/AL Locals** window and declare a variable:

Name	DataType	Subtype
CompanyEvent	Record	Company Event

9. Close the local declarations to return to the code editor and type the function code:

```
WITH CompanyEvent DO BEGIN
    "Event Type" := EventType;
    "User ID" := USERID;
    "Company Name" := COMPANYNAME;
    "Event Date" := TODAY;
    "Event Time" := TIME;
    INSERT;
END;
```

10. Open the **C/AL Globals** window, create a function `LogCompanyOpen`. Access the function properties and configure the values as shown in the following table:

Property	Value
Event	Subscriber
EventPublisherObject	Codeunit ApplicationManagement
EventFunction	OnAfterCompanyOpen

When setting the property `EventPublisherObject`, you can simply enter `codeunit 1` as the property value. The number will be replaced with the codeunit name by the code editor.

After filling in the value of `EventFunction` property, C/SIDE will request the confirmation to change the function signature. Confirm the request.

11. Close the function properties. Back in **C/AL Globals**, create one more function `LogCompanyClose`.

12. Set up the function properties as described in the following table:

Property	Value
Event	Subscriber
EventPublisherObject	Codeunit ApplicationManagement
EventFunction	OnAfterCompanyClose

Do not leave the global declarations yet. Open the **Variables** tab and declare a variable GlobalEventType of type Option. In the variable properties, modify the value of the property OptionString – add two values: Company Open, Company Close.

13. Close the declarations window and return to the C/AL editor. In the function LogCompanyOpen, insert the following code line:

```
LogEvent(GlobalEventType::"Company Open");
```

14. The function LogCompanyClose will write information on company logout events:

```
LogEvent(GlobalEventType::"Company Close");
```

15. Save the codeunit. In the **Save As** dialog box, assign ID and name 50901 Global Event.

How it works...

In the first five steps, we create a table to log the company open and close events. The primary key of the table, Event ID, is declared as an autoincrement field to delegate the record numbering from application code to the database engine.

The table itself has the property DataPerCompany changed to No, which means that the SQL Server will store a single table Company Event for all companies in the database. Most tables used by the application, have their data separated between different companies. To access data in a company other than the current active company, the developer must switch the company for the table by calling the function CHANGECOMPANY. The function call will succeed only if the user running this code has sufficient privileges to view data in the selected company.

Some tables, though, have their data shared between all companies in the database. These are, for example, the tables User, User Group, Permission, and Permission Set, that store information about user account and their data access permissions. The application code reading these tables will return the same records in any company.

The codeunit created in Step 6 will run the event subscriber code. The first function declared in the codeunit, LogEvent, does not subscribe to events. This is a helper that will receive event data from subscribers and write it into the table.

The next steps, Step 10 to Step 12, create a function that will actually subscribe to global events and call the helper function to log the event. The subscription setup is very similar to the configuration done in the previous recipe, except that the event source is always codeunit 1 ApplicationManagement.

Using database trigger events

Database trigger events give the C/AL developers the possibility to receive notifications when data in a table is being updated. There are eight events raised on data modification – before and after each of the four table actions: insert, modify, delete, and rename. Two more events are reserved for field validation – OnBeforeValidateEvent and OnAfterValidateEvent.

Unlike business and integration events, database triggers are not raised by the application code, they are managed by the NAV server.

How to do it...

In the following recipe, you will create an event subscriber function that subscribes to database trigger events to implement additional verification of the record before it is inserted into the database.

1. In the NAV codeunit designer, create a new codeunit with ID 50902 and name Database Trigger Event.
2. In **C/AL Globals**, declare a function OnInsertVerifyRecord that will subscribe to the OnInsert event of the Customer table.
3. Open the function properties. In the property Event, select the value Subscriber.

4. In the next property `EventPublisherObject`, click the lookup button and select the table 18 `Customer`. Alternatively, you can type the keyword `table` followed by the table ID or name in the **Value** field without lookup. For example, the value can be entered as `table 18`.

5. In the `EventFunction` property, select the `OnBeforeInsertEvent` function.

6. Close the function properties to return to C/AL global declarations. Create another function. Give it the name `OnValidateVerifyRecord`. Open the function properties window and change the value of the property `Event` to `Subscriber`.

7. In the `EventPublisherObject` property, choose or type the table 18 `Customer`.

8. Click on the lookup button in the property `EventFunction` and choose the event function `OnBeforeValidateEvent`.

9. After Step 8, a new property `EventPublisherElement` will appear in the list. Click on the lookup button in this property value and choose the field `Salesperson Code`. Click **OK**.

10. Return to C/AL code editor. In the function `OnInsertVerifyRecord`, type the following code:

```
Rec.TESTFIELD("Salesperson Code");
```

11. Copy the same line of code to the function `OnValidateVerifyRecord`.

12. Save and compile the codeunit. The event subscription becomes active immediately after compilation. New validation of the customer data will require the field `Salesperson Code` to be filled in for all customers. An attempt to insert a record without a salesperson code, or remove this code from an existing record, will cause an error and transaction rollback.

How it works...

Subscribing to database trigger events mostly follows the same pattern as a subscription to any other type of event. A subscriber function must be declared in a codeunit, then the `Event` property of the function is set to `Subscriber` to enable other subscription properties. The difference with an integration event is in the object that raises the event. In the case of a database trigger, you select a record as the `EventPublisherObject` (Step 4).

If you open the source code of an object raising an integration event, you can see its event functions in the code, along with explicit calls of these functions. Database trigger events are raised by the NAV runtime environment, and their implementation is hidden from the C/SIDE level.

The OnBeforeInsert event selected in Step 5, is raised when a record is prepared for insertion, but before it is actually inserted into the table. This trigger can be used for any custom verification of the data being committed to the database.

Step 6 through Step 9 introduce a handler function subscribing to a table field validation event. After selecting the event function OnBeforeValidateEvent, one additional setup step must be performed. In Step 9, you select a table field which you want to validate. The subscriber will receive only events raised by the field specified in the property EventPublisherElement.

The application code executed in the triggers, is very simple. It is shown in Step 10, in the OnInsertVerifyRecord event subscriber. The same line is run in the OnValidateVerifyRecord. The code refers to a variable Rec to verify the data, but this is not the global Rec keeping the reference to a current record in table and page objects. The variable Rec in database triggers is a local function parameter passed to the event subscriber by the NAV runtime.

Extending UI with page trigger events

Page trigger events provide a way to extend the functionality of UI actions on pages. As with other event types, the main purpose of an event is to allow developers to add custom code to base application objects without intrusion into the code.

Objects subscribing to a page trigger event are invoked when the user runs an action in the page, after the C/AL code located directly in the page, is executed.

How to do it...

This recipe shows how to use a page trigger event to assign a user account to a sales order on the `Release` action.

1. Run the NAV development environment. In the Codeunit Designer, create a new codeunit 50903 `Page Trigger Event`.
2. In C/AL Globals, declare a function `OnReleaseSalesOrderAssignUserID`.
3. Open the function properties. In the `Event` property, set the value to `Subscriber`. In the current example, `EventPublisherObject` is **Page 42** `Sales Order`. You can either choose it from the lookup list or just type `page 42` in the property value.
4. Lookup the list of events in the `EventFunction` property and choose `OnAfterActionEvent`. When `OnAfterActionEvent` is selected as the event trigger, the property `EventPublisherElement` must also be filled. Enter the name of the action `Release` in this field, or choose it from the lookup list.
5. With properties configured as described in Step 4, the event subscriber function `OnReleaseSalesOrderAssignUserID` will receive a new parameter `Rec`. You will be asked to confirm the change in the function signature.
6. Back in the C/AL editor, declare a local variable in the event subscriber function:

Name	DataType	Subtype
UserSetup	Record	User Setup

7. Then type the following function code:

```
IF UserSetup.GET(USERID) THEN BEGIN
  Rec.VALIDATE("Assigned User ID",USERID);
  Rec.MODIFY(TRUE);
END;
```

8. Save and compile the codeunit. To run this example, you need to have a record in the `User Setup` table. From the **application** menu, open the **User Setup** page under **Departments** | **Administration** | **Application Setup** | **Users** | **User Setup**.

9. Click **New** to add a setup record, then choose your user ID in the **User ID** field:

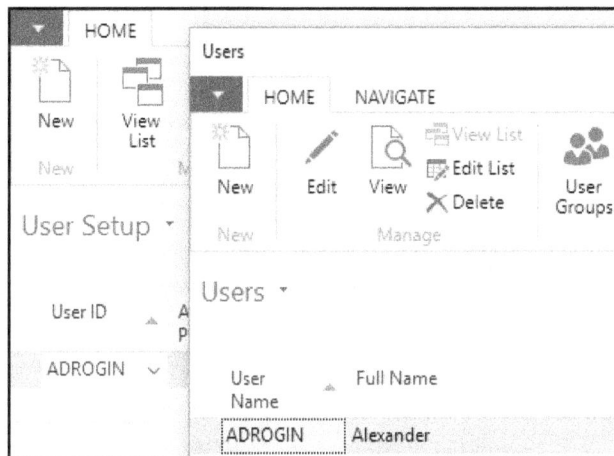

10. To verify the new function, run the NAV client and open the list of sales orders from **Departments | Sales & Marketing | Order Processing**.

11. Create a new sales order. Select any customer in the header and setup a line. For example, choose customer **10000**, then move to the lines and insert one line to sell item **1896-S** from **BLUE** location. Set **Quantity** = 1.

12. Execute the action **Release** from the **Home** tab. This is the UI action to which the codeunit 50903 subscribes:

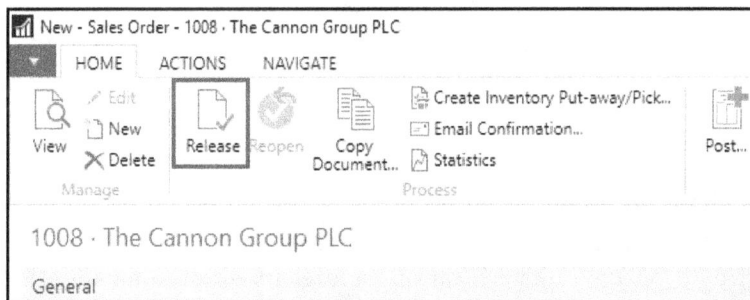

13. When the sales order is released, it is automatically assigned to the user who releases it. You can see your User ID in the field `Assigned to User ID`.

How it works...

The function `OnReleaseSalesOrderAssignUserID`, declared in the codeunit created in the beginning of the recipe, is the event subscriber handling the UI action Release on the page 42 `Sales Order`. The first step to turning a function into a subscriber of a page trigger event is to change the value of the property `Event` to `Subscriber`.

The `EventPublisherObject` set in Step 3 is the page on which the action button is located. In our case, this is page 42 `Sales Order`. To subscribe to a page UI event, you must choose the function `OnAfterActionEvent` as the event publisher. After this, the property `EventPublisherElement` will become available in the function properties list. Here, you choose a UI element to which you want to bind the subscription. The lookup button in the property value field opens a list of action elements on the page.

Step 7 gives an example of C/AL code handling the page trigger event. This code is called after the `Release - OnAction()` trigger on the page is completed, and the sales document is in the released status.

The sales order being processed is passed to the event subscriber as the function parameter `Rec`. As in the previous recipe, this local variable should not be confused with the system variable `Rec` available in tables and pages.

Creating custom events

The capabilities of custom application code are not limited by event subscription. Customized objects can raise predefined business or integration events, and publish new custom events.

How to do it...

The following recipe explains how to create a new event in codeunit 21 `Item Jnl.-Check Line.` that will fire on journal line verification, before any other line validation code.

1. In the NAV development environment, select the codeunit 21 `Item Jnl.-Check Line` and click the **Design** button to access its C/AL code.
2. Open the **C/AL Globals** window, tab to **Functions** and insert a new function in the list – `OnBeforeCheckItemJnlLine`.

3. Click the **Locals** button located in the right panel. This will open the list of function parameters. Add one parameter:

Var	Name	DataType	Subtype
True	ItemJnlLine	Record	Item Journal Line

4. Close the **C/AL Locals** to return to the list of functions, then open the properties of the function `OnBeforeCheckItemJnlLine`.

5. In the field `Event`, choose the option `Publisher`, change the value of the property `EventType` to `Integration`.

6. Return to the code editor, and modify the function `RunCheck`. Call the function `OnBeforeCheckItemJnlLine` before any other function statement. The function `RunCheck` should contain the following code:

```
RunCheck(VAR ItemJnlLine : Record "Item Journal Line")
OnBeforeCheckItemJnlLine(ItemJnlLine);

WITH ItemJnlLine DO BEGIN
```

It is insufficient to declare the subscriber with the signature matching the event publisher. The name of the parameter in the subscriber function must also exactly match the name of the corresponding parameter of the publisher, otherwise the subscriber will not be called.

The integration event `OnBeforeCheckItemJnlLine` in codeunit 21 does not execute any C/AL code, it should remain blank. All logic will be implemented in the event subscriber.

7. Save the object and close the code editor. Create a new codeunit in the codeunit designer. Assign the ID 50904 and name `Custom Integration Event` to the codeunit.

8. Create a function `VerifyJournalLineDimensions` in the new codeunit. In its properties, set `Event` to `Subscriber`. In the `EventPublisherObject` property, choose the codeunit 21 `Item Jnl.-Check Line`. Select the property `EventFunction` and click the lookup button to see the list of events available for subscription. Select the function `OnBeforeCheckItemJnlLine` you created in previous steps. Click **OK** and close the function properties.

9. In the C/AL code editor, type the function code to verify that global dimension values are set in the journal lines:

```
ItemJnlLine.TESTFIELD("Shortcut Dimension 1 Code");
ItemJnlLine.TESTFIELD("Shortcut Dimension 2 Code");
```

10. Save and compile the codeunit. To run the code, start the NAV client, open the item journal, and create a new journal line. Fill in the mandatory fields. For example, create a purchase line for two PCS of item 1900 on blank location. Do not fill in global dimensions and try to post the line. Posting will fail, notifying you that the department code dimension must have a value in item journal line.

How it works...

Codeunit 21 `Item Jnl.-Check Line` raises an event `OnBeforeCheckItemJnlLine` after performing the verification procedure for an item journal line, before the line is forwarded to the posting routine. Now we want to implement a similar event that will be raised before any other verification is started.

The event publisher function `OnBeforeCheckItemJnlLine` is declared in Step 2. Step 3 adds a parameter that will be used by the subscriber. When designing an event publisher, think of its parameter from the subscriber's viewpoint, because the subscriber will inherit the parameters list and the return value from the event publisher it subscribes to. The publisher function does not contain any C/AL code and does not use the parameter, except to pass it to all subscribers.

In Step 5, we use the already familiar property `Event` to declare the function as an event publisher by setting the value of the property to `Publisher`. C/AL code can raise either `Business` or `Integration` events. The type of the event is specified by the property `EventType`.

To raise the event, the event publisher function must be called from the application code. This is done is Step 6 – the function `RunCheck` is modified to invoke the function `OnBeforeCheckItemJnlLine`. At this point, all event subscribers bound to this event, are called consequently.

Subscribing to events in runtime

In all examples of event subscription developed in the current chapter so far, subscription is registered statically at compile time. As soon as the event subscriber codeunit is saved and compiled, it starts to receive event notifications.

Subscription binding can also be controlled from the application code at runtime, so that the subscriber can start and stop subscriptions dynamically.

How to do it...

In this recipe, we will modify the codeunit 50904 `Custom Integration Event` from the *Creating custom events* recipe to control the subscription state from the UI.

1. Start the recipe from creating a new codeunit in NAV object designer.
2. Open codeunit properties. To do this, press *Shift + F4*, or choose the option **Properties** in the **View** menu, from any place in the code editor. Change the value of the property `EventSubscriberInstance` from its default value `Static-Automatic` to `Manual`. Close the **properties** window.
3. In **C/AL Globals** declarations, create a function `VerifyJournalLineDimensions`. This is the same function that was executed in codeunit 50904. You can copy the function or create a new one.
4. Access the function properties and modify the key properties required to subscribe to an event:

Property	Value
Event	Subscriber
EventPublisherObject	Codeunit Item Jnl.-Check Line
EventFunction	OnBeforeCheckItemJnlLine

Confirm the changes of the function signature when modifying properties.

5. Insert the C/AL code that verifies the dimensions in the item journal line. This code should be placed in the `VerifyJournalLineDimensions` function:

```
ItemJnlLine.TESTFIELD("Shortcut Dimension 1 Code");
ItemJnlLine.TESTFIELD("Shortcut Dimension 2 Code");
```

6. Save the object as codeunit 50906 `Dynamic Event Subscriber`.

7. The code controlling the subscription status will be placed in a page. Create a blank page in NAV page designer.

8. Open the page **Action Designer**. Insert an action container and two action buttons inside the container: **Start** and **Stop**. These buttons will control the subscription state:

Type	SubType	Name
ActionContainer	ActionItems	Subscription
Action		Start
Action		Stop

9. Declare two global variables in the page:

Name	DataType	Substype
DynamicEventSubscriber	Codeunit	Dynamic Event Subscriber
SubscriptionActive	Boolean	

10. Select the first action button **Start** and write the code to activate the event subscription:

```
BINDSUBSCRIPTION(DynamicEventSubscriber);
SubscriptionActive := TRUE;
```

11. In the application code for the **Stop** button, write the following code:

```
UNBINDSUBSCRIPTION(DynamicEventSubscriber);
SubscriptionActive := FALSE;
```

12. The boolean variable `SubscriptionActive` is required to control the state of the action buttons – whether each of them is clickable or not. Close the code editor and open the properties for the **Start** action. In the property `Enabled` set the value: `NOT SubscriptionActive`.

13. In the properties of the action button **Stop**, modify the same value `Enabled`. Set its value to `SubscriptionActive`.

14. Close the action designer and access the code editor from the page designer. In the `OnOpenPage` trigger, insert the initialization of the global Boolean variable:

    ```
    SubscriptionActive := FALSE;
    ```

15. Before testing the new codeunit, delete the codeunit 50904 `Custom Integration Event` in the object designer.

16. Save the page and run it. When you click the **Start** button, event subscription is activated, and the custom verification of the item journal line will be imposed on posting procedure. If you now try to post a journal line without global dimensions, posting will fail. Click the **Stop** button to release the event subscription and post the same journal line – it will be posted successfully.

> Subscription is active only while the subscriber codeunit instance remains in scope. When the variable goes out of scope (for example, if the user closes the page), subscription will be removed.

Developing an extension

The concept of events finds another important application in NAV extension packages. NAV extension is a file containing application modifications. Extensions can be easily installed to extend the base NAV functionality without changing base application objects. An extension package can modify UI elements and extend the data structure, but it is not allowed to introduce modifications to application code. All changes in the code can be implemented only via event subscription.

Getting ready

You will need a command line tool `SignTool` to sign the extension package in this recipe. SignTool is a component of Windows SDK. Before starting the recipe, make sure you have the SDK installed, or download the SDK package corresponding to your version of Windows, from `developer.microsoft.com`.

How to do it...

This recipe shows how to create an extension package. As an example, we will use an object developed in the *Business and integration events* recipe, modify in and wrap the changes in a NAV extension package file.

1. Besides one modified application object and a new one, the extension package must include a codeunit managing the upgrade procedure when a new version of the extension is installed. Create a codeunit in the NAV object designer. Save it as codeunit 50905 `Upgrade Extension`.

2. In the new object, declare a function `OnNavAppUpgradePerCompany`. This must be a global function, so open function properties and change the value of the `Local` property from its default value `Yes` to `No`.

3. A single line of code executed in the function:

   ```
   NAVAPP.RESTOREARCHIVEDATA(DATABASE::"Item Ledger Entry");
   ```

4. Prepare the unchanged version of table 32 `Item Ledger Entry`. Export it into a text file. To export an object, select it in the object designer and choose the option **Export** from the **File** menu. The dialog **Export Objects** opens. In the **dialog** window, select the text file type, enter `BaseObjects` in the **File Name** field, and click **Save**.

5. If you have completed the first recipe of this chapter, *Business and integration events*, and saved your modifications, import the modified object now. Otherwise, implement changes in C/SIDE objects described in the indicated recipe.

6. Select the following objects: table 32 `Item Ledger Entry`, codeunit 50900 `Item Ledger DateTime`, and the codeunit 50905 `Upgrade Extension`. To select all three objects, switch the object designer to Table view, choose the table 32 and press *Ctrl + F1* to mark the selected table. After that, switch to codeunit view, choose the codeunit 50900 and mark it with *Ctrl + F1*. Do the same for codeunit 50905. With three objects marked, choose **All** in the object menu, then select the option **Marked Only** from the **View** menu.

7. After Step 6, only the marked objects remain visible in the objects list. Select all objects and export them into a text file `ModifiedObjects.txt`. To restore the full view, select the menu option **Show All** in the **View** menu.

8. Run **NAV 2016 Development Shell** as administrator.

9. Create a DELTA file containing the difference between the base version and modifications – run the following command in the NAV development shell:

```
Compare-NAVApplicationObject -OriginalPath BaseObjects.txt -
    ModifiedPath <ModifiedObjects.txt> -DeltaPath <Delta.txt>
```

When running the command, specify the full path to object files.

10. Create the extension manifest file describing your extension package. Run the PowerShell cmdlet in the NAV development shell:

```
New-NAVAppManifest -Name "ILE Posting DateTime" -Publisher
    "CRONUS International" -Version "1.0.0" | New-NAVAppManifestFile
    -Path <Manifest.xml>
```

11. Pack the delta file and the extension manifest into a package file `.navx` with the following command:

```
Get-NAVAppManifest -Path <Manifest.xml> | New-NAVAppPackage -Path
    <ILEPostingDateTime.navx> -SourcePath <Delta.txt>
```

12. Create a test self-signed certificate. Run the Powershell cmdlet from the NAV Development Shell:

```
New-SelfSignedCertificate -Type CodeSigningCert -Subject
    ILEPostingDateTime -CertStoreLocation "Cert:\CurrentUser\My"
```

The cmdlet will create an SSL certificate that will be installed in the `Current User\Personal` certificate store. This certificate will be used in the next step for code signing.

13. To sign the extension code, press *Win + R*, type `cmd` and press *Enter*. This will open the command line. In the command line, change the current folder by running the following command:

```
cd "C:\Program Files (x86)\Windows Kits\8.0\bin\x86"
```

Then execute the signtool:

```
signtool sign /n ILEPostingDateTime <ILEPostingDateTime.navx>
```

When running the command, provide the full path to the package file `ILEPostingDateTime.navx`.

14. Now the extension package is ready to be deployed. The deployment process is described in the next recipe, *Installing an extension*.

How it works...

Custom modifications that are to be packed in an extension package must conform to certain requirements. The first requirement is that an extension package cannot modify code in any application object. Instead, all changes in the code must be introduced through events and encapsulated in new codeunits.

Another requirement is imposed on changes in the data model. An extension can include new tables, or add new fields to existing tables, but modifications of data structure must go together with upgrade procedures for new data fields. The first three steps of the recipe introduce a function that handles the upgrade for the custom fields added to the table Item Ledger Entry. The upgrade function is placed in a separate codeunit with a Normal subtype. Since the upgrade of extensions is managed separately from upgrading the base application, this codeunit should not be marked with a subtype Upgrade. The latter is reserved for objects handling the upgrade of base objects.

The upgrade code for the table in this example is shown in Step 2 and Step 3. The code is placed into a function with a predefined name. If you need to run an upgrade for a table storing data per company, name the function OnNavAppUpgradePerCompany(). This function will be called once for each company residing in the database.

To upgrade tables containing application-wide data, place the upgrade code into a function OnNavAppUpgradePerDatabase().

The functions are called during the installation process, if the NAV server has information about a previously installed version of the same extension.

At least one of these functions – OnNavAppUpgradePerDatabase or OnNavAppUpgradePerCompany – must be included in the extension package is it contains schema changes. If the package modifies the data structure, but does not include upgrade code, the package creation will fail with an error.

The NAV extension package is based on a DELTA file that carries information about modification in object structure, and new objects. Therefore, to create this file, you must prepare an unchanged version of objects in a text file, and export modified and new objects into another file. The cmdlet Compare-NAVApplicationObject compares two files and saves the difference them into the file Delta.txt, as shown in Step 9.

Step 10 creates the last file that must be included in the extension package – `Manifest.xml`. The manifest file contains metadata describing the package, such as package name, version, developer, and so on.

After preparing all the necessary files, we can pack them into a `.navx` package file, which is done in Step 12. When running the cmdlet, provide the path to the files `Delta.txt` and `Manifest.xml`, and specify the name of the new extension package file.

In the last two steps, we sign the package file with a security certificate. This is not a required action, and can be skipped, but it is recommended to sign your code, so that users installing it can verify its genuineness. Step 13 generates a test certificate (in practice, you will receive your certificate from a third-party certification authority) and installs it into your personal certificate store. In Step 14, the name of the certificate is passed to the signing tool to update the package with the security signature.

Installing an extension

The developed NAV extension is packed into a .navx file, and is ready to be installed on the NAV server. Now we will see how to publish a package with several simple Powershell commands and install the published extension.

A significant part of the recipe is dedicated to the installation of an SSL certificate that is intended to verify the extension package security.

Getting ready

If you are testing the installation of the extension on your development database, restore the initial state of application objects included in the extension before you continue. Delete custom codeunits and import the base version of the table 32 `Item Ledger Entry`. Compile the table after importing. In the **Compile** dialog, select **Force** for the **Synchronize Schema** option.

How to do it...

This walkthrough continues the previous recipe and describes the process of installing the package created in the *Developing an extension* recipe.

1. In the following steps, we will copy the security certificate created in the previous recipe, to the NAV server where the extension package is to be installed. Start by running the Microsoft Management Console on your development computer: press *Win + R*, type mmc and press *Enter*.

2. Select the **Console Root** and press *Ctrl + M*, or choose the option **Add or remove snap-in** from the **File** menu.

3. In the list of available console snap-ins, choose **Certificates** and click the button **Add**. In the **request** window, choose the option **My user account** to manage your personal certificates.

4. Under the folder, **Certificates – Current user\Personal\Certificates**, find the certificate ILEPostingDateTime. Right-click on the certificate name, and under **All tasks**, choose **Export**. Click **Next**, then select the option **Do not export the private key**.

5. Click **Next**, and choose the certificate file format. Select **X.509 in DER encoding** for the file format. In the next window, specify the file name and location and complete the export wizard.

6. Copy the certificate file to the NAV server where the extension package will be installed.

7. If NAV server and client are running on different computers, repeat Step 1 through Step 4 on the server, but instead of the option **My user account**, choose the **Local computer account**. This step can be skipped if you work with the development installation on one computer.

8. Under the console root, expand the folder **Trusted root certification authorities**, right-click on the **Certificates** folder located under it. In the context menu, choose **All tasks\Import**. Select the certificate file copied in Step 7, choose the option **Place all certificates in the following store**. The certificate store **Trusted root certification authorities** is already selected as the default location. Confirm the selection and complete the import wizard.

9. After the security certificate is successfully imported and installed, you can publish the NAV extension. Run **NAV 2016 Development Shell** with the administrator credentials (right-click on the application name in the start menu and choose **Run as administrator**).

10. Execute the following cmdlet to publish the extension on the NAV server:

```
Publish-NAVApp -ServerInstance DynamicsNAV90 `
  -Path <ILEPostingDateTime.navx>
```

11. To retrieve information about extension published on the server, run the cmdlet:

```
Get-NAVAppInfo -ServerInstance DynamicsNAV90
```

The following is the output generated:

```
PS C:\WINDOWS\system32> Get-NAVAppInfo -ServerInstance DynamicsNAV91

Id                                        Name                    Version  Publis
                                                                           her
--                                        ----                    -------  ------
d09fa965-9a2a-424d-b704-69f3b54ed0ce      PayPal Payments S...    1.0.0.0  Mic...
da2d36ab-99f9-4fc8-89d0-0338b2966c36      ILE Posting DateTime    1.0.0    CRO...
e2743298-9ccb-49cd-9d8e-4b2d1ab91d36      Envestnet Yodlee ...    1.0.0.0  Mic...
1b80b577-772f-4e0f-bc13-50214fb3da6e      QuickBooks Data M...    1.0.0.0  Mic...


PS C:\WINDOWS\system32> _
```

12. After publishing the extension, you can install it with the following Powershell command:

```
Install-NAVApp -ServerInstance DynamicsNAV90 `
  -Name "ILE Posting DateTime"
```

13. The command in Step 12 installs the application on the default tenant. You can review installed extensions with the same cmdlet Get-NAVAppInfo, but with the tenant name in its parameters:

```
Get-NAVAppInfo -ServerInstance DynamicsNAV90 -Tenant default
```

14. After the application extension is installed, users can access the functionality it provides in the same way as they do with normally developed modifications in the database. Event subscription becomes active immediately after installing the package, and custom fields in the table Item Ledger Entry will be filled with the next posting, although, these fields are now not accessible in the NAV object designer. If you open the object in design mode, you won't see the new fields. To ensure the functionality works as expected, do the same verification Step 11 from the *Business and integration events* recipe.

10
PowerShell

In this chapter, we will cover the following recipes:

- Managing the database
- Managing users and user permissions
- Managing companies
- Administering NAV services with PowerShell
- Handling application objects
- Merging application objects

Introduction

With PowerShell, Windows system administrators received a comprehensive scripting environment with a broad set of tools for administering any application in the corporate domain and integrating all software into a common infrastructure.

The latest release of Microsoft Dynamics NAV also supports PowerShell and comes with numerous cmdlets to aid both developers and system administrators in their daily tasks. All NAV cmdlets are collected in two modules, one of them incorporating development tools, and the second containing the administration cmdlets.

The Administration module is loaded into the PowerShell environment when you run the **NAV 2016 Administration Shell** from the **Start** menu. **NAV 2016 Development Shell** loads the development module.

After starting one of the shells, you can get the list of commands available in the corresponding module by running the command `Get-Command *NAV*`

Help topics on each command can be retrieved with a standard PowerShell cmdlet `Get-Help <command>`.

Managing the database

The very first daily task of a system administrator is the database backup. Other database management tasks come right behind it. The NAV administration module does not include database backup scripts – this is a task for the SQL Server. Instead of the database backup, you can export and import data from all database tables in an internal NAV format and import the file into a new database.

How to do it...

In the first recipe, we will see how to backup and restore a database with SQL Server cmdlets, then export and import NAV data via the NAV administrator shell. Besides, the recipe gives a brief overview of the PowerShell Integrated Scripting Environment.

1. Run the **NAV 2016 Administration Shell** from the **Start** menu. Start the shell with administrator credentials.
2. To backup the demo database, run the `Backup-SqlDatabase` cmdlet with the following parameters:

   ```
   Backup-SqlDatabase -ServerInstance localhost -Database "Demo
       Database NAV (9-0)" -BackupFile <backup file name>
   ```

3. Restore the backup into a new database:

   ```
   New-NAVDatabase `
   -FilePath <backup file name> -DatabaseServer localhost `
   -DatabaseName "Copy of NAV Demo DB" `
   -DataFilesDestinationPath "C:\Program Files\Microsoft SQL`
       Server\MSSQL12.NAVDEMO\MSSQL\DATA\DemoCopy.mdf" `
   -LogFilesDestinationPath "C:\Program Files\Microsoft SQL`
       Server\MSSQL12.NAVDEMO\MSSQL\DATA\DemoCopy.ldf"
   ```

4. To view the new database, run the SQL Server Management Studio, connect to the `localhost` server, and expand the list of databases:

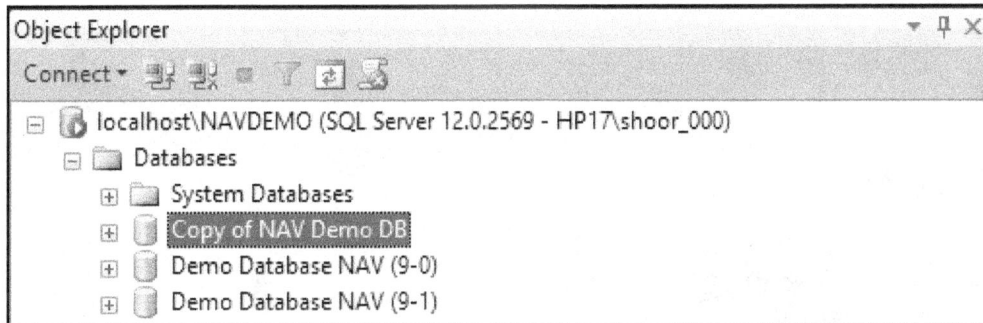

5. The previous steps involve a cmdlet from the SQL **Server Management Objects** (**SMO**) package. This is the most natural and flexible way to backup a SQL Server database. On the other hand, if you need to copy data into a new database for demonstration purposes, or require a copy of a separate company from the database, native NAV cmdlet `Export-NAVData` may be a better choice. To export data from the company CRONUS International Ltd., run the following cmdlet:

```
Export-NAVData -ServerInstance "DynamicsNAV90" -CompanyName
    "CRONUS International Ltd." -FilePath Cronus.navdata
```

> **TIP**
>
> When running the cmdlet, provide the full path to the file `Cronus.navdata`, otherwise it will be saved in your current folder. By default, NAV Administration Shell opens in `C:\Windows\System32`.

6. When the file is exported, you can retrieve information about its content in PowerShell without restoring the data with `Get-NAVDataFile`:

```
Get-NAVDataFile -FilePath Cronus.navdata
```

The following is the output generated:

```
PS C:\WINDOWS\system32> Get-NAVDataFile c:\Work\Cronus.navdata

ExportVersion          : 1
DatabaseVersion        : 91350
Description            :
IncludeApplication     : False
IncludeApplicationData : False
TenantId               : default
IncludeGlobalData      : False
CompanyName            : {CRONUS International Ltd.}
ExportDateTime         : 19.12.2016 19:29:46
FileName               : c:\Work\Cronus.navdata


PS C:\WINDOWS\system32>
```

7. Now let's import the data from the `.navdata` file into a new database. To create a database, we will use the PowerShell **Integrated Scripting Environment (ISE)**. To start the environment, type ISE in the Start menu and select the application.

8. In the ISE scripting window, type the following script:

```
[System.Reflection.Assembly]::LoadWithPartialName(
   'Microsoft.SqlServer.SMO')

$server = new-Object
   Microsoft.SqlServer.Management.Smo.Server("localhost")
$db = New-Object
   Microsoft.SqlServer.Management.Smo.Database($server,
      "CronusDB")
$db.Create()
```

9. To run the script, click the green arrow button from the actions menu:

```
NwqSQLDatabase.ps1* X
1   [System.Reflection.Assembly]::LoadWithPartialName('Microsoft.SqlServer.SMO')
2
3   $server = new-Object Microsoft.SqlServer.Management.Smo.Server("localhost")
4   $db = New-Object Microsoft.SqlServer.Management.Smo.Database($server, "CronusDB")
5   $db.Create()
```

10. Return to the NAV Administration Shell and run the following cmdlet to import the data:

```
Import-NAVData -FilePath Cronus.navdata -DatabaseServer`
    "localhost" -DatabaseName CronusDB -AllCompanies
```

How it works...

The example of the `New-NAVDatabase` cmdlet in Step 3 creates a database on the default SQL Server instance. If you want to create a database on a named instance, add the parameter `DatabaseInstance`:

```
New-NAVDatabase
-FilePath <backup file name> -DatabaseServer localhost `
-DatabaseInstance "NAVDEMO" -DatabaseName "Copy of NAV Demo DB" `
-DataFilesDestinationPath "C:\Program Files\Microsoft SQL`
Server\MSSQL12.NAVDEMO\MSSQL\DATA\DemoCopy.mdf" `-
LogFilesDestinationPath "C:\Program Files\Microsoft SQL`
Server\MSSQL12.NAVDEMO\MSSQL\DATA\DemoCopy.ldf"
```

Files `DemoCopy.mdf` and `DemoCopy.ldf` store the database itself and the transaction log. Usually, these files are managed by the SQL Server and the developer does not have to pay special attention to files. In this case filenames are stored in the backup file, and will try to overwrite the files, unless new filenames are specified explicitly.

In Step 4, we run the SQL Management Studio to view the list of databases. This can also be done with a PowerShell script.

To list the databases in PowerShell, run the PowerShell ISE and execute the following script:

```
[System.Reflection.Assembly]::LoadWithPartialName(
'Microsoft.SqlServer.SMO')
$server = New-Object ('Microsoft.SqlServer.Management.Smo.Server')
"localhost"
$dbList = $server.Databases
$dbList | Select-Object Name
```

The `Export-NAVData` cmdlet shown in Step 5 has an alternative parameter set. We specified the NAV server instance to access the database it is linked to. Alternatively, you can provide the name of the SQL server and the database in cmdlet parameters:

```
Export-NAVData -DatabaseServer localhost `
-DatabaseName "Demo Database NAV (9-0)" `
-CompanyName "CRONUS International Ltd." `
-FilePath "Cronus.navdata"
```

The same applies to the `Import-NAVData` cmdlet. You can invoke it with the server name and the database name:

```
Import-NAVData -FilePath "Cronus.navdata" `
-ServerInstance "DynamicsNAV90" -AllCompanies
```

> **TIP**
>
> When running the cmdlet `Import-NAVData`, make sure that the source and the destination databases have the same data structure. Otherwise import fails.

Managing users and user permissions

Managing user accounts and user permissions is another common task for a system administrator. With PowerShell cmdlets in NAV, this important task can also be automated.

How to do it...

This recipe shows the steps to use PowerShell to create a user account and extend the user permissions.

1. Run the **NAV 2016 Administration Shell** with administrator credentials.
2. Create a user account with `NavUserPassword` authentication:

```
New-NAVServerUser -ServerInstance DynamicsNAV90 `
-UserName TESTUSER `
-Password (Read-Host "Enter user password: " -AsSecureString)`
-ChangePasswordAtNextLogOn
```

3. When you run the cmdlet, you will be requested to enter a password for the new user:

```
PS SQLSERVER:\> New-NAVServerUser -ServerInstance DynamicsNAV91 -UserName testus
er -Password (Read-Host "Enter user password: " -AsSecureString) -ChangePassword
AtNextLogOn
Enter user password: : *****_
```

4. Assign the permission set BASIC to the user account TESTUSER:

```
New-NAVServerUserPermissionSet `
-ServerInstance DynamicsNAV90 `
-UserName TESTUSER -PermissionSetId BASIC
```

5. Run the NAV client and sign in with the new user account. You will be required to set the new password. Change the password:

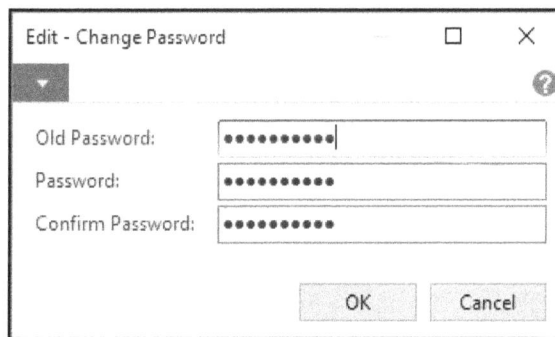

6. In the **Search** textbox, type customer price groups. Search will not return any result, since access to customer price groups is restricted for a basic user.
7. In the following steps, we will create a permission set to extend permissions of a basic user and allow access to customer price groups.

    In the NAV Administration Shell, create a permission set:

```
New-NAVServerPermissionSet
-ServerInstance DynamicsNAV91 `
-PermissionSetId CUSTPRICEGROUP `
-PermissionSetName "Customer price groups"
```

8. Include the table 6 `Customer Price Group` in the new permission set:

```
New-NAVServerPermission `
-ServerInstance DynamicsNAV91 `
-PermissionSetId CUSTPRICEGROUP -ObjectType TableData `
-ObjectId 6 -Read Yes -Insert Yes -Modify Yes -Delete Yes
```

9. Assign the permission set `CUSTPRICEGROUP` to the `TESTUSER` account:

```
New-NAVServerUserPermissionSet `
-ServerInstance DynamicsNAV90 `
-UserName TESTUSER -PermissionSetId CUSTPRICEGROUP
```

10. Sign in again as the user `TESTUSER` and search the page `Customer Price Groups`, as described in Step 5. This time, the user can open the page and edit price groups.

How it works...

The recipe begins with creating a user account that accesses the NAV server with the `NavUserPassword` authentication method. A password must be assigned to the account, but it cannot be passed directly in the command as a cmdlet parameter, since the type of the parameter is `SecureString`. This means that the password cannot be displayed in the command line – that would be a security risk. To pass the password as a parameter in the cmdlet, we ask the administrator to enter it separately in a secure string:

```
-Password (Read-Host "Enter user password: " -AsSecureString)
```

When the command is executed, a request to enter the password is displayed, and all entered text is masked.

To force the user to change the password at next logon, an additional parameter `-ChangePasswordAtNextLogOn` is added to the command.

If you sign in to the server as an administrator after running the command and review the newly created user account, you can see that the checkmark **User must change password at next login** is enabled:

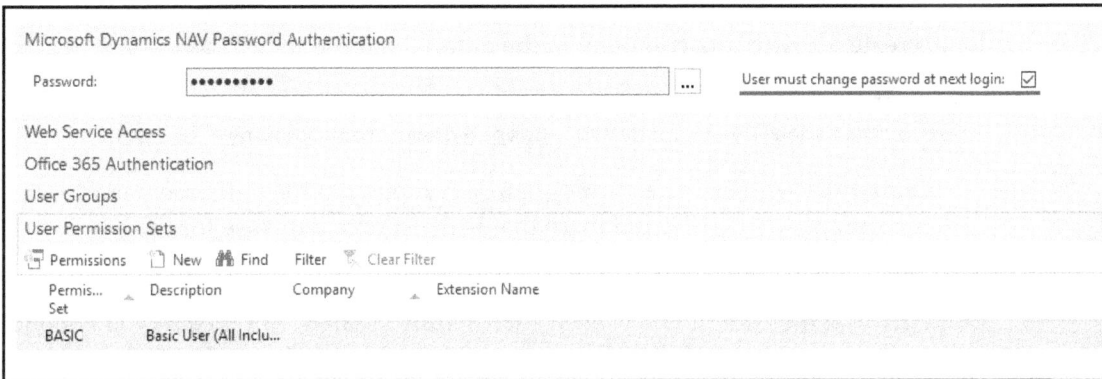

An alternative way to create a NAV server user account is to link the account with a Windows login:

```
New-NAVServerUser `
-WindowsAccount <Windows account name> `
-ServerInstance DynamicsNAV90
```

Managing companies

Individual companies inside the database can also be created, removed, or renamed with PowerShell cmdlets. Now we will run several simple examples illustrating basic operations with companies.

How to do it...

The cmdlets illustrated in this recipe, create a company in the database, create a copy of the company, and rename it.

1. First, create a new blank company in the demo database:

```
New-NAVCompany `
-ServerInstance DynamicsNAV90 -CompanyName TestCompany
```

This cmdlet will create a `TestCompany` company in the database `Demo Database NAV (9-0)` database that is the source database for the `DynamicsNAV90` service.

2. To verify that the company has been successfully created, run the NAV client and choose the menu action **Select Company** in the main application menu:

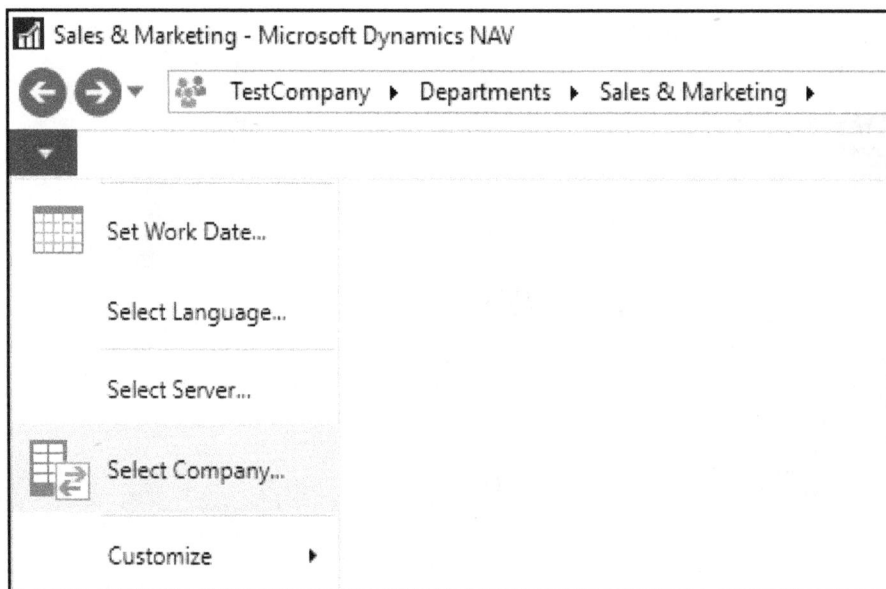

3. The new company is available in the list:

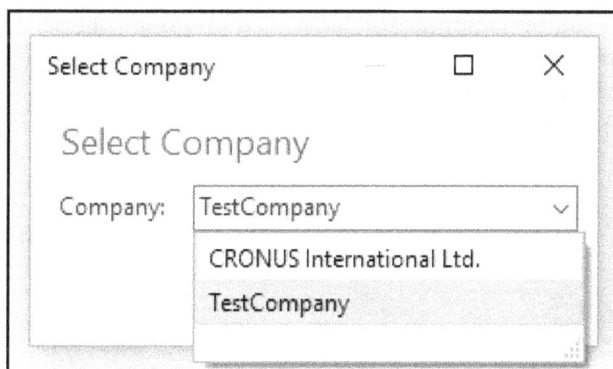

4. Cmdlet `New-NAVCompany` creates a blank company without any data. Another cmdlet, `Copy-NAVCompany`, creates a copy of an existing company in the same database:

```
Copy-NAVCompany `
-ServerInstance DynamicsNAV90 `
-SourceCompanyName "CRONUS International Ltd." `
-DestinationCompanyName CronusCopy
```

This command will create a new company `CronusCopy` and will copy all contents of `CRONUS International Ltd.` into the new company. The database for both source and destination companies is taken from the configuration of the service `DynamicsNAV90` service that is passed to the cmdlet in the `ServerInstance` parameter.

5. To rename a company, invoke the `Rename-NAVCompany` cmdlet:

```
Rename-NAVCompany `
-ServerInstance DynamicsNAV90 `
-CompanyName CronusCopy -NewCompanyName MyCompany
```

This will rename the `CronusCopy` company to `MyCompany`.

6. Delete the test company when you no longer need it:

```
Remove-NAVCompany -ServerInstance DynamicsNAV90 -CompanyName
    MyCompany
```

Administering NAV services with PowerShell

Administering NAV services becomes much easier with PowerShell, especially when the corporate infrastructure requires a large number of services running simultaneously. A simple task of restarting services may consume a lot of time when you need to do it for each service separately in the UI.

This is where PowerShell comes to aid; operations on NAV services can be automated and performed on many server instances in one cmdlet call.

How to do it...

This recipe presents PowerShell cmdlets to create and remove a NAV service, and control the state of installed services.

1. Run the NAV 2016 Administrator Shell with administrator credentials.
2. Create a NAV server instance. The name of the new instance is `NavShellTest`, and it will use the database `Demo Database NAV (9-0)`:

```
New-NAVServerInstance `
-ServerInstance "NAVShellTest" `
-DatabaseServer localhost `
-DatabaseName "Demo Database NAV (9-0)" `
-ManagementServicesPort 7065 -ClientServicesPort 7066 `
-SOAPServicesPort 7067 -ODataServicesPort 7068
```

3. The service just created in the previous step, is not started. Start the service:

```
Set-NAVServerInstance -Start -ServerInstance NavShellTest
```

4. And this is all you need to do to create a server instance in PowerShell. The service is ready to serve connections. Run the NAV client and connect to the server on the address `localhost:7066/NavShellTest` address.
5. You can obtain an overview of the server instance with a cmdlet `Get-NAVServerInstance`. The cmdlet does not require any parameters, and will list all installed services. To fine-tune the output, you can pass the result to the PowerShell pipeline and filter the dataset to see only the new service:

```
Get-NAVServerInstance | Where-Object `
-Property 'ServerInstance' -Like "*NavShellTest"
```

6. The example in Step 5 shows information on a single server instance NavShellTest. Similarly, you can see the result filtered by other criteria. For example, run the following command to view all stopped NAV services:

```
Get-NAVServerInstance | Where-Object `
-Property 'State' -eq 'Stopped'
```

The following is the output generated:

```
Администратор: Dynamics NAV 2016 Administration Shell                    —   □   ×

ServerInstance  : MicrosoftDynamicsNavServer$WebService
DisplayName     : Microsoft Dynamics NAV Server [WebService]
State           : Stopped
ServiceAccount  : NT AUTHORITY\NETWORK SERVICE
Version         : 7.1.35871.0
Default         : False


PS SQLSERVER:\>
```

7. Now use the result obtained from the previous command to start all stopped services:

```
Get-NAVServerInstance | Where-Object `
-Property 'State' -eq 'Stopped' | Set-NAVServerInstance -Start
```

8. When you don't need the test service anymore, stop it with the `Set-NAVServerInstance` cmdlet:

```
Set-NAVServerInstance -Stop -ServerInstance NavShellTest
```

9. And delete the server instance:

```
Remove-NAVServerInstance -ServerInstance NavShellTest
```

At this step, the cmdlet will require a confirmation to remove the server instance. The default response value is `Yes`, so just press *Enter* for confirmation.

How it works...

Parameters for the cmdlet `New-NAVServerInstance` in Step 2 are given on the assumption that the NAV demo database is hosted on the default instance of SQL Server. If a named instance is used instead, include a parameter `-DatabaseInstance`. The full list of parameters will be as follows:

```
New-NAVServerInstance -ServerInstance "NAVShellTest" `
-DatabaseServer localhost `
-DatabaseInstance "NAVDEMO" `
-DatabaseName "Demo Database NAV (9-0)" `
-ManagementServicesPort 7065 `
-ClientServicesPort 7066 `
-SOAPServicesPort 7067 `
-ODataServicesPort 7068
```

This cmdlet has five mandatory parameters: the name of the new server instance and four ports for external connections. Other parameters are optional, and can be configured via Microsoft Management Console or directly in the server configuration file `CustomSettings.config`.

Optional parameters not specified in the command, are initialized with default values, and the example of the preceding command is sufficient to create a workable server instance.

Handling application objects

In previous examples of this chapter, we used PowerShell cmdlets available via the NAV Administration shell. These are commands intended to automate administration tasks.

Another set of cmdlets is accessible in the **NAV 2016 Development Shell** and aimed for application developers to help them in their routine work with application objects. In the current recipe, we will illustrate several basic scripts for application objects manipulation.

How to do it...

In this recipe, you will learn how to export, import, compile, and run application objects from the PowerShell command line.

1. Start **Dynamics NAV 2016 Development Shell**. To do it, open the **Start** menu and start typing the application name.

2. One of the typical tasks for a NAV application developer is to export application objects from C/SIDE and store them in separate text files in a source control system. This is easily done in NAV Development Shell. Export custom application objects into a text file:

```
Export-NAVApplicationObject -DatabaseServer "localhost" `
-DatabaseName "Demo Database NAV (9-0)" `
-Filter "Type=Codeunit|Table;Id=50000..59999" `
-Path "NavObjects.txt"
```

   This command will export all tables and codeunits with IDs between 50000 and 59999. The full file path must be provided in the parameter `-Path`. The default path is the same as for the administrator shell, `C:\Windows\System32`.

3. Create a `NavObjects` folder where the object files will be stored. Split the file into separate objects:

```
Split-NAVApplicationObjectFile `
-Source "NavObjects.txt" `
-Destination "NavObjects"
```

4. Object files can be imported from a source code storage via a PowerShell cmdlet. Import the codeunit 50000 from a text file. Codeunit 50000 was introduced in the recipe, *Basic C/AL programming,* in Chapter 1, *Writing Basic C/AL Code.* You can copy it from the book's source files. To import the object to the database, run the following command:

```
Import-NAVApplicationObject `
-Path "NavObjects\COD50000.txt" `
-DatabaseServer "localhost" `
-DatabaseName "Demo Database NAV (9-0)" `
-ImportAction Overwrite -SynchronizeSchemaChanges Force
```

5. In the next step, we will illustrate error reporting when compiling an object from the command line. Let's introduce an error to the object code to see the error report. Open the codeunit 50000 in the object designer and change the first line from IF VerifyCheckSum(79927398712.0) THEN to IF VerifyCheckSum('79927398712.0') THEN.

Apostrophes around the number in the function parameter present it as a text constant rather than the expected big integer number. This is a compiler error.

Save the object without compiling (remove the checkmark **Compiled** in the **Save As** dialog).

6. Now compile all uncompiled objects in the database:

```
Compile-NAVApplicationObject -DatabaseServer "localhost"
-DatabaseName "Demo Database NAV (9-0)" -Filter "Compiled=No"
```

The result of the compilation will be displayed in the Development Shell console:

7. To fix the error, return to the object designer and remove the erroneous apostrophes in the codeunit 50000. The first line in the OnRun trigger should be as follows:

```
IF VerifyCheckSum(79927398712.0) THEN
```

8. Now compile the codeunit again with the following command:

```
Compile-NAVApplicationObject `
-DatabaseServer "localhost" `
-DatabaseName "Demo Database NAV (9-0)" `
-Filter "Type=Codeunit;ID=50000"
```

9. With PowerShell cmdlets, you can even invoke NAV code units or codeunit methods. Run object from NAV Administration Shell:

```
Invoke-NAVCodeunit `
-ServerInstance DynamicsNAV90 -CodeunitId 50000
```

> `Invoke-NAVCodeunit` in the preceding example calls the codeunit's OnRun method. Any UI messages raised by the codeunit will be posted in the console.

10. With the same cmdlet, any global function in a codeunit can be called. To demonstrate this, let's invoke the codeunit 50800 from Chapter 8, *Web Services*. Import the codeunit and open it in the object designer. Replace the EXIT in the last line of the GetCityByPostCode method with a MESSAGE:

```
MESSAGE(PostCodeCatalog.City);
```

11. Save and compile the modified codeunit.

12. Now run the Invoke-NAVCodeunit cmdlet with the following parameters:

```
Invoke-NAVCodeunit `
-ServerInstance DynamicsNAV90 `
-CodeunitId 50800 `
-MethodName GetCityByPostCode `
-Argument "ES-46007" `
-CompanyName "CRONUS International Ltd."
```

> The GetCityByPostCode method name is passed as a parameter to the cmdlet. This function returns the city name by the post code that is received in a parameter. The method receives the post code parameter in the cmdlet parameter -Argument.

> As a result of the execution, the message text **Valencia** will be posted to the PowerShell window.

How it works...

The second step of the recipe illustrates the export of application objects into a text file. The database server and database where the objects must be exported from, are specified in parameters -DatabaseServer, and -DatabaseName, respectively. If the database is located on a default SQL Server instance, it is sufficient to specify the NetBIOS name of the server (for example, localhost) where the service is running. In case of a named instance, the name of the instance is specified after the computer name, separated with a backslash (for example, localhost\NAVDEMO):

```
Export-NAVApplicationObject `
-DatabaseServer "localhost\NAVDEMO" `
-DatabaseName "Demo Database NAV (9-0)" `
-Filter "Type=Codeunit|Table;Id=50000..59999" `
-Path "NavObjects.txt"
```

The -Filter parameter specifies the filters that will be applied to the list objects. The filter structure is similar to the filters used in NAV user interface. The filter begins with a field name which you want the filter to be applied on, followed by the filtered values.

To specify several values, separate them with a vertical bar (Type=Codeunit|Table). A range of values is defined with two dots (Id=50000..59999). Several filters that must be applied to different fields are divided with a semicolon.

Step 4 shows how to import objects from a text file into the development environment with the Import-NAVApplicationObject cmdlet. You specify the file name where the object is stored, and the server and the database to import the objects to.

Two parameters to pay special attention to are ImportAction and SynchronizeSchemaChanges.

The first one, ImportAction, defines the cmdlet behavior if an object being imported already exists in the database. It accepts one of the values Default, Overwrite, Skip.

- Default: Object is not imported, and the error is logged
- Overwrite: Object in the database is replaced with the new one
- Skip: Conflicting object is skipped

The SynchronizeSchemaChanges parameter can take one of three values: Force, No, Yes. This parameter manages the schema synchronization for imported tables if there are any among the imported objects. For a detailed description of database schema synchronization, refer to the recipe *Creating custom tables* in Chapter 1, *Writing Basic C/AL Code*.

In Step 5, the imported objects are compiled with the compilation log dumped on the screen. This way of reporting compilation errors may be extremely inconvenient, so it would be a good idea to include a `LogFile` parameter to the cmdlet to duplicate its output into a text file:

```
Compile-NAVApplicationObject `
-DatabaseServer "localhost" `
-DatabaseName "Demo Database NAV (9-0)" `
-Filter "Compiled=No" `
-LogPath "NavObjects"
```

The value of the `LogPath` parameter is a folder where the two resulting files are generated:

- The `navcommandresult.txt` file contains the command execution summary with a reference to the error log if the command fails:
- The `naverrorlog.txt` file lists compilation errors.

Merging application objects

A dedicated set of PowerShell cmdlets in NAV Development Shell is available to aid in the tedious task of merging modifications in application objects. Application developers turn to this collection of cmdlets when applying modifications made by the Microsoft development center to customized objects.

How to do it...

The following recipe illustrates the benefits and limitations of automated object merge:

1. Import the unchanged version of the codeunit 50800 from `Chapter 8` source files. This version of the object will serve as a base for comparison.
2. Create a folder `MergeObjects` and copy the source file with the unchanged codeunit in the folder as `COD50800_Original.txt`.
3. Open the codeunit 50800 in the object designer. Modify the function `GetCityByPostCode` as follows:

```
PostCodeCatalog.SETRANGE(Code,PostCode);
IF PostCodeCatalog.FINDFIRST THEN
EXIT(PostCodeCatalog.City);
```

4. Save the codeunit and export it to the same `MergeObjects` folder as `COD50800_Target.txt`.

5. Import the unchanged version of the codeunit again (replacing the original object), and create a new function, `GetCountryByPostCode`:

```
GetCountryByPostCode(PostCode : Code[20]) : Text[30]
PostCodeCatalog.SETRANGE(Code,PostCode);
PostCodeCatalog.FINDFIRST;
EXIT(PostCodeCatalog.County);
```

The function is a copy of `GetCityByPostCode` with minor changes in the code, so you can copy the original function and rename the copy.

The variable `PostCodeCatalog` is also a copy of a variable from the original function `GetCityByPostCode`. It should be declared as a local variable of type `Record` with subtype `Post Code`.

6. Export the third version of the object to the `MergeObjects` folder. Save it as `COD50800_Modified.txt`.

7. In NAV Development Shell, run the `Merge-NAVApplicationObject` cmdlet:

```
Merge-NAVApplicationObject `
-OriginalPath "MergeObjects\COD50800_Original.txt" `
-ModifiedPath "MergeObjects\COD50800_Modified.txt" `
-TargetPath "MergeObjects\COD50800_Target.txt" `
-ResultPath "COD50800_Result.txt"
```

8. When the command completes, the digested log is displayed, informing that one object was successfully merged:

9. Open the result file `COD50800_Result.txt`. It contains merged code from both versions Modified and Target. The following code sample is the result of the successful merge:

```
PROCEDURE GetCityByPostCode@1(PostCode@1001 : Code[20]) :
  Text[30];
VAR
  PostCodeCatalog@1000 : Record 225;
BEGIN
  PostCodeCatalog.SETRANGE(Code,PostCode);
  IF PostCodeCatalog.FINDFIRST THEN
    EXIT(PostCodeCatalog.City);
  END;


PROCEDURE GetCountryByPostCode@2(PostCode@1001 : Code[20]) :
  Text[30];
VAR
  PostCodeCatalog@1000 : Record 225;
  BEGIN
    PostCodeCatalog.SETRANGE(Code,PostCode);
    PostCodeCatalog.FINDFIRST;
  EXIT(PostCodeCatalog.County);
END;
```

10. Now let's review another example. Suppose, we want our modified version of the function to look for cities only in Great Britain. Import the original version of the object from the `COD50800_Original.txt` file and make another modification:

```
PostCodeCatalog.SETRANGE(Code,PostCode);
PostCodeCatalog.SETRANGE("Country/Region Code",'GB');
PostCodeCatalog.FINDFIRST;
EXIT(PostCodeCatalog.City);
```

11. Save the object and export it as a modified version into the `COD50800_Modified.txt` file.

12. Run the cmdlet with the same parameters as in Step 7. Now the log in the console notifies you that the automatic merge of modifications failed because there is conflicting code in two modified versions of the object:

The `COD50800.CONFLICT` file created in the `MergeObjects` folder after the merge also indicates a failed merge attempt.

13. To review the conflicting code, open the `COD50800_Result.txt` file. Conflicting blocks of code are marked as `ORIGINAL`, `MODIFED`, and `TARGET`. Code lines taken from corresponding files are listed under marks to highlight the conflict:

```
PostCodeCatalog.SETRANGE(Code,PostCode);
{>>>>>>>} ORIGINAL          PostCodeCatalog.FINDFIRST;
EXIT(PostCodeCatalog.City);          {=======} MODIFIED
PostCodeCatalog.SETRANGE("Country/Region Code",'GB');
PostCodeCatalog.FINDFIRST;          EXIT(PostCodeCatalog.City);
{=======} TARGET        IF PostCodeCatalog.FINDFIRST THEN
EXIT(PostCodeCatalog.City);          {<<<<<<<}
```

How it works...

Almost a half of this recipe (the first six steps, to be precise) is a preparation of source files for an automated merge. The merge is executed on three files:

- The original, unchanged version of the object (baseline code). This version is stored in the file COD50800_Original.txt file. The path to this version is sent to the cmdlet as an OriginalPath parameter.
- A customized version of the same object. This is the version implemented at a customer's site, where NAV developers make their modifications. In the recipe example this is the COD50800_Modified.txt file and ModifiedPath parameter.
- An updated object (for example, received from Microsoft Development Center as a part of a cumulative update). This is COD50800_Target.txt and TargetPath.

The Merge-NAVApplicationObject cmdlet compares Modified and Target versions with the base and inserts modifications from both changed files into the baseline if there are no conflicting modifications. The result is saved as a new file specified in the ResultPath parameter. A successful merge without conflicts is shown in Step 7 through Step 9. Here, we can see that the Target version modifies the baseline function, while the Modified version contains a new function that does not overlap with the modification introduced in the Modified.txt file.

Conflicts arise when both changed versions try to modify the same piece of code. This situation is illustrated in Step 10 through Step 13. Both Modified and Target versions of the codeunit 50800 changed the GetCityByPostCode function, and the merge script cannot prioritize one over another. This object cannot be merged automatically, and the conflict has to be resolved manually.

Index

www.ingramcontent.com/pod-product-compliance
Lightning Source LLC
Chambersburg PA
CBHW080132220326
41598CB00032B/5043